Putting Crime in its Place

Putting Crime in its Place

Units of Analysis in Geographic Criminology

Edited by

David Weisburd
Institute of Criminology
Hebrew University, Jerusalem, Israel and
Department of Administration of Justice
George Mason University, Manassas, VA
USA

Wim Bernasco
Netherlands Institute for the Study of Crime
and Law Enforcement (NSCR)
Leiden, The Netherlands

and

Gerben J.N. Bruinsma
Netherlands Institute for the Study of Crime
and Law Enforcement (NSCR)
Leiden, The Netherlands and
Department of Criminology
Leiden University, The Netherlands

 Springer

Editors

David Weisburd
Institute of Criminology
Hebrew University, Jerusalem
Israel
and
Department of Administration of Justice
George Mason University
Manassas, VA
USA
msefrat@mscc.huji.ac.il

Wim Bernasco
Netherlands Institute for the Study of Crime
    and Law Enforcement (NSCR)
Leiden, The Netherlands
wbernasco@nscr.nl

Gerben J.N. Bruinsma
Netherlands Institute for the Study of Crime
    and Law Enforcement (NSCR)
Leiden, The Netherlands
and
Department of Criminology
Leiden University
The Netherlands
bruinsma@nscr.nl

ISBN 978-0-387-09687-2 (hardcover)   e-ISBN 978-0-387-09688-9
ISBN 978-1-4419-0973-2 (softcover)
DOI 10.1007/978-0-387-09688-9
Springer Dordrecht Heidelberg London New York

Library of Congress Control Number: 2009931093

springer.com

Preface

This book is about the unit of analysis in studies of crime and place. The quick expansion of this field demands a reflection on what the units of its analysis are and should be. Crime analysts working for the police or government are confronted routinely now with the dilemma of identifying what the unit of analysis should be when reporting on trends in crime or crime hot spots, or when mapping crime and drug problems in cities. Also, in the field of policing new developments can be observed in place-based policing instead of offender-based policing in which the choice of the level of aggregation plays a critical role.

We hope that this volume will contribute to crime and place studies by making explicit the problems involved in choosing units of analysis in the criminology of place or in crime mapping. Although the chapters have been written by experts in the field, the book has not been written for experts only. Those who are involved in the practice of crime mapping and academic researchers studying the spatial distributions of crime and victimization can learn from the arguments and tools presented in this volume.

The book is the result of a three-day workshop on the unit of analysis held in September 2006 at the Netherlands Institute for the Study of Crime and Law Enforcement (NSCR) in Leiden, the Netherlands. At the workshop, all participants presented the first drafts of their papers and others commented on them in the following discussions. After rewriting, all the papers were subsequently reviewed (single-blind) by three other workshop participants and by us, the editors. Besides the authors of the volume, we would like to thank Lieven Pauwels of Ghent University, Belgium; Danielle Reynald, Margit Averdijk, and Henk Elffers of the NSCR for their time and efforts to review the papers.

We owe George Tita and Robert Greenbaum credit for borrowing a variation on the subtitle of their paper as the main title of the whole volume. We also want to thank the NSCR for organizing and financing the workshop at Leiden, and the Netherlands Organization of Scientific Research for additional funding. At the NSCR, Ariena van Poppel, Jörgen de Gooijer, and Soemintra Jaghai helped to organize the workshop smoothly and supplied support when necessary. Lastly, we are grateful to Welmoed Spahr of Springer who supported us from the beginning and managed the production process.

Israel and USA   David Weisburd
The Netherlands   Wim Bernasco
The Netherlands   Gerben J.N. Bruinsma

Contents

Part I Introduction

1 Units of Analysis in Geographic Criminology: Historical
   Development, Critical Issues, and Open Questions   3
   David Weisburd, Gerben J.N. Bruinsma, and Wim Bernasco

**Part II What Is the Appropriate Level of Investigation of Crime at Place?
Theoretical and Methodological Issues**

2 Why Small Is Better: Advancing the Study of the Role of Behavioral
   Contexts in Crime Causation   35
   Dietrich Oberwittler and Per-Olof H. Wikström

3 Where the Action Is at Places: Examining Spatio-Temporal
   Patterns of Juvenile Crime at Places Using Trajectory Analysis
   and GIS   61
   Elizabeth Groff, David Weisburd, and Nancy A. Morris

4 Crime Analysis at Multiple Scales of Aggregation: A Topological
   Approach   87
   Patricia L. Brantingham, Paul J. Brantingham, Mona Vajihollahi,
   and Kathryn Wuschke

5 Geographical Units of Analysis and the Analysis of Crime 109
   George F. Rengert and Brian Lockwood

6 Waves, Particles, and Crime 123
   Michael D. Maltz

**Part III   Empirical Examples of Crime Place Studies:
What Can We Learn?**

7 **Crime, Neighborhoods, and Units of Analysis: Putting Space in Its
   Place** 145
   George E. Tita and Robert T. Greenbaum

8 **Predictive Mapping of Crime by ProMap: Accuracy, Units of
   Analysis, and the Environmental Backcloth** 171
   Shane D. Johnson, Kate J. Bowers, Dan J. Birks, and Ken Pease

9 **Urban Streets as Micro Contexts to Commit Violence** 199
   Johan van Wilsem

10 **Determining How Journeys-to-Crime Vary: Measuring Inter-
   and Intra-Offender Crime Trip Distributions** 217
   William Smith, John W. Bond, and Michael Townsley

About the Authors 237

Index 245

Contributors

Wim Bernasco
Netherlands Institute for the Study of Crime and Law Enforcement, Leiden,
The Netherlands, wbernasco@nscr.nl

Daniel J. Birks
School of Criminology and Criminal Justice, Griffith University, Brisbane,
Australia, d.birks@griffith.edu.au

John W. Bond
Northamptonshire Police, and University of Leicester, United Kingdom,
john.bond@northants.pnn.police.uk

Kate J. Bowers
UCL Jill Dando Institute of Crime Science, London, United Kingdom,
k.bowers@ucl.ac.uk

Paul J. Brantingham
Institute for Canadian Urban Research Studies, Simon Fraser University,
Vancouver, BC, Canada, branting@sfu.ca

Patricia L. Brantingham
Institute for Canadian Urban Research Studies, Simon Fraser University,
Vancouver, BC, Canada, pbranting@sfu.ca

Gerben J.N. Bruinsma
Netherlands Institute for the Study of Crime and Law Enforcement,
Leiden, and Department of Criminology, Leiden University, The Netherlands,
bruinsma@nscr.nl

Robert T. Greenbaum
John Glenn School of Public Affairs and Center for Urban and Regional Analysis,
The Ohio State University, Columbus, OH, USA, greenbaum.3@osu.edu

Elizabeth Groff
Department of Criminal Justice, Temple University, Philadelphia, PA, USA,
groff@temple.edu

Shane D. Johnson
UCL Jill Dando Institute of Crime Science, London, United Kingdom,
shane.johnson@ucl.ac.uk

Brian Lockwood
Department of Criminal Justice, Temple University, Philadelphia, PA, USA,
brianl@temple.edu

Michael D. Maltz
Criminal Justice Research Center, The Ohio State University, Columbus, OH, and
University of Illinois at Chicago, IL, USA, mdm@sociology.osu.edu

Nancy A. Morris
Crime, Delinquency and Corrections Center, Southern Illinois University,
Carbondale, IL, USA, nmorris@siu.edu

Dietrich Oberwittler
Department of Criminology, Max Planck Institute for Foreign and International
Criminal Law, Freiburg, Germany, and University of Freiburg, Germany,
d.oberwittler@mpicc.de

Ken Pease
UCL Jill Dando Institute of Crime Science, London, and University of
Loughborough and Chester University, United Kingdom, K.Pease@lboro.ac.uk

George F. Rengert
Department of Criminal Justice, Temple University, Philadelphia, PA, USA,
grengert@temple.edu

William Smith
Thames Valley Police, United Kingdom, Will.Smith@thamesvalley.pnn.police.uk

George E. Tita
Department of Criminology, Law and Society, University of California – Irvine,
CA, USA, gtita@uci.edu

Michael Townsley
School of Criminology and Criminal Justice, Griffith University, Brisbane,
Australia, m.townsley@griffith.edu.au

Mona Vajihollahi
Institute for Canadian Urban Research Studies, Simon Fraser University,
Vancouver, BC, Canada, monav@sfu.ca

David Weisburd
Institute of Criminology, Hebrew University, Jerusalem, Israel, and Department
of Administration of Justice, George Mason University, Manassas, VA, USA,
msefrat@mscc.huji.ac.il

Per-Olof H. Wikström
Institute of Criminology, University of Cambridge, United Kingdom,
pow20@cam.ac.uk

Johan van Wilsem
Department of Criminology, Leiden University, The Netherlands,
j.a.van.wilsem@law.leidenuniv.nl

Kathryn Wuschke
Institute for Canadian Urban Research Studies, Simon Fraser University,
Vancouver, BC, Canada, wuschke@sfu.ca

Part I
Introduction

Chapter 1
Units of Analysis in Geographic Criminology: Historical Development, Critical Issues, and Open Questions

David Weisburd, Gerben J.N. Bruinsma, and Wim Bernasco

Abstract Social scientists have had a long and enduring interest in the geography of crime and the explanation of variation of crime at place. In this introductory chapter, we first describe the history of crime and place studies, showing that in the course of two centuries, scholars have increasingly focused their interest on smaller spatial units of analysis. In the 19th century, they typically studied large administrative districts such as regions and countries. The Chicago School focused on much smaller urban communities. More recently, interest has moved toward geographic units as small as street blocks or addresses. After this historical account, we address specific questions regarding how the unit of analysis should be chosen for crime and place studies. We address substantive theoretical, statistical, and practical problems that are raised in choosing appropriate levels of geography for research and practice. We discuss issues of theory and data and consider the factors that have inhibited the study of units of analysis of crime at place to date, mentioning the specific contributions to the unit of analysis problem that are made by the chapters that follow.

Introduction

Criminologists have had a long and enduring interest in the idea of place and its role in the production of crime (Weisburd and McEwen 1997). In 1829 Adriano Balbi and Andre-Michel Guerry compared education levels and crime across large French administrative areas ("departments") and discovered not only that crime varied across them, but that places with higher levels of education also had higher levels of property crime (Balbi and Guerry 1829; Kenwitz 1987). This finding, though surprising at the time given popular assumptions about the role of poverty in crime and reflective of a new fascination with the ability of social scientists to bring insights

D. Weisburd
Institute of Criminology, Hebrew University, Jerusalem, Israel; Department of Administration of Justice, George Mason University, Manassas, VA, USA
e-mail: msefrat@mscc.huji.ac.il

D. Weisburd et al. (eds.), *Putting Crime in its Place*,
DOI 10.1007/978-0-387-09688-9_1, © Springer Science+Business Media, LLC 2009

into the nature and causes of social problems, was reinforced in similar studies conducted during the period. For example, the Belgian astronomer and statistician Lambert Adolphe Quetelet (1831/1984) also observed the variability of crime across large administrative areas, noting that some of the poorest areas of France and the Low Countries had the lowest crime rates (see Beirne 1987). Quetelet concluded that poverty was not in itself the cause of crime, but rather that crime develops when the poor and disadvantaged "are surrounded by subjects of temptation and find themselves irritated by the continual view of luxury and of an inequality of fortune" (1831/1984, p. 38).

The interest of criminologists in geographic criminology did not end with these early contributions to the birth of a "positivist criminology" in Europe. Across the Atlantic Ocean, new and important insights about crime and place were to be brought in the early 20th century by criminologists associated with the University of Chicago (Burgess 1925/1967; Park 1925/1967; Thrasher 1927; Shaw 1929; Shaw and McKay 1942/1969). Led by Robert Park, these scholars looked to characteristics of the urban environment to explain the crime problem in American cities. They found that crime was strongly linked to social disorganization and poverty in urban settings. In turn, just as 19th-century studies of crime at place helped to spawn the science of criminology in Europe, study of crime and place in the Chicago School was to encourage the development of a strong empirical science of criminology in the United States.

In recent years, interest in crime and place has reemerged, and scholars in this area are once again at the cutting edge of major theoretical and empirical advances in criminology. In this case, the focus is not on the large administrative areas that were studied by European scholars in the 19th century or the middle level focus on neighborhoods and communities that sparked many of the important insights of the Chicago School and that continue to be an important concern of criminologists (e.g., see Reiss and Tonry 1986; Sampson et al. 1997), but rather a new concern with micro units of place such as addresses or street segments or clusters of these micro units of geography (e.g., see Eck and Weisburd 1995; Taylor 1997; Sherman 1995; Weisburd and Green 1995). Findings that 50 percent of crime is found at three or four percent of the micro crime places in a city (e.g., Sherman et al. 1989; Weisburd et al. 2004) has generated not only scholarly interest in crime at place but also strong policy and practitioner interest in what has been termed "hot spots of crime" (see Sherman and Weisburd 1995; National Research Council 2004; Weisburd and Braga 2006; Weisburd and Eck 2004).

While study of crime and place has thus had an enduring role in criminology and has often occupied an important position in advancing theoretical insights, there has to date been little sustained theoretical and methodological interest in understanding and defining the units of analysis that should be used. Criminologists have long been interested in the variability of crime at place, but they have given little thought to the level of geography that should be used in exploring such relationships. "What is a place? Should we study place at the micro or macro level? Is the action of crime at the level of regions, communities or micro place hot spots?" These questions are critical if we are to develop a systematic understanding of the role of place in crime, and we think it is surprising that to date, scholars have focused little systematic attention upon them.

Importantly, the unit of analysis problem is not unique to study of crime at place. These questions have formed an important focus of study in geography more generally in the context of what has been termed the "modifiable area unit problem" or MAUP (Openshaw 1984). The MAUP is a potential source of error that can affect the outcomes of the analysis of aggregated spatial data. There are numerous ways to aggregate individual point data and the results of the spatial analysis of aggregated data depend on the particular way in which individual points on the surface of the earth are aggregated into areal units. The MAUP consists of two parts, the problem of *scale* (how large should aggregated units be) and the problem of *aggregation* (how should points be allocated to larger units, i.e., how to aggregate). The MAUP is a significant problem in studies of crime at places, partly because these studies often depend on aggregated data that are provided by third parties, such as law enforcement agencies or the census administration, and there is often no way to study what the results would look like under alternative aggregations (Ratcliffe and McCullagh 1999).

The unit of analysis problem, in turn, is not restricted to problems of spatial aggregation in crime research. Criminologists over the last few decades have often criticized empirical studies of offenders for failing to recognize and examine critically the nature of the unit of analysis that is examined. The literature on co-offenders, for example, has cautioned criminologists regarding the simplistic assumption that we can explore the causes of individual offending without reference to the fact that crime is often carried out not by single offenders but by offenders working together in smaller groups (Erickson 1971; Erickson and Jensen 1977; Gold 1970; Klein 1969; Reiss 1986; Sarnecki 1986; Shaw and McKay 1931; Warr 1996). Co-offending in turn raises important questions about our examination not only of criminality, but also of the activities of criminal justice, for example of sentencing or processing of offenders (Reiss 1988; Short and Moland 1976; Waring 1998, 2002).

Our goal in this volume is to focus critical attention on units of analysis in what Sherman and colleagues (1989) have called the "criminology of place." We think that the growing interest in crime and place over the last few decades makes it particularly important to shed light on this question. Indeed, we are too far along in the scientific study of crime and place to leave unit of analysis to the serendipitous interest of singular scholars. For crime and place studies to advance significantly over the coming decades, we need to subject not only crime places to empirical inquiry, but also the spatial unit of analysis that we use in studying crime and place.

Our volume raises a series of core questions that we believe are critical to the development of crime and place studies. Would our understanding of crime at place be advanced most significantly if we focused on very small units of geography such as street addresses or street segments, or is the study of crime better served by examining larger aggregates such as administrative areas, census tracts, or communities? Or should we continue to examine differing geographic units depending on the questions we ask? Should the unit of analysis be defined by the nature of the problem that is studied or the policy questions that are examined? What statistical advances are needed for developing our understanding of units of analysis and especially for differentiating such units?

We begin this introductory chapter with a history of the role of place in criminology. While the chapters that follow focus on substantive questions related to the unit of analysis problem, we thought it important to begin by placing the criminology of place in context. Importantly, our historical review suggests that in the course of two centuries of study of geographic criminology, scholars have increasingly focused their interest on smaller spatial units of analysis. We then turn to specific questions that are raised regarding how the unit of analysis should be chosen for crime and place studies and the substantive theoretical and practical problems that are raised in choosing appropriate levels of geography for research and practice. The next section of our chapter is concerned with problems of theory and data and considers the factors that have inhibited study of units of analysis of crime at place to date. In these last two sections, we also describe the specific contributions of the chapters that follow and place them in the context of their contributions to the unit of analysis problem.

Putting Place in Criminological Context

As we have already noted, the story of the development of interest in geographic criminology starts in the early 19th century. Since that period interest has ebbed and flowed, though crime and place has played a part in many of the most important theoretical and practical crime prevention advances over the last two hundred years. Below we trace that history, noting the shifting interests of criminology in different geographic units of analysis and the tendency over time for the action at crime at place to be focused on increasingly smaller units of geography.

The First Geographical Crime Research in France and Belgium: Macro Level Studies of Regions and Counties

Geographical criminology begins with the publication of crime statistics on the French population by the French Home Office in the 1820s. The publication of the *Comptes Générales de l'administration de la justice criminelle en France* inspired many statisticians and other scholars to explore in more detail data on crime. Among the very first was Baron Charles Dupont who spoke for the first time about statistics on morality of people and the nation in a meeting of the *Conservatoire des Arts et Métiers* in November 1826 (Beirne 1993). As a cartographer, he published in 1816 tables on the "distribution of illiterates" across the regions of France. During this meeting, he promised to publish a map on crime and criminals soon. However, the Belgian Edouard Ducpétiaux was the first to publish a table with crime and suicide figures of regions in Spain, France, Italy, and England (Ducpétiaux 1827).

He observed remarkable differences between regions and countries and concluded that the morality of nations differed (ibid., pp. 11–12). The Lower Lands (The Netherlands) were especially praised for their low crime rates and for a low number of homeless people (ibid., p. 29).

In 1829 the first geographical map of crime was published. Partly based on the *Comptes Générales de l'administration de la justice criminelle en France*, Michel-André Guerry and the Venetian cartographer Adriano Balbi published on one large sheet, three maps on the distribution of crime in France in the years 1825–1827. It was a novelty in the new field of criminology that they made use of a cartographic method of presenting statistical material. They concluded from their work that (1) in certain regions in France (departments) with higher numbers of personal[1] crimes, there was less property crime; (2) that the area above the line of Orléans and Lyon showed the highest rate of property crimes in France; and (3) in urban areas, especially in the capital of Paris, the highest numbers of property and personal crimes could be observed. Later, when Guerry became head of the Crime Statistics Unit of the France Ministry of Justice, he continued his work on mapping crime. In 1833 his influential *Essai sur la statistique morale de la France* was published (Guerry 1833). Inspired by the Reform Movement[2] of the 19th century, Guerry examined whether poverty and density of population might lead to higher crime rates. He observed, however, an empirical complexity. The rich north *departements* were confronted with higher property crime rates than the poor *departements* in the south of France. He concluded that the level of poverty was not the direct cause of crime. Similarly, his data suggested that population density was not a cause of crime.

The studies by Guerry (1832; 1833) soon became the subject of a heated debate between proponents and opponents of the Reform Movement, especially in England. A British Member of Parliament defended the work of Guerry, but the industrialist William Greg criticized Guerry's conclusions (Greg 1839; Beirne 1993, pp. 129–131). In 1864 Guerry published again a comparison of crime rates between England and France (Guerry 1864). We can hardly imagine today the work he had to carry out collecting and analyzing the data, which included over 226,000 cases of personal crime in the two countries over 25 years and, for France only, over 85,000 suicide records (Friendly 2007). The results of this effort reinforced the findings he had published 30 years before.

His friend Alexandre Parent-Duchâtelet published in 1836 an empirical study containing maps on the distribution of prostitution from 1400 till 1830 in Paris (Parent-Duchâtelet 1837). Because of the official control of brothels by the Paris authorities, systematic data were available on prostitutes, especially from the years 1817 to 1827. Even information regarding the "*departements*" they came from were collected. Not surprisingly, the center of the city had the highest number of prosti-

---

[1] We would now label them as violent crimes.

[2] In France and England, the Reform Movement focused its policy on public health and education for the poor.

tutes, especially "*quartier 6*". He used neighborhoods as defined by administrative boundaries as units of analyses.

The French scholar Michel-André Guerry is often bracketed together with the Belgium statistician and astronomer Adolphe Quetelet who discovered the normal distribution in statistics with which deviations can be observed and calculated (Quetelet 1847; Landau and Lazarsfeld 1968). In 1828, Quetelet (1831/1984) examined the French *Comptes Générales de l'administration de la justice criminelle en France* in a lecture for the Academy of Science to show how crime rates vary with the seasons of the year. He demonstrated that June had the highest numbers of violent crimes of the year. He also examined crime data in each *arrondissement* and added, "It appeared to me that these numbers were able to give a sufficiently satisfactory idea of the state of knowledge in each department and especially for the inferior classes where most crimes are committed" (ibid. p. 30). He used provinces and countries as units of analyses. Groningen, South-Brabant, Anvers, Limburg and Drenthe had the highest crime rates of all provinces of the Lower Lands (including Flanders). He discussed these observations as was common in the period, in the context of social factors such as poverty, heterogeneity, composition of the population, and attractiveness of cities. He explained the higher rates of property crimes of the richer provinces, as we noted in our introduction, by the unequal distribution of wealth: a great number of people possess nothing compared to the relatively few rich citizens (1984, p. 38).

The French and Belgian scholars were the first who scientifically analyzed crime at place. These scholars focused on the administrative and political borders of their time in their geographical crime analyses. Nations, regions, counties, provinces, departments, and *quartiers* were the units of analyses and they were used as a unit for systematic comparisons of crime figures. They were fully dependent on official crime data and other data that the government supplied arranged within these larger geographic units. While the early French and Belgian researchers concerned with crime and place also examined some variability of crime within cities, their overall focus was generally on larger administrative units. Importantly, these early criminologists in their focus on crime rates and official statistics also helped to encourage the more general development of a positivist empirical criminology (Beirne 1987).

Pioneers in England in the 19th Century

France and Belgium were not the only countries where geographical studies on crime were carried out in the 19th century. Members of *the Statistical Society of London* also regularly published on crime topics in their statistical journal.[3] Two articles on crimes were included in the second volume. One was by a prison chaplain who wrote on *Criminal Statistics of Preston* and the other was a short article about the distribution and kinds of robberies in London and Liverpool (mentioned in

---

[3] Their journal was published in 1838 for the first time.

Morris 1957, p. 53). In this and later papers of members of the society, the influence of the work of Guerry can be observed.

In the year 1839, a lecture by William Greg on the spatial distribution of population density, fertility, education, and crime in the Netherlands[4] for the *British Association for the Advancement of Science* of August 1835 was published by Ridgway and Sons. He compared the crime figures on property crimes, violent crimes, and on serious crimes like rape, murder, and manslaughter in the Netherlands with those of England and France. The overall crime figures showed remarkable differences: for the year 1826 the data indicated that the Netherlands had less crime than the other two countries: 1:28,900 inhabitants, in England 1:23,400, and in France 1:17,570 (Greg 1839, p. 15). Greg also studied in more detail large areas of the Lower Lands. He counted the most crimes for the province of Overijssel, followed by South-Brabant, Groningen and Drenthe, and West-Flanders.[5] The lowest overall crime rates were found in the province of Friesland. For that period the highest position of Overijssel in the crime ranking was striking because this province also showed the highest education level for all of Europe (Greg 1839, p. 24). Serious crime was more likely to be present in the provinces of South-Brabant, Liege, Groningen, and East-Flanders.

Rawson R. Rawson, then secretary of the society, correlated variables such as age and sex with crime, but also presented the number of crimes for the districts of England and Wales (Rawson 1839). He discussed the variability in crime across the districts and concluded that climate and ethnic differences in the population could not be the causes of crime. He rejected the conclusions of Guerry on the relationship between education and crime. He assumed that the type of labor could be a cause of crime and divided regions in England into (1) rural areas with farms; (2) industrial areas; (3) mining areas; and (4) big cities. Rawson's research illustrates the critical role that the unit of analysis can play in the development of our understanding of crime at place. He is the first scholar to go beyond the usual administrative and political borders (Morris 1957, p. 55). Based on official data, he found that large cities had the highest crime rates and mining areas the lowest.

His successor at the society, Joseph Fletcher, continued the work of Guerry and Rawson. He studied for many years the relationship between education and crime by producing maps showing the levels of crime and illiteracy of England and Wales (later published in Fletcher 1850). According to Fletcher, there were four causes of the level of "immorality" of populations: (1) population density; (2) the distribution of property across societies; (3) the number of people earning their own income; and (4) the level of illiteracy of the population.[6] He indicated the level of immorality of the population by the number and nature of crimes committed; the number of marriages with a man younger than 21[7]; the number of illegitimate children and

---

[4] In those days, parts of Belgium and Luxembourg were also included in the Netherlands.

[5] As discussed in the former paragraph, Quetelet observed similar findings 25 years later.

[6] Measured by the number of crosses instead of signatures in the registers of marriage!

[7] This indicator pointed then at forced marriages because of pregnancy.

the number of bank accounts in the population. He argued (1850) that not only were differences between regions important in the explanation of crime rates, but so was the speed with which these regions changed over time economically and demographically. With these ideas Fletcher can be seen as a precursor of the French sociologist Emile Durkheim who introduced the concept of anomie to explain the impact of societal changes on people and society (Durkheim 1893/1964).

John Glyde (1856) was the first to question the validity of the research findings when large areas were chosen as units of analysis in geographic criminology. In his paper *Localities of crime in Suffolk* he showed very clearly that larger units of analysis hide underlying variations in crime. When smaller units than districts or *departements* were taken into account, significant differences in crime rates across smaller areas appeared. As Morris (1957, p. 58) notes, "Of the regional studies, a major criticism is that the county was the smallest territorial unit considered, but Glyde, by breaking Suffolk down into its seventeen Poor Law Unions was able to demonstrate that the 'County Aggregate' masked considerable differences between the smaller geographical units of which it was composed." Glyde also observed that middle-sized cities situated along main roads had higher crime rates than the mean of the large area they were part of. Jelinger Symons (1857/2000, p. 281) also examined the relationship between urbanization and crime through ecological analyses of crime in Liverpool, Bristol, and Cardiff. In his view, it was the speed with which the population increases that explains higher crime figures.

In studies of crime and place in England in the 19th century, the work of Henry Mayhew cannot be neglected. He is well known in criminology (and cited therefore) for his descriptive studies of the underworld of London in the middle Victorian Age (1851/1950). However, his detailed studies on the distribution of crime in England and London are also a rich source for those studying crime. He was an excellent observer of his time, describing in four voluminous books precisely and in detail the daily life of the Londoners, their habits, their cloths, their quarters, and streets in the Victorian era (Mayhew 1865). Mayhew also tried to uncover patterns in the distribution of crime in the city of London combining ethnographic methods and statistical data.[8] He interviewed prostitutes, criminals, and other citizens about alcoholism, poverty, housing conditions, and economic uncertainty. He was the first scholar who focused on small areas like squares, streets, and buildings as a unit of analysis in criminological research, predating modern interests in micro crime places (see later) by over a century. Mayhew also used police data of the seven Metropolitan Police Divisions and revealed that two of these divisions produced about 65 percent of all the suspects in London.

After 1870 the interest of French and English academics in geographic and statistical analyses diminished. At the same time, there are important exceptions. In one of them, Cesare Lombroso studied the geographical distribution of homicide, infanticide, parricide, and suicide across very large geographic areas in Italy

---

[8] In a sense, Mayhew already practised the methodology that Robert Park (1925) advocated 70 years later in the 1920s in Chicago.

(Lombroso 1878/2006). He explained the different violent crime rates between the north and the south of the country in reference to the "racial inferiority" of the southern population. The French criminologist Jean-Gabriel Tarde studied the relationship between urbanization and crime from a different perspective than earlier scholars (Tarde 1890/1912, p. 338). By comparing the crime levels of larger areas, he argued that cities were exporting crime to the rural areas. He wrote, ". . . today we can see crime spreading from the great cities to the country, from the capitals to the provinces, and these capitals and great cities having an irresistible attraction for the outcasts and scoundrels of the country, or the provinces, who hasten to them to become civilized after their own manner, a new kind of ennobling" (Tarde 1890/1912, p. 338).

Chicago and the Dynamics of Cities: Neighborhoods and Square Miles as Unit of Analyses

After the turn of the century, the locus of geographic research on crime moved to the United States, and especially to the city of Chicago. At the University of Chicago, a group of sociologists[9] took the initiative to undertake new research on urban problems, which centered in part on crime (Faris 1967; Bulmer 1984; Harvey 1987; Beirne and Messerschmidt 1991). They also moved the action of crime and place research from broad comparisons across large geographic areas to more careful comparisons within cities. Interestingly, the Chicago School scholars were either not aware of or ignored till 1933 the work of 19th-century crime and place researchers in Europe (Elmer 1933).

American cities grew in the second part of the 19th century and first part of the 20th century faster than ever before in history, with all the social problems associated with such growth. Chicago itself played an important role in the integration of large numbers of Italian, Irish, German, Chinese, Polish, Jewish, and Scandinavian immigrants. The city evolved from a very small settlement in 1840 (with 4,470 inhabitants) to a city with a half-million inhabitants in 1880. Ten years later, the population had increased to one million, and in 1930, to about 3.5 million. Crime was perceived as one of the most important urban problems:

> After World War I (1914–1918), Chicago sociologists turned their ecological attentions to a variety of social problems. Exacerbated by the severe hardships of the Great Depression, Prohibition, and by the well-publicized rise of gangland warfare and union racketeering, crime itself came to be seen as a major social problem in Chicago. Crime, therefore, was one of the chief topics studied by members of the Chicago School (Beirne and Messerschmidt 1991, p. 362).

Now a group of American sociologists, among them, Robert Park, William Thomas, Louis Wirth, Ernest Burgess, Clifford Shaw, and Henry McKay, took a

---

[9] As Burgess and Bogue (1964, p. 1) demonstrated, other disciplines and governmental agencies also studied urban life in Chicago extensively (also see Bulmer 1984; Faris 1967).

leadership role in the development of the criminology of place, in contrast to the statisticians, criminal lawyers, or psychiatrists who dominated criminology more generally in Europe (Vold et al. 2002).

William Thomas contributed to the criminology of place by introducing the important concept of *social disorganization*, referring to "a decrease of the influence of existing social rules of behavior upon individual members of the group" (Thomas 1966, p. 3). The concept naturally focused on neighborhoods or communities. Robert Park (1864–1944), who was recruited by Thomas, was the initiator of urban social research on crime places, shifting the unit of analyses from countries and large areas to cities and their neighborhoods (Park 1925/1967). The city in his opinion was more than "... a congeries of individual men and of social conveniences – streets, buildings, electric lights, tramways, and telephones, etc; something more, also, than a mere constellation of institutions and administrative devices – courts, hospitals, schools, police and, civil functionaries of various sorts. The city is, rather, a state of mind, a body of costumes and traditions, and of the organized attitudes and sentiments that inhere in these costumes and are transmitted with this tradition. The city is not, in other words, merely a physical mechanism and an artificial construction. It is involved in the vital process of the people who compose it; it is a product of nature, and particularly of human nature" (Park 1925/1967, p. 1). Park argued that urban life must be studied in this context in terms of "its physical organization, its occupations, and its culture" and especially the changes therein (Park, 1925/1967, p. 3). Neighborhoods in his view were the elementary form of cohesion in urban life.

His younger colleague, Ernest Burgess, drawing from an inventory of price changes in housing values in Chicago areas developed a concentric zone model of the distribution of social problems and crime for cities (especially for Chicago) (Burgess 1925/1967).[10] Burgess suggested that Chicago included five concentric[11] zones, each containing various neighborhoods, four of them situated around "The Loop" (the business center of the city): "the typical processes of the expansion of the city can best be illustrated, perhaps, by a series of concentric circles, which may be numbered to designate both the successive zones of urban extension and the types of areas differentiated in the process of expansion" (Burgess 1925/1967, p. 50). Burgess' unit of analysis was a series of neighborhoods within cities that share similar characteristics. He assumed that depending on the distances to the center and the special features of these zones, the levels of crime would vary.

Clifford Shaw was one of the first Chicago sociologists to carry out extensive empirical research on the geographical distribution of crime on the basis of Burgess' zone model (Shaw 1929). This study can be seen as a landmark in the history of crime and places studies because of its detailed data collection, advanced methods, and innovative statistical tools. Based on the concentric zone model of Burgess,

---

[10] The real-estate agent had discovered zones in the city of Chicago when he made up an inventory of price changes of houses and real estate. He contacted Burgess regarding his findings, which led to the now famous geographic model of crime and social problems in the urban context.

[11] In reality only half circles because Chicago is situated at the border of Lake Michigan.

he studied the distribution of truancy of young people, juvenile delinquents, and adult offenders in Chicago. Assisted by young researchers like Henry McKay, Frederick Zorbaugh, and Leonard Cottrell, he took natural areas as units of analyses (Abbott 1997) but in more detail than ever before in these kinds of studies.[12] Shaw introduced new units of analyses. First, he introduced *spot maps* by plotting the home address of thousands of offenders on a map of Chicago. Second, he combined the offender address data with census data to create *delinquency rate maps* of square-mile areas. And finally, he constructed *radial maps* and *zone maps*, which displayed delinquency rates at regular distances from the city center.

For further analyses on the distribution of crime across Chicago, Shaw divided the city into 431 census tracts in 1910 and 499 in 1920 (Shaw 1929). Each census tract included convenient age and sex groups of the population. Subsequently, these census tracts were combined into square-mile areas with a minimum population of 500 residents. The technique was to allocate delinquents to their place of residence and to divide the number of delinquents by the number of boys of juvenile court age, in order to compute rates for small areas. These rates were used by Shaw and his associates to make shaded maps or compute correlations.

In the same year Shaw's research assistant Harvey Zorbaugh published his PhD in which he compared a slum neighborhood (The Lower North Side) with a wealthy area (Gold Coast) in Chicago, both situated in close proximity (Zorbaugh 1929). In this more qualitative study, Zorbaugh presented only a few maps, all of them less detailed in information than Shaw's study. However, his research demonstrated clearly that two areas in close physical proximity did not illustrate that physical and social distances coincide. As Park wrote in his foreword of Zorbaugh's study, "a situation in which people who live side by side are not, and – because of the divergence of their interests and their heritages – cannot, even with the best good will, become neighbors" (1929, p. ix), pointing to the invalid assumption of policy makers (and criminologists) that people living in the same locality shared the same backgrounds and interests. This conclusion is very important for the choice of the unit of analysis in criminological research. This PhD study made explicit that administrative and political areas and social spaces are not identical. Depending on the size of the area, a variety of social communities with different identities can exist. Importantly, he concluded that the smaller the unit of analysis, the greater the chance of a homogeneous community.

In 1942, Clifford Shaw and Henry McKay published their magnum opus *Juvenile Delinquency and Urban Areas* in which they presented not only their geographical

---

[12] It is interesting to note that a similar approach was taken by Cyrill Burt (1883–1971) who studied the location of the home addresses of delinquent boys and girls in the years 1922 and 1923 in London. Following the Chicago School findings, he noted that the highest concentrations in crime were found in three neighborhoods situated closely to the city center: Holborn, Finsbury, and Shoreditch (Burt 1924/1944). According to Burt, these oldest but not poorest neighborhoods of London were for offenders of strategic importance, because they were situated closely to attractive crime targets in the inner city and – if necessary – they could function as a place to hide from the police.

and etiological analyses of crime rates in the city of Chicago, but also those of other cities: Philadelphia, Boston, Cincinnati, Cleveland, and Richmond. In principle, they used similar analytic tools as introduced in their study of 1929. Again, they employed spot maps, rate maps, radial maps, and zone maps to illustrate concentrations of crime and offenders in the city of Chicago over a long period of time (up to 60 years). In all of the studied cities, they found similar patterns in the geographical distribution of crime. However, the units of analysis differed a good deal between the various cities. These differences were due to the lack of detailed official crime data in cities other than Chicago. The rapid changes in the city Chicago over a long period of time enabled them also to study the effects of the dynamics of the city on crime and other phenomena. One of their findings was that "The data on trends also demonstrate with equal sharpness the rapid rise in rates of delinquents in certain areas when a population with a different history and different institutions and values takes over areas in a very short period of time" (Shaw and McKay 1942/1969, p. 382).

The Chicago studies inspired other criminologists to carry out empirical crime and place research in other cities (e.g., see Burgess and Bogue 1964a).[13] At the same time, as the decades passed, empirical and methodological critics of the Chicago approach began to emerge (Lander 1954). First, it was argued that Shaw (1929) and Shaw and McKay (1942/1969) could not distinguish between the dwelling place of the offender and the location where he or she committed a crime, neglecting the variability in the mobility of offenders (see also Boggs 1965). Second, by relying on official crime figures, their research was seen as biased because offenders of the lower class had (and still have) a greater chance to be processed in the criminal justice system (for instance, Gordon 1967; Chilton 1964; Chilton and Dussich 1974; Beirne and Messerschmidt 1991). Third, delinquency rates after 1945 in Chicago did not conform to the distribution patterns of Shaw and McKay's early assumptions (Bursik 1984, 1986). European studies also showed contradicting results. Morris (1957) examined the offender rates of the county of Croydon, but could not confirm the zone model of Burgess. Twenty years later, Morris' findings were replicated in the city of Sheffield (Baldwin and Bottoms 1976). In Europe, the direct and indirect consequences of the operation of housing markets confounded the results of the geographical distribution of crime in American cities.

Another criticism that is key to our concern with units of analysis for crime place studies is that brought by Robinson (1950) who discussed the use of ecological correlations in geographical studies like that of Shaw and McKay (1942/1969). According to Robinson (1950, p. 351) the object of an ecological correlation is a group of persons, not a person: "... the individual correlation depends on the internal frequencies of the within-areas individual correlations, while the ecological

---

[13] Interesting to mention here is the relatively unknown policy report of Edwin Sutherland (1883–1950) on the geographical distribution of juvenile delinquency of the city of Bloomington, Indiana (Sutherland 1937). Inspired by the work of Shaw and McKay and using the zone model of Burgess, he revealed, like in Chicago, certain delinquent neighborhoods with high numbers of adult and juvenile offenders.

correlation depends upon the marginal frequencies of the within-areas individual correlations" (Robinson 1950, p. 354). He concluded that ecological correlations cannot validly be used as substitutes for individual correlations. Such an ecological fallacy leads to meaningless conclusions. Looking back, these empirical and methodological critics diminished the attention of criminologists to studies of crime and place for almost twenty years.

Reemerging Interest in Communities and the Emergence of Study of Micro Crime Places

In the 1980s, Albert J. Reiss Jr. was to encourage a group of younger criminologists to return to the interests of the Chicago School where he had received his PhD in 1949. Reiss (1986) saw the criminological tradition as including two major theoretical positions, one that focused on individuals and a second that focused on crimes. Communities and crime was a main focus of the latter tradition and he sought to rekindle criminological interest in understanding variability of crime within and across communities. Editing an early volume in the *Crime and Justice* series, Reiss and Michael Tonry sought to bring *Communities and Crime* (1986) to the forefront of criminological interests.

Reiss did not see the new interest as simply mimicking the insights of the Chicago School criminologists. Rather, he sought to raise a new set of questions about crime at place that had been ignored in earlier decades: "Recent work on communities and crime has turned to the observation that Shaw and McKay neglected: not only do communities change their structures over time but so often do their crime rates (Kobrin and Schuerman 1981; Bursik and Webb 1982; Bursik 1986; Schuerman and Kobrin 1986; Skogan 1986), a recognition that communities as well as individuals have crime careers" (Reiss 1986, p. 19). Many of the contributors to the Reiss and Tonry volume would become leaders of a new generation of criminologists, once again suggesting the important and enduring role of crime and place in advancing the criminological enterprise more generally. Among the contributors were Wes Skogan, Robert Sampson, Douglas Smith, Robert Bursik, Ralph Taylor, Stephen Gottfredson, and Lawrence Sherman.

This volume and other work developed in this period drew upon the identification of neighborhoods and communities to expand insights about the development of crime (Brantingham and Brantingham 1981/1991; Bursik and Webb 1982; Clarke 1983; Hunter 1988; LeBeau 1987; Rengert 1980, 1981; Roncek and Bell 1981; Sampson 1985; Sampson and Groves 1989). Smith (1987), for example, identified neighborhood variation in the behavior of the police, suggesting the importance of place in understanding not only the etiology of crime, but also the etiology of criminal justice. Skogan brought new insights not only to our understanding of the interaction of community characteristics and policing (Skogan 1986), but also more generally to the developmental processes that led to the emergence of crime and disorder in urban communities (Skogan, 1990). More recently, scholars led by Robert Sampson have used a focus on the community to draw new insights into developmental crime patterns, arguing that social cohesion within communities and shared expectations of community members combine to affect both crime and social disorder (Sampson and Raudenbush 1999; Sampson et al. 1997).

Consistent with Reiss' call for investigation of the criminal careers of communities, Bursik (1986; see also Bursik and Webb 1982) revisited crime in Chicago neighborhoods over time and challenged earlier views of the stability of crime within neighborhoods and communities, arguing that stability in crime patterns was a result of long-term stability in the social characteristics of places, and that instability in such patterns would also lead to instability in crime rates. Similarly, Schuerman and Kobrin (1986) identified stability and variability in criminal careers of places, focusing on the residences of juvenile delinquents as had Shaw and McKay (1942). Using the number of residential addresses of officially known delinquents by census tracts in Los Angeles as an indicator of aggregate crime they found three general patterns that led to high crime rates in 1970. The first pattern they termed "emerging" and referred to those clusters that were relatively crime free in 1950 but had moderate to high crime in 1960 and 1970, respectively. The second pattern, "transitional", refers to those clusters that had moderately high crime in 1950, a higher level in1960 and an even higher level in 1970. The last pattern is referred to as "enduring" and refers to those clusters that had persistently high crime rates at all points in time. The vast majority of census tracts within the clusters were designated as having enduring crime rates over the time span with fewer census tracts in the transitional and emerging categories.

Interestingly, though the approach of the Chicago School called for the identification of units of geography that would not be drawn from administrative data collection, but from the social units that defined neighborhoods or communities, this new generation of scholars concerned with communities and crime have generally used officially defined units for drawing their data and conclusions. In this case, the US Census definitions, most often census tracts or the smaller census block groups, have become the main source for defining the units of geography that are the focus of research in the United States, despite the fact that the goals of the census in creating physically contiguous geographic units are often inconsistent with the goals of community and crime researchers (see Rengert and Lockwood, this volume). Often such studies will simply assume that census units such as census tracts reflect actual community boundaries (Hipp 2007), though some scholars in this area combine census units with the idea of creating boundaries of communities that are more consistent with the theoretical interests of researchers (e.g., see Sampson et al. 1997). Importantly, this new focus on communities and crime often led to the study of much smaller geographic units of analysis than had drawn the interests of the Chicago School scholars.

While a reemergence of interest in communities and crime had been one important source for renewed study of crime and place in recent decades, the 1980s produced a more radical reformulation of the unit of geography that should form the basis of crime place studies, continuing to push the unit of geographic analysis to a more micro level. Traditional criminological interest in place has focused on higher level geographic units such as regions, cities, communities, or neighborhoods. One reason for this focus on macro levels of geography is simply that data were often not available at geographic levels lower than the standard administrative or census divisions. But even when data were available, statistical and analytic tools were not readily available for linking crime easily with micro units of geography.

Certainly, the difficulty of mapping crimes to specific places and of analyzing geographic data were factors that prevented study of crime at micro units of geography, but another barrier was the lack of consistent theoretical interest in micro places as contrasted with research on individual criminality or crime across macro geographic units (Weisburd and McEwen 1997; Weisburd et al. 2004). Such theoretical interest was not to emerge until the late 1970s and 1980s, about the time that computerized crime mapping and more sophisticated geographic statistical tools were to emerge (Weisburd and McEwen 1997). A new group of theorists challenged traditional criminological interests and began to focus more on the "processes operating at the moment of the crime's occurrence" (Birkbeck and LaFree 1993, p. 114). One influential critique that was to have strong influence on the development of interest in micro units of geography was brought out by Lawrence Cohen and Marcus Felson (1979). They argued that the emphasis placed on individual motivation in criminological theory failed to recognize the importance of other elements of the crime equation. They argued that crime rates could be affected by changing the nature of targets or of guardianship, irrespective of the nature of criminal motivations. The "routine activities" perspective they presented established the spatial and temporal context of criminal events as an important focus of study.

Canadian criminologists Patricia and Paul Brantingham (1993) made the connection between routine activities and place even more directly in their development of "crime pattern theory." Crime pattern theory focuses directly upon places by asking how targets come to the attention of offenders and how that influences the distribution of crime events over time and across places. Like Cohen and Felson, Brantingham and Brantingham see routine human social and economic activities as a critical feature of the crime equation, but in this case the place is made an explicit rather than implicit part of this equation, providing a "backcloth" for human behavior.

Drawing upon similar themes, British scholars led by Ronald Clarke began to explore the theoretical and practical possibilities of "situational crime prevention" in the 1980s (Clarke 1983, 1992, 1995; Cornish and Clarke 1986). Their focus was on criminal contexts and the possibilities for reducing the opportunities for crime in very specific situations. Their approach turned traditional crime prevention theory on its head. At the center of their crime equation was opportunity. And they sought to change opportunity rather than reform offenders. In situational crime prevention, more often than not, "opportunity makes the thief" (Felson and Clarke 1998). This was in sharp contrast to the traditional view that the thief simply took advantage of a very large number of potential opportunities. Importantly, in a series of case studies situational crime prevention advocates showed that reducing criminal opportunities in very specific contexts can lead to crime reduction and prevention (Clarke 1992, 1995).

One implication of these emerging perspectives is that micro crime places were an important focus of inquiry. Places in this "micro" context are specific locations within the larger social environments of communities and neighborhoods (Eck and Weisburd 1995). They are sometimes defined as buildings or addresses (e.g., see Green (Mazerolle), 1996; Sherman et al. 1989), sometimes as blockfaces, "hundred blocks", or street segments (e.g., see Taylor 1997; Weisburd et al. 2004), sometimes as clusters of addresses, blockfaces, or street segments (e.g., see Block et al. 1995; Sherman and Weisburd 1995; Weisburd and Green 1995). Research in this area began with attempts to identify the relationship between specific aspects of urban design (Jeffery 1971) or urban architecture and crime (Newman 1972) but broadened to take into account a much larger set of characteristics of physical space and criminal opportunity (Brantingham and Brantingham 1991 [1981]; e.g., see Brantingham and Brantingham 1975; Duffala 1976; Hunter 1988; LeBeau 1987; Mayhew et al. 1976; Rengert 1980; Rengert 1981). In 1989, Sherman and colleagues coined the term the "criminology of place," to describe this new approach that drew its theoretical grounding from routine activities and situational crime prevention to emphasize the importance of micro crime places in the etiology of crime.

Recent studies point to the potential theoretical and practical benefits of focusing research on micro crime places. A number of studies, for example, suggest that there is a very significant clustering of crime at places, irrespective of the specific unit of analysis that is defined (Brantingham and Brantingham 1999; Crow and Bull 1975; Pierce et al. 1986; Roncek 2000; Sherman et al. 1989; Weisburd and Green 1994; Weisburd et al. 1992; Weisburd et al. 2004). The extent of the concentration of crime at place is dramatic. In one of the pioneering studies in this area, Sherman et al. (1989) found that only three and a half percent of the addresses in Minneapolis produced 50 percent of all calls to the police. Fifteen years later in a study in Seattle, Washington, Weisburd et al. (2004) reported that between four and five percent of street segments in the city accounted for 50 percent of crime incidents for each year over 14 years. These studies and others (Brantingham and Brantingham 1984; Clarke 1983; Curtis 1974; Maltz et al. [1990] 2000; Pyle 1976; Rengert 1980; Skogan 1990) have established crime places as an important focus of criminological inquiry. In turn, a number of recent crime prevention programs that focused on specific places often defined as crime "hot spots" have been found to reduce crime and disorder without evidence of spatial displacement of crime to other areas (Braga 2001; Eck and Weisburd 2004; Weisburd et al. 2006).

At What Unit of Geography?

Our review suggests not only the enduring importance of research and theorizing about places in criminology, but also the diversity of units of analysis that have informed criminological study over the last two centuries. Interest in crime places began for the most part with the study of large administrative districts such as regions or even countries, in good part because that is how data were organized and available. In the Chicago School, scholars focused interest on social units that could not simply be defined using administrative units, but their interests still focused primarily on larger geographic units such as neighborhoods or communities. More recent interest in communities and crime has tended to focus on smaller, more specific, and targeted definitions of neighborhoods, often analyzing crime at place using data provided by the US census. Over the last two decades, interest in micro crime places has begun to attract significant criminological interest, in this case, bringing scholars to geographic units that operate much below the neighborhood level and sometimes in units as small as addresses or street blocks.

While criminologists have had a sustained interest in crime at place, the unit of analysis for study of geographic criminology has received little systematic theoretical or empirical attention. There is consensus about some basic rules of defining spatial units, such as the requirement that boundaries should be well defined, that units can only have a single boundary and cannot overlap each other, but the choice of spatial units is typically made on the basis of pragmatic arguments. Researchers today generally define the geographic boundaries for their studies based on data that are readily available, much as criminologists in the 19th century used data drawn from administrative areas defined by government departments. As George Rengert and Brian Lockwood note in this volume,

> The problem is that most of these boundaries are constructed for administrative purposes rather than for reasons of sound research designs. For example, census boundaries are constructed for administrative purposes of the enumeration of the population, zip code boundaries for postal delivery, police districts for allocation of resources, and political boundaries for purposes of administrative responsibility.

Even when researchers have defined boundaries based on theoretical domains, as did Shaw and McKay (1942/1969), they do not often examine critically the geographic unit of analysis employed.

At what level should we study crime at place? As we have described above there is an important trend over time toward study of crime at place at smaller units of geography. But does that trend reflect a fact about the level of geography that is important to understanding crime, or is it simply a result of the specific data available or theoretical interests of scholars? Of course, we might question why the unit of geography should matter at all. Perhaps the best approach is one that is eclectic in its understanding of crime at place.

While we do not discount the relevance of studying varying geographic units in coming to a more complete understanding of crime at place, it is important to recognize at the outset that studying crime at the "wrong" geographic unit may lead to a very misleading portrait of how place and crime interact. This was pointed out more than half a century ago by Robinson (1950) in his identification of what he termed the "ecological fallacy." In this volume, Liz Groff, David Weisburd, and Nancy Morris suggest that such biases in our understanding of crime may be present even when the units of geography used for study are measured at such levels as census tracts or census block groups. Groff and her colleagues examine street-to-street variability in juvenile crime patterns across time in the city of Seattle over a 14-year period. While they find that there is greater clustering of street segments with similar patterns or trajectories than would be expected by chance, their analyses show that there is also very strong street-to-street variability suggesting "independence" of street blocks in terms of crime patterns over time.

Such results imply (as had Glyde's observations more than 150 years earlier; see also Zorbaugh 1929) that when examining crime patterns at larger geographic levels, even such commonly used "smaller" units such as census tracts or census block groups will mask significant lower order geographic variability. If, for example, a census tract included both increasing and decreasing crime trajectories as identified by Groff et al., the portrait gained when aggregating segments to the census tract would likely lead a researcher to conclude that there is overall a stable trend of crime over time (masking the contrasting trends at the street block level). More generally, when there is a good deal of variability at a very local level of geography (e.g., a street segment or group of street segments), we might in measuring higher order geographic units miss local area effects. This can be referred to as "averaging" and presents today as in earlier decades an important challenge to crime and place research.

Such averaging can manifest itself in a number of ways that would lead to misleading interpretation of geographic data. A number of very active crime areas within a larger geographic unit might for example give the impression of an overall crime-prone area, when in fact most places in the larger geographic unit have low levels of crime. Similarly, when the vast majority of places have very little crime but a few very active places have very high crime counts, there can be a "washing out" of effect. In some sense, a conclusion in such a case that the area overall has little crime is correct. However, such a conclusion would miss the very important fact that some places within the larger unit are "hot spots of crime."

Of course, the ecological fallacy may not only apply to studies which rely on larger geographic units. If the "action of crime" is at higher levels of geography, an approach that focuses only on lower level variability can also be misleading. In this case, we might assume that there are important local effects, when they are simply reflecting higher order influences. Take for example a study that examines street blocks and finds that a relatively small number of street blocks are responsible for a large proportion of crime. It may be that all of those street blocks are in one central area of the city. In this case, the focus on micro units of geography might obscure the importance of larger community or neighborhood effects.

Contributors to this volume certainly show that there are local as well as higher order influences on crime at place. We have already noted the findings of Groff, Weisburd, and Morris. Oberwittler and Wikström employing a large survey in Peterborough (UK) that was structured to allow comparison of small area with larger area effects also find strong evidence of the contribution of very local area influences to crime. Their study emphasizes the homogeneity of responses in areas with 300–1,500 inhabitants as contrasted with units of greater than 5,000 inhabitants and finds that much variability in juvenile delinquency can be attributed to environmental characteristics at the local level. These data once again point to the importance of focusing on smaller more micro units of geography.

Importantly, beginning with a micro level approach also allows the researcher to examine the influences of larger geographic units, while starting at higher levels of geography may preclude examination of local variability. This problem is similar to that presented when choosing levels of measurement. The general admonition is to collect data at the highest level of measurement (interval or ratio scales), since such data can be converted to lower levels of measurement (Weisburd and Britt 2007). At the same time, data collected at lower levels of measurement (e.g., ordinal or nominal scales) cannot simply be disaggregated to higher levels. The same principle applies to geographic information, though the language is reversed. Collecting data at the lowest geographic level, or smallest units of analysis, allows aggregation up to higher levels but data collection at higher units may not allow conversion to more micro units of analysis. For this reason, Brantingham and Brantingham argue in this volume that crime analysis at places must begin with small spatial units and build larger units that reflect the reality of crime patterns. Their article presents a statistical methodology for building up from smaller units to levels that fully reflect variability in the data analyzed.

One problem, however, as Michael Maltz (this volume) notes is that there just may not be enough data at a very micro level from which to draw inferences (see also in this volume Brantingham et al.; Rengert; and Oberwitter and Wikström). Especially if one is interested in specific types of crime, they may be too rare in any single micro place unit, such as a street segment, to allow the identification of patterns or trends. Importantly, as well, the reality of the study of crime is that we are often dependent on social and demographic data that are drawn from data sources meant for other purposes. This will often create a dilemma for researchers, who need to do the best they can with the information available. Our point is not that researchers should not use the data at hand, but that they should be critical of the data used and recognize the potential fallacies of interpretation that may lead from the unit of analysis problem. In this context, George Rengert and Brian Lockwood's chapter in this volume both identifies the nature of such problems and presents methods for dealing with averaging and other problems in aggregated geographic data, including the difficult problem of drawing edges or geographic boundaries when such boundaries are difficult to define.

Moving Forward: Problems of Theory and Data

In focusing attention on units of geography for study of crime and place, we think it is important to also consider the factors that have inhibited study of this question to date. Why has the unit of analysis not been a more critical issue in the criminology of place? How can we move beyond prior studies and advance our understanding of how units of analysis influence our portrait of crime and place? Our view is that the "criminology of place" has reached a critical juncture, at which real advancement will require scholars to critically assess the unit of analysis problem. This volume was developed with this goal in mind and, before concluding this introductory chapter, we want to focus on specific barriers to advancement of our identification and understanding of units of analysis in crime and place research.

Perhaps the most important barrier to date develops from the relatively uncritical theoretical approach that crime and place researchers have brought to units of geography. This is in some sense understandable given the fact that most criminological theory has been focused on people and not on places (Brantingham and Brantingham 1990; Eck and Weisburd 2004; Nettler 1978; Sherman 1995; Weisburd 2002). The critical concern for most criminologists over the last half a century has been "why do people commit crime" not "why does crime occur in certain places"? Recent study of crime places suggests that this emphasis has provided a biased portrait of the crime problem and that the study of crime and place should be central in criminology (see Eck and Weisburd 1995; Weisburd 2002). Lawrence Sherman, for example, using data from Minneapolis, Minnesota, and comparing these to the concentration of offending in the Philadelphia Cohort Study (see Wolfgang et al. 1972), notes that future crime is "six times more predictable by the address of the occurrence than by the identity of the offender" (1995, pp. 36–37). Sherman asks, "why aren't we doing more about it? Why aren't we thinking more about wheredunit, rather than just whodunit?"

While there is growing evidence indicating the importance of crime places in criminology and crime and justice practice, theoretical attention to place and its definition has lagged far behind theoretical advances in study of individuals. But it is important to note that even those theories that have addressed directly the importance of place have failed to provide clear guidance as to the appropriate units of geography for understanding particular theories. For example, as we described earlier, social disorganization theory suggests the importance of macro level area effects, usually identified in such geographic units as neighborhoods or communities. But in defining social disorganization theory, scholars rarely provide specific guidance as to how to define the boundaries of these units of analysis. What is a community or neighborhood? This is still an issue of debate among scholars (Hipp 2007).

Routine activities or crime pattern theory suggest a very different, micro rather than macro level of geography, for crime place studies. But again, we are left with very little guidance as to how to define such "hot spots" or local contexts. Sometimes, places are measured as street segments or block faces, sometimes as addresses, and sometimes as small micro clusters of places (such as drug market areas). And this raises another issue, which we noted earlier, which is whether there is a competition between units of analysis or whether the units themselves depend on the nature of the problems studied. There may be no correct unit of geography for criminological study. And in this case we would have to recognize that units of analysis will change from study to study. Another important issue is the extent to which there needs to be integration of the person, context, and place levels in theory and in research. Oberwittler and Wikström (in this volume) and Wikström and Butterworth (2006) have begun to explore this question. But our knowledge is still at a very early stage of development.

Another critical problem for criminologists in the study of crime at place is that the data rather than theory have often driven empirical analysis. Our review of the history of geographic criminology suggests how this problem has been a consistent one beginning with the choice of large administrative areas in early 19th-century studies, to examination of much smaller, though still not micro crime place units developed by the US Census Bureau. In this case, geographic criminologists perhaps face a much more difficult problem than criminologists more generally, since most data sets in this area are not created by criminologists but rather drawn from such official agencies as the police or other local government. This means, as George Rengert and Brian Lockwood and Michael Maltz note in this volume, that the present data that define the boundaries of units for crime and place studies often have little to do with what is important in the criminology of place.

Clearly, new databases scaled to the units of geography that fit theories of crime and place will have to be developed if we are to advance our understanding of the criminology of place. Two chapters in this volume illustrate the importance of new data collection for developing such an understanding. The chapter by Oberwittler and Wikström described earlier is based on a major data collection effort that included information on "(i) *the individual* and his and her individual and social characteristics and experiences (data is collected through an interview, interviewer-led questionnaires and psychometric tests); (ii) *the environment* and the characteristics of different small-area environments of Peterborough (data is collected through a community survey); and (iii) *individuals' exposure to different environments* in Peterborough (data is collected using a Space-Time Budget technique)" for a sample of 6,600 respondents. Tita and Greenbaum also collect original data, in this case on the perceptions and attitudes of gang members to understand the geographic context of gang violence. Their contribution to our volume is particularly important because it emphasizes that specific geographic units may not always be easily defined in trying to understand social phenomena. Indeed, the geographic distribution of gang violence as reflected in their data is conditioned by the "socio-spatial dimensions of the gang rivalry network." While place clearly matters in understanding gang violence, place is only one part of a more complex story. We suspect that such social contexts play an important role as well in many other types of crime.

While original and innovative data collection, such as that represented by these chapters in our volume, must form an important part of crime and place studies, such data collection is very expensive and we cannot expect for advances in this area to rely solely on costly new databases given present support for crime research and social research more generally. Our volume also shows that we can learn much using existing data. Advances in geographic information systems have meant that local governments are now collecting and keeping detailed information on places at lower levels of geography. While they are not doing so to advance criminological inquiry, the data they keep for routine administrative purposes can provide important insights into our understanding of crime and place.

Johnson, Bowers, Birks, and Pease draw from official police data on burglaries from Merseyside (UK) over a fourteen-month period to assess how well crime locations can be predicted based on prior patterns. Their study reinforces the predictive value of repeat victimization (Anderson et al. 1995; Farrell and Pease 2001; Forrester et al. 1988; Polvi et al. 1990, 1991), but also raises important questions about the level at which police activities should be brought to address burglary problems. Johan van Wilsem also uses crime data collected by the police, but supplements such data with social information collected by the Center for Research and Statistics of the Rotterdam municipality to examine the factors that influence the commission of violent crime. Van Wilsem finds that street-level characteristics and routine activities are important to understanding the geographic concentration of crime reinforcing recent interest in micro place units of analysis. Finally, Smith, Bond, and Townsley use official data to draw new insights about the geographic distances that typify offender journeys to crime. One very important insight from this work is that there are a considerable minority of offenders in their sample that travel relatively long distances, contradicting research that emphasizes the relatively short journeys to crime of offenders (e.g., see Rossmo 2000; Rengert et al. 1999; Rhodes and Conly 1981; Paulsen and Robinson 2004; Chainey and Ratcliffe 2005). This finding emphasizes that units of analysis for geographic criminology may at times be shifting because of the social context of offender behavior, reminding us of the observations of Tita and Greenbaum described earlier. The unit of analysis for geographic crime studies cannot be divorced from the social contexts of crimes and criminals.

A final critical issue to be mentioned concerns the statistical issues raised by spatial data in general, and by small spatial units of analysis in particular. It is well recognized that in most spatial crime research, the spatial units of analysis are not independent observations. In fact, many substantive questions focus directly on how adjacent spatial units interact. For example, we are interested in whether crime prevention activity in one place displaces crime to nearby places (Weisburd et al. 2006). The interdependence between spatial units of analysis requires statistical techniques and models that are geared to spatial structures (Anselin et al. 2000), and many of them are utilized in the other chapters in this volume.

The trend toward increasingly smaller units of analysis that has been documented here not only implies that we need to consider more closely the interactions between adjacent and nearby units, but also gives rise to additional statistical challenges. For example, the distributions of dependent variables will typically be skewed (e.g., a large percentage of the units experience no crime at all), which poses additional (non-linearity) requirements to the statistical models employed. In addition, some spatial relations are also hierarchical, for example, all street segments within a police beat or other administrative boundary are subject to the same policies and procedures, irrespective of their spatial arrangement vis-à-vis each other. In those cases the statistical models used need to account for hierarchical and spatial structure simultaneously (e.g., Morenoff et al. 2001).

Conclusions

Our intention in this book is to bring attention to the problem of units of analysis in geographic criminology. We recognize at the outset that no single volume can explore the myriad of issues that are important in this area, but we try to cover a broad spectrum of critical questions and concerns in the chapters that follow. Our book is divided into two main sections, reflecting the broad themes that we have raised in this introductory chapter. The first section deals directly with the substantive question of the unit of analysis that should be the focus of criminologists and suggests a number of methodological approaches to identifying units appropriate for analysis and investigation. The second part of the book focuses on case studies of crime at place, illustrating how we can advance our understanding of units of analysis for geographic criminology through specific empirical studies.

In this introductory chapter, we have focused on the history of crime and place studies and the specific challenges that geographic crime researchers face in advancing this promising area of criminological inquiry. We hope that this exploratory effort in identifying the problem of units of analysis in crime and place studies will spur interest in advancing geographic criminology and strengthening its influence in criminology more generally. While by necessity our book takes a broad approach to the problem of units of analysis, we think that the contributions share a common theme in that they make explicit the importance of clearly defining and specifying geographic units of analysis. This is a theoretical problem as well as a practical question of data and methods. It is time to "put crime in its place."

References

Abbott, A. (1997). Of time and space: The contemporary relevance of the Chicago school. *Social Forces*, 75(4), 1149–1182.

Anderson, D., Chenery, S., & Pease, K. (1995). *Biting back: Tackling repeat burglary and car crime*. Crime Detection and Prevention Series Paper 58. London: Home Office.

Anselin, L., Cohen, J., Cook, D., Gorr, W., & Tita, G. (2000). Spatial analyses of crime. In: D. Duffee, (Ed.), *Criminal justice 2000: Volume 4. Measurement and analysis of crime and justice* (pp. 213–262). Washington, DC: National Institute of Justice.

Balbi, A., & Guerry, A.-M. (1829). *Statistique comparée de l'état de l'instruction et du nombre des crimes dans les divers arrondissements des Académies et des Cours Royales de France*. Paris.

Baldwin, J., & Bottoms, A. E. (1976). *The urban criminal*. London: Tavistock.

Beirne, P. (1987). Adolphe Quetelet and the origins of positivist criminology. *American Journal of Sociology*, 92(5), 1140–1169.

Beirne, P. (1993). *Inventing criminology: Essays on the rise of 'homo criminalis.'* New York: State University of New York Press.

Beirne, P., & Messerschmidt, J. (1991). *Criminology*. San Diego: Harcourt Brace Jovanovich.

Birkbeck, C., & LaFree, G. (1993). The situational analysis of crime and deviance. *Annual Review of Sociology*, 19, 113–137.

Block, C., Dabdoub, M., & Fregly, S. (Eds.) (1995). *Crime analysis through computer mapping*. Washington, DC: Police Executive Research Forum.

Boggs, S. L. (1965). Urban crime patterns. *American Sociological Review*, 30(6), 899–908.

Braga, A. A. (2001). The effects of hot spots policing on crime. *The Annals of the American Academy of Political and Social Science*, 578, 104–115.

Brantingham, P. L., & Brantingham, P. J. (1975). Residential burglary and urban form. *Urban Studies*, 12, 104–125.

Brantingham, P. J., & Brantingham, P. L. (1984). *Patterns in crime*. New York: Macmillan.

Brantingham, P. J., & Brantingham, P. L. (1990). Situational crime prevention in practice. *Canadian Journal of Criminology*, 32(1), 17–40.

Brantingham, P. J., & Brantingham, P. L. (1991). The dimensions of crime. In: P. J. Brantingham & P. L. Brantingham (Eds.), *Environmental criminology* (pp. 7–26). Beverly Hills, CA: Sage. (Original work published 1981).

Brantingham, P. L., & Brantingham, P. J. (1993). Environment, routine, and situation: Toward a pattern theory of crime. In R. V. Clarke & M. Felson (Eds.), *Routine activity and rational choice: Advances in criminological theory*, Vol. 5. New Brunswick, NJ: Transaction.

Brantingham, P. L., & Brantingham, P. J. (1999). Theoretical model of crime hot spot generation. *Studies on Crime and Crime Prevention*, 8, 7–26.

Bulmer, M. (1984). *The Chicago school of sociology: Institutionalization, diversity, and the rise of sociological research*. Chicago & London: The University of Chicago Press.

Burgess, E. W. (1967). The growth of the city: An introduction to a research project. In: R. E. Park & E. W. Burgess (Eds.), *The city: Suggestions for the investigation of human behaviour in the urban environment*. Chicago: The University of Chicago Press. (Original work published 1925).

Burgess, E. W., & Bogue, D. J. (1964a). Research in urban society: A long view. In: E. W. Burgess & D. J. Bogue (Eds.), *Contributions to urban sociology* (pp. 1–14). Chicago & London: The University of Chicago Press.

Burgess, E. W., & Bogue, D. J. (1964b). The delinquency research of Clifford R. Shaw and Henry D. McKay and associates. In: E. W. Burgess & D. J. Bogue (Eds.), *Contributions to urban sociology* (pp. 591–615). Chicago & London: The University of Chicago Press.

Bursik, R. J. Jr. (1984). Urban dynamics and ecological studies of delinquency. *Social Forces*, 63, 393–413.

Bursik, R. J. Jr. (1986). Ecological stability and the dynamics of delinquency. In: A. J. Reiss, Jr. & M. Tonry (Eds.), *Communities and crime. Crime and justice: A review of research* (Vol. 8, pp. 35–66). Chicago: The University of Chicago Press.

Bursik, R. J. Jr., & Webb, J. (1982). Community change and patterns of delinquency. *American Journal of Sociology*, 88(1), 24–42.

Burt, C. (1944). *The young delinquent*. London: University of London Press. (Original work published 1924).

Chainey, S., & Ratcliffe, J. (2005). *GIS and crime mapping*. Hoboken, NJ: John Wiley.

Chilton, R .J. (1964). Continuity in delinquency area research: a comparison of studies for Baltimore, Detroit, and Indianapolis. *American Sociological Review*, 29, 71–83.

Chilton, R. J., & Dussich, J. P. (1974). Methodological issues in delinquency research: Some alternative analysis of geographical distributed data. *Social Forces*, 53(1), 73–82.

Clarke, R. V. (1983). Situational crime prevention: Its theoretical basis and practical scope. In M. Tonry & N. Morris (Eds.), *Crime and justice: An annual review of research* (Vol. 14, pp. 225–256). Chicago: The University of Chicago Press.

Clarke, R. V. (1992). *Situational crime prevention: Successful case studies*. Albany, NY: Harrow and Heston.

Clarke, R. V. (1995). Situational crime prevention. In: M. Tonry & D. Farrington (Eds.), *Building a safer society: Strategic approaches to crime prevention. Crime and justice: A review of research* (Vol. 19, pp. 91–150). Chicago: The University of Chicago Press.

Cohen, L. E., & Felson, M. (1979). Social change and crime rate trends: A routine activity approach. *American Sociological Review*, 44(4), 588–605.

Cornish, D., & Clarke, R. V. (Eds.). (1986). *The reasoning criminal: Rational choice perspectives on offending*. New York: Springer-Verlag.

Crow, W., & Bull, J. (1975). *Robbery deterrence: An applied behavioral science demonstration – Final report*. La Jolla, CA: Western Behavioral Science Institute.

Curtis, L. A. (1974). *Criminal violence: National patterns and behavior*. Lexington MA: Lexington Books.

Ducpétiaux, E. (1827). *De la Justice de prévoyance, et particulièrement de l'influence de la misère et de l'aisance, de l'ignorance et de l'instruction sur le nombre des crimes*. Bruxelles: J. J. de Cautaerts.

Duffala, D. C. (1976). Convenience stores, armed robbery, and physical environmental features. *American Behavioral Scientist*, 20, 227–246.

Durkheim, E. (1964[1893]). *The division of labour in society*. New York: Free Press. (Original work published 1893).

Eck, J. E., & Weisburd, D. (1995). Crime places in crime theory. In: J. E. Eck & D. Weisburd (Eds.), *Crime and place* (pp. 1–33). Monsey, NY: Willow Tree Press.

Eck, J. E., & Weisburd, D. (2004). What can the police do to reduce crime, disorder, and fear? *The Annals of the American Academy of Political and Social Science*, 593, 42–65.

Elmer, M. C. (1933). Century-old ecological studies in France. *American Journal of Sociology*, 39(1), 63–70.

Erickson, M. L. (1971). The group context of delinquent behavior. *Social Problems*, 19(1), 114–129.

Erickson, M. L., & Jensen, G. F. (1977). Delinquency is still group behavior! Toward revitalizing the group premise in the sociology of deviance. *The Journal of Criminal Law and Criminology*, 68(2), 262–273.

Faris, R. E. L. (1967). *Chicago sociology 1920–1932*. San Francisco: Chandler.

Farrell, G., & Pease, K. (Eds.), (2001). *Repeat Victimization*. Crime Prevention Studies Vol. 12. Monsey: Criminal Justice Press.

Felson, M., & Clarke, R. V. (1998). *Opportunity makes the thief: Practical theory for crime prevention*. Police Research Series Paper 98. London: Policing and Reducing Crime Unit; Research, Development and Statistics Directorate.

Fletcher, J. (1850). *Summary of the moral statistics of England and Wales*. London: Private distribution of the author.

Forrester, D., Chatterston, M., & Pease, K. (1988). *The Kirkholt burglary reduction project, Rochdale*. London: Home Office Crime Prevention Unit.

Friendly, M. (2007). A.-M. Guerry's moral statistics of France: Challenges for multivariable spatial analysis. *Statistical Science*, 22, 368–399.

Glyde, J. (1856). Localities of crime in Suffolk. *Journal of Statistical Society of London*, 19, 102–106.

Gold, M. (1970). *Delinquent behavior in an American city*. Belmont, CA: Brooks/Cole.

Gordon, R. A. (1967). Issues in the ecological study of delinquency. *American Sociological Review*, 32, 927–944.

Green (Mazerolle), L. (1996). *Policing places with drug problems*. Thousand Oaks, CA: Sage.

Greg, W. R. (1839). *Social statistics of the Netherlands*. London: Ridgway, Harrison and Crosfield.

Guerry, A.-M. (1832). La Statistique comparée de l'état de l'instruction et du nombre des crimes. *Revue Encyclopédique*, 55, 414–424.

Guerry, A.-M. (1833). *Essai sur la statistique morale de la France*. Paris: Crochard.

Guerry, A.-M. (1864). *Statistique morale de l'Angleterre compare avec la Statistique Morale de la France*. Paris: Bailliére.

Harvey, L. (1987). *Myths of the Chicago school of sociology*. Hong Kong: Avebury.

Hipp, J. R. (2007). Block, tract, and level of aggregation: Neighborhood structure and crime and disorder as a case in point. *American Sociological Review*, 72, 659–680.

Hunter, R. D. (1988). *Environmental characteristics of convenience store robberies in the state of Florida*. Paper presented at the meeting of the American Society of Criminology, Chicago.

Jeffery, C. R. (1971). *Crime prevention through environmental design*. Beverly Hills, CA: Sage.

Kenwitz, J. W. (1987). *Cartography in France: 1660–1848*. Chicago: The University of Chicago Press.

Klein, M. (1969). On the group context of delinquency. *Sociology and Social Research*, 54, 63–71.

Kobrin, S., & Schuerman, L. A. (1981). *Ecological processes in the creation of delinquency areas: An update*. Paper presented at the meeting of the American Sociological Association, Toronto, Canada.

Landau, D., & Lazarsfeld, P. F. (1968). Quetelet, Adolphe. *International Encyclopedia of the Social Sciences*, 13, 247–257.

Lander, B. (1954). *Towards an understanding of juvenile delinquency*. New York: Columbia University Press.

LeBeau, J. L. (1987). The methods and measures of centrography and the spatial dynamics of rape. *Journal of Quantitative Criminology*, 3, 125–141.

Lombroso, C. (2006). *Criminal man* (translated and with a new introduction by M. Gibson & N. Han Rafter),.Durham, NC: Duke University Press. (Original work published 1878).

Maltz, M. D., Gordon, A. C., & Friedman, W. (2000). *Mapping crime in its community setting: Event geography analysis*. Originally published New York: Springer-Verlag. Internet edition available at http://www.utc.edu/depts/lib/forr. (Original work published 1990).

Mayhew, H. (1865). *London labour and the London poor. Volume 4: Those that will not work*. London: Charles Griffin.

Mayhew, H. (1950). *London's underworld: Being selections from 'Those that will not work', the 4th volume of 'London labour and the London poor'* (edited by P. Quennell). London: Spring Books. (Original work published 1851 & 1862).

Mayhew, P., Clarke, R. V., Sturman, A., & Hough, M. (1976). *Crime as opportunity*. Home Office Research Study, Vol. 34. London: Home Office, H.M. Stationary Office.

Morenoff, J., Sampson, R. J., & Raudenbush, S. W. (2001). Neighborhood inequality, collective efficacy and the spatial dynamics of homicide. *Criminology*, 39, 517–560.

Morris, T. (1957). *The criminal area: A study in social ecology*. London: Routledge & Kegan Paul.

National Research Council. (2004). *Fairness and effectiveness in policing: The evidence*. Committee to Review Research on Police Policy and Practices. In: W. Skogan & K. Frydl (Eds.). Committee on Law and Justice, Division of Behavioral and Social Sciences and Education. Washington, DC: The National Academies Press.

Nettler, G. (1978). *Explaining crime*. Montreal: McGraw-Hill.

Newman, O. (1972). *Defensible space: Crime prevention through environmental design*. New York: Macmillan.

Openshaw, S. (1984). *The modifiable areal unit problem*. Norwich: Geo Books.

Parent-Duchâtelet, A. J. B. (1837). *Prostitution dans la ville de Paris*. Paris.

Park, R. E. (1967). The city: Suggestions for the investigation of human behaviour in the urban environment. In: R. E. Park & E. W. Burgess (Eds.), *The city: Suggestions for the investigation of human behaviour in the urban environment* (pp. 1–46). Chicago: The University of Chicago Press. (Original work published 1925).

Paulsen, D. J., & Robinson, M. B. (2004). *Spatial aspects of crime: Theory and practice*. Boston, MA: Pearson.

Pierce, G., Spaar, S., & Briggs, L. R. (1986). *The character of police work: Strategic and tactical implications*. Boston, MA: Center for Applied Social Research, Northeastern University.

Polvi, N., Looman, T., Humphries, C., & Pease, K. (1990). Repeat break and enter victimisation: Time course and crime prevention opportunity. *Journal of Police Science and Administration*, 17, 8–11.

Polvi, N., Looman, T., Humphries, C., & Pease, K (1991). The time course of repeat burglary victimization. *British Journal of Criminology*, 31(4), 411–414.

Pyle, G. F. (1976). Spatial and temporal aspects of crime in Cleveland, Ohio. *American Behavioral Scientist*, 20, 175–198.

Quetelet, A. (1847). Statistique morale de l'influence du libre arbitre de l'homme sur les faits sociaux, et particulièrement sur le nombre des mariages, *Bulletin de la Commission Centrale de Statistique*, III, 135–155.

Quetelet, A. (1984). *Research on the propensity for crime at different ages, translated and with an introduction by S.F. Sylvester*. Cincinnati: Anderson Publishing. (Original work published 1831).

Ratcliffe, J. H., & McCullagh, M. J. (1999). Hotbeds of crime and the search for spatial accuracy. *Geographical Systems*, 1, 385–398.

Rawson, R. W. (1839). An inquiry into the statistics of crime in England and Wales. *Journal of the Statistical Society of London*, 2, 316–344.

Reiss, A. J., Jr. (1986). Why are communities important in understanding crime? In: M. Tonry & N. Morris (Eds.), *Communities and crime. Crime and justice: A review of research* (Vol. 8, pp. 1–33). Chicago: The University of Chicago Press.

Reiss, A. J. Jr., & Tonry, M. (1986). Preface. In: A. J. Reiss Jr. & M. Tonry (Eds.), *Communities and crime. Crime and justice: A review of research*, (Vol. 8, pp. vii–viii). Chicago: The University of Chicago Press.

Reiss, A. J. Jr. (1988). Co-offending and criminal careers. In: A. J. Reiss Jr., & M. Tonry (Eds.), *Communities and crime. Crime and justice: A review of research* (Vol. 10, pp. 117–170). Chicago: The University of Chicago Press.

Rengert, G. F. (1980). Spatial aspects of criminal behavior. In: D. E. Georges-Abeyie & K. D. Harries (Eds.), *Crime: A spatial perspective* (pp. 47–57). New York: Columbia University Press.

Rengert, G. F. (1981). Burglary in Philadelphia: A critique of an opportunity structure model. In: P. Brantingham & P. Brantingham (Eds.), *Environmental criminology* (pp. 189–201). Prospect Heights, IL: Waveland Press.

Rengert, G. F., Piquero, A. R., & Jones, P. R. (1999). Distance decay reexamined. *Criminology*, 37(2), 427–446.

Rhodes, W. M., & Conly, C. (1981). Crime and mobility: An empirical study. In: P. J. Brantingham & P. L. Brantingham (Eds.), *Environmental criminology*. Beverly Hills, CA: Sage.

Robinson, W. S. (1950). Ecological correlations and the behavior of individuals. *American Sociological Review*, 15, 351–357.

Roncek, D. W. (2000). Schools and crime. In: V. Goldsmith, P. G. McGuire, J. H. Mollenkopf, & T. A. Ross (Eds.), *Analyzing crime patterns: Frontiers of practice* (pp. 153–165). Thousand Oaks, CA: Sage.

Roncek, D. W., & R. Bell. (1981). Bars, blocks, and crimes. *Journal of Environmental Systems*, 11(1), 35–47.

Rossmo, D. K. (2000). *Geographic profiling*. New York: CRC Press.

Sampson, R. J. (1985). Neighborhoods and crime: The structural determinants of personal victimization. *Journal of Research in Crime and Delinquency*, 22, 7–40.

Sampson, R. J., & Groves, W. B. (1989). Community structure and crime: Testing social disorganization theory. *American Journal of Sociology*, 94(4), 774–802.

Sampson, R. J., & Raudenbush, S. W. (1999). Systematic social observation of public spaces: A new look at disorder in urban neighborhoods. *American Journal of Sociology*, 105(3), 603–651.

Sampson, R. J., Raudenbush, S. W., & Earls, F. (1997). Neighborhoods and violent crime: A multilevel study of collective efficacy. *Science*, 277(5328), 918–924.

Sarnecki, J. (1986). *Delinquent networks*. Stockholm: National Council for Crime Prevention.

Schuerman, L., & Kobrin, S. (1986). Community careers in crime. In: A. J. Reiss Jr. & M. Tonry (Eds.), *Communities and crime. Crime and justice: A review of research* (Vol. 8, pp. 67–100). Chicago: The University of Chicago Press.

Shaw, C. R. (with F. M. Zorbaugh, H. D. McKay, & L. Cotrell) (1929). *Delinquent areas: A study of the geographical distribution of school truants, juvenile delinquents, and adult offenders in Chicago*. Chicago & London: The University of Chicago Press.

Shaw, C. R., & McKay, H. D. (1931). *Social factors in juvenile delinquency*. Report on the Causes of Crime, National Commission of Law Enforcement and Observance, vol. 2. Washington, DC: Government Printing Office.

Shaw, C. R., & McKay, H. D. (1969). *Juvenile delinquency and urban areas: A study of rates of delinquency in relation to differential characteristics of local communities in American cities*. Chicago & London: The University of Chicago Press (Rev. ed.). (Original work published 1942).

Sherman, L. W. (1995). Hot spots of crime and criminal careers of places. In: J. E. Eck & D. Weisburd (Eds.), *Crime and Place*. Monsey, NY: Willow Tree Press.

Sherman, L. W., & Weisburd, D. (1995). General deterrent effects of police patrol in crime 'hot spots': A randomized, controlled trial. *Justice Quarterly*, 12(4), 625–648.

Sherman, L. W., Gartin, P., & Buerger, M. E. (1989). Hot spots of predatory crime: Routine activities and the criminology of place. *Criminology*, 27(1), 27–55.

Short, J. F. Jr., & Moland, J. Jr. (1976). Politics and youth gangs: A follow-up study. *The Sociological Quarterly*, 17, 162–179.

Skogan, W. (1986). Fear of crime and neighbourhood change. In: A. J. Reiss Jr. & M. Tonry (Eds.), *Communities and crime. Crime and justice: A review of research* (Vol. 8, pp. 203–229). Chicago: The University of Chicago Press.

Skogan, W. (1990). *Disorder and decline: Crime and the spiral of decay in American cities*. New York: Free Press.

Smith, D.A. (1987). Police response to interpersonal violence: Defining the parameters of legal control. *Social Forces*, 65(3), 767–782.

Symons, J. (2000). On crime and density of population. In: D. M. Horton (Ed.), *Pioneering perspectives in criminology: The literature of 19th century criminological positivism* (pp. 279–285). Incline Village, NV: Copperhouse. (Original work published 1857).

Tarde, J.-G. (1912). *Penal philosophy* (translated by R. Howell). Boston: Little, Brown and Company. (Original work published 1890).

Taylor, R. B. (1997). Social order and disorder of street blocks and neighborhoods: Ecology, microecology, and the systemic model of social disorganization. *Journal of Research in Crime and Delinquency*, 34, 113–155.

Thomas, W. I. (1966). Social disorganization and social reorganization. In: M. Janovitz (Ed.), *On social organization and social personality: Selected papers* (pp. 3–11). Chicago and London: The University of Chicago Press.

Thrasher, F. M. (1927). *The gang: A study of 1,313 gangs in Chicago*. Chicago, IL: Phoenix Books. (Abridged ed. 1963).

Vold, G. B., Bernard, T. J., & Snipes, J. B. (2002). *Theoretical criminology* (5th ed.). New York: Oxford University Press.

Waring, E. J. (1998). Incorporating co-offending in sentencing models: An analysis of fines imposed on antitrust offenders. *Journal of Quantitative Criminology*, 14(3), 283–305.

Waring, E. J. (2002). Co-offending as a network form of social organization. *Advances in Criminological Theory*, 10, 31–48.

Warr, M. (1996). Organization and instigation in delinquent groups. *Criminology*, 34(1), 11–37.

Weisburd, D. (2002). From criminals to criminal contexts: Reorienting criminal justice research and policy. *Advances in Criminological Theory*, 10, 197–216.

Weisburd, D., & Braga, A. (2006). Hot spots policing as a model for police innovation. In: D. Weisburd & A. Braga (Eds.), *Police innovation: Contrasting perspectives* (pp. 225–244). Cambridge: Cambridge University Press.

Weisburd, D., & Britt, C. (2007). *Statistics in criminal justice* (3rd ed.). New York: Springer.

Weisburd, D., Bushway, S., Lum, C., & Yang, S.-M. (2004). Trajectories of crime at places: A longitudinal study of street segments in the city of Seattle. *Criminology*, 42(2), 283–321.

Weisburd, D., & Eck, J. (2004). What Can Police Do to Reduce Crime, Disorder and Fear? The Annals of the American Academy of Political and Social Science, 593 (May), 42–65.

Weisburd, D., & Green, L. (1994). Defining the drug market: The case of the Jersey City DMA system. In: D. L. MacKenzie & C. D. Uchida (Eds.), *Drugs and crime: Evaluating public policy initiatives*. Newbury Park, CA: Sage.

Weisburd, D., & Green, L. (1995). Policing drug hot spots: The Jersey City DMA experiment. *Justice Quarterly*, 12(4), 711–735.

Weisburd, D., & McEwen, T. (1997). Introduction: Crime mapping and crime prevention. In: D. Weisburd & T. McEwen (Eds.), *Crime mapping and crime prevention* (pp. 1–23). Monsey, NY: Criminal Justice Press.

Weisburd, D., Maher, L., & Sherman, L. (1992). Contrasting crime general and crime specific theory: The case of hot spots of crime. In: F. Adler & W. S. Laufer (Eds.), *Advances in criminological theory* (Vol. 4, pp. 45–70). New Brunswick, NJ: Transaction Publications.

Weisburd, D., Wyckoff, L. A., Ready, J., Eck, J. E., Hinkle, J. C., & Gajewski, F. (2006). Does crime just move around the corner? A controlled study of spatial displacement and diffusion of crime control benefits. *Criminology*, 44(3), 549–592.

Wikström, P.-O., & Butterworth, D. A. (2006). *Adolescent crime: Individual differences and lifestyles*. Devon: Willan.

Wolfgang, M. E., Figlio, R., & Sellin, T. (1972). *Delinquency in a birth cohort*. Chicago: The University of Chicago Press.

Zorbaugh, H. W. (1929). *The gold coast and the slum: A sociological study of Chicago's near north side*. Chicago: The University of Chicago Press.

Part II
What Is the Appropriate Level
of Investigation of Crime at Place?
Theoretical and Methodological Issues

Chapter 2
Why Small Is Better: Advancing the Study of the Role of Behavioral Contexts in Crime Causation

Dietrich Oberwittler and Per-Olof H. Wikström

Abstract In this chapter we argue, both from a theoretical (Situational Action Theory) and methodological (homogeneity of environmental conditions) point of view, that small environmental units are preferable to large in the study of environmental effects on crime.

Most empirical research in the field of communities and crime utilizes fairly large spatial units of several thousand residents, such as U.S. census tracts or even clusters of census tracts, thus evoking doubts about internal homogeneity. If geographical areas are heterogeneous in their environmental conditions, associations between structural conditions, social organization, and outcomes such as crime may be clouded or rendered insignificant. On the other hand, due to common financial restrictions, choosing more units often (but not necessarily) imply fewer subjects per units which may cause a 'small number problem', that is, that the prediction of events as rare as crime will lose precision (compared to the use of larger units with more subjects). The question then is how small can you go before this potential problem outweighs the benefits of more homogeneous areas? This chapter assesses the added value of using very small area units in a community survey on environmental influences on crime. This survey was carried out in 2005 as part of the Peterborough Adolescent and Young Adult Development Study (PADS+) and covers the UK city of Peterborough and some rural surroundings. For the purpose of this study, we used the smallest administrative unit which subdivides the city, isolating 550 areas with about 300 residents each. We sampled an average of 13 respondents per unit for a total sample of 6,600 respondents. Multilevel analyses and Raudenbush and Sampson's (1999) ecometric approach are applied to compare the aggregate-level reliability of survey scales on this very small geographical level to the larger spatial level conventionally used for geographical analysis. The results show a considerable increase in between-neighborhood variance, reflecting a higher degree of homogeneity and statistical power for detecting particularly moderate to weak area-level effects. We use the collective efficacy scale and its subscales to illustrate these results.

D. Oberwittler
Department of Criminology, Max Planck Institute for Foreign and International Criminal Law, Freiburg, Germany; University of Freiburg, Germany
e-mail: d.oberwittler@mpicc.de

D. Weisburd et al. (eds.), *Putting Crime in its Place*,
DOI 10.1007/978-0-387-09688-9_2, © Springer Science+Business Media, LLC 2009

Introduction

The role of the social environment is probably one of the least understood aspects of crime causation. One important reason for that is the lack of well-developed theoretical models of *how* social environments influence individual acts of crime and the development of crime propensity. Another important reason is the lack of well-developed methodologies to study and measure the influence of social environments on individual acts of crime and the development of crime propensity (Wikström 2007a).

A major aim of *the Peterborough Adolescent and Young Adult Development Study* (PADS+) is to advance theory and methodology in the study of crime causation, with a particular focus on the role of the social environment. A specific aim of this chapter is to advocate, on theoretical and methodological grounds, the advantages of using small area units to study the effects of the social environment on human development and action.

PADS+ is based on a newly developed theoretical framework, the *Situational Action Theory* (see Wikström 2004, 2005, 2006, 2007a, 2007b, 2007c; Wikström and Treiber 2007, 2008) which is specifically designed to address the role of the interaction between individuals and the social environment in crime causation. The cornerstone of the theory is that individual actions (like acts of crime) are an outcome of how people *perceive their action alternatives* and (on that basis) *make choices* when confronted with the particularities of *behavior-settings*. A *behavior-setting* may be defined as the part of the environment which an individual, at a particular moment in time, can access with his or her senses, including any media present (Wikström 2006).

According to the theory, only those individual and environmental characteristics that (directly or indirectly) influence how people perceive action alternatives and make choices are relevant to the study of crime causation. That is, those individual characteristics and experiences, and features of the environments to which an individual is exposed, which (directly or indirectly) influence whether or not he or she sees acts of crime as action alternatives and his or her choice to act upon such perceptions are relevant factors in a theory of crime causation.

In brief, the theory proposes that crimes are moral actions (actions which are guided by rules about what it is right or wrong to do) and have to be explained as such. It further proposes that individual differences in morality (moral values and emotions) and ability to exercise self-control, on the one hand, and the moral contexts (applicable moral rules and their enforcement and sanctions) of the behavior-settings in which individuals take part, on the other, interact to determine what action alternatives an individual will perceive, what choices he or she will make and, consequently, what kind of action will follow (e.g., an act of crime). Individual differences in crime involvement are thus, according to the theory, an outcome of differences in individuals' characteristics and experiences (morality and ability to exercise self-control) *and* their exposure to particular behavior-settings (their moral contexts). In other words, the theory proposes that some kinds of individuals in some kinds of settings are more likely to commit crimes than others, depending on the interaction of their morality (and ability to exercise self-control) and the moral contexts to which they are exposed. Individuals' exposure to behavior-settings is, according to the theory, not only directly relevant to their moral actions but also (in the longer term) to the development of individual characteristics related to their crime propensity (their morality and ability to exercise self-control).

This implies that individuals' exposure to behavior-settings, and changes over time in their exposure to behavior-settings, are key in understanding their crime involvement, and changes over time in their crime involvement (i.e., individual crime trajectories) because they affect the development and change of individuals' crime propensities and exposure to environmental inducements and, particularly, the interaction between the two.

The Situational Action Theory's strong emphasis on the role of the social environment (and its changes) in individuals' involvement, and changing involvement, in crime, highlights the need to adequately measure relevant aspects of the social environment, and its changes. Therefore a specific aim of PADS+ is to utilize better techniques (i) to measure relevant *characteristics* of the social environment (behavior-settings) and (ii) to measure individuals' *exposure to* different social environments (their activity fields) than have been previously used in longitudinal studies of individuals' crime involvement and its development and changes.

Since the theory proposes that human development and action is influenced by the behavior-settings in which individuals take part, it is crucial to develop methods to measure units that approximate behavior-settings. Because behavior-settings are the parts of the social environment the individual can access with his or her senses, these units have to be geographically small. Since the theory also proposes that it is the moral context of behavior-settings that influences an individual's moral action, it is important to develop measures that tap into the moral context of the studied units. In other words, the theory implies that we need to develop measurements which capture the moral context of small units which approximate behavior-settings to adequately study the role of the environment in crime causation.

The theory also proposes that it is the behavior-settings to which an individual actually is *exposed* that are of relevance to his or her development and actions. An individual does not, for example, only act and develop in the area surrounding his or her place of residence (i.e., his or her neighborhood). Thus we also need to develop techniques to measure individuals' exposure to different behavior-settings (within or outside their neighborhoods). The configuration of settings to which an individual is exposed within a certain period of time may be referred to as his or her *activity field* for that period (see further, Wikström 2005, 2006). To measure activity fields we have developed a *space-time budget* technique which measures an individual's hourly exposure, over a specific time period, to different kinds of behavior-settings, i.e., his or her activity field (Wikström and Ceccato 2004; Wikström and Butterworth 2006).

In this chapter, we will deal only with the problems related to advantages and disadvantages of using small units of analysis in ecologically oriented research. The equally important problem of measuring individuals' *exposure* to behavior-settings (through the space-time budget technique) will be dealt with elsewhere.

The 'Unit of Analysis' Problem

The unit of analysis is rarely a problem when we study individuals. An *individual* is defined by his or her body and when we study individuals we study characteristics of their bodies (e.g., weight and height) or internal to their bodies (e.g., values and emotions). Deciding on the best unit of analysis is also relatively uncomplicated when we study *action* (such as acts of crime) because actions[1] are always taken by individuals (an aggregate cannot act[2]) and therefore action is linked to the individual (and to the individual as a unit of analysis). To study the influence of individual characteristics and experiences on action is therefore usually straightforward in regards to the basic unit of analysis (i.e., the individual).

However, the unit of analysis problem becomes much more complex when we introduce the *environment* and particularly when studying environmental influences on human action (such as acts of crime). There is no simple universal criterion to define the boundaries of 'the environment' (or of what it consists). The environment has to be defined in relation to something. What is a valid unit of environment depends on the nature of the research.

If the research question concerns the study of environmental influences on action, it is reasonable to argue that the valid unit of analysis is the part of the environment (the behavior-setting) in which an individual actually takes part. However, this is further complicated by the fact that individuals are not environmentally stationary but move around in space and are therefore likely to be *exposed* to a range of different kinds of settings (a generally neglected problem and one we will not deal with further in this chapter).

Most studies of the role of the environment in crime causation operate on an *aggregate* level, that is, the outcome variable represents aggregated data of individual acts of crime occurring in a geographic unit (and sometimes some or all of the predictors are aggregates of individual characteristics, such as mean income or percent from a particular ethnic background). Using aggregates of action as outcome variables (and, in addition, also using aggregates of individual characteristics as predictors) when trying to assess the environmental impact on individual action introduces numerous analytical problems.

To draw conclusions about causes of crime from aggregate associations between environmental characteristics and acts of crime, one has to be able to justify at least the assumption that the aggregate relationship holds up at the individual level (because, strictly speaking, it is not possible to argue for a causal relationship at the aggregate level, i.e., between aggregates). For example, if one studies the relationship between the level of informal social control and frequency of crime at the area level of analysis and finds a relationship between people's stated willingness to intervene to prevent crime (e.g., percent willing to intervene) and crime (e.g., mean

---

[1] Action consists of all movements of the body (e.g., talking or hitting) under the guidance of the individual (the latter implies the exclusion of reflexes).

[2] Although individuals can, of course, act jointly.

number of crimes committed per resident) it is not justifiable to argue that the *mean* is causally dependent on the *percent*. However, this association *may* reflect a causal relationship between individuals' exposure to settings with a certain level of informal social control and their decisions in those settings (as a consequence of the perceived level of informal social control) whether or not to commit acts of crime.

To avoid any misunderstandings, we do not argue that environmental (non-individual) conditions (such as opportunity or social climate) cannot be the causes of individual action. However, we do argue that ultimately it has to be shown (on the individual level) that such environmental conditions are directly linked to individual actions[3] (e.g., that individuals who commit more acts of crime *actually* have been exposed more often to settings with poor informal social control, and crucially, that their acts of crime *actually* have occurred in such settings).

A common problem in the study of aggregate relationships is knowing when it is justified to argue that an aggregate relationship reflects a (causal) relationship at the individual level. There are many important methodological issues to consider when inferring individual-level relationships from the study of aggregate data (a common problem in studies of environmental effects on acts of crime); although it is out of the scope of this chapter to deal with them all, we will mention a few.

In this chapter we will focus on *one* important problem: the size of the environmental unit of analysis. We advocate the (theoretical and empirical) advantages of using small-scale units of measurement when studying environmental factors in crime causation. We submit that this is important not only when analyzing data on the aggregate level (using aggregated data as outcomes) but also when analyzing corresponding relationship on the individual level. However, the empirical examples we use in this study only refer to analyses on the aggregate level and are selected to illustrate methodological points rather than present new substantive findings.

The dominant research tradition in the study of environmental influences on crime is the study of neighborhoods and crime. The methodological discussions in this tradition illustrate many problems related to the choice of units of analysis and, in our opinion, support our view that smaller is generally better.

Neighborhood Studies of Crime and the Unit of Analysis Problem

Notwithstanding different theoretical approaches, various methodologies and often conflicting results, the terms 'community' and 'neighborhood' in criminological research generally imply that areas within cities (or somewhere on the urban-rural

---

[3] Although this is a minimal criterion for causal dependency, it does not imply that such a relationship is potentially causal. One must also provide a plausible causal mechanism that would explain *why* the environmental factor in question would cause (independently or in interaction) an individual to act in a certain way (e.g., to commit an act of crime). And of course, being able to manipulate putative causes and show that their outcomes vary as expected is the best way to demonstrate causal dependency (but rarely a realistic possibility when studying environmental influences on acts of crime).

continuum) constitute discernable spatial entities characterized by certain features of social organization which are relevant for behavior. While the collective social organization or 'social climate' of communities has always been theoretically considered a relevant characteristic of the behavioral context – for residents or visitors (Shaw and McKay 1942) – survey-based measurement of community social organization started much later, really progressing only during the last decade, both theoretically and methodologically (e.g., Kubrin and Weitzer 2003; Sampson et al. 2002; Wikström and Dolmen 2001).

In community or neighborhood-based studies, the problem of defining area size and boundaries is awkwardly inescapable and is typically solved pragmatically. Empirical studies usually depend on 'official' data regarding the socio-demographic and physical make-up of neighborhoods, and these data are normally available only for pre-defined administrative units; therefore, most studies simply use these administrative units. In the context of U.S. cities, these units represent street blocks, census blocks groups, or census tracts; in Britain, they represent electoral wards, enumeration districts, or, more recently, output (and super output) areas. Similar definitions and labels apply for other countries.

The problems connected with the choice of area units are well known in geography and other spatially oriented social sciences under the heading 'modifiable area unit problem' (MAUP) and have been debated extensively for decades. While a review of this debate is beyond the scope of this chapter (see further, Bailey and Gatrell 1995; Openshaw 1984; Openshaw and Taylor 1981; Reynolds 1998), it is useful to consider the two basic problems identified and their relevance to the study of the influence of environmental conditions on human action (such as acts of crime).

First, the 'zonation effect' relates to the difficulty of drawing meaningful boundaries within an area which reflect rather than blur the spatial patterns of important variables. For example, if an ethnic enclave is artificially cut in half by an administrative boundary such that the residents appear to live in two separate neighborhoods amongst the native population, indices of segregation will grossly underestimate the degree of segregation in this ethnic group. Social scientists using census and other official data are hardly ever in a position to change administrative boundaries. However, it seems fair to say that boundaries have often been intentionally defined to avoid such problems. The question then remains of how successful these attempts to preserve 'natural' patterns have been. Moreover, even if the boundaries follow 'natural' patterns for one dimension of segregation it is not certain it does so for other dimensions of segregation. However, when the research task is to study the influence by environmental conditions on human action, this problem is only relevant insofar as the boundaries of the units under study are drawn in such way so that they create large within-area heterogeneity in terms of the environmental conditions under study. Regardless of how boundaries are drawn, the smaller the units of analysis, the less likely it is that they will be significantly heterogeneous in their environmental conditions.

The 'scale effect' or 'aggregation effect' (or 'aggregation bias') concerns the susceptibility of statistical results to changes in the size of units. If the magnitude or even the direction of correlations between relevant variables depends on the level of spatial aggregation employed, results are less than robust and the question of which spatial level is the most appropriate for analysis then arises. Smith et al. (2000, p. 494), for example, discuss the possible interaction effects between routine activity variables and individual risk factors for victimization. A concentration of non-residential land use in one part of an area may be irrelevant for a household at the other end of this area if the area is large, or if activity patterns are constrained. McCord's et al. (2007) recent study shows that respondents' perceptions of neighborhood crime and disorder are in fact systematically linked to the distance from their household to non-residential areas within their neighborhood. On the whole, therefore, it seems fair to assume that smaller geographical units are more homogenous, and hence more accurately measure environments. In other words, smaller is better.

Contrary to the 'zonation effect', researchers can often choose between and compare results using different spatial levels such as census blocks versus census tracts. Some studies have investigated the 'scaling effect' or 'aggregation bias' by comparing statistical analyses of socio-demographic factors and crime rates on two levels of aggregation. Ouimet (2000) compared census tracts (averaging 3,500 inhabitants) to groups of census tracts ('neighborhoods' averaging 21,000 inhabitants) in an aggregate-level analysis of crime rates in the city of Montreal (Canada). He found higher bivariate correlation coefficients, beta-coefficients, and R-squares for the larger neighborhoods which he suggests is due to inflated random variation in the smaller census tracts due to low absolute numbers of crimes. However, some associations, such as that between subway stations and violent juvenile crime, are stronger and more significant for the smaller census tract level. The effect of land use patterns on crime may be attenuated by aggregating small area units to larger but more heterogeneous units as discussed by Smith et al. (2000). Ouimet's (2000) decision to use larger 'neighborhood' units seems misguided, because by looking exclusively at *standardized* coefficients, which reflect the amount of variation around a regression line, he misses the likewise important information contained in *un*standardized coefficients, i.e., how strong a predicted effect is in terms of the change of units. We will demonstrate this point in the empirical part of this chapter.

Wooldredge (2002) reported a similar comparison based on data from Cincinnati (USA), which is divided into 129 census tracts and 48 neighborhoods. He employed multilevel analysis, entering individual data on arrestees on the first level and contextual data on the second (tract or neighborhood) level. Two significant area-level effects were rendered insignificant when switching from the smaller tract to the larger neighborhood level. However, further tests revealed that the coefficients were not significantly different. Wooldredge concluded that there were no substantial differences between aggregation levels apart for the effects of aggregate sample sizes (Wooldredge 2002, p. 699).

In the light of these results, Sampson's (2006, p. 35) comment that 'empirical results have not varied much with the operational unit of analysis' and that the social stratification of communities is 'a robust phenomenon that emerges at multiple levels of geography' seems warranted. In fact, many survey-based studies employ relatively large units of analysis such as census tracts (US) or wards (UK) which typically encompass 4,000–10,000 residents (e.g., Bellair 1997; McVie and Norris 2006; Sampson et al. 1997). Only some studies, such as the Seattle Victimization Survey (Miethe and Meier 1994) use smaller units, mainly street blocks. In Ralph Taylor's (2001) Baltimore study, some analyses are carried out on the street block level, although the main focus remains on census tracts.

Statistical Power Considerations in Multi-level Sampling Designs

There is an additional reason why the 'unit of analysis' issue is of particular relevance for survey-based community studies on crime causation. In contrast to studies employing recorded crime data, which usually represent complete samples, survey-based community studies using random samples of respondents are subject to the problems of statistically inferring relationships using standard errors and significance levels. Considerations of statistical power for hypothesis testing are more complicated in multi-level studies where respondents are clustered in neighborhoods (or other social groups) and hypotheses refer not only to individual-level effects between respondents, but also to aggregate-level effects between neighborhoods or cross-level effects between individuals and neighborhoods.

Recent methodological research has advanced knowledge concerning statistical power analysis in complex survey designs (Murrey et al. 2004; Raudenbush 1999). A detailed technical discussion of this research is beyond the scope of this chapter; however, it is important for any community-based study working on a restricted budget to balance the number of neighborhoods, and the number of individual respondents within neighborhoods, surveyed in order to achieve an optimal statistical power to test hypotheses of interest (Snijders and Bosker 1999, p. 140). Consider a study on community-level effects on crime which aims to measure the social organization of all neighborhoods in a given city. Assume, for example, that this study has resources to survey 1,000 respondents. These respondents may theoretically be allocated to 10 neighborhoods with 100 respondents each, or to 100 neighborhoods with 10 respondents each, or to any other combination of areas and individuals within areas, depending on the existing levels of administrative units in the city. Statistical power analysis for this task is complex and depends on the focus of the hypotheses. However, generally and within certain limits, more statistical power is gained by choosing more areas with fewer respondents rather than fewer areas with more respondents (Murrey et al. 2004, p. 424; Snijders and Bosker 1999, p. 152). This is mainly due to the large incremental increase in statistical power for detecting significant area-level effects if the initial number of areas is small. As Snijders and Bosker (1999, p. 140) remark, 'requirements on the sample size at the highest level... are at least as stringent as requirements on the sample in a single level design'. Ten, fifty, or even hundred aggregate-level units still represent a small sample size for multivariate analyses. Using simulation studies, Snijders and Bosker (1999, p. 152) show that depending on the focus of the hypotheses, as few as 8–15 respondents per area are sufficient to achieve statistical significance in multi-level models including area-level effects.

Taking together the issue of homogeneity of small areas and power considerations for area-level sample size, we are not satisfied with Wooldredge's and Sampson's conclusions that area size does not matter. Instead, we posit that using smaller units of analysis has important advantages over using larger units. First, the studies just mentioned clearly evidence differences, even if these were marginal. Second, both studies started with units of analysis which were already quite large, and therefore insufficiently homogenous for the measurement of behavioral contexts. Hence, the crucial question is whether geographical areas large enough to encompass 5,000–8,000 inhabitants can approximate behavior-settings which influence human development and action in any meaningful sense. We would argue they cannot. Thus, we deem it worth digging deeper into the issue of scale effects in a multilevel framework which employs very small units of analysis averaging only 300 residents.

The Peterborough Adolescent and Young Adult Development Study (PADS+)

The Peterborough Adolescent and Young Adult Development Study (PADS+) is an ongoing Economic and Social Research Council (ESRC) financed longitudinal study of young people's development and crime involvement during adolescence and young adulthood. The study includes 716 subjects randomly selected from a cohort of young people who were 12 years old in 2003 and living in the city of Peterborough (UK) or several surrounding villages.

The overall aim of PADS+ is to contribute to a better understanding of the causes and prevention of young people's crime involvement by studying (i) the interaction between individual characteristics and experiences and the features of the social environments in which young people develop and act and (ii) how these interactions change and shape criminal involvement over two critical developmental phases: adolescence and the transition into young adulthood.

The data collected in the Peterborough longitudinal study (PADS+) covers three main topics: (i) *the individual*: his and her individual and social characteristics and experiences (data is collected through an interview, interviewer-led questionnaires and psychometric tests); (ii) *the environment*: the characteristics of different small-area environments of Peterborough (data is collected through a community survey); and (iii) *individuals' exposure to different environments* in Peterborough (data is collected using a Space-Time Budget technique).

The study has to date (2008) successfully completed five waves of data collection, with a 98% retention rate by wave five. Data was also collected via a special community survey in 2005 which covered a random sample of the Peterborough population and received responses from approximately 6,600 residents. The purpose was to gather detailed information at a small area level (approximating behavior-settings) about key environmental characteristics within the city and nearby villages of Peterborough. The data used in this chapter is taken from the 2005 Peterborough Community Survey (PCS)

The Community Survey Data

The PCS was conducted in 2005. The sample is a clustered random sample of adult residents living in the city of Peterborough and several adjacent villages. Peterborough has approximately 160,000 inhabitants. Respondents aged 18 and over were randomly selected from the electoral register, which comprises 104,281 eligible voters; 4.9% of the adult population in Peterborough is not included in the electoral register, mainly because of non-British citizenship. In addition, 35% of registered voters 'opt out' which means their address cannot be used for purposes like surveys. It is generally assumed that those who opt out are more likely to be middle class and have a better than average education.

The PCS used the smallest available administrative units called 'output areas' (OAs). OAs have been empirically derived using individual-level census data and geographical and physical information to approach homogeneity both in terms of socio-demographic composition and population size (Martin 2000). OAs, on average, have around 300 inhabitants. This means that in densely populated areas there are more smaller OAs than in sparsely populated areas.

We grouped all OAs according to the official 'Index of Multiple Deprivation' (IMD) into 'normal' and 'deprived' OAs. The IMD is an overall index measuring deprivation in seven domains, including income, employment, education, and health

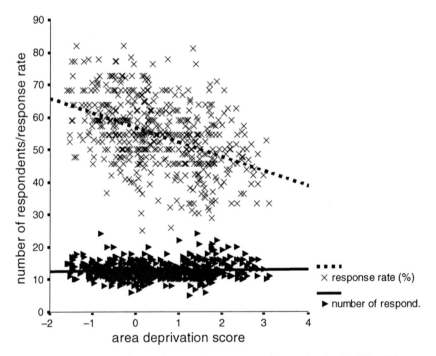

Fig. 2.1 Absolute number of respondents and response rates by area deprivation (N = 518 output areas with N = 6, 615 respondents)

(Office of the Deputy Prime Minister 2004). Anticipating a lower response rate in deprived areas, we randomly selected 22 addresses from 'normal' OAs and 33 addresses from 'deprived' OAs. Respondents were sent a 20-page questionnaire and, if needed, a reminder letter. In OAs where we initially received less than 15 respondents, we sent up to four additional reminder letters. The overall response rate was 53%. By oversampling respondents in deprived OAs and sending up to four reminder letter to non-responding persons in OAs which lacked a sufficient number of respondents, we counter-balanced the well-known effect of low response rates in deprived areas. As can be seen in Fig. 2.1, this strategy worked well in the sense that the absolute number of respondents does not co-vary with area deprivation. The average number of respondents per OA was 12.8 (standard deviation 2.7).

In the questionnaire, we introduced questions on the respondents' residential areas as follows: 'We would like you to think about the area within a short walking distance (say a couple of minutes) from your home. That is the street you live in and the streets, houses, shops, parks and others areas close to your home'. We intended for this definition to focus respondents' answers on the immediate area around their homes (approximating the size of a behaviour setting).

Analytic Strategy

By asking respondents questions about their immediate area of residence, we intend to measure collective properties of these local contexts. As with any social science measurement, however, respondents' answers will not represent a 'true' picture of their area but will be biased and affected by measurement error to some extent. For example, a respondent who spends little time in his or her immediate neighborhood and does not care about his or her neighbors will probably know less about community life than respondents who spend more time in their immediate neighborhood and have more contacts with their neighbors. A very old respondent may evaluate victimization risks differently from a younger respondent or may report less alcohol-related disorder because he or she seldom leaves his or her home at night. Some aspects of community life, such as social cohesion and trust among neighbors, are more subjective and depend on individual experiences, while others, such as the presence of litter in front gardens, are more objectively measurable, and depend less on (but are not entirely independent of) respondents' individual characteristics.

We start with some simple examples to illustrate the accuracy of responses by exploiting external spatial information. In the questionnaire, respondents were asked to state whether certain aspects of infrastructure like shops, police stations, etc. were close to their homes. Figure 2.2 shows the percentage of respondents who reported the presence of a police station in their local area as well as the actual location of police stations (symbolized by stars). The close congruence, which was also found for fire stations (graph not shown), shows that people were quite accurate in reporting spatial aspects of infrastructure which we are able to check. We also found, for example, a close spatial match between survey respondents' frequency

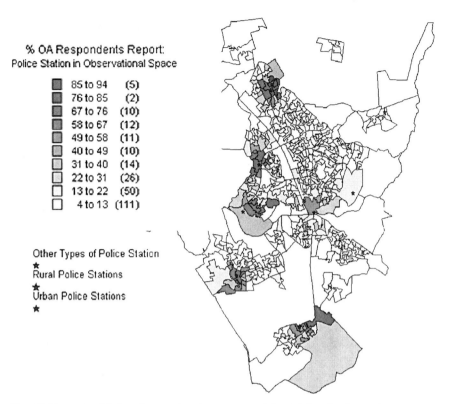

% OA Respondents Report:
Police Station in Observational Space

■	85 to 94	(5)
■	76 to 85	(2)
■	67 to 76	(10)
■	58 to 67	(12)
■	49 to 58	(11)
■	40 to 49	(10)
□	31 to 40	(14)
□	22 to 31	(26)
□	13 to 22	(50)
□	4 to 13	(111)

Other Types of Police Station
★
Rural Police Stations
★
Urban Police Stations
★

Fig. 2.2 External validation of respondents' assessment of the vicinity of police stations

of reporting noisy neighbors and the frequency of police calls regarding nuisance neighbors (finding not shown). These and other similar tests make us confident that the respondents reporting of their observable local conditions are largely accurate. However, in matters concerning latent dimensions of social organization, the same opportunity for external validation does not exist.

The question then remains as to how we can evaluate the quality of survey data on contexts and determine the degree to which respondents' answers reflect the actual social conditions of their common environment rather than their subjective views. As in any kind of empirical research, data quality refers to validity and reliability. Validity is the degree to which data actually measures what it is supposed to measure, while reliability is the degree to which a measure is consistent (or precise).

Until recently, the reliability of community-level survey data has been generally neglected, as no standardized statistical tools comparable to scale reliability measures like Cronbach's alpha existed. This has changed largely thanks to the 'ecometric' approach recently developed by Raudenbush and Sampson (1999) which is specifically designed to assess the reliability of data on collective entities, such as neighborhoods, schools, or companies. This statistical method is based on the idea, analogous to the concept of interrater reliability, that information given by individuals concerning a common environment is reliable to the extent that it is concurrent. If all respondents in a neighborhood answer questions identically, their information is deemed perfectly reliable. On the other hand, if every respondent gives a different answer, they do not provide a consistent picture of neighborhood conditions. Raudenbush and Sampson call the consistency of residents' reports on their shared environment '*ecological reliability*'.

The same approach can be exploited to address the issue of homogeneity within area units. If smaller output areas are more homogeneous in terms of environmental conditions than larger super output areas (which represent clusters of smaller output areas), then we can expect answers (the subjects' observations) on the smaller spatial level to be more similar, and hence more reliable.

Statistically, the measurement of ecological reliability is based on multilevel (or hierarchical linear) modeling (Hox 2002; Raudenbush and Bryk 2002). One of the basic features of multilevel modeling is a decomposition into within- and between-group variance, where the share of the between-group variance represents the degree of consistency of answers by members of the same group. The more concurrent the answers from respondents in one area are, the lower the within-group variance, and the higher the between-group variance. Computed from this variance decomposition, the intra-class correlation coefficient (ICC) is defined as the share of the between-group variance of the sum of between- and within-group variance. The coefficient of ecological reliability called lambda is based on the intra-class coefficient weighted by the number of respondents, just as Cronbach's alpha is weighted by the number of items in a scale. Thus, the ecological reliability increases with the number of respondents. Finally, using a Bayesian approach, estimates of group-level values are 'smoothed' by pulling them towards the mean of all groups if the reliability is low due to very few respondents (see below).

One of the important findings from Raudenbush and Sampson's research is that a relatively small number of respondents are sufficient to achieve a high reliability of information on neighborhood conditions. Little incremental improvement of the ecological reliability is observed beyond 30 or 40 respondents (Raudenbush and Sampson 1999, p. 9). The fact that ecological reliability is dependent on the number of respondents is particularly critical in the case of the PCS considering its relatively low number of respondents per small OA. It is important to determine if an average of 13 respondents is enough to achieve a reliable measurement of neighborhood characteristics.

On the following pages, we will use the ecometric approach to assess the reliability of survey scales measuring behavioral contexts in Peterborough comparing smaller and larger area units. We will try to answer to what extent respondents' observations represent concurrent and reliable views on their local area and how much internal homogeneity is dependent on the level of aggregation. The ecometric approach will enable us to assess the advantage of our sampling design based on many very small units compared to more conventional designs which use fewer but larger units. Subsequently, we will then investigate how both levels of aggregation compare in multi-level regression models which include area-level effects. Here, the important question is whether the increase in area-level sample size enhances the statistical power to detect significant effects.

We start with the smaller spatial units of output areas; in a second step, we compare these results with those from larger spatial units (super output areas) and try to assess the advantages and disadvantages of our focus on the smaller output area level. We use the 'social cohesion/trust' and the 'informal social control' scales which jointly constitute the 'collective efficacy' scale as an example. Incidentally, the collective efficacy scale can theoretically be viewed as a measure of an area's moral context.

Results: 'Social Cohesion/Trust' and 'Informal Social Control' (Collective Efficacy)

Collective efficacy has emerged as an important dimension in recent community research, consisting of questions about trust and cohesion among neighbors (social cohesion) and the capability of neighbors to exert informal social control over misbehaving children and adolescents (informal social control). Sampson et al. (1997) argued, in their seminal paper on the attenuating effects of collective efficacy on violence in Chicago neighborhoods, that both aspects of collective efficacy – trust among neighbors and their shared expectation about counteracting disorder and crime – are so closely associated theoretically and empirically to justify a unified concept. Other studies and analyses keep these subscales separate or focus on informal social control (Wikström and Dolmen 2001; Silver and Miller 2004; Taylor 2002). We will do likewise, assessing each scale separately and look to informal social control as the dependent variable in the final analysis.

The first four items displayed in Table 2.1 were introduced in the questionnaire as follows: 'For each of the following, please state if it is very likely, likely, unlikely, or very unlikely that people in your neighborhood would act in the following manner.' Respondents were asked about the likelihood 'that your neighbors would do something about it' if neighborhood children were skipping school, hanging out on a street corner or spraying graffiti on a local building or, if they were fighting.

Confirming the results of previous studies, principal component analysis with oblimin rotation of all nine items yields two closely related dimensions representing social cohesion/trust and informal social control (Table 2.1). The two dimensions are clearly correlated ($r = 0.45$ on the individual level, $r = 0.77$ on the area level). The individual-level reliabilities are very high for both sub-scales of collective efficacy (Cronbach's alpha $= 0.83$).

To evaluate the ecological, neighborhood-level reliability of these scales, the first step within multilevel modeling is to compute ICCs in a so-called 'empty model' without any individual-level predictors, comparable to variance decomposition in a conventional analysis of variance. As reported in Table 2.2, about 19% of the variance of 'social cohesion/trust' and about 11% of the variance of 'informal social control' is due to differences between output areas. Weighted by the number of

Table 2.1 Principal component analysis of 'collective efficacy' scale (individual level, N = 6, 615 respondents)

Variables	'informal social control' (Eigenvalue 4.4, 48.5% variance)	'social cohesion' (Eigenvalue 1.3, 14.5% variance)	Extraction
	Dimensions		
Skipping school and hanging out	0.82		0.67
Spray-painting graffiti on a local building	0.82		0.71
Fight in front of your house	0.77		0.59
Child showing disrespect to an adult	0.81		0.64
People around here are willing to help their neighbours	0.34	0.57	0.62
This is a close-knit neighbourhood	0.30	0.58	0.58
People in this neighbourhood can be trusted		0.74	0.67
People in this neighbourhood generally do not get along with each other		−0.84	0.63
People in this neighbourhood do not share the same values		−0.81	0.58
Cronbach's alpha	0.83	0.83	

Table 2.2 Variance components of 'social cohesion/trust' and 'informal social control' scales (N = 518 OAs with N = 6, 615 respondents)

	Social cohesion/trust		Informal social control	
	Empty model	Conditional model[a]	Empty model	Conditional model[a]
variance components between respondents (r_{ij})	0.41126	0.40716	0.81604	0.81235
explained variance on respondent level	–	1.0% of 0.41126	–	0.5% of 0.81604
between areas (u_{0j})	0.09878	0.0891	0.10425	0.10042
explained variance on output area level	–	9.8% of 0.09878		3.7% of 0.10425
ICC[b]	19.4%	18.0%	11.3%	11.0%
lambda ('ecological' reliability)	0.75	0.72	0.61	0.60

[a] *Controlling for socio-demographic composition*
[b] *Intraclass correlation coefficient* $= r_{ij}/(u_0 + r_{ij})^* 100$

respondents, this ICC translates to lambdas of 0.75 for 'social cohesion/trust' and 0.61 for 'informal social control'. Whereas the result for the former scale is very good, the value for the latter is at best satisfactory. We can interpret these reliability measures as showing that respondents are more concurrent in giving their impression of social cohesion and trust in their area of residence than assessing the likelihood that their neighbors would intervene in situations of child and adolescent misbehavior.

In the Chicago Project on Human Development in Chicago Neighborhoods' (PHDCN) community survey (which uses substantially larger area units than this study), the ICCs reported for the same scales were slightly higher, at 24% for social cohesion/trust and 13% for informal social control (Raudenbush and Sampson 1999, p. 8). In a community survey in two German cities using the same scales (but, again, larger area units), the ICC was 17% for 'social cohesion/trust' and 10% for 'informal social control', mirroring findings from Peterborough (Oberwittler 2003).

In a second step, individual-level variables are introduced to the multilevel model to control for neighborhoods' socio-demographic composition. If differences in measurement between neighborhoods are mainly due to socio-demographic variables, for example, the fact that older respondents answer survey questions differently than younger respondents, or poorly educated respondents answer differently than highly educated respondents, this would be reflected in the so-called conditional model. The stronger the effect of individual-level variables, the more the ICC would be reduced between the empty and conditional model. The second column in Table 2.2 ('conditional model') reveals that socio-demographic variables have only a very small effect on area-level measurements, reducing the ICC of 'social cohesion/trust' by 10% and the ICC of 'informal social control' by 4%. Socio-demographic variables also have a very marginal effect on within-area differences between individual respondents (1% for 'social cohesion/trust', 0.5% for 'informal social control'). This result underlines the fact that perceptions of area social organization are largely independent of individual socio-demographic factors, and thus area differences are hardly attenuated if controlling for respondents' socio-demographic composition. What really drives area differences in these dimensions of collective efficacy, then, is the effect of the *collective* makeup of areas, such as the concentration of social deprivation. We will turn to these collective dimensions later.

In the case of Peterborough, an average of four to five output areas constitutes one super output area. Any additional information gained on the smaller level can be assessed by aggregating the survey data to the super output area level and comparing the results from both (Fig. 2.3). If we look to the ecological reliability of the social cohesion/trust scale, its ICC (share of between-group variance) is only 14% on the superoutput areas (SOA) level compared to 19% on the smaller OA level, indicating that SOAs are internally more heterogeneous.[4]

On the other hand, because there are more respondents per SOA unit, the ecological reliability lambda rises from 0.75 to 0.91. The same holds true for the 'informal social control' scale. The ICC of 'informal social control' drops from 11 to 8.5% if

---

[4] However, it should be noted that the super output areas are still generally smaller (averaging about 1,500 inhabitants) than the units commonly used in ecological studies. We would therefore expect that the difference in heterogeneity would be even greater had our comparison with OAs involved larger units than the SOAs.

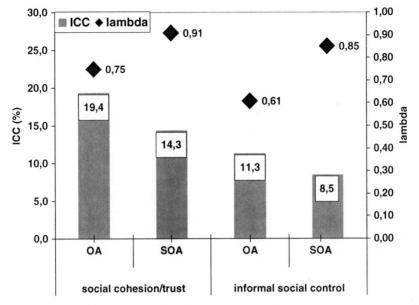

Fig. 2.3 ICCs and ecological reliability (lambda) of 'social cohesion/trust' and 'informal social control', OA and SOA levels compared (N=518 OAs, N=90 SOAs with N=6, 615 respondents)

one move from OA to SOA level; lambda, on the other hand, increases from 0.61 to 0.85.

Thus, one faces a trade-off between the (theoretically important) aim to target small and homogenous areas approximating behavior-settings and the need for sufficiently reliable measurements (methodologically important). The mean of 13 respondents per output area certainly marks the lower bound of a reasonable sampling design. In the Chicago survey (PHDCN study), using much larger area units, the average number of respondents per neighborhood cluster was 26 (Raudenbush and Sampson 1999). As we will see below, a rather unintended positive side-effect of lower reliability and larger measurement errors is the reduction in multicollinearity between neighborhood-level variables.

We can achieve a more detailed picture on the gains in homogeneity on the smaller OA level by utilizing multilevel analyses to build three-level models where the variance is more accurately decomposed into shares of variance for each level. In this model, level 1 represents respondents nested in OAs, level 2 represents OAs nested in SOAs and level 3 represents SOAs. Figure 2.4 displays the results of this variance decomposition. For both scales, the larger share of between-group variance is between the SOAs, with around 30% of the additional variance lying between the OAs within these SOAs. Thus, the heterogeneity between OAs within one SOA is lower than the heterogeneity between SOAs. Still, there is a considerable increase of around 30% in spatial homogeneity.

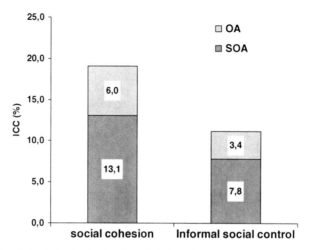

Fig. 2.4 ICC's of 'social cohesion/trust' and 'informal social control' in three-level models
N = 6,615 respondents nested in N = 518 OA's nested in N = 108 SOA's)

Multiple Regression Models with Area Level Predictors

How does the decision to use 518 smaller instead of 102 larger spatial units change
the results of substantive statistical analyses? We will explore this in this final section by modeling stepwise multiple regression models on both levels of aggregation
with informal social control as the dependent variable (Tables 2.3 and 2.4). Models
on both levels are kept as similar as possible in order to facilitate the comparison and
to focus on the 'scaling effect'. These models are pure area-level models because we
are dealing with area-level dimensions of social structure (measured by census data)
and social organization (measured by survey data). However, all survey scales are
empirical Bayes estimates (which 'smoothen' unreliable values at the extreme ends
of the distribution) adjusted for individual-level socio-demographic composition, as
recommended by Sampson et al. (1997).

The models are built in three steps. First, only structural (census) variables are
used to predict the outcome. In a second step, observed disorder and area neighbor
contacts are introduced, which are assumed to correlate negatively (disorder) respectively positively (contacts) with expectations for informal social control. In the final
step, the predictive power of the second component of collective efficacy, social
cohesion/trust, is also tested. The 'R squared change' value indicates how much the
model improves with each step. We report unstandardized coefficients which can be
easily compared as all predictors have been standardized to a mean value of 0 and a
standard deviation of 1.

Comparing the models at the two levels of aggregation, the first thing which is
clear is that, on the whole, the results are concurrent. No predictor behaves in a
completely different manner or changes signs when moving from the smaller OA to

Table 2.3 Aggregate-level OLS regression of 'informal social control' (N = 518 OAs with N = 6, 615 respondents)

N = 518 OAs	1		2		3	
	unst. B	t-value	unst. B	t-value	unst. B	t-value
Constant	3.172	323.8	3.132	333.495	3.106	362.911
deprivation (factor score)	**−0.096**	**−9.896**	**−0.040**	**−4.008**	−0.011	−1.192
asian ethnicity (factor score)	**−0.034**	**−2.753**	−0.012	−1.126	0.014	1.405
asian ethn. square	**0.006**	**3.639**	0.002	1.728	−0.001	−.775
fluctuation	**−0.020**	**−2.041**	−0.014	−1.675	0.003	0.399
fluctuation * deprivation	0.015	1.681	0.011	1.374	0.007	0.942
fluctuation * asian ethn.	**−0.015**	**−2.147**	−0.010	−1.604	−0.006	−1.192
pop density	**−0.070**	**−5.699**	**−0.037**	**−3.349**	−0.016	−1.597
non-residential land use	**−0.035**	**−3.430**	**−0.018**	**−2.034**	−0.015	−1.909
R square	*0.45*					
observed (youth) disorder	–		**−0.118**	**−11.110**	**−0.072**	**−7.131**
neighbourh contacts	–		**0.041**	**5.135**	0.011	1.518
neighbourh contacts * depriv.	–		−0.012	−1.651	**−0.016**	**−2.359**
neighbourh contacts * asian ethn	–		**0.015**	**2.776**	**0.017**	**3.570**
R square change			*0.13*			
social cohesion	–		–		**0.132**	**12.085**
R square change					*0.09*	
Total adj. R square (F-value)	*0.44*	*(51.5)*	*0.58*	*(58.2)*	*0.68*	*(80.4)*

bold coefficients: $p < 0.05$; all predictors are z-standardized

Table 2.4 Aggregate-level OLS regression of 'informal social control' (N = 102 SOAs with N = 6, 615 respondents)

N = 102 SOAs	1		2		3	
	unst. B	t-value	unst. B	t-value	unst. B	t-value
Constant	3.231	170.520	3.155	153.702	3.109	155.439
deprivation (factor score)	**−0.175**	**−9.055**	**−0.074**	**−3.051**	−0.026	−1.096
asian ethnicity (factor score)	**−0.072**	**−2.638**	−0.019	−0.767	0.033	1.344
asian ethn. square	**0.010**	**2.957**	0.004	1.102	−0.002	−0.761
fluctuation	−0.017	−1.083	−0.019	−1.361	−0.003	−0.252
fluctuation * deprivation	−0.015	−0.805	−0.021	−1.331	−0.011	−0.811
fluctuation * asian ethn.	−0.012	−1.018	0.000	0.038	−0.006	−0.657
pop density	**−0.042**	**−2.260**	**−0.038**	**−2.340**	−0.015	−0.966
non-residential land use	−0.014	−0.768	−0.018	−1.111	−0.021	−1.542
R square	*0.76*					
observed (youth) disorder			**−0.129**	**−5.614**	**−0.083**	**−3.756**
neighbourh contacts			0.024	1.785	0.005	0.416
neighbourh contacts * depriv.			−0.004	−0.260	0.002	0.133
neighbourh contacts * asian ethn			0.020	1.856	0.012	1.260
R square change			*0.07*			
social cohesion					**0.146**	**5.261**
R square change					*0.04*	
Total adj. R square (F-value)	*0.74*		*0.81*		*0.86*	

bold coefficients: $p < 0.05$; all predictors are z-standardized the larger SOA level (see Table 2.4). Thus Sampson's assertion that most results are robust across level of aggregation is at least supported by these empirical findings. Yet differences are noticeable in the more subtle parts of the models, mainly concerning the moderate and weak predictions. For example, in the first step there are significant but weak effects of residential stability and land use at the OA level which are insignificant at the SOA level. There is also a significant interaction effect between residential instability and Asian ethnicity, suggesting that negative effects on informal social control are exacerbated if both dimensions go hand in hand. In the second model, the significant effect of neighborhood contacts as well as its interaction term between Asian ethnicity disappears when moving to the larger spatial level.

It appears, then, that there is a general tendency for weaker, more subtle effects to disappear when data in analyzed at a higher level of aggregation. This could be due to watering down the degree of spatial homogeneity by aggregating small areas. For example, if there are small ethnic enclaves or 'pockets' of non-residential land use, their effect may be masked to the extent of non-significance if they are lumped together with neighboring areas. More detailed research into geographical micro-spaces would be needed to elaborate this hypothesis.

There is another, more technical reason why regression models on the lower level of spatial aggregation yield more nuanced and complex findings. The statistical power to detect significant effects of predictors necessarily increases with the sample size of area units, which renders the standard errors of coefficients smaller. This is reflected by higher t-values in the OA models reported in Table 2.3 compared to the SOA models in Table 2.4. Logically, it is the more subtle effects on the lower end of significance – like interaction effects typically are – which profit from this increase in power. An important finding, therefore, is that a sufficient number of area units are an important requirement for more complex modeling.

Finally, the share of explained variance (R squared) is considerably higher in models on the larger SOA level than on the smaller OA level. This should, however, not be interpreted as a decisive advantage, as Ouimet (2000) did, since the unstandardized coefficients are not affected by spatial aggregation. This effect can be graphically illustrated in the scatterplots displayed in Fig. 5a and 5b. In both scatter plots, the association between deprivation and expectations for informal social control are overlaid for both spatial levels, where every dot represents one area. The steepness of the regression line (the slope) represents the strength of the effect of deprivation on informal social control. In Fig. 2.5a, the lines are virtually the same, yet the cloud of dots is much more widely dispersed around the regression line on the OA level; there are some particularly extreme outliers on both ends of the scale which 'disappear' when the data is aggregated to the larger SOA level. It is important to understand that although the correlation coefficient and the R squared value are necessarily much higher at the SOA level due to less random variation, the predicted effect of deprivation on informal social control (the steepness of the regression line, formally expressed by the *unstandardized* beta coefficient) is practically the same. This is the reason why a focus on correlation coefficients, standardized regression coefficients, and value of R squared often is unhelpful and even misleading, and why

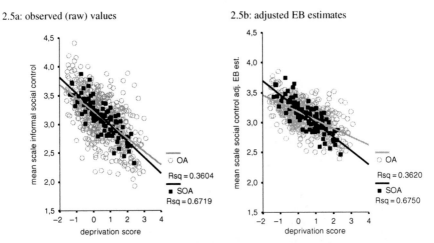

Fig. 2.5 a,b Scatter plots of the association between area deprivation and informal social control, OA and SOA levels compared (N = 518 for OAs, N = 108 for SOAs and N = 6,615 for respondents)

the information carried in the unstandardized beta coefficient is more meaningful if one is interested in prediction.

However, the Bayesian approach to the estimation of group means does impact the strength of the relationships at the smaller OA level. The scatter plot on the right (Fig. 2.5b) displays the same association using the empirical Bayes estimates adjusting for individual socio-demographic composition which we used in the regression models. As one can easily see, in comparison to the 'raw value' on the left side, the Bayes method 'pulls' the extreme values at both ends of the distribution towards the mean for all neighborhoods, rendering the distribution of the OA level group means more similar to that of the SOA level. This happens to the extent that outlying estimates of group means are deemed unreliable, which has been shown to be a function of low sample sizes of respondents within areas. As result of this, the regression line is rendered flatter than that of the scatter plots using either the raw or the SOA values. In effect, the empirical Bayes 'smoothing' procedure attenuates the empirical association and proposes a more conservative estimate. This can be observed in the regression models discussed above where the unstandardized coefficient of deprivation is −0.175 at the SOA level but only −0.096 at the OA level. Generally speaking, if the number of respondents per spatial unit is very small and estimates of survey results become too unreliable, the Bayesian method built into multi-level modeling software will tend to produce very conservative estimates which may in extreme cases effectively 'kill' substantial results. However, the comparison of models shows that, on balance, more significant effects are observed at the lower spatial level because the effect of increased statistical power due to a larger number of area units is stronger than the effect of attenuated reliability of area estimates due to the smaller number of respondents in areas.

There is yet another side-effect of using smaller spatial units which enables more nuanced and complex models and the testing of more differentiated hypotheses. At the lower spatial level of OAs, there is a much higher degree of randomness or random variation due to the 'small number problem' where a change of one or two individual values can cause a significant change in rates. While this random variation or random noise could be viewed as a nuisance, it also has the paradoxically positive effect of attenuating the problem of multicollinearity which hampers aggregate data analysis in particular (Land et al. 1990). If independent variables are strongly intercorrelated, with bivariate correlations greater than $r = 0.70$, the basic task of multiple regression analysis (to disentangle the effects of intercorrelated variables) becomes very difficult. From this perspective, using data on a smaller level of aggregation, where correlations are generally lower, can actually be advantageous (Sampson and Raudenbush 1999, p. 625). At the SOA level, correlations between deprivation, informal social control and social cohesion all surpass 0.80, whereas they range between 0.60 and 0.80 at the OA level.

Conclusions

In this chapter, we have made a number of arguments about how to advance the study of the role of the social environment in crime causation. We have, on theoretical grounds (based on Situational Action Theory), criticized the common practices of (i) using large area units and (ii) neglecting the importance of individuals' exposure to different kinds of environments (within and outside their neighborhoods). We have advocated the use of small area units (which resemble behavior-settings as closely as possible) combined with a measure of individuals' exposure to different behavior-settings (within and outside their neighborhoods) to advance empirical study of the role of the social environment in crime causation. In this chapter, we focused on exploring the pros and cons of using small area units. The equally important problem of measuring individuals' exposure to different environments will be dealt with elsewhere.

First, we have shown that differences in subjects' assessments of the environment of their immediate area of residence (e.g., social cohesion, informal social control) are in fact due to area characteristics and largely independent of respondents' socio-demographic characteristics, which gives us some confidence that we are actually measuring environmental features when using small area units.

Second, we have demonstrated that the use of smaller area units produces more homogenous observations of the environment (as judged by the ICCs), indicating that the environment of smaller areas tends to be more homogeneous than that of larger areas. It should be stressed that when we talk about a homogenous environment in this context we could, in fact, refer to heterogeneous characteristics, such as ethnic diversity. For example, if all observers agree that an area is ethnically diverse their observations are homogeneous although this aspect of their environment is heterogeneous (but homogeneously heterogenic within its area boundaries). This is an important point because heterogeneity in environmental conditions is often of particular interest in the study of the role of the environment in crime causation (e.g., diversity in aspects of the area's population composition or land use). Thus when we refer to area homogeneity this includes (within-area) *homogeneous heterogeneity* in environmental conditions.

In our study, we compared area units averaging 300 inhabitants to area units averaging 1,500. Many ecological studies use area units averaging between 5,000 and 8,000 inhabitants (and some even more) and we would expect that the observed gain in area homogeneity using smaller area units would have been even more dramatic had our comparison involved such large units (although a city the size of Peterborough could not have been divided into enough units of this size to allow the ecometric analyses we have conducted).

Third, we have shown that an additional advantage of using more smaller area units rather than fewer larger units is an increase in statistical power for detecting significant area level effects. This result is in line with recent research on power analysis in multi-level survey designs showing that, in general, maximizing the number of area units is preferable to maximizing the number of respondents within each unit.

However, we have also demonstrated that using smaller areas with a lower number of respondents rather than fewer areas with more respondents inevitably affects reliability (as judged by the lambdas), which is a methodological disadvantage. In such case, the researcher must compromise between area homogeneity and reliability. This compromise will preferably be taken based on relevant theoretical and methodological concerns, such as aiming to approximate behavior-settings without losing too much in terms of reliability of data.

In this context it should, however, be stressed that there are no reasons, in principle, why the use of smaller area units should imply lower numbers of respondents. In practice, this is often the case generally because of financial constraints, which are a reality in almost all empirical research. It is more expensive, for example, to conduct a survey which has 30 respondents in each of 300 (small) areas than one which has 30 respondents in each of 100 (large) areas. However, we have shown that, on balance, the advantage of having more small areas (which are more homogenous) outweighs the loss of reliability.

So why is smaller better? Small units of analysis are better on *theoretical* grounds because they more closely approximate behavior-settings. Individuals' actions and development are only influenced by the environments they can access with their senses and the part of the environment which individuals can access with their senses is, arguably, generally small. Small units are also better from a *methodological* point of view because smaller units are more likely to be homogeneous in terms of environmental characteristics (although it is important to note that these homogenous environmental characteristics, in fact, can constitute heterogeneity, such as ethnic diversity or diversity in land use). Small units are also better because using more small areas provides more statistical power than using fewer large areas, making it easier to establish statistical significance. The only major drawback we have identified is that researchers may (purely for financial reasons) have to choose between the number of units and the number of respondents per unit which they include in a survey; opting for smaller units will mean they have fewer respondents per unit, which will affect the reliability of their estimates. By and large, however, in our evaluation, in order to advance the study of the role of the environment in crime causation small is certainly better.

References

Bailey, T. C., & Gatrell, A. C. (1995). *Interactive spatial data analysis*. London: Longman.
Bellair, P. E. (1997). Social interaction and community crime: Examining the importance of neighbor networks. *Criminology*, 35, 677–703.
Hox, J. (2002). *Multilevel analysis: Techniques and applications*. Mawhaw: Erlbaum.
Kubrin, C. E., & Weitzer, R. (2003). New directions in social disorganization theory. *Journal of Research in Crime and Delinquency*, 40(4), 374–402.
Land, K. C., McCall, P. L., & Cohen, L. E. (1990). Structural covariates of homicide rates: Are there any invariances across time and space. *American Journal of Sociology*, 95(4), 922–963.
Martin, D. (2000). Towards the geographies of the 2001 UK census of population. *Transactions of the Institute of British Geographers*, 25, 321–332.
McCord, E. S., Ratcliffe, J. H., Garcia, R. M., & Taylor, R. B. (2007). Nonresidential crime attractors and generators elevate perceived neighborhood crime and incivilities. *Journal of Research in Crime and Delinquency*, 44(3), 295–320.
McVie, S., & Norris, P. (2006). *Neighbourhood effects on youth delinquency and drug use (Edinburgh study of youth transitions and crime, working paper 10)*. Edinburgh: Centre for Law and Society.
Miethe, T. D., & Meier, R. F. (1994). *Crime and its social context: Towards an integrated theory of offenders, victims, and situations*. Albany: State University of New York Press.
Murrey, D. M., Varnell, S. P., & Blitstein, J. L. (2004). Design and analysis of group-randomized trials: A review of recent methodological developments. *American Journal of Public Health*, 94(3), 423–432.
Oberwittler, D. (2003). Die Messung und Qualitätskontrolle kontextbezogener Befragungsdaten mithilfe der Mehrebenenanalyse - am Beispiel des Sozialkapitals von Stadtvierteln. *ZA-Informationen*, 53, 11–41.
Office of the Deputy Prime Minister. (2004). *The English Indices of Deprivation 2004: Summary*. London.
Openshaw, S., & Taylor, P. J. (1981). The modifiable areal unit problem. In: N. Wrigley & R. J. Bennet (Eds.), *Quantitative geography: A British view* (pp. 60–70). London: Routledge.
Openshaw, S. (1984). *Modifiable areal unit problem*. Norwich: GeoBooks.
Ouimet, M. (2000). Aggregation bias in ecological research: How social disorganization and criminal opportunities shape the spatial distribution of juvenile delinquency in Montreal. *Canadian Journal of Criminology*, 42, 135–156.
Raudenbush, S. W. (1999). Statistical analysis and optimal design in cluster randomized trials. *Psychological Methods*, 2(2), 173–185.
Raudenbush, S., & Bryk, A. (2002). *Hierarchical linear models: applications and data analysis methods (2.A.)*. Thousand Oaks: Sage.
Raudenbush, S. W., & Sampson, R. J. (1999). Ecometrics: Toward a science of assessing ecological settings, with appliance to the systematic social observation of neighborhoods. *Sociological Methodology*, 29, 1–41.
Reynolds, H. D. (1998). *The modifiable area unit problem: empirical analysis and statistical simulation*. PhD thesis, University of Toronto.
Sampson, R. J., Raudenbush, S. W., & Earls, F. J. (1997). Neighborhoods and violent crime: A multilevel study of collective efficacy. *Science*, 277, 918–924.
Sampson, R. J., & Raudenbush, S. W. (1999). Systematic social observation of public spaces: A new look at disorder in urban neighborhoods. *American Journal of Sociology*, 105(3), 603–651.

Sampson, R. J., Morenoff, J. D., & Gannon-Rowley, T. (2002). Assessing "neighborhood effects": Social processes and new directions in research. *Annual Review of Sociology*, 28, 443–478.

Sampson, R. (2006). How does community context matter? Social mechanisms and the explanation of crime rates. In: P.-O. H. Wikström & R. Sampson (Eds.), *Crime and its explanation: Contexts, mechanisms and development*. Cambridge: Cambridge University Press.

Shaw, C., & McKay, H. D. (1969 [1942]). *Juvenile Delinquency and Urban Areas*. Chicago: Chicago University Press.

Silver, E., & Miller, L. L. (2004). Sources of informal social control in Chicago neighborhoods. *Criminology*, 42(3), 551–583.

Smith, W. R., Frazee, S. G., & Davison, E. (2000). Furthering the integration of routine activity and social disorganization theories: Small units of analysis and the study of street robbery as a diffusion process. *Criminology*, 38(2), 489–523.

Snijders, T., & Bosker, R. (1999). *Multilevel Analysis: An introduction to basic and advanced multilevel analysis*. London: Sage.

Taylor, R. (2001). *Breaking away from broken windows: baltimore neighborhoods and the nationwide fight against crime, grime, fear, and decline*. Boulder, CO: Westview Press.

Taylor, R. (2002). Fear of crime, social ties, and collective efficacy: Maybe masquerading measurement, maybe Deja Vu all over again. *Justice Quarterly*, 19(4), 773–792.

Wikström, P.-O. H. (2004). Crime as alternative: Towards a cross-level situational action theory of crime causation. In: J. McCord (Ed.), *Beyond empiricism: Institutions and intentions in the study of crime* (pp. 1–37). New Brunswick: Transaction.

Wikström, P.-O. H. (2005). The social origins of pathways in crime. Towards a developmental ecological action theory of crime involvement and its changes. In: D. P. Farrington (Ed.), *Testing integrated developmental/life course theories of offending* (pp. 211–145). New Brunswick: Transaction.

Wikström, P.-O. H. (2006). Individuals, settings and acts of crime. situational mechanisms and the explanation of crime. In: P.-O. H. Wikström & R. J. Sampson (Eds.), *The explanation of crime: Context, mechanisms and development*. Cambridge: Cambridge University Press.

Wikström, P.-O. H. (2007a). The social ecology of crime: The role of the environment in crime causation. In: H.-J. Schneider (Ed.), *Internationales Handbuch der Kriminologie* (Vol. 1). Berlin: de Gruyter.

Wikström, P.-O. H. (2007b). Deterrence and deterrence experiences: Preventing crime through the threat of punishment. In: S. Shoham, O. Beck, & M. Kett (Eds.), *International handbook of penology and criminal justice* (pp. 345–378). London: CRC Press.

Wikström, P.-O. H. (2007c). In search of causes and explanations of crime. In: R. King & E. Wincup (Eds.), *Doing research on crime and justice* (2nd ed.). Oxford: Oxford University Press.

Wikström, P.-O. H., & Dolmen, L. (2001). Urbanisation, neighbourhood social integration, informal social control, minor social disorder, and fear of crime. *International Review of Victimology*, 8, 121–140.

Wikström, P.-O. H., & Ceccato, V. (2004). *Crime and social life: A space-time budget study*. Paper presented at the annual meeting of the American Society of Criminology. Nashville, TN. November 2004.

Wikström, P.-O. H., & Butterworth, D. (2006). *Adolescent crime: Individual differences and lifestyles*. Collumpton: Willan Publishing.

Wikström, P.-O. H., & Treiber, K. (2007). The role of self-control in crime causation: Beyond Gottfredson and Hirschi's general theory of crime. *European Journal of Criminology*, 4(2), 237–264.

Wikström, P.-O. H., & Treiber, K. (2008). What drives persistent offending? The neglected and unexplored role of the social environment. In: J. Savage (Ed.), *The development of persistent criminality*. Oxford: Oxford University Press.

Wooldredge, J. (2002). Examining the (Ir)Relevance of aggregation bias for multilevel studies of neighborhoods and crime with an example comparing census tracts to official neighborhoods in Cincinnati. *Criminology*, 40(3), 681–709.

Chapter 3
Where the Action Is at Places: Examining Spatio-Temporal Patterns of Juvenile Crime at Places Using Trajectory Analysis and GIS

Elizabeth Groff, David Weisburd, and Nancy A. Morris[1]

Abstract "Crime Places" have recently emerged as an important focus of crime prevention theory and practice. Interest develops in part from the underlying assumptions of recent theoretical perspectives that focus on opportunity structures for crime. Building upon these theoretical innovations a number of studies beginning in the late 1980s show that crime is concentrated in specific places in urban areas. This has led many scholars to argue that crime places would be a more effective focus of crime prevention activities than people involved in crime. Previous studies have shown that crime is concentrated at such micro places, but they have not examined critically whether our understanding of crime across place would have been seriously altered if we had used larger geographic units of analysis to characterize changes in crime rates over time. Our study uses trajectory analysis and GIS to examine this question. Our geographic analysis reveals a tendency for members of the same trajectory to be clustered. However, tremendous block by block variation in temporal patterns of juvenile crime is also exposed. These findings show that much would have been lost if we would have aggregated up from the street block and examined only units such as census block groups. We think these data suggest that much of the action of crime at place occurs at very micro units of geography such as street blocks, and that researchers should begin with micro units of analysis before moving to larger aggregates such as census block groups.

Introduction

Traditionally, research on the spatial distribution of crime has been cross-sectional and focused on relatively "macro" units of geography that have been seen as linked to broad social units such as neighborhoods or communities (Eck and

[1]The authors gratefully acknowledge the financial support of the University of Pennsylvania via grant #2001-JN-FX-K001from the Office of Juvenile Justice and Delinquency Prevention, US Department of Justice.

E. Groff
Department of Criminal Justice, Temple University, Philadelphia, PA, USA
e-mail: groff@temple.edu

Weisburd 1995). The most frequently chosen units of study in turn, tend to be those for which additional data are available from census organizations. Researchers have consistently relied on official census data to characterize the socio-economic status of neighborhoods in the city. In this way, census boundaries have become the de facto standard because they are easily accessible, longitudinal, and free. As a result, not only has our understanding at crime across geography tended to center on units that fit theories that are at the neighborhood or community level, but specific analyses have often been linked to census boundaries. The result is that study of crime at the area level has seldom been focused on what has recently been termed "crime places" (Eck and Weisburd 1995).

Since the 1970s the study of "crime places" has emerged as an important focus of crime prevention and practice (see Chapter 1 for a complete review). The interest in studying places grows in part from the underlying assumptions of recent theoretical perspectives that focus on opportunity structures for crime. Opportunity theories such as environmental criminology (Brantingham and Brantingham 1991[1981]) situational crime prevention (Clarke 1980), and routine activity theory (Cohen and Felson 1979; Felson 2002) emphasize the role of places in inhibiting or encouraging criminal activity. Building upon these theoretical innovations a number of studies beginning in the late 1980s show that crime is concentrated in specific places in urban areas, which might be termed "crime hot spots" (Sherman et al. 1989; Weisburd and Green 1995; Eck et al. 2000; Weisburd et al. 2004). These hot spots can take the form of micro place units such as addresses (Sherman et al. 1989) or street hundred blocks (Weisburd et al. 2004). Importantly, such crime places are at a more micro level of geography than are the neighborhoods or communities that have been the focus of most studies of crime across geography, or even the smallest geographic units for which significant census data are available.[2]

These studies consistently show that a relatively small number of places measured at micro units of geography account for a majority of crime in a city. More recently longitudinal analyses have also established that macro level crime trends are produced by changes in specific types of crime places in a city (Weisburd et al. 2004). At the same time, existing studies have conducted only exploratory analyses of local level variability in crime trends. The question of whether examination of micro place crime trends is simply an exercise of breaking up what are consistent higher geographic level trends has not been critically examined in prior work. For example, is there important variation in crime within neighborhoods (i.e., from block to block), or do we find overall similar micro crime places within larger geographic units? Are street blocks with similar crime trajectories over time concentrated in one place or spread throughout the city?

---

[2] Census block groups in Seattle average about 295,462 square meters while blocks average 21,665 square meters. Additionally, the census block has relatively few data items available and its geographic definition does not fit recent crime and place conceptions. By definition a census block groups the interior block faces of four adjacent streets together to form a square. We believe that grouping the block faces on both sides of the same street is a more theoretically defensible approach.

Such questions are critical, since there is little reason for developing understanding of crime at "places" if we could have gained a very similar portrait of the crime trend at higher levels of geographic analysis. In turn, the existence of strong local level variability at places would suggest that our reliance on larger units of geography such as those that are found when using census data are problematic for gaining valid portraits of crime across geography.

To answer these questions, our study extends earlier longitudinal work that employed trajectory analysis to classify street blocks into groups of streets that evidence similar patterns of juvenile crime over a 14-year period (Weisburd et al. unpublished manuscript). These data provide eight groups of places that have distinct temporal patterns of juvenile crime which we then examine to see whether their spatial distribution suggests that the action for crime and place research is at the micro-level or a higher level of aggregation. Our focus is squarely on whether we should be looking at the micro level, not what is causing crime at the micro level.

Background

Opportunity theories have been important in providing a theoretical framework for why examining crime at places in general, and more specifically at micro places, is critical to furthering our understanding of crime events. As a group, opportunity theories emphasize the importance of place characteristics such as housing, employment, shopping, and recreation in shaping the timing and spacing of the convergence of motivated offenders and suitable targets in places with a lack of capable guardians. They also recognize the important role of the structure of the transportation network in influencing human activity. Four theories have exemplified this approach: situational crime prevention (Clarke 1983, 1997), rational choice perspective (Clarke and Cornish 1985), routine activity theory (Cohen and Felson 1979), and environmental criminology (Brantingham and Brantingham 1991 [1981]).[3] Since the size of the unit of analysis is what is at issue here we should note that opportunity theories, even routine activity theory, are recognized as predominantly micro level theories (Eck 1995).

Environmental criminology emphasizes how micro level places can play different roles in stimulating crime. Two of the most frequently identified are as crime attractors or crime generators (Brantingham and Brantingham 1995). For example, a school may be a crime generator because it attracts large groups of people including potential offenders and victims who attend the school. A fast food restaurant may also serve as a crime generator because its inexpensive food and relatively anonymous atmosphere are conducive to "hanging out" in groups that is favored by many juveniles. In both cases, it is the characteristics of individual places that are underlying crime patterns.

---

[3] See Stark (1987) for a related theory based on the ecology of places which emphasizes the role of place characteristics in affecting human behavior.

Empirical research has also noted the existence of extensive block by block variation in characteristics of the physical environment as it is related to criminal activity. Specifically, the relationship between calls for service and burglaries (Groff and LaVigne 2001) as well as auto thefts (Potchak et al. 2002) have been examined.[4] In addition, the relationship between crime and accessibility has been established (Hillier 1999). Both theoretical developments in opportunity theories and empirical studies testing those theories have led to an increasing recognition of the importance of micro-level places in driving crime patterns.

But why did we choose the street block and not some other level of analysis? There are several reasons to focus on street blocks as the preferred unit of analysis, as opposed to U.S. census block groups or single addresses, for examining the micro level variation in patterns of juvenile crime trajectories at places (see Weisburd et al. 2004). First, a street block constitutes a single behavior setting bounded by time and space and both must be considered if we are to understand the dynamics of place (Jacobs 1961; Taylor 1997a, b). Taylor views street blocks as "a key mediating social and spatial construct" (1997b, p. 115).[5] While we know of no research that has attempted to test the notions of behavior settings internationally, it is plausible that similar mechanisms would be at work regardless of country. Specifically, barring some personal relationship, people tend to have more interaction with those individuals on the same block than individuals from other blocks (Taylor 1997b). Second, using micro places such as individual addresses, intersections and street blocks minimizes the aggregation in the analysis and consequently, the risk of ecological fallacy (Brantingham et al. 1976). Third, when considering policing strategies as they relate to place, a key aspect is how much of the variation in crime involves factors the police are able to address (Taylor 1997a). Street blocks offer a manageable size for police and police-coordinated interventions to be identified and applied.

Finally, on a more technical note, the use of street blocks to define places reduces the problem of spatial heterogeneity among the units of observation that has been shown to exist when larger areal units were used (e.g., block groups and census tracts) (Smith et al. 2000). Spatial heterogeneity refers to within-observation variation in measures. This phenomenon is observed when a measure that is valid for a larger areal unit does not accurately represent the within-area variation. For example, a measure such as single family housing may label a neighborhood "sixty percent single-family housing" but that label masks street to street variation in the proportion of housing. One street may be one hundred percent single-family residential, another may be ten percent. Street blocks, on the other hand, offer relatively homogenous units of analysis and thus minimize possible reductions of the size of effects (Smith et al. 2000). In addition, as noted by earlier researchers, the use of street blocks minimizes the error from miscoding of an address in official data and

---

[4] There has also been much work focused on the differences in risk between individual properties (Johnson et al. 1997; Tseloni et al. 2002).

[5] See Taylor (1997b) for a comprehensive discussion of street blocks and their role in maintaining social control.

allows for the coding of events that may occur at no particular address but rather unfold on a particular street (Weisburd et al. 2004; Weisburd et al. in progress).

The major question of this study is whether the processes underlying crime patterns are occurring at micro places rather than higher levels of aggregation. To examine this question, the research extends an earlier analysis by Weisburd et al. (in progress) that used trajectory analysis to identify groups of street blocks with similar juvenile crime profiles. Their analysis used the TRAJ procedure developed by Dan Nagin to group street hundred blocks together that experience similar juvenile crime profiles over time (Nagin 2005).[6] Here we address the following research questions: (1) What is the spatial pattern of street blocks that follow specific trajectories of juvenile crime?; (2) Are trajectories of street blocks related to the trajectories of nearby blocks?; and (3) Are street blocks of certain trajectories found near one another or are they spatially independent? The answers to these questions are critical to identifying whether the processes underlying the observed data are occurring at the micro-level and to quantifying the strength and spatial extent of those processes. In the end, we offer a determination on whether variation in juvenile crime at the micro level is significant enough to justify the effort involved in examining it.

Methodology

We attempt to provide insights into these questions by examining a data set originally developed to study all crime events across street hundred blocks (Weisburd et al. 2004) and later narrowed to focus on only those crimes committed by juveniles (Weisburd et al. unpublished manuscript). Weisburd et al. (unpublished manuscript) conducted a group-based trajectory analysis of juvenile crime in Seattle, WA over a 14-year period.[7] For ease of description we refer to their "hundred blocks" as street blocks throughout the rest of the paper. Street blocks were defined as containing all addresses ending in 0–99 for each primary number (e.g., the 300 block of Main Street would include addresses from 300 to 399 on Main Street). This is consistent with the US pattern of numbering blocks in non-rural areas from x00 to x99 and is used with both gridded and non-gridded street layouts. This definition produced 29,849 street blocks for the city of Seattle which became the units of analysis. Using a combination of official crime and arrest data, the researchers identified 30,004 crimes that were committed by juveniles age 8–17 inclusive (i.e., crimes for which a juvenile was arrested). They referred to that subset of crime as juvenile crime; we follow the same convention here.[8]

---

[6] Please see the original and subsequent papers by Weisburd et al. for details of how the trajectories were identified (Weisburd et al. 2004; Weisburd et al. unpublished manuscript).

[7] They used the same base data as the initial study by Weisburd et al. (2004). A hundred block consists of a spread of 100 addresses and includes both sides of the street.

[8] Only juvenile crimes for which an arrest was made were included in the study. Juvenile crimes were identified by linking incident and arrest data. A more complete description of the data lineage and creation is available in the original publications.

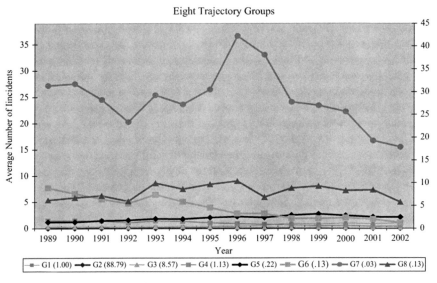

Fig. 3.1 Juvenile crime trajectories

Their trajectory analysis identified eight unique trajectories (Fig. 3.1). While three of the trajectories have low and stable levels of juvenile crime over the entire time period, the others evidence significant changes in the number of juvenile crimes committed. These trajectories also capture streets with higher rates of juvenile crime per year. The number of street blocks in each trajectory varies widely with the largest group, group 2, having no juvenile crime (Table 3.1). For purposes of analysis we focus here on the five trajectories with the most distinctive patterns over time, Groups 4, 5, 6, 7, and 8 (Table 3.1).

Three simple point maps provide basic information about the geography of the street blocks in each trajectory (Figs. 3.2–3.4). Tremendous block by block variation in trajectory group is present. Often adjacent streets are part of different trajectories indicating they experienced different temporal patterns of juvenile crime over the

Table 3.1 Number of street blocks per trajectory group

Trajectory	Number of original street blocks	Number of geocoded street blocks
1	297	296
2	26, 503	26, 067
3	2, 558	2, 553
4	338	336
5	67	67
6	40	40
7	8	8
8	38	38
Total	29, 849	29, 405

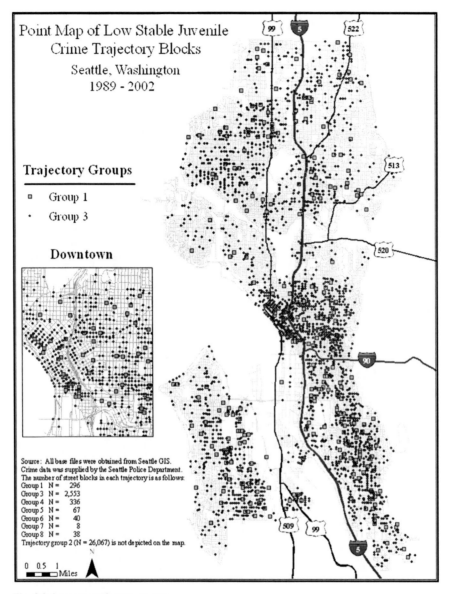

Fig. 3.2 Low rate trajectory groups

study period. The maps also demonstrate that street blocks sharing the same trajectory are not clustered in a single area but rather appear over much of Seattle.

Using trajectory analysis the researchers demonstrated that temporal changes in juvenile crime were not uniform; there was much variation among individual street blocks. They also found that juvenile crime was concentrated in a few places and that the majority of places were stable with low rates of juvenile crime.

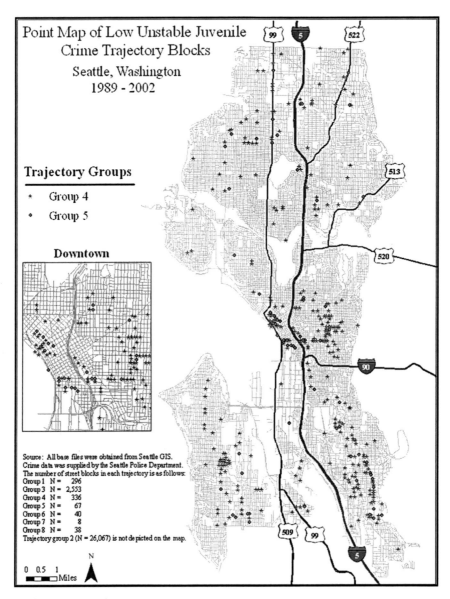

Fig. 3.3 Low rate trajectory groups

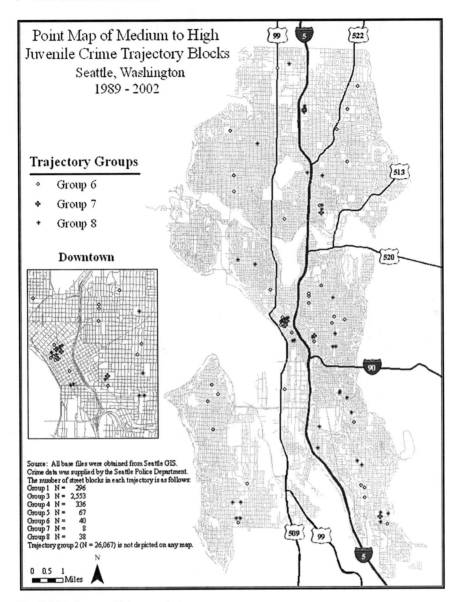

Fig. 3.4 Moderate to high rate trajectory groups

Examining the Geographic Distribution of Trajectory Group Members

The trajectories developed by Weisburd et al. (unpublished manuscript) provide the opportunity to examine the micro level spatial distribution of places that we know experienced the same rate of change in juvenile crime over time. Once again, the study area is the city of Seattle, Washington and the base data used are the list of street "hundred blocks" that make up the street network. The variable of interest in the study is the trajectory group designation which characterizes the temporal change in juvenile crime over time which is a limited categorical variable. In addition to the juvenile crime trajectory designation for each street block, the study uses street centerline data from Seattle GIS. Data analysis and display are done using a variety of software packages because no single software package combines both spatial statistics and a powerful cartographic display engine.[9]

Geocoding Process

In order to examine the spatial patterns in the data, the first step is to assign each street block (e.g., 100 Main St) record a geographic location (i.e., X, Y). The process of assigning geographic coordinates is called geocoding. A multi-step geocoding process is used here to ensure the highest accuracy level possible.[10] In the end, 29,405 (98.6%) of the original street blocks were able to be geocoded and are used in this analysis. There was very little loss of juvenile crime data from the geocoding process. Only, eleven of the street blocks that were not geocoded (and thus dropped from the geographic analysis) experienced any crime during the time period. The other 394 street blocks that were not geocoded had zero crimes for the entire period.

Definition of Juvenile Crime

As Weisburd et al. noted (unpublished manuscript), their study was the first to examine *where* juveniles commit crime. Historically, the dependent measure used in juvenile research has been either the number of juvenile delinquents in a com-

---

[9] Ripley's K values are calculated in CrimeStat (Levine 2005). The spatial autocorrelation analyses are calculated in GeoDa© (Anselin 2003) and the results displayed using ArcGIS©. Splancs© extension to R© is used to calculate a cross K-function. All mapping is done using ArcGIS© 9.1.

[10] First the records were geocoded in batch mode using the following parameters: (1) Spelling Sensitivity = 80; (2) Minimum candidate score = 10; (3) Minimum Match Score = 85; and (4) Do not match if candidates tie. These settings are considered rigorous for geocoding. While they result in more records that have to be manually inspected, they reduce the probability of a record being matched to an incorrect location. Thus they enable greater confidence that the records from the database have been assigned the correct physical location in Seattle. The remaining 901 records were individually inspected using interactive geocoding.

munity or the number of crimes that juvenile delinquents in a community report committing. Studies in both these literatures routinely attribute the spatial aspects of juvenile delinquency to the community where the juvenile resided, rather than the community where the crime was committed. Because this research is interested in the changes in crime at places, the location of crimes committed by juveniles captures this construct best. However, this measure is not without limitations.[11]

In the interests of completeness, the sources of bias in the measure are discussed briefly here. Since the measure relies on official crime and arrest data from the Seattle Police Department it is subject to the standard limitations of those data types discussed elsewhere (Gove et al. 1985). Several factors in combination indicate that the sample of juvenile crime used to generate the trajectory designations over-represents violent crime incidents committed by juveniles and under-represents property crime incidents (e.g., police focus on violent crime in patrol and clearance activity). Since offenders tend to travel farther to commit property crime than violent crime, the juvenile crimes in this sample also may over represent juveniles who live close to the location of the offense. In addition, to the extent that violent crimes cluster in different places than property crimes, the spatial distribution of events may be biased. However, the degree of bias is unknown since the total distribution of property and violent crimes committed by juveniles is also unknown. The differences between arrested individuals and those that avoided arrest are unknown and could introduce bias into the measure (Blumstein and Wallman 2000; McCord et al. 2001).

Despite its shortcomings, this measure of juvenile crime location has several benefits. First and most importantly, this measure characterizes juvenile crime in terms of where it is committed and thus is measuring a different construct than the traditional measure of juvenile crime which represents juvenile crime by offender residence location. The present characterization of juvenile crime better reflects the study's focus on juvenile crime at place by capturing the number of crimes on each street block that are committed by juveniles. Second, the measure offers no disadvantages in comparison with those studies which use juvenile arrests. Both are limited to studying only those events in which an arrest is made. Third, unlike primary data collection where longer time periods incur greater costs, because the measure is based on official crime data it is easier to examine a long time period for no additional cost (Kerlinger and Lee 2000). Finally, the measure enables the exploration of how the geographic location of places factors into the processes at work in the onset, persistence and desistance in the criminal careers of places (Jefferis 2004; Smith et al. 2000).

Applying Trajectory Analysis to Places as Individuals

Before proceeding, it should be noted that there are two potential shortcomings to the application of trajectory analysis to places rather than people. The assignment of

---

[11] Please see Weisburd et al. (unpublished manuscript) for a full discussion of the limitations of characterizing juvenile crime as crimes for which a juvenile was arrested.

trajectories was done without regard to the life cycle stage (i.e., age) of a particular street block. Thus the trajectory assignment may have grouped places at different stages of development in the same group. However, any impact on the current study would have been lessened because the substantive goal was to better understand changes in crime over a particular time period, rather than to describe life-cycle changes in general; the impact of similar historical circumstances changing in concert was the focus. Second, the trajectory technique is inherently aspatial and thus ignores the geography of places. In doing so it did not account for spatial effects that may have been at work.

Future studies could ameliorate the impact of different street ages through the use of a joint trajectory analysis that incorporates age of street. This would enable the trajectory analysis to take into account the age of the street at the start of the study period. Addressing the second issue would require incorporating geography into trajectory analysis. Spatio-temporal measures exist that can identify local and global clustering across both time and space. But those statistics are not group-based and consequently would not produce the same type of output as the TRAJ procedure and could not answer the research questions posed here. We follow the sequential approach taken by previous studies when dealing with this issue (i.e., conducting a spatial analysis of the output of the developmental statistic) (Griffiths and Chavez 2004; Kubrin and Herting 2003; Weisburd et al. 2004).

Analytical Approach

We use a variety of spatial statistics to describe the spatial distribution of trajectory group members and in doing so address the main question of this chapter – is there micro-level variation among street blocks that would be lost at higher levels of aggregation. Since this research involves the initial systematic investigation of the geography of trajectory groups, an exploratory data analysis (EDA) approach was warranted.[12] EDA is often used when the goal of the research is to identify patterns and suggest hypotheses from a data set while employing as few assumptions about the structure of the data as possible (Tukey 1977). Exploratory spatial data analysis (ESDA) represents a variation on EDA that explicitly examines the spatial distribution of a phenomenon to recognize spatial outliers, discover spatial association in attributes, identify clusters of events, suggest spatial heterogeneity, and recognize spatial trends (Anselin and Getis 1992; Bailey and Gatrell 1995; Fotheringham et al. 2000; Haining 1990; Messner et al. 1999).

---

[12] Only two previous studies used ESDA and a group-based trajectory analysis to examine the spatial distribution of trajectories of places (Griffiths and Chavez 2004; Weisburd et al. 2004). Griffiths and Chavez (2004) used census tracts rather than street blocks as their unit of analysis, and thus their experience informs the macro analysis of trajectories. Weisburd et al. (2004) limited their geographic analysis to density maps of the different trajectories and Weisburd et al. (unpublished manuscript) to point maps.

The analysis of spatial patterns is divided into two main sections that address the following research questions: (1) What is the spatial pattern of street blocks within the same trajectory of juvenile crime (i.e., clustered, dispersed, or random)?; (2) Are trajectories of street blocks related to the trajectories of nearby blocks?; and (3) Are street blocks of certain trajectories found near one another or are they spatially independent (e.g., do trajectory 5 and trajectory 7 tend to be found close to each other)? If there is a systematic pattern present in the data, a next logical question would concern the scales over which it operated. For instance, if blocks of a certain trajectory are clustered, is the clustering at the geographic level of the closest neighbors or does it extend to all spatial scales? The exercise of quantifying the patterns in the data is conducted to further our understanding of the "underlying process that generated the points" (Fotheringham et al. 2000). A series of point pattern statistical techniques are used to analyze the spatial patterns of street blocks. Each street block is represented by a dot (i.e., a point) on the map.

Analysis of the Spatial Patterns of Trajectory Group Members

A series of formal tests of the spatial distribution of crime events are employed to characterize the spatial patterning. Local statistics describe the variation in the immediate area of an observation, quantifying the distances between a street block and other street blocks of the same trajectory. Local statistics can also be used to describe how the attributes of street blocks tend to vary (i.e., how likely a street block of a certain trajectory is to be in the vicinity of another member of that trajectory). Local statistics specifically examine the second order effects (i.e., local relationships) related to spatial dependence (Bailey and Gatrell 1995; Fotheringham et al. 2000).

Second order or local variation in the data is examined using the Ripley's K-function and local indicators of spatial association (LISA). Together the two provide a more nuanced picture of local variation than would be possible with either one alone. Ripley's K describes the proximity of street blocks in the same trajectory to one another. For each street block, it counts the number of street blocks of the same trajectory that fall within a specified distance band and then repeats for each distance band in use. In this way, it characterizes spatial dependence at a wide range of scales. In order to make more formal statements about the point patterns, it is necessary to compare the summary statistics calculated from the observed distribution of street blocks with those calculated from a model distribution: for example, complete spatial randomness (CSR). When used in this way, the K-function is able to identify whether the observed pattern is significantly different than what would be expected from a random distribution (Bailey and Gatrell 1995). Ripley's K is calculated and then compared to a reference line that represents CSR: if $K(h) > \pi d^2$, then clustering is present (Bailey and Gatrell 1995, 90–95; Kaluzney et al. 1999, 162–163).

The LISA statistic is calculated in order to measure the degree of spatial autocorrelation in the pattern (i.e., how likely a street block of one group is to be near a street block of the same or another group). This statistic identifies four types of autocorrelation; two characterize positive spatial autocorrelation and two negative spatial autocorrelation. In positive spatial autocorrelation, observations with high values are near other observations with high values or low values are near other observations with low values. Negative correlation describes situations in which high values are near low values or vice versa.

The limited nature of the dependent variable, in this case trajectory group membership, provides a challenge to measuring spatial autocorrelation. Typically, measures of spatial autocorrelation such as Moran's I and LISA measure the pattern in the deviation of an observation from the mean for the distribution. This requires a ratio level variable such as the number or rate of juvenile crime. For example, if number of crimes was the dependent variable, Moran's I would characterize the existence and strength of the relationship between the number of juvenile crimes on one street block and the number on nearby street blocks. However, the focus of this research is on the distribution of street blocks by type of trajectory, which involves a limited dependent variable and makes the use of spatial autocorrelation techniques inappropriate without recoding. Following recent research, this study dummy coded the dependent variable to allow a series of comparisons; each trajectory group, in turn, was compared to all others (Griffiths and Chavez 2004).

Finally, a cross K (also called a bivariate-K) function is used to test for independence between movement patterns. This statistical technique answers whether the pattern of street blocks belonging to one trajectory is significantly different than the pattern of street blocks in another trajectory (Bailey and Gatrell 1995; Rowlingson and Diggle 1993). As described by Rowlingson and Diggle (1993) and applied here, the cross K-function expresses the expected number of street blocks of a particular trajectory (e.g., decreasing) within a distance of an arbitrary point of a second type of street block (e.g., increasing), divided by the overall density of increasing street blocks.

As with both Ripley's K and LISA, simulation is used to test whether two patterns are independent. This is accomplished by using a series of random toroidal shifts on one set of points and comparing the cross K-function of the shifted points with another fixed set (Rowlingson and Diggle 1993).[13] If the K value falls within the envelope of independence, then the two patterns are independent of each other; there is no evidence of spatial interaction (i.e., attraction or dispersion). If the K value falls above the envelope, significant attraction exists at that distance.[14] If the K value line is below the envelope, significant dispersion is present between the

---

[13] A toroidal shift provides a simulation of potential outcomes under the assumption of independence. This is accomplished by repeatedly and randomly shifting the locations for one type of street block and calculating the cross K-function for that iteration. The outcomes are used to create test statistics in the form of an upper and lower envelope. One thousand iterations were used for each simulation except those involving group 2 which used one hundred to save computing time.

[14] Since street blocks are stationary, attraction in this context refers to a tendency for street blocks of one trajectory to be found in closer proximity to street blocks of another trajectory than would be expected under independence (i.e., their patterns are similar).

two patterns. The x-axis (s) represents the distance in feet and the y-axis the cross K value.

Results

An examination of local relationships among the locations of street blocks within the same trajectory offers information critical to understanding the existence and extent of spatial dependence among streets that experienced similar trajectories of juvenile crime. Ripley's K provides information on whether blocks of the same trajectory are clustered in space and whether that clustering is greater or less than would be expected under an assumption of complete spatial randomness. The statistic reported from Ripley's K in CrimeStat is the L value. This is a rescaled Ripley's K where CSR is represented by a horizontal zero line. In order to provide a measure of significance, one-hundred Monte Carlo simulations were used to develop an envelope of the minimum and maximum values under CSR. The odds of getting a result outside the envelope were one in one-hundred (or 0.01). The presence of the L-value line (dark line) above and outside the simulation envelopes (CSR MIN and CSR MAX) indicates that the members of the trajectory are closer together than would be expected under CSR (i.e., the distances between street blocks of the same trajectory group are shorter than would be expected under CSR).

Figure 3.5 depicts the results for the three trajectory groups that showed some variation over distance.[15] Groups 6 and 8 which started at about the same level of crime (i.e., approximately 6–10 per year) in 1989 and then diverge are each significantly more clustered then would be expected under the assumption of complete spatial randomness but the distances over which the clustering is significant differ. The clustering persists up to about 2.5 miles in group 6 but ends at approximately 1.4 miles for group 8. Street blocks in group 5 are more clustered up to about 2.6 miles. The relatively large distances for clustering indicate a community-level rather than micro-level process may be at work.

However, the use of CSR as a comparison measure has its limits. We know that human activities and urban development are not randomly distributed. To get a more realistic estimate of the clustering among trajectory group members we instead use the intrinsic clustering in the population of street blocks as a comparison measure (Fig. 3.6).

The L-value for each of the trajectory groups is higher than that for all blocks at short distances. At both one-half mile and one mile, all trajectory groups are more clustered than would be expected based on the pattern of street blocks. This finding

---

[15] Results for the low stable groups (1–3) and group 4 are not shown because the members of the trajectory group are significantly more clustered than would be expected under an assumption of a random distribution across all distances and thus the visual representation is uninformative. Group 7 was significantly more clustered up to about 0.30 miles but has only eight observations reducing the reliability of the analysis and thus is not shown. Results are available from authors.

Group 5

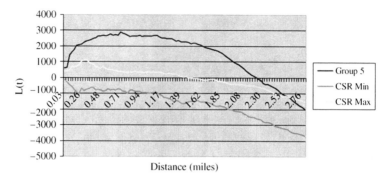

Group 6

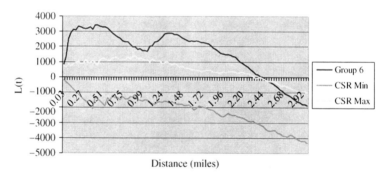

Group 8

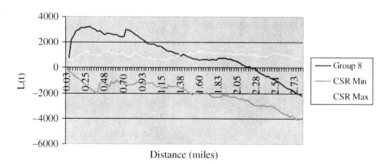

Fig. 3.5 Ripley's K for groups 5, 6 and 8

provides evidence that another process, other than the configuration of the street network, is driving the observed clustering.

Overall, the results of Ripley's K show that trajectory group members are not randomly distributed across Seattle. Rather, clustering is the dominant spatial pattern for all trajectory groups. The relatively large distances across which clustering

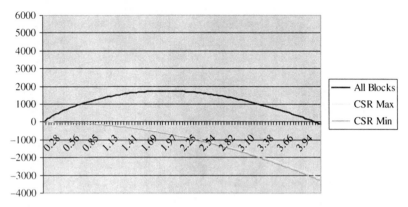

Fig. 3.6 Ripley's K results for all street blocks in Seattle

remained significant (for all groups except group 7) could point to a community-level process or a cluster of local processes with slight geographic separation. Thus, the answer to the first research question is that the pattern of trajectory groups is clustered rather than random or dispersed. However, the clustering is significant at a range of distances from micro to community level.

Spatial Autocorrelation Among Trajectory Groups

For this analysis, we examine each of the eight trajectories, one at a time. We present the graphical results grouped by the level of juvenile crime (low, medium, and high). As explained earlier, the use of local measures of spatial autocorrelation such as the Univariate LISA enables the measurement of the extent to which street blocks of a single trajectory group are near other members of the same group or stand isolated. Because of the limited dependent variable, group membership, each of the patterns of the eight trajectory groups needs to be analyzed separately. For example, when Group 8 trajectory blocks are the focus, all the Group 8 blocks are coded as "1" and all street blocks of other trajectories are coded as "0" (i.e., other). To continue the example, there are four potential outcomes of the analysis. For an analysis of the members of trajectory group 8 positive spatial autocorrelation refers to: (1) the tendency of trajectory group 8 blocks to be near other trajectory group 8 blocks (dark red) and (2) the tendency of "other" street blocks to be spatially proximal to one another (dark blue). Negative spatial autocorrelation occurs in the following two situations: (1) where "other" trajectory blocks are associated with the presence of trajectory group 8 blocks (light blue) and (2) where trajectory group 8 blocks are associated with the presence of "other" trajectory blocks (light red). These places are important because they indicate where there is significant block to block variability at the micro level.

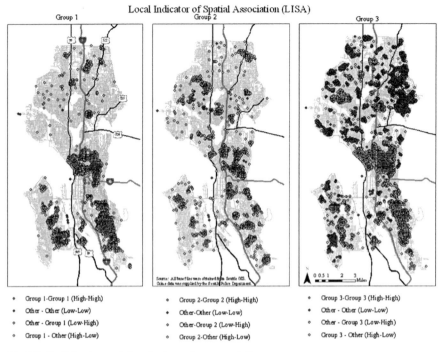

Fig. 3.7 Spatial autocorrelation for low rate groups, 1–3

Figures 3.7–3.9 depict the results of the Univariate LISA. Only those street blocks with significant differences ($p < 0.05$) are drawn on the map. We include these maps so that the patterns are available for inspection. However, the maps are most important for their general findings. Regardless of group, there are instances of predominantly negative spatial autocorrelation (i.e., light blue blocks or light red blocks). In these areas, other trajectory groups are correlated with the presence of group 1 blocks demonstrating significant variation in trajectory types at the micro level. However, there are also significant clusters of positive spatial autocorrelation (i.e., dark red dots); places where blocks of the same trajectory are in close proximity. Since we are examining one trajectory group at a time and aggregating all the others into the "other" group it is not surprising that we find many cases where "other" group blocks (i.e., blocks of another trajectory group) are found in proximity to one another providing evidence of positive spatial autocorrelation.

While the specifics of the patterns are difficult to describe because of their complexity, the degree of negative spatial autocorrelation in the distribution offers strong evidence that there are localized processes operating at the street block level of analysis. The finding of both negative and positive autocorrelation in each of the patterns of trajectory groups indicates that the presence of street blocks of one type of trajectory is related to the presence of other trajectories. In some cases, the block is located among blocks of the same trajectory. These cases point to a process affecting the nearby blocks in the same direction. In other cases, a street

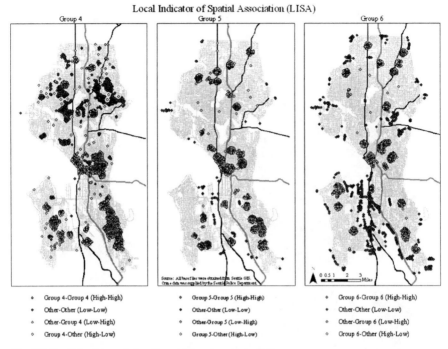

Fig. 3.8 Spatial autocorrelation for middle rate groups, 4–6

block of one trajectory is isolated (i.e., surrounded by street blocks with differing temporal trajectories) indicating that the local process is affecting one street block differently than the rest. However, this analysis did not enable relationships between two specific trajectory groups to be identified. For example, the question of whether street blocks from group 5 tend to be found near street blocks of group 7 could not be answered without the use of the cross K-function described in the next section.

The uniqueness of the patterns revealed by the spatial autocorrelation analysis deserves recognition. It is especially unusual to observe negative spatial autocorrelation in distributions describing human-related processes (Fotheringham et al. 2000). Typically, human-related processes reflect positive, not negative spatial autocorrelation. Using the street block level of analysis is the only way to discover these interesting processes because higher levels of aggregation would mask these potentially important variations.

Comparing the Spatial Distribution of Trajectory Groups

The question of whether street blocks of one trajectory have a similar pattern to the street blocks of another trajectory is addressed through the calculation of a cross K-function. The use of a cross K-function can reveal also whether two patterns are independent of each other. The advantage to this technique over the previous ones

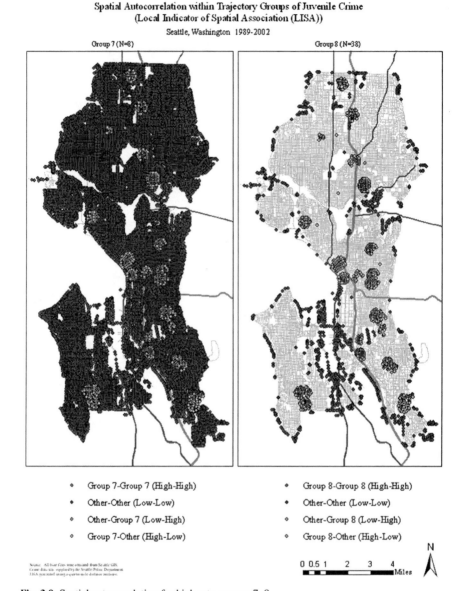

Fig. 3.9 Spatial autocorrelation for high rate groups, 7–8

is that two point patterns can be compared directly. Results from the cross K-function provide evidence regarding whether the process or processes under-lying the spatial pattern of one group may be related to those of another trajectory group. For example, if we assume that there are similar processes driving a decline in juvenile crime wherever it occurs, we would expect trajectory groups that have a temporal pattern of predominantly decreasing juvenile crime rates to have a similar spatial distribution. Thus, a finding that street blocks of similar trajectories are dependent would support a community level explanation while a finding of independence would support the argument for micro level examination of crime.

We conduct a series of pairwise comparisons to evaluate the patterns of each group as compared to those of every other group (i.e., group 1 to group 2, group 1 to group 3, etc.). Although $K(i,j)$ is consistently above the line of independence, it never falls outside the simulation envelope; thus the pattern of street blocks in each trajectory is independent of all others.[16] The results of the cross K-function with simulation indicate that while most group comparisons indicate attraction, the relationship was not significant. Although this result provides evidence that the same underlying processes may be influencing the spatial distribution of two different trajectory groups, the effect was not statistically strong enough to be significant. Interpreting these results further would require data describing the characteristics of the street blocks. Once the characteristics are known, we can begin to identify the specific processes at work. In sum, the finding that the patterns of street blocks in different trajectories are statistically independent of each other demonstrates that the processes underlying the spatial distribution of each of the trajectories are likely to be different and thus supports the importance of micro level studies of crime.

Discussion

The preceding analysis applies formal spatial measures to uncover whether the "action" at crime places is at the micro level of analysis. We use the changes in juvenile crime rates across time and space at the street block level of analysis to examine this issue. Three main findings emerge from the analysis and are discussed below. Together they point toward a combination of micro and macro level processes underlying juvenile crime patterns and illustrate that an exclusive focus on macro levels such as neighborhoods is missing significant intra-unit variation.

First, places in the same trajectory group (i.e., with similar temporal trends in juvenile crime) are distributed across much of Seattle. The large spatial extent of each of the temporal trajectories points toward the existence of global/societal factors that are interacting with micro level street blocks in different ways (e.g., societal changes that increase time spent with peers (Felson and Gottfredson 1984); appearance of crack cocaine; increase in hand gun use, and employment opportunities (Blumstein and Wallman 2000)). These types of factors could potentially influence all street blocks but their actual affect would be dependent upon the micro level characteristics of places.

Second, we also find that street blocks of the same trajectory group are not randomly distributed across Seattle but rather are more likely to be found "near" one

---

[16] Since all the results indicated independence, the individual graphs are not shown here. Graphs and results are available upon request from the authors.

another. Non-stable (groups that increased or decreased over time) trajectory blocks were more clustered than would be expected based on the street network for up to about a mile; a distance of roughly 13 blocks in Seattle. This finding suggests there are particular physical or social characteristics that affect clusters of street blocks in the same manner and thus the processes driving the clustering may be occurring at a more aggregate scale such as the neighborhood rather than at the street block level.

Clustering at scales of about a mile could also be a reflection of development patterns in Seattle. Often land use tends to cluster in certain areas. For example, street blocks in the downtown area tend to have more retail and restaurants on them than the average block in Seattle. The concentration of food and shopping tends to draw large numbers of juveniles to the area focusing juvenile activities and increasing the likelihood of high rates of convergence between juveniles and crime opportunities (Bichler-Robertson 2006). The clustering observed among street blocks within the same trajectory could also be driven by the mobility of juveniles. Empirical research has found smaller activity spaces for juveniles than adults (Chapin and Brail 1969; Orleans 1973). Smaller activity spaces reflect the concentration of juvenile activities near home and other important anchor points such as schools and malls (Rengert 1992).

Third, we find a great deal of block to block variation in the trajectory group classification of street blocks. In many instances, adjacent blocks have different and sometimes opposite temporal trends. This negative spatial autocorrelation among human-related patterns is very unusual and violates Tobler's (1970) first rule of geography that things closer to one another tend to be more alike.[17] Formal comparisons of the spatial patterns of each trajectory group's members with every other trajectory group's members reveal that they are independent of one another. Thus, it is likely that the specific spatial processes underlying the temporal patterns captured in trajectory analysis are slightly different for each of the trajectory groups. The finding of block by block variation in juvenile crime lends support for the examination of micro level places. In sum, whatever the macro level effects that influence crime across geography these findings suggest that there are strong local level trends that should not be ignored by researchers.

These findings fit closely with the conception of street blocks as "behavior settings" in and of themselves, even though they are situated within a larger social unit such as a neighborhood (Jacobs 1961; Taylor, 1997a, b). Urban studies have frequently noted the variation from block-to-block within the same neighborhood. In addition, opportunity theories emphasize that motivated offenders, suitable targets, and capable guardians must converge at the same place and time for a crime to occur. But time/space convergence at places is a complex combination that is driven by the characteristics of the place, the structure of the street network, and the routine activities of the people in a city.

---

[17] Tobler's First Law of Geography states "Everything is related to everything else, but near things are more related than distant things." (Tobler 1970).

The characteristics of a place contribute to the context in which crime decisions are made. As mentioned previously, street blocks with facilities that attract large numbers of people increase the possibility of crime because they are likely to attract motivated offenders as well as targets and guardians. However, traffic levels are not the only characteristic that drives crime. Since each street block can have unique characteristics, it is plausible that two street blocks with similar levels of traffic might have different juvenile crime levels depending on their situational characteristics. Places that have businesses or settings that attract juveniles are more likely to have higher levels of juvenile crime. Except for the downtown core, these places are relatively isolated within neighborhoods. Their particular "behavior setting" is heavily influenced by the neighborhood in which they are situated.

Taken together, our findings clearly demonstrate the importance of micro level "crime places" in understanding patterns of juvenile crime. We think opportunity theories are likely to have strong explanatory power but it is also plausible that social disorganization perspectives play a significant role. Until more data are collected, what we know for sure is that there is important variation at the micro level and that macro level examinations of crime at place would be unable to tease out these intra-neighborhood nuances.

Implications for Practice

The study's results have immediate potential to assist police practice. Many of the current policing strategies require identifying and understanding problems. Any and all of these policing strategies would be strengthened by better information on *where* to concentrate police efforts. Street blocks represent discrete "places" that are consistent with the language of policing, in that law enforcement officers tend to communicate in "hundred blocks" (i.e., street blocks). Thus, these units have immediate relevance to law enforcement officers and the results of studies that use street blocks will be immediately understandable to them. In addition, street blocks are both small enough to see an immediate impact from prevention and enforcement efforts and large enough to provide an aggregate effect toward changing their immediate context. Finally, the power of spatial analysis and display cannot be overstated. Tabular data describing crime does not convey how those addresses might be related to one another on the ground.

One concrete way in which these findings could be used by law enforcement is to identify those street blocks in the city that have changing trajectories (i.e., are not low and stable). In the case of Seattle, there were 86 street blocks that had moderate to high levels of crime and are spread throughout the city. This type of analysis provides important information on where those street blocks are located and how they relate to one another. Officers could further drill down to focus on the eight street blocks which decreased slightly over the study period but at the same time experienced the highest level of juvenile crime, averaging about 400 crimes per year. These places have the best potential for providing the highest reduction in juvenile crimes per street block.

The aspatial identification of places that exhibit similar juvenile crime trajectories over time by Weisburd et al. (unpublished manuscript) was the first step in providing more empirically-based evidence for deployment of police and community resources. Achieving a better understanding of the geography of particular trajectories advances the effort and makes the results more actionable for police. However, more information on the characteristics of street blocks and how they change over time is necessary before we can begin to explain what is causing crime at the micro level.

Conclusions

This research examines whether study of micro crime places is critical to gain an understanding of crime across geography. Most studies of the geography of crime have ignored the micro level conception of crime that we have proposed in favor of neighborhood or community definitions, or census boundaries that provide significant social data for analysis. Our study suggests that such an approach is likely to miss very significant local variation of crime at the micro place level, analyzed in our study as the street segment. We find a great deal of the "action" is indeed at micro places such as street blocks. Our geographic analysis suggests that there is some clustering of street blocks; street blocks of the same trajectory type are more likely to be near one another than to other types of trajectories. However, there is also evidence of negative spatial autocorrelation which points toward significant and important block to block variation in places. Together these findings identify processes at both the local and neighborhood levels of analysis that are affecting the distribution of juvenile crime. This mixed view is consistent with opportunity theories of crime that recognize both micro and macro level processes at work in determining both temporal and spatial patterning of crime. At the same time, these findings do not preclude the salience of more traditional perspectives such as social disorganization, collective efficacy, and social ecology; it could very well be that they are at work.

In sum, these analyses show that much would have been lost if we would have aggregated up from the street segment and examined only units such as census block groups. That is, there is much spatial "independence" as well as "dependence" among street blocks. We think these data suggest that researchers should begin with micro units of analysis such as street blocks before moving to larger aggregates such as census block groups or tracts.

References

Anselin, L., & Getis, A. (1992). Spatial statistical analysis and geographic information systems. *Annals of Regional Science*, 26, 19–33.
Bailey, T. C., & Gatrell, A. C. (1995). *Interactive spatial data analysis*. Essex: Longman Group Limited.
Bichler-Robertson, G. (2006). Personal Communication. Vancouver, BC.
Blumstein, A., & Wallman, J. (2000). *The crime drop in America*. Cambridge: Cambridge University Press.

Brantingham, P. J., & Brantingham, P. L. (1991 [1981]). *Environmental criminology.* Prospect Heights, IL: Waveland Press, Inc.

Brantingham, P. J., Dyreson, D. A., & Brantingham, P. L. (1976). Crime seen through a cone of resolution. *American Behavioral Scientist,* 20(2), 261–273.

Brantingham, P. L., & Brantingham, P. J. (1995). Criminality of place: Crime generators and crime attractors. *European Journal on Criminal Policy and Research,* 3(3), 5–26.

Chapin, F. S. J., & Brail, R. K. (1969). Human activity systems in the metropolitan United States. *Environment and Behavior,* 1(2), 107–130.

Clarke, R. V. (1980). "Situational" crime prevention: Theory and practice. *British Journal of Criminology,* 20(2), 136–147.

Clarke, R. V. (1983). Situational crime prevention: Its theoretical basis and practical scope. In: M. Tonry & N. Morris (Eds.), *Crime and justice: An annual review of research* (Vol. 14, pp. 225–256). Chicago: University of Chicago Press.

Clarke, R. V. (1997). *Situational crime prevention: Successful case studies* (2nd ed.). Albany, NY: Harrow and Heston Publishers.

Clarke, R. V., & Cornish, D. B. (1985). Modeling offender's decisions: A framework for research and policy. In: M. Tonry & N. Morris (Eds.), *Crime and justice: An annual review of research* (Vol. 6). Chicago: University of Chicago Press.

Cohen, L. E., & Felson, M. (1979). Social change and crime rate trends: A routine activity approach. *American Sociological Review,* 44, 588–608.

Eck, J. E. (1995). Examining routine activity theory: A review of two books. *Justice Quarterly,* 12(4), 783–797.

Eck, J. E., Gersh, J. S., & Taylor, C. (2000). Finding Crime Hot Spots Through Repeat Address Mapping. In Goldsmith, V., McGuire, P.G., Mollenkopf, J. H., & Ross, T. A. (eds.), *Analyzing Crime Patterns: Frontiers of Practice* (pp. 49–64). Thousand Oaks, CA: Sage.

Eck, J. E., & Weisburd, D. L. (1995). Crime places in crime theory. In: J. E. Eck & L. Weisburd David (Eds.), *Crime and place* (pp. 1–33). Monsey, NY: Willow Tree Press.

Felson, M. (2002). *Crime in everyday life* (3rd ed.). Thousand Oaks, CA: Sage.

Felson, M., & Gottfredson, M. (1984). Social indicators of adolescent activities near peers and parents. *Journal of Marriage and the Family,* 46, 709–714.

Fotheringham, A. S., Brundson, C., & Charlton, M. (2000). *Quantitative geography.* London, UK: Sage Publications.

Gove, W. R., Hughes, M., & Geerken, M. (1985). Are uniform crime reports a valid indicator of the index crimes? An affirmative answer with minor qualifications. *Criminology,* 23, 451–501.

Griffiths, E., & Chavez, J. M. (2004). Communities, street guns, and homicide trajectories in Chicago, 1980–1995: Merging methods for examining homicide trends across space and time. *Criminology,* 42(4), 941–978.

Groff, E. R., & LaVigne, N. G. (2001). Mapping an opportunity surface of residential Burglary. *Journal of Research in Crime and Delinquency,* 38(3), 257–278.

Haining, R. (1990). *Spatial data analysis in the social and environmental sciences.* Cambridge, UK: Cambridge University Press.

Hillier, B. (1999). The common language of space: A way of looking at the social, economic and environmental functioning of cities on a common basis. Retrieved February 17, 2004, from http://www.spacesyntax.org/publications/commonlang.html

Jacobs, J. (1961). *The death and life of great American cities.* New York: Vintage Books.

Jefferis, E. (2004). *Criminal places: A micro-level study of residential theft.* Unpublished Dissertation, University of Cincinnati, Cincinnati.

Johnson, S. D., Bowers, K., & Hirschfield, A. (1997). New insights into the spatial and temporal distribution of repeat victimization. *British-Journal-of-Criminology,* 37(2), 224–241.

Kaluzny, S. P., Vega, Cardoso, T. P., & Shelly, A. A. (1997). *S+SpatialStats User's Manual.* New York: Springer.

Kerlinger, F. N., & Lee, H. B. (2000). *Foundations of behavioral research* (4th ed.). US: Wadsworth.

Kubrin, C. E., & Herting, J. R. (2003). Neighborhood correlates of homicide trends: An analysis using growth-curve modeling. *The Sociological Quarterly,* 44(3), 329–350.

McCord, J., Widom, C. S., & Crowell, N. A. (2001). *Juvenile crime juvenile justice.* Washington DC: National Academy Press.

Messner, S. F., Anselin, L., & Baller, R. D. (1999). The spatial patterning of county homicide rates: An application of exploratory spatial data analysis. *Journal of Quantitative Criminology*, 15(4), 423–450.

Nagin, D. (2005). *Group-based modeling of development over the life course.* Cambridge, MA: Harvard University Press.

Orleans, P. (1973). Differential cognition of urban residents: Effects of social scale on mapping. In: R. M. Downs & D. Stea (Eds.), *Image & environment: Cognitive mapping and spatial behavior* (pp. 115–130). Chicago: Aldine Publishing Company.

Potchak, M. C., McGloin, J. M., & Zgoba, K. M. (2002). A spatial analysis of criminal effort: Auto theft in Newark, New Jersey. *Criminal Justice Policy Review*, 13(3), 257–285.

Rengert, G. (1992). The journey to crime: Conceptual foundations and policy implications. In: D. J. Evans, J. J. Fyfe & D. T. Herbert (Eds.), *Crime, policing and place: Essays in environmental criminology* (pp. 109–117). London: Routledge.

Rowlingson, B. S., & Diggle, P. J. (1993). Splancs: Spatial point pattern analysis code in S-Plus. *Computers and Geosciences*, 19, 627–655.

Sherman, L., Gartin, P. R., & Buerger, M. E. (1989). Hot spots of predatory crime: Routine activities and the criminology of place. *Criminology*, 27, 27–56.

Smith, W. R., Frazee, S. G., & Davison, E. L. (2000). Furthering the integration of routine activity and social disorganization theories: Small units of analysis and the study of street robbery as a diffusion process. *Criminology*, 38(2), 489–523.

Stark, R. (1987). Deviant places: A theory of the ecology of crime. *Criminology*, 25(4), 893–909.

Taylor, R. B. (1997a). Crime and small-scale places: What we know, what we can prevent, and what else we need to know. In: R. B. Taylor, G. Bazemore, B. Boland, T. R. Clear, R. P. J. Corbett, J. Feinblatt, G. Berman, M. Sviridoff, & C. Stone (Eds.), *Crime and place: Plenary papers of the 1997 conference on criminal justice research and evaluation* (pp. 1–22). Washington, DC: National Institute of Justice.

Taylor, R. B. (1997b). Social order and disorder of street blocks and neighborhoods: Ecology, microecology, and the systemic model of social disorganization. *Journal of Research in Crime and Delinquency*, 34(1), 113–155.

Tobler, W. (1970). A computer model simulation of urban growth in the Detroit region. *Economic Geography*, 46(2), 234–240.

Tseloni, A., Osborn, D. R., Trickett, A., & Pease, K. (2002). Modelling property crime using the British Crime Survey. *British Journal of Criminology*, 42, 109–128.

Tukey, J. (1977). *Exploratory data analysis.* Reading, MA: Addison-Wesley.

Weisburd, D. L., Bushway, S., Lum, C., & Yang, S.-M. (2004). Trajectories of crime at places: A longitudinal study of street segments in the city of Seattle. *Criminology*, 42(2), 283–321.

Weisburd, D. L., Lum, C., & Yang, S.-M. (2004). *The criminal careers of places: A longitudinal study.* Washington DC: US Department of Justice, National Institute of Justice.

Weisburd, D. L., Morris, N., & Groff, E. R. (unpublished manuscript). Hot spots of juvenile crime: A longitudinal study of street segments in Seattle, Washington. *Manuscript submitted for publication.*

Weisburd, D., & Green, L. (1995). Police drug hot spots: the Jersey City Drug Market Analysis experiment. *Justice Quarterly*, 12(4), 711–735.

Chapter 4
Crime Analysis at Multiple Scales of Aggregation: A Topological Approach

Patricia L. Brantingham, Paul J. Brantingham, Mona Vajihollahi, and Kathryn Wuschke[1]

Abstract Patterns in crime vary quite substantially at different scales of aggregation, in part because data tend to be organized around standardized, artificially defined units of measurement such as the census tract, the city boundary, or larger administrative or political boundaries. The boundaries that separate units of data often obscure the detailed spatial patterns and muddy analysis. These aggregation units have an historic place in crime analysis, but increasing computational power now makes it possible to start with very small units of analysis and to build larger units based on theoretically defined parameters. This chapter argues for a crime analysis that begins with a small spatial unit, in this case individual parcels of land, and builds larger units that reflect natural neighborhoods. Data are limited in these small units at this point in time, but the value of starting with very small units is substantial. An algorithm based on analysis of land unit to unit similarity using fuzzy topology is presented. British Columbia (BC) data are utilized to demonstrate how crime patterns follow the fuzzy edges of certain neighborhoods, diffuse into permeable neighborhoods, and concentrate at selected high activity nodes and along some major streets. Crime patterns that concentrate on major streets, at major shopping centers and along the edges of neighborhoods would be obscured, at best, and perhaps missed altogether if analysis began with larger spatial units such as census tracts or politically defined neighborhood areas.

---

[1] The authors would like to thank "E"-Division, Royal Canadian Mounted Police, for provision of data and for generous support. The authors would like to thank Jordan Ginther for preparation of the maps shown in Fig. 4.2.

P.L. Brantingham
Institute for Canadian Urban Research Studies, Simon Fraser University, Vancouver, BC, Canada
e-mail: pbranting@sfu.ca

D. Weisburd et al. (eds.), *Putting Crime in its Place*,
DOI 10.1007/978-0-387-09688-9_4, © Springer Science+Business Media, LLC 2009

Introduction

Crime is a complex event occurring in a real spatio-temporal environment. Understanding crime patterns requires both theory and research. In many situations, the requirements of understanding crime patterns lead to the development of new theories or new research methods or techniques. The choice of unit of analysis constitutes a fundamental issue for criminologists interested in spatial patterns in crime. Crime can form very different patterns at different scales of analysis (Brantingham et al. 1976; Lim et al. 2007). Standard spatial aggregations such as census tracts or politically defined neighborhood or city borders often fail to reflect the underlying socio-spatial distributions of people, land uses, or criminal events (Schmid 1960a, b).

Our study builds on criminology's history of interest in spatial patterns in crime (e.g., Quetelet 1842; Shaw and McKay 1942; Brantingham and Brantingham 1984) and focuses on the importance of starting with small units of information and aggregating them in a fashion that permits both the construction of theoretically relevant spatial units of analysis and the maintenance of a capacity for micro analysis of crime. We pay particular attention to crime pattern theory (Brantingham and Brantingham 1993a) to set the stage for presentation of a topological aggregation technique that facilitates understanding where offenders choose targets as they move through their urban surrounds.

Following a brief background review of crime pattern theory our study explores the spatial patterning of residential burglary in a suburban municipality in metropolitan Vancouver, British Columbia. The study analyses address level burglaries over a four year time period in relation to high activity nodes, major travel arteries, and well-defined edges distinguishing topologically constructed, coherent, small neighborhood areas.

Crime Pattern Theory and Scale of Analysis

Crime pattern theory maintains that criminal events occur in persistent, identifiable patterns in time and space. These patterns are temporally structured by routine human social and economic activities and are spatially structured by physical and social nodes, paths, and edges that constrain physical activity. They are shaped more deeply by the cultural, social, economic, and physical backcloth that underlies any place of human habitation (Brantingham and Brantingham 1993a, b, 2008).

Most people spend their days in very routine ways: time is spent at home; in travel to work or school; at work or school; in travel to visit friends or entertainment sites; and in travel back home. This routine may cover a small area or a large area depending on the social context, network of friends, work and home locations, the design of the city, the means of transit, and the reasons for moving around. People learn routes between destinations and tend to follow those routes repeatedly. These routes and their end points or *nodes* form an *activity space* and the basis for an *awareness space*. For most people the activity space stabilizes for long periods of time but changes when there is a life course or lifestyle change.

People who commit crimes mostly engage in non-criminal behavior. Offenders usually base their criminal activities on the time constraints or normal time expenditures of the routines they have primarily developed for their non-criminal activity. (See Wikström and Butterworth 2006; Ratcliffe 2006 for recent research that addresses the role of situational time and time budgeting in offending patterns.) In understanding criminal behavior in an urban environment, it is important to understand general variations both in the legitimate and criminal activities of offenders and in the legitimate activities of people more generally.

In the aggregate, certain locations such as drinking establishments, entertainment areas, large and small shopping areas, major transit stops, and schools are found to be at the center of clusters of crimes. These "hot spots" can attract intending offenders, that is serve as *crime attractors*, or can serve as *crime generators* simply by attracting large volumes of people including some who commit opportunistic crimes (Brantingham and Brantingham 1995; McCord et al. 2007). At the same time, the networks of paths formed by the roadways and transit systems connecting activity points channel and cluster criminal events (Beavon et al. 1994). This study explores general paths and nodes but places special emphasis on neighborhood *edges* to see how they influence patterns in criminal activity.

Crime is a rare event. This poses problems for analysts in several ways: First, because crime is rare analysts are tempted to aggregate information into larger spatial agglomerations in order to achieve sufficient counts for statistical analysis (e.g., Shaw and McKay 1942). Second, in the agglomeration process there is a temptation to use existing spatial units such as census tracts or city planning department "neighborhoods" for ease of statistical comparison between crime and information collected specifically for that spatial unit. Results from such a procedure are often misleading either because they assume a smooth distribution of crime across the entire unit or because they assume that the pre-defined unit correlates spatially with natural social neighborhoods as understood by residents of the area. However, it has long been known that both assumptions are usually wrong (Wilcox 1973; Schmid 1960a, b; Brantingham and Brantingham 1984). Third, analysts are tempted to agglomerate discrete crime categories such as assault and robbery or burglary and theft into larger categories such as "violent crime" or "property crime" even though the spatial and temporal patterns of the specific crime types may be very different. Fourth, spatial and temporal crime patterns can be very different at different spatial and temporal scales: agglomeration obscures these differences (Brantingham et al. 1976; Lim et al. 2007). Moreover, crime patterns vary at the individual location and land use levels. For example, some drinking establishments experience few crimes; some experience a lot of crimes. Similarly, some transit stops experience high crime levels; some do not.

In all aggregate spatial information, there are ongoing issues that relate to modifiable area unit boundaries; to the limitations of statistics in dealing with data with high levels of spatio-temporal autocorrelation; and to the lack of independence that bedevils statistical analysis of data generated by high levels of repeat offending. Contemporary research into spatio-temporal crime patterns has an expanding interest in understanding extremes in the spatio-temporal patterning of crime and in finding ways to move through a continuum of analysis from the micro level individual offender's activities and characteristics through many levels of aggregate patterns without being restricted to choosing either a single micro or meso or macro level.

Ideally, analysis would be nested, that is information about individual criminal events – specific location or address, specific time of occurrence, detailed description of crime type – would be the base unit of analysis. This base unit would be aggregated to different, larger units depending on the research question, but the basic information would be maintained for aggregation along a different schema for a different research question. This implies that no single level of aggregation can constitute the "best" unit of analysis for studying the spatial or temporal patterns in crime. Data should be collected at the most detailed level possible and aggregated upward to fit the requisites of theory or the limitations of data unit aggregations of those elements of urban backcloth thought to be important. That is, in looking at different levels of aggregation, researchers must consider aggregation of crime units into different areal units for comparison against the urban backcloth.

It is a simple fact that, until recently, the tedium and expense of manual data collection and analysis as well as the limitations of computer storage and analysis capabilities, meant that aggregation was often necessary to facilitate any type of analysis. Advancements in computational power and the availability of extensive data at detailed spatial and temporal levels now make it possible to start small, at discrete locations in space-time and have theory help direct aggregation into larger units for analysis.

The recent emergence of *computational criminology*, grounded on improvement in the computational power available to researchers, provides, potentially, a way to link theory and research at a micro level with theory and research at the meso levels of analysis. The research made possible by computational criminology is nascent, but rapidly evolving. Several chapters in this book use extensive computing that would not have been possible ten years ago, let alone in the time of Shaw and McKay.

Computational modeling is particularly important in its requirement that the structure of the model and the rules of computation be made explicit. Computational criminology is also an invitation to more criminologists to use artificial intelligence, agent-based modeling, and graph theory in modeling crime and testing related crime theories (See, e.g., Groff 2007; Xue and Brown 2006; Brantingham et al. 2005; Liu et al. 2005; Townsley et al. 2003; Brantingham et al. 2005; Brantingham and Brantingham 2004; Adderley 2004; Brown 1998). This study uses a computationally intensive mathematical technique called *fuzzy topology* to build nested models of paths, nodes, and edges in order to study the discrete distribution of specific crime types across the urban backcloth of a British Columbia municipality.

Methodology

This study attempts to provide an example of a new approach to looking at crime by placing discrete crime locations on a model of the urban backcloth based on common paths and activity nodes, and on identification of the boundaries and cores of neighborhood areas that stand out as different from their surrounds. This chapter should be seen as a compliment to the other chapters in this section: *Oberwittler and Wikström's* study of behavioral contexts and *Groff, Weisburd, and Morris'* exploration of juvenile crime against block level crime trajectories over time.

We explore the patterns of residential burglary for 2004 for a suburban municipality in Metro Vancouver. During 2004, more than 12,000 criminal code offences and more than 350 drug offences were reported to police in this municipality. There were 552 residential burglaries reported to police in 2004 and 2,296 over the four year period from 2001 through 2004.

The rapidly growing suburb used in this analysis is relatively near the core city of Vancouver and is primarily residential. Its population of about 124,000 grew by 24% between 1993 and 2004, and by slightly more than 7% over the period 2001–2004. In 2005, the suburb had almost 37,000 separately tracked parcels of land.

This study suburb is similar to many other Vancouver Metro suburbs with an older section dating back to the first half of the 20th century when this was more on the edge of suburb development. A major growth spurt in the last quarter of the 20th century has seen some increase in higher density housing. Overall, however, this municipality remains primarily a residential suburb with single family dwelling units as the primary type of residence. There is no core business/commercial area.

The analysis presented in this chapter builds on micro level address data for residential burglaries and then analyzes the patterning of these crimes using the ideas of common nodal activity points, routine common pathways, and roads within the suburb and the edges of neighborhood spaces. The analysis is primarily done using an agglomeration algorithm that will be described below.

Data Sources

The analysis was done using four categories of data: officially reported crimes; British Columbia Assessment Authority (BCAA) data that provides individual lot level land use information; detailed street information from GIS Innovations; and Canadian Census data for the 2001 census.

The reported crime data was made available by "E" Division of the Royal Canadian Mounted Police (RCMP). "E" Division provides local municipal policing services to over 180 jurisdictions in British Columbia, including the suburban municipality used in this study. The British Columbia Assessment Authority is a provincial government agency that is responsible for the provision of tax assessment information for every separate parcel of property in the province. More than 200 detailed land use types are tracked. This information is used by municipalities for property taxation purposes. The assessment data set contains detailed land use information that makes it possible to distinguish between and identify many detailed types of residential, commercial, civic, and industrial land uses by address.

The crime and land use data were geocoded using a street network file developed by GIS Innovation and used by many BC government ministries. The information contained in this street network file is very detailed. It even identifies traffic calming speed bumps. For the purposes of this analysis, the street network was used to identify local and arterial roads. More detailed information about foot paths, unpaved logging roads, and other types of pathways is available and will be analyzed in future studies.

The final type of data used in this analysis is Canadian census information. Canada undertakes a census every five years; at the time of this study the latest available census data was for the year 2001. This created a time lag for census data. However, the census provides detailed socio-demographic household and housing information on a five-year cycle; so, data are fresh in comparison with census data used in many criminological studies.

As is common in much criminological research, there was some necessary mixing of time ranges. Crime data was available for 2001–2004; BCAA data was available for 2005; GIS Innovation street files were available for 2006. Census data was from 2001. This creates uncertainty about some of the data and should be kept in mind in interpreting the results. We are engaged in creating archives for these and other data sources; so, over time it should become possible to eliminate such temporal mixing, at least for specific census years.

Micro-Meso-Micro Analysis

The unit of analysis is fundamental in any study and the central issue for this book. As mentioned before, we are entering a period where we can undertake analysis at the most fundamental address level, aggregate to some larger summary unit to look for patterns, and return to a more micro level of analysis to better understand any interesting patterns that are found.

Following geocoding, the burglary data was explored visually at the address level in comparison to the BCAA taxable parcel database.[2] We used census data at the smallest available level. This small unit is called a Dissemination Area (DA) and consists of a cluster of blocks. Eight to ten Dissemination Areas, when combined, form a Census Tract. BCAA data was aggregated to the DA level. The census data was used mathematically to depict an empirical version of the urban backcloth for analysis of crime in relation to major activity nodes, major streets, and the sharpness of the edges of coherent neighborhoods. The technique will be described in

---

[2] The effective geocoding rate for the burglary data was 94.9%; some 98.3% of the BCAA land use data successfully geocoded.

summary below. Detailed description of the technique is presented in the mathematical appendix.

Commercial areas reported in the BCAA data set are used to identify likely activity nodes for the study city. Schools, parks, and recreation areas were not used in this initial beta testing of the new algorithm. In this study city, road arteries were consistent with commercial areas. Census information about age of housing and type of housing was used in this exploratory analysis. Older housing built before 1946 and middle aged housing built between 1946 and 1960 and small apartment buildings were identified as reasonably good visual identifiers of residences that would be more likely to experience burglary (See, e.g., Brantingham and Brantingham 1977; Waller and Okihiro 1978; Bennett and Wright 1984; Clarke and Hope 1984; Cromwell et al. 1991; Rengert and Wasilchick 2000).

Urban Backcloth

What surrounds us in an urban environment includes centers of activity, roads and pathways, well known landmarks, and parks as well as neighborhoods with different socio-economic and demographic character. We move around in the urban environment from one activity node to another sometimes with fixed location goals (such as a specific restaurant) and sometimes with general area goals (the entertainment district). This movement takes people through well defined areas with crisp, clear borders, and through less clearly identifiable areas. Crimes occur within this backcloth, and can even shape the backcloth. Individuals have personal nodes, paths, and edges that shape their activities within the backcloth. In the aggregate some nodes, paths, and edges stand out.

Common aggregate activity nodes that are studied in criminology are shopping areas, entertainment districts (including pubs or bars), and schools. Aggregate awareness spaces are likely to be located the areas around these types of nodes. Of course, activity nodes vary by individual, but areas of activity concentration reflect the activity nodes for many people. In a similar way, major roads and mass transit shape and reflect paths used by many people. Individual movement patterns vary, but groups of individuals shape aggregate patterns of movement (WAAG Society 2007).

What is of particular importance is what shapes the edges of the awareness spaces around major paths and nodes. A new algorithm described below is being developed to model the shape of the aggregate awareness spaces around major activity centers, major roads, and homogenous neighborhoods. The algorithm helps identify sharp or gradual breaks or barriers between aggregate awareness spaces. The algorithm is designed to reflect the dynamics of an urban environment and move towards softer definitions of distance.

We are currently in a period of innovation in spatial analysis. Part of the originality of research is in the development of new measures to articulate ideas. (Bittner 2001; Bafna 2003; Elffers 2003; and Weisburd et al. 2004 for examples of the creation of interesting measures to address differing theoretical approaches in spatial analysis.)

Common GIS software makes it relatively easy for researchers to create fixed distance buffers around points, streets, or shapes (polygons) and look at crime concentrations within these buffered areas. This chapter tries to go beyond the fixed distance buffers, utilizing a new algorithm, TOPO$_{©}$, for aggregation of fine grained spatial units into larger, coherent aggregates that reflect probable awareness spaces – cognitive buffers of flexible size and power. The algorithm has value in understanding the impact of perceptual edges on crime patterns. In highly varied areas in particular, sharp perceptual edges may block awareness and activity at the boundary, keeping people and events from crossing into spatially adjacent but perceptually different areas. Flexible buffer size may be of particular importance where space, place, and context are important and where there are high levels of dissimilarity from spatial unit to spatial unit.

TOPO provides a tool for research construction of cognitive buffer areas around activity locations. Cognitive buffers need not be of equal length in all directions but can reflect the actual structure and use of areas around an activity node or common path. Rengert and Wasilchick (2000) show a cardinality in the direction of offending patterns consistent with a non-circular awareness space (Pyle 1974; Costanzo et al. 1986). Ratcliffe (2006) defines time constrained buffers that take a teardrop shape.

TOPO is a fuzzy topology algorithm. The details of the algorithm are set out in appendix A. As a brief summary, topology is an area of mathematics that has a focus on continuity and discontinuity. Continuity within TOPO means that one unit of analysis is similar to an adjacent unit to some degree. This area of mathematics has links to interpretation of images in medicine, satellite images, and in linguistics, among others.

Fuzzy topology measures the amount of difference from block to block. When changes between adjacent blocks are gradual, someone travelling past them may have trouble noticing the change until it has cumulated into a very large difference. It is possible to move from one neighborhood to the next; recognize when you are in the core area of a neighborhood; but not be able to say exactly when you move from one neighborhood to another. Gradual change produces a *fuzziness* in neighborhood membership in that a block may partially belong to two or more neighborhoods.

Fuzzy topology also tracks crisp or sharp changes between neighborhoods.[3] When there is a crisp change from one block to the next, people tend to notice the difference. The border between an industrial district and an adjacent residential area is sharp and noticeable; everybody experiences the sharp change when they turn off a commercial block with stores and move into a quieter residential area.

In TOPO, an adjacency table is used to compare a series of adjacent units and measure the rate of change in the variables of interest as observation moves from one adjacent unit to another. This measure of rate of change from one unit to the next adjacent unit makes it possible to identify core areas (groups of contiguous spatial units) with higher homogeneity and to identify spatial transitions between core areas by gradual change or by sharp, abrupt difference, that is, where there

---

[3] These are the sorts of neighborhood edges described by Kevin Lynch (1960) in his classic book *The Image of the City*.

is much less similarity from block to block on the variable of interest. The places on the fuzzy edges or border areas may partially belong to two or more disparate but homogenous neighborhoods. The places on crisp edges represent a sharp break between adjacent neighborhoods.

To help measure the crispness or softness of the borders between adjacent units, the algorithm is written so that it allows for consideration of neighborhood sets across a range of levels of difference in the variable of interest. In this study, a lattice was used that agglomerated sets of similar blocks and identified their fuzzy and crisp boundary edges by allowing 30% variation in value of the variable of interest, 20% variation, and 10% variation to be set as the measure of similarity. Using this lattice (30%, 20%, and 10%), the sharpest edges would be dissimilar at 30% variation (which means that the adjacent units would be dissimilar at 20% and 10% as well). A softer edge would be similar in adjacent units at 30% difference and 20% difference and only show dissimilarity at 10% variation.

The softness or crispness of neighborhood edges can vary greatly depending on the number of variables considered and the number of levels of dissimilarity considered. In this study four primary variables with three dissimilarity levels are used on the lattice. As a result, the number of edge components assigned to a particular unit could range from 0 to 16. The lowest value would be *zero* where adjacent units were similar for all variables of interest and at the 30%, 20%, and 10% difference levels of variation. The highest measure in the sharp edges or border areas would be 16 where there was a difference for adjacent units for 10, 20, 30% variation levels. This provides an index of the extent to which any given unit belongs to a single unique neighborhood.

This approach is different from traditional clustering algorithms where a set of units is divided into well-defined subsets. A unit either belongs to a subset or it does not. TOPO assigns a *level* of membership to basic sets. It is developed to handle, in spatial analysis, something equivalent to how it is possible to say someone is "tall" or "short" in some situations, but that there are many people who are neither "tall" nor "short" but are "taller" or "shorter". As you might infer from the example, fuzzy topology and fuzzy logic are used heavily in such fields as computational linguistics.

The TOPO algorithm is used in this study to identify the clear centers or interiors of neighborhoods within a suburb of Vancouver and to identify both the gradual and sharp changes between neighborhoods, that is, the fuzzy edges. The edges define many of the structures of the urban backcloth.

Crime is relatively rare. It is expected that sharp edges form cognitive barriers and locations where crime is likely to cluster (remembering that relationships are not isomorphic). A sharp border does not necessarily produce crime, just a locale that is frequently compatible with crime because the activity of both neighborhood insiders and outsiders is channeled and held there. Insiders are reluctant to cross the sharp border into a very different neighborhood; outsiders are reluctant to leave the sharp border zone. A soft border – a highly fuzzy area – and less crime would be expected in the broader fuzzy areas. In a topological sense this could be visualized by considering a buffer along a road with equal risk within the buffer. A crisp edge compacts the buffer, moving the crimes into a smaller area. A large, soft, fuzzy area expands the buffer and spreads the crime over a larger area.

Results

Overview of Residential Burglary

Figure 4.1 provides a kernel density map for residential burglary in the suburb of Vancouver covered in this chapter. Residential burglary is varied across the city with a concentration along its south western jurisdictional limit. As presented in this chapter, data from adjacent municipalities were not used, but some preliminary testing indicated that the adjacent municipal areas represented crisp, sharp breaks with the area covered in the analysis particularly along the western edge. One municipal boundary is on a sharp transition to industrial storage; the other municipal boundary runs along a major road with a large regional shopping complex with mass transit and bus exchange stations across the street in the other municipality; shops associated with the mall complex are found on the study community side of this road.

   Figure 4.2 provides additional general display information for the study municipality. The upper panel shows the general distribution of residential developments. The lower panel shows the distribution of multi-family residences and higher density dwelling types. As is typical of many North American suburban cities, there is no high density core area. The study city is dominated by single family residential land uses. It should be noted that as part of a planning scheme to develop a city

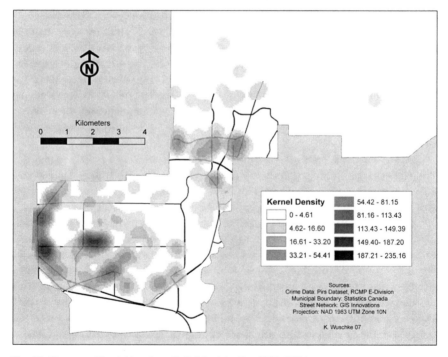

Fig. 4.1 Repeat residential burglary: B.C. Municipality, 2001–2004

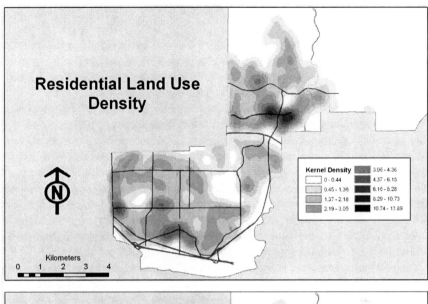

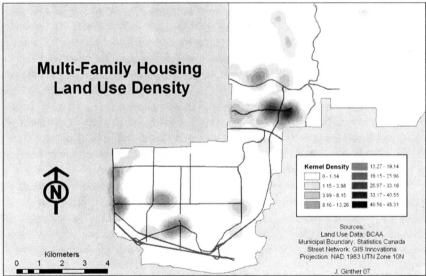

Fig. 4.2 Study area land use, 2005

center, the municipal government has encouraged construction of new multi-story condominium developments in an area near a shopping mall where it has also built a large park and recreation center, a series of new city service buildings including the city hall, the police station, a library, and allocated land to a new community college. There is a clustering of some residential burglaries in this area, but, as will be shown, the volume is small in relation to the number of residential units.

Fuzzy and Sharp Borders

The paths, nodes, and edges in this municipality are explored using the TOPO©
algorithm. For Dissemination Areas (DAs), the smallest census area unit available,
burglaries are analyzed for clustering in areas along major arteries, near shopping
areas (common activity nodes) and for their border/edge areas.

The results of this exploratory testing are very interesting. Most Dissemination
Areas have some measure of dissimilarity with contiguous areas, that is, there are
many fuzzy boundary areas in the city. The fuzzy borders or edges for commercial
areas, older housing, and small apartments were calculated allowing a 30% change
from adjacent unit to adjacent unit. These borders or edges show a difference in
the average number of burglaries (see Table 4.1). There is enough diversity in this
suburb that there are few areas that are interiors for all variables and many more that
are borders or edges for all three variables. Even with this diversity, the range of
values runs from 1.67 for the interiors or areas surrounded by similar areas to 13.81
where the fuzzy borders cumulate to produce strong edges.

The variation, however, is large within each fuzzy boundary category and with
some outliers or extreme values. Figure 4.3 presents the box-plot for the fuzzy
boundary/edge values. The results are very interesting given that this exploratory
analysis was planned primarily to test the algorithm. It is expected that results should
be even more interesting using a broader range of variables with smaller units of
analysis for the aggregation into homogeneous and less clear, fuzzy areas.

For descriptive purposes, Table 4.2 shows the impact of both individual and combined boundaries for the three variables. Zero represents an interior; the value 1 is
used for a single boundary. As can be seen from the figure, the highest average number of burglaries (about 14) is for Dissemination Areas that are fuzzy borders/edges
of commercial, older housing, and small apartment areas. Areas that are interiors for
all variables or a boundary for only one of the variables have much lower numbers
of burglaries than the high boundary areas.

The small apartment variable and the older housing variable were used with the
boundary counts as a factor in a General Linear Model (GLM). As is usually the
case with crime data, the assumptions of GLM could not be met. The variances are
unequal (Levene's Test); cell sizes vary; and clear outliers exist. The largest variance
is, as expected, with the boundary category with the largest n. This and the small

Table 4.1 Mean and standard deviation of number of burglaries (2001–2004) by number of fuzzy
boundaries

Number of fuzzy boundaries	Mean	Standard deviation	N
0	1.67	2.887	3
1	4.3	3.323	23
2	9.29	6.979	62
3	13.81	9.594	93
Total	10.85	8.788	181

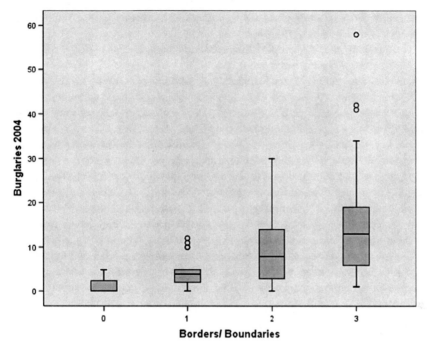

Fig. 4.3 Box-plot for the fuzzy boundary/edge values

Table 4.2 Mean and standard deviation of number of burglaries (2001–2004) by boundaries/ borders

Construction 1946–1960 boundary	Commercial boundary	Small apartment boundary	Mean	Std. deviation	N
0	0	0	1.67	2.89	3
		1	4.07	2.95	14
	1	0	4.50	0.71	2
		1	7.86	6.97	29
1	0	0	4.71	4.61	7
		1	10.68	7.04	31
	1	0	8.50	2.12	2
		1	13.81	9.59	93

n for interior areas are likely to under-identify relationships. With the exclusion of the three outliers (worth special study separately in a crime attractor analysis), the boundary impact is reasonable. The boundary/interior difference was significant for the number of borders and for the covariates. The η_p^2 values, however, are small for all the variables.

An additional GLM was run with natural log transformations, exclusion of outliers, and a collapsing of the boundary edge variable into two categories (zero and one boundary; and two or three variables). The GLM model, consistent with the variance equality assumption, continues to show significance for the transformed variables. The η_p^2 values remain small.

The analysis was repeated for different lattice values (20% and 10%, as well as 30%). The results were similar.

Crime is rare, but clustered. Research needs a focus on extreme values. Table 4.3 shows the difference in the extreme values for the interior (0/1) and boundary (1/2) divisions used in the GLM just described. As can be seen by the information in the table, there is a large difference in the high and low values. The five high values for the interiors range from 5 to 12. The five high values for the borders range from 33 to 58. The low values for both categories are zeros. There are low crime borders or edges just like there are low crime interiors, but the high crime edges are of a magnitude greater than high crime interiors. Similarly, the weighted averages for the 95th percentile for interiors start at 11.65 for interiors and 26 for borders.

In general, this initial testing provides support for expanding work using fuzzy set theory and topology in computational criminology. The importance of moving to block level analysis is strongly supported. Dissemination Areas are aggregations of blocks. By using street blocks, it will be possible to create a model that reflects micro level perceptual changes as well as one that moves closer to block level concentration of crime and to begin to add individual cognitive awareness spaces.

Table 4.3 Extreme values for borders and interiors

				Case Number	Value
Burglaries	Interior	Highest	1	72	12
			2	75	11
			3	83	10
			4	87	10
			5	124	5[a]
		Lowest	1	181	0
			2	178	0
			3	177	0
			4	174	1
			5	171	1
	Border	Highest	1	1	58
			2	2	42
			3	3	41
			4	4	34
			5	5	33
		Lowest	1	180	0
			2	179	0
			3	176	0
			4	175	0
			5	173	1[b]

[a] Only a partial list of cases with the value 5 are shown in the table of upper extremes.
[b] Only a partial list of cases with the value 1 are shown in the table of lower extremes.

Table 4.4 Number of land uses and burglaries at selected high and low border areas

Dissemination area	Borders	Land uses	Crimes	Residential units	Crime rate
High Border 1	14	5	58	270	21.48
High Border 2	13	8	42	350	12.00
High Border 3	14	9	41	370	11.08
Low Border 1	4	2	3	125	2.40
Low Border 2	4	3	3	195	1.54
Low Border 3	5	1	4	115	3.48

Return to the Micro Level of Analysis

The difference between the crisp border areas and the more homogeneous interiors is rather strong. This exploratory analysis used a limited number of variables. To bring the study full circle, we identified Dissemination Areas with the highest and lowest counts and explored how the residential burglaries varied from building to building, that is, in essence we took the similarity idea in TOPO and applied it to lot or individual parcel level data in some selected locations.

As Table 4.4 shows, the three highest residential burglary Dissemination Areas had border/edge counts of 14, 13, and 14. The three lowest Dissemination Areas had border/edge counts of 4, 4, and 5.

Conclusions

This research strongly supports the move in criminology towards using micro units of analysis, aggregating them when necessary, but maintaining the detailed units of analysis for additional research purposes. One level of natural aggregation is to small locales such as neighborhoods and to major roads and activity centers. We explored using fuzzy topology to develop small locales or neighborhoods and identify the edges or borders of these neighborhoods. We found that even using an aggregate unit of a Dissemination Area (the smallest census area with available data) there were fairly strong differences in the amount of burglaries in homogeneous interiors and in their fuzzy edges or borders. Burglaries were higher for crisp borders than for more gradually changing edges.

It was particularly interesting to explore the residential burglary patterns within a selection of high border/ high crime Dissemination Areas (DAs) and the low border/ low crime DAs. While the TOPO algorithm only used three variables, the actual land uses in the high border/high crime DAs were highly varied. There were many micro edges within these areas. The land uses in the lower edge/lower crime DAs were less varied, more homogeneous. Our conclusion is that the basic spatial unit of analysis in crime pattern research should be the individual address or parcel of land. Larger aggregates should be constructed from this spatial level in a way that makes it possible to look back within the aggregates. Future research in crime patterns should begin by using a fine, small unit of analysis, and aggregating up to street blocks, neighborhoods, major activity spaces, or other larger units when the theoretical orientation calls for it.

Mathematical Appendix: Fuzzy Topology Algorithm

This appendix contains a brief summary of the fuzzy topology algorithm developed for this study. Topology is an area of mathematics that has a focus on sets, continuity, and discontinuity. In fuzzy topology, sets can have partial membership in a set instead of the traditional set theory where an element is either a member of a set or not a member. The degree of membership fits well into the use of words like "near" or "similar". The fuzzy set membership fits well into urban concepts like "neighbourhood" where there may be agreement about the core of a neighbourhood, but lack of agreement about its borders or edges. Similarly, a person's awareness space can have well-defined centres but fuzzy edges.

Background

A *topology* on a space T is the collection of subsets, X_i, such that:

- The $\emptyset \in T$ and $T \in T$
- If $X_1, \ldots, X_n \in T$ then $\cup X_i \in T$
- If $X_1, \ldots, X_n \in T$ then $\cap X_i \in T$

An important concept which must be considered is that of a *basis* or *base*. A basis of a topology T is a sub-collection B of T with the property that every open set X of T is the union of the basis sets. Formally, if $X_i \in T$ then $X_i = \cup B_j$ where B_j is a basis set. Another important concept is the difference between finite point-set topology and infinite topology. Topologies in criminology are built on a finite number of sets when the unit of analysis is something like crimes or addresses or where the unit of analysis is a city block.

Probably one of the most important aspects of topology useful to criminologists is that the individual sets can be of different sizes. Unions of adjacent sets, that are sets themselves, create a natural way to aggregate information. With property lots, for example, these can be aggregated to block faces, to blocks, to nearest intersection, to groups of blocks joined by specified criteria, to neighbourhoods, to urban areas, and to larger units. While the modifiable area unit problem in spatial analysis of government data sources cannot be eliminated completely, aggregating and disaggregating elements of topology provide the potential for forming natural neighbourhoods or creating a cognitive unit like an awareness space.

Edges (boundary), *interiors*, and *neighbourhoods* are concepts in topology that are very helpful in crime analysis and spatial analysis. These concepts will be defined mathematically. These are concepts that distinguish between the relative position of points in sets and sets that have been joined into a union of sets

$(S_i = \cup X_j$ where $X_j \in T)$. Fundamentally, in topology, you can have a point x that is in a set. That set may be surrounded by other sets. When a set is surrounded by other similar sets in the topology it is called an open set. The open sets around point x form the neighbourhood of x. Generally for sets a neighbourhood has the following properties: if T is a topological space and S is a subset of T, then X is a neighbourhood of S if X is open and X is contained in another subset Y that is contained in T. Symbolically, $S \subseteq X \subseteq Y \subseteq T$. The *interior* of a set $(int(S))$ is the union of open sub-sets within the set and points within these open sub-sets. The *boundary* or *edge* of a set $(bd(S))$ is the union of the closed sub-sets, that is, sets that are not open sets.

Topological Aggregation Algorithm

The focus of this algorithm is to develop aggregate awareness spaces shaped by a distinction between neighbourhoods or districts with sharp or fuzzy boundaries defined by gradual change. This topology algorithm is different from the common statistical methods of clustering where there are classifications of areas using some k-mean values, high or low values, density/connectivity measures or grid-based methods as the basis of alternative mathematical rules for similarity that use a set common value. TOPO$^©$ uses rules for determining similarity that are based on the differences in adjacent block units only. What this means is that there can be a series of adjacent blocks where a highly visible attribute like the age of the buildings can vary in small amounts from one block to another so that the block at the beginning of the series is very different from the block at the end, but where there is little difference between the any two adjacent blocks. Strong differences are more easily recognized than small changes.

Fuzzy set theory was developed by Zadeh (1965). Fuzzy topology is a growing area of applied research. Readers who have an interest in fuzzy logic and fuzzy topology should review the work of Li and Li (2004), Winter (1998), Haq and Zimring (2003), Yeung et al. (2005), and Liu and Shi (2006) to see the uses of fuzzy sets and fuzzy topology. The article by Liu and Shi (2006) is of particular interest. It describes a fuzzy topology algorithm with some similarity to the algorithm presented in this chapter.

In fuzzy set theory there is a membership function that is used to assess a level of membership. That is, there is a membership function μ such that $\mu \rightarrow [0, 1]$ where the values 0 and 1 are non-membership and complete membership. The 0/1 is like traditional Cartesian *true/false* logic. The values between 0 and 1 measure the degree of membership.

A fuzzy set on the types of sets previously described uses the following notation: $\tilde{A} = \{(x, \mu_A(x))|x \in X\}$. For all elements of a set, X, the fuzzy set is the elements and their associated membership based on the fuzzy membership function, μ_A. The intersection of two fuzzy sets is denoted as $(A \cap B)(x) = \min[A(x), B(x)]$. The union of two fuzzy sets is denoted as: $(A \cup B)(x) = \max[A(x), B(x)]$.

The associated membership functional value that is used to set the limit for similarity can be changed. Every time the inter-unit variation is changed, new basis sets are constructed. Many sets are created as the percentage variation is allowed to range up or down. For example, let B_i be a basis set and b_j be a block. Let $f(b_j)$ be a functional value associated with block b_j, such as average cost of housing, average rent, or percent apartment houses. Then a basis set is:

$$B_j = \left\{ b_i \mid \| f(b_j) - f(b_i) \| \leq \max\{af(b_j), af(b_i)\} \right\} \text{ Where}$$

$$b_i \in B \text{ and } b_i \cap b_j \neq \phi; \text{ and } 0 < a < 1; b_i \neq b_j; \ i = 1, \ldots, n; \ j = 1, \ldots, m$$

The contours of the *neighbourhood* change and develop as the permitted inter-block variation is changed and new basis sets are formed. A set constructed from a fixed level of inter-block variation contains sets constructed from lower levels of inter-block variation. If $a_{i-1} < a_i < a_{i+1}$ are real numbers between zero and one and $B_j(a_j)$ is a set formed by allowing a fixed a_i inter-block variation then:

$$\ldots \subseteq B_j(a_{i-1}) \subseteq B_k(a_i) \subseteq B_l(a_{i+1}) \ldots$$

It is worth special consideration to note that as the associated membership function value decreases additional boundary blocks will be created. When a block is a boundary block for one level of variation it will be a boundary block for a set created by a smaller inter-block variation. Let $\bar{b}_j$ be a boundary block in a basis set constructed by allowing an a_i inter-block variation, then another chain is formed as the inter-set variation changes:

$$\ldots \subseteq \{\bar{b}_j(a_{i+1})\} \subseteq \{\bar{b}_j(a_i)\} \subseteq \{\bar{b}_j(a_{i-1})\} \subseteq \ldots$$

It should be noted that boundary blocks for sets constructed from lower levels of variation will not always be boundary blocks for sets constructed from higher levels of variation. Boundaries may change as the value of a changes; this is a gradual change. The boundaries will be the same when there is a sharp, crisp, difference between neighbourhoods.[4]

TOPO© uses multiple characteristics in a *product topology*, that is, we consider different characteristics of urban areas co-jointly. If we let $\{X_\alpha\}$ $\alpha \in J$ be a finitely indexed family of topological spaces. $\prod_\alpha X_\alpha$, the Cartesian product of the X_α's, is the product space. The basis for this product space is the collection of all sets of the form $\prod_\alpha B_\alpha$ where B is an open set in X_α and J is a finite index set.

Once again, as with the simple topologies, the interesting properties emerge as the permitted variation is allowed to increase and decrease in the basis sets for the component topologies. For example, in a given residential area, the component topologies may have the same basis sets; that is, within an area B_α the basis set for characteristic α (topology α) could contain the same blocks as B_β, a basis set for topology T_β for many levels of contiguous variation. This area would have a very

---

[4] See Brantingham and Brantingham (1978) for a more detailed exploration of the boundary effect.

high level of internal homogeneity and clear-cut boundaries with adjacent areas. An area that has the same basis sets for all the component topologies at many levels of variation has a high level of perceptual distinctiveness.

Many complex nests and chains are created when the boundary blocks are different for each component topology (each characteristic or attribute) and when the boundary blocks change as the permitted variation increases or decreases. The range of types of transitions between the centres or interiors of neighbourhoods is part of how this type of neighbourhood model may approach cognitive images. Sharp or crisp boundaries are relatively rare except when there is a physical feature such as a lake or a highway or an abrupt land use change such as a move from a shopping area to a residential area.

For the purposes of analysis, the ideas just described are written in the following functional form: Consider f a functional value for the unit of analysis. Let the membership function μ have two values: $\mu = 0$ when $b_i \cap b_j = \phi$; and has the following value when the basis sets intersect.

$$\mu = 1 - \left(\frac{\| f(b_j) - f(b_i) \|}{\max(f(b_j), f(b_i))} \right)$$

The fuzzy sets have values for every adjacency in the matrix described earlier. For example, when block$_1$ is adjacent to block$_2$, block$_3$, and block$_4$, then fuzzy values would be numbers such as {.8, .7, .3} when the functional value between block$_1$ and block$_2$ is an 80% similarity, the similarity for block$_1$ and block$_3$ is 70%; and the similarity between block$_1$ and block$_4$ is 30%. In a fuzzy sense, blocks 1, 2, and 3 are highly similar; block$_4$ is dissimilar.

The topology just described creates an urban backcloth that identifies sharp changes from one spatial area to the next. It also identifies gradual changes. The model identifies neighbourhood interiors for single and multiple variables. It creates a fabric of changes, a fabric that may start to identify the location of potential cues and cue clusters that identify locations as unique. The nodes (other than home locations) are likely to be in boundary areas; paths may fall along boundaries, particularly when in strip commercial development or when the main roads run along the edge of water or open spaces. The paths, when large enough, create a boundary themselves. It is expected that sharp boundaries influence the permeability of urban areas. The sharper the boundary, the more likely it is that people passing through an area stay in the boundary area. It is also expected that the boundary areas are areas where everyone feels like an outsider. There is lack of similarity. Each turn or block can seem different. With most people feeling like outsiders there is little likelihood that there are many natural guardians.

References

Adderley, R. (2004). The use of data mining techniques in operational crime fighting. *Intelligence and Security Informatics*. Second Symposium on Intelligence and Security Informatics, Tucson, AZ, USA, June 10–11, 2004. Proceedings.

Bafna, S. (2003). SPACE SYNTAX A brief introduction to its logic and analytical techniques. *Environment and Behavior*, 35(1), 17–29.

Beavon, D. J. K., Brantingham, P. L., & Brantingham, P. J. (1994). The influence of street networks on the patterning of property offenses. *Crime Prevention Studies*, 2, 115–148.

Bennett, T., & Wright, R. (1984). *Burglars on burglary: Prevention and the offender*. Brookfield, Vermont: Gower Publishing Company.

Bittner, T. (2001). The qualitative structure of built environments. *Fundamenta Informaticae* 46, 97–128.

Brantingham, P. J., & Brantingham, P. L. (1977). Housing patterns and burglary in a medium-sized American city. In: J. Scott & S. Dinitz (Eds.), *Criminal justice planning* (pp. 63–74). New York: Praeger.

Brantingham, P. J., & Brantingham, P. L. (1984). *Patterns in crime*. New York: Macmillan.

Brantingham, P. J., Dyreson, D. A., & Brantingham, P. L. (1976). Crime seen through a cone of resolution. *American Behavioral Scientist*, 20, 261–273.

Brantingham, P. L., & Brantingham, P. J. (1978). A topological technique for regionalization. *Environment and Behavior*, 10, 335–353.

Brantingham, P. L., & Brantingham, P. J. (1993a). Environment, routine and situation: Toward a pattern theory of crime. *Advances in Criminological Theory*, 5, 259–294.

Brantingham, P. L., & Brantingham, P. J. (1993b). Nodes, paths and edges: Considerations on the complexity of crime and the physical environment. *Journal of Environmental Psychology*, 13, 3–28.

Brantingham, P. L., & Brantingham, P. J. (1995). Criminality of place: Crime generators and crime attractors. *European Journal on Criminal Policy and Research*, 3, 5–26.

Brantingham, P. L., & Brantingham, P. J. (2004). Computer simulation as a tool for environmental criminologists. *Security Journal*, 17(1), 21–30.

Brantingham, P. L., & Brantingham, P. J. (2008). The rules of crime pattern theory. In: R. Wortley, L. Mazerolle, & S. Rombouts (Eds.), *Environmental criminology and crime analysis*. Devon, UK: Willan Publishing.

Brantingham, P. L., Brantingham, P. J., & Glässer, U. (2005). Computer simulation as a research tool in criminology and criminal justice. *Criminal Justice Matters*, 58, 19–20.

Brantingham, P. L., Glässer, U., Kinney, B., Singh, K., & Vajihollahi, M. (2005). A computational model for simulating spatial aspects of crime in urban environments. *Proceedings of the IEEE international conference on systems, man and cybernetics* (pp. 3667–3674). Hawaii, October 2005.

Brown, D. (1998). The Regional Crime Analysis Program (ReCAP): a framework for mining data to catch criminals. *Proceedings of the 1998 IEEE international conference on systems, man and cybernetics*, 3, 2848–2853.

Clarke, R. V. G., & Hope, T. (1984). *Coping with burglary: Research perspectives on policy*. Boston: Kluwer-Nijhoff.

Costanzo, C. M., Halperin, W. C., & Gale, N. (1986). Criminal mobility and the directional component in journeys to crime. In R. M. Figlio, S. Hakim, & G. F. Rengert (Eds.) *Metropolitan Crime Patterns*. (pp. 73–95). Monsey, New York: Criminal Justice Press.

Cromwell, P. F., Olson, J. N., & Avary, D. W. (1991). *Breaking and entering: An ethnographic analysis of burglary*. Newbury Park, CA: Sage Publications.

Elffers, H. (2003). Analysing neighbourhood influence in criminology. *Statistica Neerlandica*, 57(3), 347–367.

Groff, E. R. (2007). Simulation for theory testing and experiments: An example using routine activity theory and street robbery. *Journal of Quantitative Criminology*, 23(2), 75–103.

Haq, S., & Zimring, G. (2003). Just down the road a piece: The development of topological knowledge of building layouts. *Environment and Behavior*, 35(1), 132–160.

Li, Y., & Li, S. (2004). A fuzzy sets theoretic approach to approximate spatial reasoning. *IEEE Transactions on Fuzzy Systems*, 12(6), 745–754.

Lim, M., Metzler, R., & Bar-Yam, Y. (2007). Global pattern formation and ethnic/cultural violence. *Science*, 317, 1540–1544.

Liu, K., & Shi, W. (2006). Computing the fuzzy topological relations of spatial objects based on induced fuzzy topology. *International Journal of Geographical Information Science*, 20(8), 857–883.

Liu, L., Wang, X., Eck, J., & Liang, J. (2005). Simulating crime events and crime patterns in a RA/CA model. In: F. Wang (Ed.), *Geographic information systems and crime analysis* (pp. 197–213). Reading, PA: Idea Publishing.

Lynch, K. (1960). *The image of the city*. Cambridge, Massachusetts: MIT Press.

McCord, E. S., Ratcliffe, J. H., Garcia, R. M., & Taylor, R. B. (2007). Nonresidential crime attractors and generators elevate perceived neighborhood crime and incivilities. *Journal of Research in Crime and Delinquency*, 44(3), 295–320.

Pyle, G. F. (1974). *The spatial dynamics of crime*. Chicago: Department of Geography, University of Chicago.

Quetelet, L. A. J. (1842). *A treatise on man and the development of his faculties*. Edinburgh: W & R Chambers.

Ratcliffe, J. H. (2006). A temporal constraint theory to explain opportunity-based spatial offending patterns. *Journal of Research in Crime and Delinquency*, 43(3), 261–291.

Rengert, G. F., & Wasilchick, J. (2000). *Suburban burglary: A tale of two suburbs*. Springfield, IL: C.C. Thomas.

Schmid, C. (1960a). Urban crime areas – Part I. *American Sociological Review*, 25, 527–543.

Schmid, C. (1960b). Urban crime areas – Part II. *American Sociological Review*, 25, 655–678.

Shaw, C., & McKay, H. D. (1942). *Delinquency and Urban Areas*. Chicago: University of Chicago Press.

Townsley, M., Homel, R., & Chaseling, J. (2003). Infectious burglaries: A test of the near repeat hypothesis. *British Journal of Criminology*, 43, 615–633.

WAAG Society. (2007). *Amsterdam real time project*. http://realtime.waag.org. Accessed November 27, 2007.

Waller, I., & Okihiro, N. (1978). *Burglary: The victim and the public*. Toronto: University of Toronto Press.

Weisburd, D., Bushway, S., Lum, C., & Yang, S.-U. (2004). Trajectories of crime at places: A longitudinal study of street segments in the city of Seattle. *Criminology*, 42(2), 283–321.

Wikström, P. O., & Butterworth, D. A. (2006). *Adolescent crime: Individual differences and lifestyles*. Portland: Willan Publishing.

Wilcox, S. (1973). *The geography of robbery*. [The Prevention and Control of Robbery, Vol. 3]. Davis: The Center of Administration of Justice, University of California at Davis.

Winter, S. (1998). Location-based similarity measures of regions. In: D. Fritsch, M. Englich, & M. Sester (Eds.), *ISPRS Commission IV Symposium "GIS Between Visions and Applications"* (Vol. 32(4), pp. 669–676). International Archives of Photogrammetry and Remote Sensing, Stuttgart, Germany.

Xue, Y., & Brown, D. E. (2006). Spatial analysis with preference specification of latent decision makers for criminal event prediction. *Decision Support Systems*, 41(3), 560–573.

Yeung, D., Chen, C., Tsang, E., & Lee, J. (2005). On the generalization of fuzzy rough sets. *IEEE Transactions on Fuzzy Systems*, 13(3), 343–361.

Zadeh, L. A. (1965). Fuzzy sets. *Information and Control*, 8, 338–353.

Chapter 5
Geographical Units of Analysis and the Analysis of Crime

George F. Rengert and Brian Lockwood

Abstract When spatial analysis of crime is conducted, the analyst should not ignore the spatial units that data are aggregated into and the impact of this choice on the interpretation of findings. Just as several independent variables are considered to determine whether they have statistical significance, a consideration of multiple spatial units of analysis should be made as well, in order to determine whether the choice of aggregation level used in a spatial analysis can result in biased findings. This chapter considers four classes of problems that can arise when data bounded in space are analyzed. These problems, inherent in most studies of space, include: issues associated with politically bounded units of aggregation, edge effects of bounded space, the modifiable aerial unit problem (MAUP), and ways in which the results of statistical analyses can be manipulated by changes in the level of aggregation. Techniques that can be used to alleviate each of the methodological difficulties described in this chapter are then discussed.

Introduction

The first law of geography is that everything is related to everything else, but near things are more related than distant things (Tobler 1970). The most important point about this law is that we are comparing the spatial arrangement of at least two phenomena. If just one variable is mapped, Reboussin et al. (1995) refer to this as a "mapless map." A mapless map is a mere description since it describes how one variable is distributed in space; whether it is clustered or uniformly distributed for example. In order to determine "why" it is distributed the way it is, the spatial distribution of at least one other variable needs to be considered. The choice of this additional variable is determined by the underlying theory we wish to test. In other words, theory suggests "why" a variable such as juvenile delinquency is spatially

G.F. Rengert
Department of Criminal Justice, Temple University, Philadelphia, PA, USA
e-mail: grengert@temple.edu

D. Weisburd et al. (eds.), *Putting Crime in its Place*,
DOI 10.1007/978-0-387-09688-9_5, © Springer Science+Business Media, LLC 2009

distributed the way it is. Data are then collected to determine whether or not one variable is spatially associated with another. This data often is arranged in spatial units. In geographic analysis, it is important to understand the nature of the units of analysis that determine the level of aggregation of the data. This is because the way data are regionalized may partly determine the nature of the spatial associations identified.

At the most basic level, units of analysis are commonly differentiated between spaces and places. Places are generally depicted as points in space while spaces have an aerial extent. The appropriate unit of analysis to be used depends both on the research question we wish to address and the availability of data. If the data are available, research generally begins with the smallest level of aggregation possible which is a point pattern of places. Point patterns can always be aggregated into spaces but spaces cannot always be disaggregated into places. However, in almost all the cases, even place data are gathered with respect to some aerial unit such as a postal zip code, police district, or census tract.

Researchers commonly accept the space boundaries that are available to them uncritically. With a few notable exceptions such as Shaw and McKay's (1942) Chicago study, analysts seldom draw their own spatial boundaries. This is unfortunate since the purpose of regionalization for analytical purposes is to construct regions so that the variance in the dependent variable is minimized within the bounded region and maximized between the regions. In other words, the objective is to construct boundaries around like areas.

Unfortunately, crime analysts commonly take the bounded space that is available to them rather than construct their own boundaries. The problem is that most of these boundaries are constructed for administrative purposes rather than for reasons of sound research designs. For example, census boundaries are constructed for purposes of enumeration of the population, zip code boundaries for postal delivery, police districts for allocation of resources, and political boundaries for purposes of administrative responsibility. Generally, these administratively defined boundaries violate the research objective of minimizing internal variance and maximizing between unit variance.

When analysts uncritically accept the data that is available to them, they encounter problems that often are not recognized. These problems can be categorized into classes. In the following discussion, four classes of problems that arise when we analyze data that is bounded in space are identified and solutions suggested. The first class of problems is associated with the somewhat arbitrary nature of the boundaries that are drawn for purposes other than scientific research. The second class of problems is associated with the edge effects of bounded space that can truncate data and skew the results of subsequent analyses. The third class of problems surrounds the issue of the relative size of the units of analysis. The critical issue here is that the results of spatial analyses can be influenced by selecting different levels of aggregation, a phenomenon commonly referred to as the modifiable aerial unit problem. The final class of problems stems from the fact that the selection of appropriate statistical models in spatial analysis is affected by changes in the level of aggregation employed in the analysis. This chapter describes these common difficulties encountered in spatial analyses and puts forth alternative methods that can be applied to address these methodological issues. The discussion begins with the problems associated with politically bounded space.

Problems Associated with Politically Bounded Space

When we regionalize space, our objective is to maximize the variance between regions and minimize variance within regions for whatever feature(s) we are analyzing. In other words, we wish our regions to contain space that is as alike as possible and the boundaries to be drawn so that the region is as unalike its neighbors as possible. This can not be accomplished if we use boundaries that are drawn for political or administrative rather than research purposes. Boundaries drawn for political or administrative purposes often have little concern for bounding like populations or features and therefore are difficult to compare statistically. More commonly, political boundaries follow physical features such as rivers and land features. For example, the Rio Grande River separates much of the United States from Mexico although most of the residents on the United States side of the border speak Spanish rather than English and are culturally of Mexican origin.

An associated problem is when political boundaries are not adjusted when the space they bound has changed. An example of this is the political boundaries of old east coast cities in the United States that follow physical features in most cases and have not changed their locations in decades even though the metropolitan region continues to grow outward. Other cities in the south and western areas of the country have recently annexed most of their suburban and some of their rural neighbors. Therefore, the politically bounded cities of the east are not comparable with those in the south and west of the country.

In order to correct for this fact, we often analyze data by Metropolitan Areas rather than by politically bounded cities. These Metropolitan Areas include the central cities with their well established political boundaries and the built up suburban areas surrounding the central cities. The suburban areas are separate political entities but are part of the larger built up metropolitan area. They are more similar to other metropolitan areas than are politically bounded cities to each other. In statistical terms, we have minimized the variance within regions and maximized the variance between these regions and the surrounding area (metropolitan and nonmetropolitan areas). In layman's terms, we have added space to some cities so they are more alike other cities in a country.

Edge Effects of Bounded Space

When we analyze the spatial arrangement of data within spaces, even carefully drawn boundaries can create analytical problems. For example, we may wish to determine whether or not our data are clustered, uniformly, or randomly distributed in space. Statistical techniques such as Nearest Neighbor Analysis are used to address this research question (Boots and Getis 1988). However, near a boundary, the nearest neighbor of a place in space may not be contained within the depicted region since it is outside the mapped area. Entire classes of techniques that rely on the analysis of the spatial arrangement of places in spaces are similarly impacted. Especially important is the recent development of Geographic Profiling. Geographic Profiling is an investigative methodology that examines the patterns of criminal events committed by a serial offender in an attempt to determine the likely location of the offender or the offender's next victim(s). Through the use of geographic profiling, a "high probability surface" is created that estimates the relative likelihood of an offender living or offending in a region. If data are collected by an urban police department near a city boundary, they may not have information on places victimized by a serial offender in a neighboring suburb. An administrative boundary where information is not available outside the boundary has the effect of moving the predicted anchor point of a serial offender toward the center of the city (point B in Fig. 5.1). If data from the neighboring suburb becomes available, the high probability surface of the offender's residence or other anchor point will shift toward the suburb (point A in Fig. 5.1). In any case, a boundary that truncates data creates a problem when we wish to analyze the point pattern of places.

Geographers have identified several solutions to this boundary or edge effect problem. One solution is to create a buffer in from the actual boundary approximately the distance to an existing nearest neighbor. Although it does not address the edge problems of geographic profiling, it does allow techniques such as Nearest Neighbor Analysis to be completed using a smaller area but with existing nearest neighbors. However, it creates a smaller space and measures such as density are, therefore, likely to be affected. Furthermore, it does not satisfy the requirements of a more general or global cluster analysis such as Moran's I.

Global cluster analysis considers the arrangement of points with all other points in the region. In this case, creating a new region by buffering in from an existing

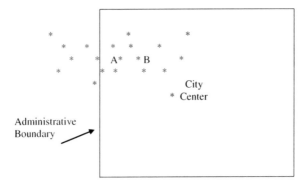

Fig. 5.1 Effects of a city boundary on a geographic profile

region does not solve the problem. Rather, we wish data to be continuous in space with places across the boundary to be arranged like places near the boundary within the region. This can be accomplished by creating a cylinder by rolling the map so that the east and west edges (or north and south edges) come together. Then the cylinder can be rolled into a doughnut-shaped figure so that there are no more edges (see Fig. 5.2). This figure is referred to as a Torus (Dacey 1975; Griffith and Amrheim 1983). Edge effects of boundaries can be corrected in this manner.

In practice, the effect of the Torus is created by making eight copies of a point pattern map. Then, each edge of the central map is connected with an identical map always using the same directional orientation so that the nine squares are identical (the top, bottom and sides of each map is identical). Then the point pattern of the central square can be computed using points in the surrounding squares whenever they are nearest neighbors of a point in the central map. This is a method for correcting for the edge effect. In this case, we are assuming that the same processes responsible for the location of the points in the study area are operating beyond its boundaries. In other words, the point pattern on the opposite side of the map is used to replace data that are missing due to the boundary effect. This would be similar space with the same processes operating if a Metropolitan Area is considered so that the city is bounded by non-urban area on each side. In this example, moving in a short distance from the non-urban area into the city from the east side would entail the same processes as moving into the city from the west side. The same is true for north and south boundaries (moving from non urban to urban areas). This technique can only be used if the study area contains a regular boundary such as a square or rectangle. If boundaries are irregular, they must be "squared off." The squaring off of boundaries will result in the loss of data and may not be practical in cases of highly irregularly bounded space.

Another method is termed the disregard solution. This method includes in the analysis only those values of d_i (distance between a point and its nearest neighbor) that are less than the distance between this point and the boundary of the study area (Boots and Getis, 1988). In other words, we are ignoring all points in the pattern that are closer to the study area boundary than they are to another point in the pattern. This disregard factor results in reducing the number of distances that can be measured. Since this method results in a loss of information, it

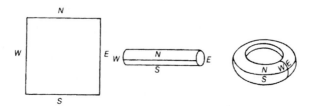

Fig. 5.2 Creation of a torus to correct for edge effects. Adopted from Boots and Getis (1988).

is not appropriate when the number of points being analyzed is small. It is only useful when the number of points is so large that the loss of information is not critical.

Finally, Donnelly (1978) has proposed adding a correction factor to the nearest neighbor equation to account for the boundary effects. It is especially useful when the disregard and buffer strategies previously mentioned reduce the number of distances prohibitively. Donnelly (1978) has shown that when N is greater than seven and the study area is not highly irregular, the value of E(di) is approximated by:

$$E(di) = 0.5 \sqrt{(A/N)} + (0.041/\sqrt{N}) \, B/N$$

And:

$$Var(d) = 0.070 \, A/N2 + 0.037 \, B \, \sqrt{(A/N5)}$$

Where:

E(di) is the correction factor to be added to the Nearest Neighbor value.
B is the length of the perimeter of the study area.
A is the size of the area of study.
N is the number of points in the area.

Since these equations were obtained by examining simulated point patterns in study areas of various shapes including circles, ellipses, squares, and rectangles, they should not be used for irregularly shaped study areas.

These are possible solutions to problems associated with the analysis of a point pattern that has boundaries or edges that truncate the data. The solutions include disregard, buffering, cartographic, and statistical methods. Except for the case of buffering, the size of the region under analysis remains the same. In the following section, we address the issue of what happens when the size of the region or regions under analysis change in size. More directly, what happens when the units of aggregation that the data are collected within change during or between analyses. This is the problem associated with the aggregation of data that is referred to as the Modifiable Aerial Unit Problem or MAUP.

Modifiable Aerial Unit Problem

Another set of problems is associated with the aggregation and disaggregation of data. An example was mentioned above when a new region is created by buffering in from an original region for Nearest Neighbor Analysis. If the data are clustered in space, Fig. 5.3 illustrates that drawing a smaller region may result in a clustered spatial pattern becoming a random or uniform spatial pattern when the boundary changes from the outer boundary to the inner boundary which bounds less space. Modifying the size of the region almost always affects such measures as density

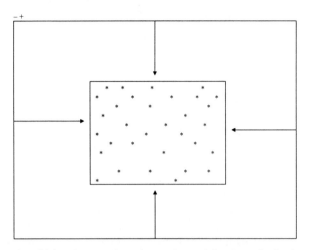

Fig. 5.3 Effect of modifying the area of a region on the spatial pattern of point data

A							B					
1	7	3	5	7	5		1	7	3	5	7	5
								4.50		3.75		5.75
3	7	3	3	3	8		3	7	3	3	3	8
4	9	5	8	4	2		4	9	5	8	4	2
								6.25		5.00		3.50
6	6	7	0	0	8		6	6	7	0	0	8
9	3	4	5	2	7		9	3	4	5	2	7
								4.50		5.00		4.75
5	1	3	8	6	4		5	1	3	8	6	4

Fig. 5.4 Problems of aggregation. The numbers in **A** indicate the number of drug sales arrests per street face. The center number in **B** is the average number of drug sales arrests per block when four street faces are aggregated together. Note that the average masks a considerable amount of variation
Adopted from Yeates (1974).

and degree of clustering of points in space. As will be demonstrated later, it also affects the mean and standard deviation of the data.

Another aspect of the Modifiable Area Unit problem is that as the level of aggregation increases, the more likely it is that variables being analyzed will be significantly associated. In other words, the larger the level of aggregation, the more likely it is that two or more variables will be statistically significantly related. This is because the variance in the data decreases as the level of aggregation increases. This will be discussed more fully in Fig. 5.4 below.

The Modifiable Area Unit problem is best addressed when the boundaries are first drawn. Again, the boundaries should be drawn so that between region variance is maximized and within region variance is minimized. Even so, the analyst must keep in mind that patterns are impacted by the way regions are constructed. In this case, analysis might proceed at several levels of aggregation to determine the impact of regionalization and the MAUP on observed spatial statistics. This is especially important with the increased use of Geographic Information Systems (GIS) that allow new regions to be created easily by buffering and overlaying of spaces.

Units of Analysis and Statistical Criteria

Figure 5.4 illustrates the effect of aggregating point patterns into space. These aggregations may conceal more information than they reveal. For example, in Fig. 5.4A, we depict the number of arrests for illegal drug sales by street face (one side of a street to each intersection). Notice that the variation is quite large. The variance is 6.01. There are several streets containing zero to three, and seven to nine values. In Fig. 5.4B, these street faces have been aggregated into blocks, each cell containing four street faces.

The bold number in the center is the average number of arrests for illegal drug sales per city block (the four street faces one would encounter if one were always to turn to the left at each intersection as they walked around a city block). The extreme values no longer exist in these means. The averages are similar, varying from a low of 3.75 to a high of 6.25 with the variance of these averages being 0.71. Therefore, the effect of this aggregation is to reduce the variance since like areas were not aggregated and separated from unalike areas, as is the goal of regionalization. The aggregation of the data has, in this case, concealed a large amount of information. If it were possible to group the data into spatially contiguous units in such a way as to minimize the variance within each block, and to maximize the variance between blocks, then the spatial variance in the data would be preserved. This rarely can be done perfectly so that in almost all cases, aggregation results in the loss of variance and units of analysis become more similar, although the grand mean value remains the same.

Units of analysis cause potential problems related to the requirements of various statistical techniques. For example, Ordinary Least Squares (OLS) regression analysis requires normally distributed data. If the data are skewed, the analyst will receive misleading results. Standard errors tend to be overestimated leading to problems of accurately interpreting the level of significance and the magnitude of a parameter. However, with the disaggregation possible with GIS, data tends to become more skewed toward zero values as spaces become smaller and smaller.

GIS Enhanced Spatial Data

Most research in criminology has used spatial units that are convenient such as census boundaries, police districts, and postal codes. If data were not available at these units of analysis, it was simply added as counts – the number of a certain feature located in the administrative units. There are several problems with this simple addition. First, it assumes that the impact of the feature is uniform across the spatial unit. Secondly, a feature near a boundary of a unit is assumed to have no impact on the surrounding spatial unit. Finally, the impact is assumed to be the same even if spatial units vary in size. For example, five taverns are assumed to have the same impact on a large spatial unit as a small one. These problems can be addressed with the use of a GIS system. Two methods are discussed: the first is termed GIS Enhanced Census Spatial Units; the second is termed Census Enhanced GIS Spatial Units.

GIS Enhanced Census Spatial Units

The following example explains how GIS can be used to enhance census spatial units. Figure 5.5 depicts two census tracts, 1 and 2 respectively. As explained above, in traditional analysis before the advent of GIS, place features were added to the census tract data in the following manner. Census tract 1 contains all the census data for the tract and also contains two bars and a check cashing center. Census tract 2 contains only one check cashing center and no bars although one exists very near its boundary with Census tract 1. Furthermore, the impact of these features is assumed to be uniformly distributed across the census tracts although the bar is located at the extreme right hand side of Census tract 1. It is assumed to have no impact on Census tract 2 although it is very near its left hand boundary. At this level of aggregation, if dependent variables are nearly normally distributed, OLS analysis is appropriate.

With the use of GIS, the problem of assuming the same amount of effect from each built facility no matter the relative size of the census tract, and the problem of no effect of a facility located near the boundary but in another census tract can be addressed. In this case, it is assumed and can be computed with Location Quotients (Rengert et al. 2005) that the facilities have a spatial impact beyond their places in space. For example, alcohol-impaired customers leaving a bar may attract strong-armed robbers (Roncek and Maier 1991). Patrons of check cashing stores often

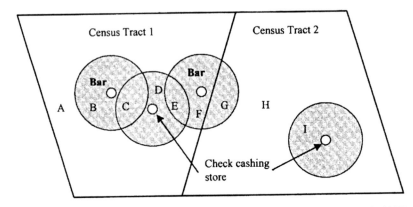

Fig. 5.5 Creating new geographies using census material. Adapted from Rengert et al. (2005).

have drug dependencies and attract illegal drug dealers (Rengert 1996). Buffers can be constructed around each facility to the extent that they negatively affect their surroundings. That is, census tract data can be enhanced by computing the proportion of the area within a census tract that is also within the buffer of a facility. In this case, small census tracts will have more of their area covered than a larger census tract with an equal number of facilities. Furthermore, a facility may impact a census tract even if it is not located in that tract. For example, Census tract 1 in Fig. 5.5 may have 40 percent of its area within the buffers of a bar and twenty percent of its area within the buffer of a check cashing store. Census tract 2 may have 20 percent of its area within the buffer of a check cashing store and seven percent of its area within the buffer of a bar although a bar does not exist within the census tract. Again, statistical techniques requiring a nearly normal distribution may be appropriate if the dependent variable has a nearly normal distribution.

This technique addresses the problem of the original assumption that neighboring census tracts are not influenced even though a facility may exist very near its boundary. It also addresses the idea that the impact of the facilities depends on the proportion of the census tract that is covered by the buffers around the facilities. However, it does not address the fact that the aerial impact of the facilities is assumed to be uniformly distributed across the census tract. The analyst must rely on a modification of boundaries originally created by the census bureau for this analysis. This technique is termed Census Enhanced GIS Spatial Units.

Census Enhanced GIS Spatial Units

Using GIS, new spatial units can be created that do not rely entirely on census boundary lines. In this case, rather than aggregating up to the census tract by adding non-census information to the census data, census data are added to the new spatial units created by the buffers and their overlays. For example, in Fig. 5.5, new spatial units are created in this manner. Region A has the characteristics of census tract 1 with no impact from a built facility. Region B has the characteristics of census tract 1, plus the impact of a bar. Region C has the characteristics of census tract 1, plus the impact of a bar, and a check cashing store. Region D has the characteristics of census tract 1, plus the impact of a check cashing store. Region E has the characteristics of census tract 1, plus the impact of a bar and a check cashing store, and region F has the characteristics of census tract 1, plus the impact from a bar. Then we move to census tract 2. Region G has the characteristics of census tract 2, plus the impact of a bar, region H has only the characteristics of census tract 2, and finally, region I has the characteristics of census tract 2, plus the impact of a check cashing store.

These new boundaries of the new spatial units can circumscribe rather small spaces. Therefore, a dependent variable is not likely to be normally distributed across the regions. Rather, it will be skewed with an abundance of areas with zero values in the dependent variable. In this case, the requirements of statistical techniques that a normal distribution of the dependent variable exists are violated. A statistical technique that is designed to analyze a skewed distribution with an abundance of zeros is required. For example, a Zero Inflated Poisson (ZIP) model assumes that an overabundance of zero values exist in the dependent variable (Zorn 1998).

In general, when data are disaggregated using GIS, the mean, variance, and standard deviation of the dependent variable become smaller. In the following example, this issue is examined using data on illegal drug sales, census boundaries, and boundaries created by buffering around built facilities and adding Census data to the new spatial units to create new geographies with GIS.

Aerial Units and Statistical Analysis

To begin, we will examine what happens when using empirical data if aerial units of analysis are disaggregated from census tracts to smaller block group units, and how this affects the mean and standard deviation during analysis. Using the 29 census tracts in Wilmington, Delaware, the mean number of drug sales arrests per census tract over a ten-year period is 263.36. The standard deviation of the distribution is 286.97. The standard deviation is larger than the mean. This indicates that there is a high degree of spatial dispersion in drug sales arrests in Wilmington at the census tract level.

When the data are disaggregated to the 93 block groups in Wilmington, Delaware, the mean number of illegal drug sales arrests over the ten-year period decreases to 73 while the standard deviation decreases to 106.11. Again, the standard deviation is larger than the mean and both are less than the example at the census tract level.

Our next step is to create new spatial units by buffering around built facilities within the city of Wilmington that may attract illegal drug dealers and combine this with the census block group boundaries as was done in Rengert et al. 2005. Here we can begin to answer the question of what happens when new spatial units are created and spatial data are attached to these new spatial units rather than to rely on boundaries created by the Census Bureau. When the new geographies are created by overlaying the boundaries of the census block groups on the buffers around built facilities that attract illegal drug dealers, the mean number of drug sales arrests drops to 5.2 while the standard deviation decreases to 16.98. When these two statistics are compared, it is clear that there is a highly dispersed distribution that likely contains an abundance of zero values. In fact, when the new boundaries are created, there are a total of 1,310 new areas of which 831 have no drug sales arrests in them. Clearly this is a zero inflated distribution that requires statistical techniques that do not assume a normal distribution in the data.

Finally, a further problem associated with using different levels of aggregation to analyze the same data is that different variables may become significant at different levels of aggregation. As the units of analysis become larger, there is a tendency for more variables to be statistically significantly associated. Chainey and Ratcliffe (2005) demonstrate how this occurs in Great Britain while Rengert et al. (2005) demonstrate how this occurs in the United States. Since the variance changes with different levels of aggregation, it is to be expected that different explanatory variables will gain and lose significance. Therefore, the meaning of variables is generally aggregation dependent. What is significant at one level of aggregation may be insignificant at another level of aggregation. This is the idea underlying hierarchical linear models that explicitly analyze varying units of analysis (Snijders and Bosker 1999). In this case, the spatial units are nested with the smaller units contained within the larger units. However, different variables become significant with changes in the size of the units of analysis even though the same study area is used.

Of course, how the regions are constructed plays a large part in this since boundaries may contain or split spatial clusters of an independent variable. One must be careful that the way boundaries are drawn do not obscure spatial patterns or lead to misleading results. Most important, the theory being analyzed needs to be reflected in the manner in which the data are managed including how it is regionalized. This is to say that micro-level theories should be analyzed with micro-level regionalization and macro-level theories with macro-level regionalization. Clearly, how we draw our boundaries in our regionalization of the data is an important aspect of the total analysis package.

Conclusions

The purpose of this chapter was to explore the consequences of aggregating data into areal units. Although data may be initially collected as points in space, it is commonly aggregated into areal units for administrative reasons as well as for purposes of analysis. Geographic analysis attempts to explain why one phenomenon is spatially associated with the spatial arrangement of another phenomena. The interpretation of the nature of this association can be impacted by the manner that data are aggregated into spatial units.

There are a variety of problems and concerns that occur when point patterns of place data are aggregated into areal units. Other problems occur when space data are disaggregated so that many places have zero values of the dependent variable. These problems and concerns are classified into problems associated with boundaries created for other than research purposes, edge problems associated with spatially truncated data, modifiable aerial unit problem associated with dispersion metrics changing as aerial boundaries change, and the dispersion of data and the appropriate statistical model to use as aerial units change in size. Possible solutions to these problems are addressed. Many of these solutions have been discussed in previous research.

A new set of problems arise with the increasing use of GIS to draw new boundaries rather than rely on data provided from administrative units. This new GIS data tends to be skewed as smaller units of analysis are created. It deviates from a normal distribution required for OLS analysis. For example, as areal units are disaggregated into smaller units of analysis using GIS, the mean also decreases and the number of units with zero values on the dependent variable increases so that the analyst must carefully select the appropriate technique to use when analyzing data at various units of spatial aggregation. Rather than relying on OLS analysis, newer methods that account for skewed data such as ZIP models are more appropriate.

This chapter concludes with the admonition that when spatial analysis is conducted, the analyst should not ignore space; that is, the spatial units that data are aggregated into and the impact of this choice on the interpretation of findings. Just as several independent variables are considered to determine whether they have statistical significance, perhaps the spatial units of analysis should be considered to determine whether the choice of which level and type of aggregation used has biased our analysis.

References

Boots, B., & Getis, A. (1988). *Point pattern analysis*. Beverly Hills, CA: Sage Publications.

Chainey, S., & Ratcliffe, J. (2005). *GIS and crime mapping*. London: John Wiley & Sons.

Dacey, M. (1975). Evaluation of the Poisson approximation to measures of the random pattern in a square. *Geographical Analysis*, 7, 351–367.

Donnelly, K. (1978). Simulations to determine the variance and edge effects of total nearest-neighbor distance. In: I. Hodder (Ed.), *Simulation methods in archaeology* (pp. 91–95). Cambridge: Cambridge University Press.

Griffith, D., & Amrheim, C. (1983). An evaluation of correction techniques for boundary effects in spatial statistical analysis: Traditional methods. *Geographical Analysis*, 15, 352–360.

Reboussin, R., Warren, J., & Hazelwood, R. (1995). Mapless mapping in analyzing the spatial distribution of serial rapes. In: C. Block, M. Dabdoub, & S. Fregley (Eds.), *Crime analysis through computer mapping* (pp. 69–74). Washington, DC: Police Executive Research Forum.

Rengert, G. (1996). *The geography of illegal drugs*. Boulder, CO: Westview Press.

Rengert, G., Ratcliffe, J., & Chakravorty, S. (2005). *Policing illegal drug markets: Geographic approaches to crime reduction*. Monsey, NY: Criminal Justice Press.

Roncek, D., & Maier, P. (1991). Bars, blocks and crimes revisited: Linking the theory of routine activities to the empiricism of 'hot spots.' *Criminology*, 29(4), 725–753.

Shaw, C., & McKay, H. (1942). *Juvenile delinquency and urban areas: A study of rates of delinquents in relation to different characteristics of local communities in American cities.* Chicago, IL: University of Chicago Press.

Snijders, T., & Bosker, R. (1999). *Multilevel analysis: An introduction to basic and advanced multilevel modeling.* London: Sage Publications.

Tobler, W. (1970). A computer model simulation of urban growth in the Detroit region. *Economic Geography*, 46(2), 234–240.

Yeates, M. (1974). *An introduction to quantitative analysis in human geography.* New York: McGraw Hill Publications.

Zorn, C. (1998). An analytic and empirical examination of zero-inflated and hurdle Poisson specifications. *Sociological Methods and Research*, 26(3), 368–400.

Chapter 6
Waves, Particles, and Crime

Michael D. Maltz

Abstract One sees different features from different points of view. Flying over a region provides a view of geographical and geological features not visible from the ground, while ground-level observations show details not apparent from the air. Similarly, different units of analysis applied to crime data can bring out different patterns in crime. This chapter describes how two different units of time, one measured in years, the other in weeks, can be used to extract two different types of geographical patterns. One, the "wave" analysis, traces the actions of whole groups over a long time period. In particular, it should be of use in investigating the effect of in- or out-migration of racial/ethnic groups in neighborhoods in a metropolitan area and the effect that these population shifts have on crime. The "particle" analysis, on the other hand, focuses on the career trajectories of individuals, from an early age, as they experience noteworthy events during their lives and move (or are moved) from place to place in a city. This view of a neighborhood's at-risk youths can be used to describe the role of residential mobility in crime.

Preliminary Considerations

The choice of unit of analysis has statistical consequences. This is especially true in mapping crime over time: a geographical unit that is too small will not have enough activity to permit much generalization, and one that is too large will not provide sufficient discrimination. But the choice of unit of analysis used can have ethical consequences as well. There is a great deal of important variation in neighborhood-level studies that is often blurred over:

> "[I]n driving through the neighborhood in question I was struck by the great degree of deterioration of the housing stock on all blockfaces, except those that sported "Neighborhood Watch" signs: "these were relatively untouched by urban decay. To my mind, aggregating

M.D. Maltz
Criminal Justice Research Center, The Ohio State University, Columbus, OH, and University of Illinois at Chicago, IL, USA
e-mail: mdm@sociology.osu.edu

D. Weisburd et al. (eds.), *Putting Crime in its Place*,
DOI 10.1007/978-0-387-09688-9_6, © Springer Science+Business Media, LLC 2009

these blockfaces with the adjacent blockfaces in some ways devalues the efforts of these residents, by lumping them in statistically with their less diligent neighbors. Nor is it necessarily a wise statistical practice to ignore this variation" (Maltz 1996).[1]

The blockface is not often used as a unit of analysis for two reasons: first, as noted above, it may be too small; and second, there is very little block-level information available from the census. But if distinct patterns emerge at the blockface level that are not apparent at higher levels of aggregation, it may be better to tailor the methods to the data rather than the data to the methods.

Not only is the size of the geographical unit of analysis important, so is the scope of the crimes included in the analysis. One aspect of the role of units of analysis that is not explored in this chapter, but is of major importance, is the crime itself. Crime categories are based on legal definitions, which are overly broad for understanding the nature of crime in a community. For example, in the U.S. sex crimes have been much in the news of late, as legislatures try to prevent sexual predators from living in areas near places where children congregate. States and cities have created map-based databases showing (or purporting to show[2]) where these offenders live. No distinction is made, however, between pedophiles and people convicted of other sex crimes like date rape or acquaintance rape (or even stranger rape), and these latter offenders rarely if ever overlap with the former and pose a danger to school children (Levenson and Hern 2007). Although crime analysts are made aware of the differences within crime categories by reading the offense reports and looking for commonalities, when these incidents get translated into a mapping program or, even worse, a statistical package, there often is no way of easily distinguishing crimes of the same type, but with different etiologies, from each other. This has a tendency to diminish the utility of crime analysis, the very opposite of the goal of using these techniques.

It is with this prologue that I would like to describe how the selection of appropriate units of analysis in crime mapping can help in gaining insights beyond the tactical. In tactical situations, we have seen crime mapping put to good use in geographic profiling of offenders and looking for crime patterns (e.g., Brantingham and Brantingham 1984, 1993); in studying the "journey to crime" (e.g., Rengert & Wasilchick 1985; Rengert et al. 1999); in studying the "foraging patterns" of serial killers and rapists (e.g., Rossmo 1995, 1999); in the investigation of "hot spots" of crime and drug dealing (e.g., Weisburd and Green 1993, 1995). In all of these cases, the space- and time-related aspects of the relevant crimes are considered, since the goal is to trace the behavior of individuals as they commit sequences of (what appear to be) related crimes. The supposition is that the crime-space-time patterns will recur, or will provide information about future recurrences by the same offenders or groups, as to when (time) and where (space) they might occur.

---

[1] Block-to-block variation in crime was also noted (more quantitatively) by Weisburd et al. (2004).
[2] There are major errors in many of these databases (Monmonier 2002, p. 7).

The time dimension is, in most cases, relatively short-term, covering intervals that are normally measured in months, or perhaps one or two years.[3] Using a longer time span, however, crime mapping can be used to study other issues of theoretical interest to policy analysts and criminologists, uses that are no less important than tactical uses.

In this chapter, I describe two different areas in which crime mapping can also prove useful, each using different units of analysis and different time intervals. For lack of better terms, I borrow from physics and consider "wave" and "particle" analyses of geographic crime data. As might be inferred, a wave analysis looks at large numbers of crimes committed in a region (city blocks), and a particle analysis traces individual criminality. The wave analysis is conducted over relatively long periods of time, measured in several years rather than days, weeks, or months, while the particle analysis may cover a few years.

In both cases, however, there is a departure from standard social science methodology. The blocks and individuals that are studied are not sampled; rather, (for blocks) they are contiguous and (for individuals) they live on contiguous blocks. Sampling breaks up the "fine structure" of the behavior, the relationship between activity on one block and activity on other blocks, or between one individual and other individuals.

Tracing crime patterns over space is facilitated by mapping and geographic information systems (GIS), and tracing them over time can be accomplished by animating the maps, i.e., by taking snapshots of crime patterns at different time periods and displaying them sequentially on a computer. Chronological animation of such data provides insight into patterns of activity that are not otherwise apparent. Lodka and Verma (1999) describe how Virtual Reality Modeling Language (VRML) can be used to animate a "pin map" of crime in Vancouver, permitting the user to see how crime hot spots evolve over time. And no one who has seen Hans Rosling's (2006, 2007) parsing of UN health and economic data (using the software Gapminder – see www.gapminder.org) can deny the utility of such animation. This paper is an attempt to show how animation might also be applied to "wave" and "particle" crime data.[4]

I focus on this type of analysis to show areas in which the standard analytic approaches to studying crime data may be deficient. These approaches ordinarily rely on assumptions (often ignored) about linearity, normality, and independence of the data, which are rarely the case in the social sciences. Visualizing data, on the other hand, holds out the promise of finding patterns in the data that do not adhere to these assumptions, and can lead to the development of new statistical tools that are not dependent on them.

I first discuss the concept of wave-particle duality in the physical world. I then show how it can be related to criminal activity. The data available for these types of analyses are then described. I end with a discussion of the potential benefits of taking a longer-term view of the geography of crime.

---

[3] Some serial murderers and rapists do operate for decades, but these are rare – as far as we know.

[4] Obviously, in a book chapter it is not possible to display animated crime maps. Perhaps the next generation of e-books will permit insertions of this sort!

Waves and Particles in the Physical World

Many people have heard of the wave-particle duality in physics, but are unclear as to what it means. In classical optics, a continuous beam of light can be studied as a wave phenomenon, where it is refracted and reflected using lenses and prisms. The characteristics of light are usually described in terms of its wavelength or its frequency: light waves vibrate at frequencies measured in terahertz, thousands of billions of times each second.

Light can also be studied by considering the characteristics of the individual particles, the photons, which are packets of pure energy. Individual photons can be detected by photoelectric devices, but the photons behave as (or can be treated as) waves when they pass through a diffraction grating. Thus, a light wave traces out the aggregate activity of a collection of particles.

This duality is present in other areas as well. Wind, for example, is merely an aggregation of molecules that, on average, move in a particular direction with a particular velocity. Yet the individual particles that, in aggregate, become the wind, the molecules of air, can each move in entirely different directions with entirely different velocities.[5] In essence, the wind's behavior is a statistical property of an ensemble of particles, their average behavior.

The average properties of wind are, however, useful. When we measure the wind's velocity and direction, we can use these quantities to predict its direction and velocity at a future time. But an extremely small number of the gas molecules in the wind are moving in that direction at that velocity; rather, they are ricocheting against each other, moving in all different directions and velocities. Their individual trajectories are not predictable,[6] even though their aggregate behavior can be predicted.

Waves and Particles in Human Interactions

Some human behaviors can be viewed in the same way. Road traffic can be seen as either particle or wave motion, depending on the volume of traffic. As traffic builds it becomes more wavelike in its behavior. From the air one can see the effect of the sudden braking of a car in heavy traffic. Even if that car subsequently continues on at its previous speed, it propagates a backward wave: the cars immediately behind it brake sharply (assuming no "ricocheting"), then continue as before, but this action starts a wave of braking cars behind them that continues far longer (in both time and distance) than the action that initiated it.

---

[5] This is not true of photons, which all travel at the speed of light.

[6] They are not even theoretically predictable. Heisenberg's Uncertainty Principle comes into play; we cannot know the exact position and momentum (the product of mass and velocity) of any single particle at the same time, let alone a collection of them.

Moreover, as traffic builds the probability of a collision increases. We cannot predict which particle, in this case, which impatient driver, will collide with another particle – say, a car whose driver is distracted by a conversation with a passenger or on a cell phone. We know, however, that the number of possible interactions of this nature increases as traffic builds.[7]

In some sense one can see the same wave-particle duality in analyzing crime as either a sociological-structural (wave) or psychological-individual (particle) phenomenon. A region may experience a wavelike increase in crime due to, say, a downturn in the economy[8], a social-structural cause; but why this causes Person A, and not Person B, to commit crimes concerns the state of mind of the individuals in question, requiring the analyst to consider the trajectories of individual "particles."

Crime and Wave Analysis

As with the wind and with traffic, the aggregate behavior of individuals in a neighborhood can be viewed as a wave. Aggregating, of course, precludes viewing the "fine structure" of the wave, but different features can be seen at this level of analysis. Determining when (or whether) to move from the particle (individual) to the wave (aggregate) level of analysis depends in part on the number of particles involved and in part on the focus of the analysis.

In the context of crime, wave analysis traces the actions of whole groups over a long time period. In particular, it should be of use in investigating the effect of in- or out-migration of racial/ethnic groups in neighborhoods in a metropolitan area and the effect that these population shifts have on crime.

Analyses of this sort may be of more than just theoretical benefit. Many countries are currently experiencing tensions arising from the immigration of other racial and ethnic groups into countries that had once been fairly homogeneous. One manifestation of these tensions is the clustering of crime in neighborhoods that are undergoing transition.

The phenomenon of "crime waves" in the context of changing neighborhoods was an aspect of the Chicago School of Sociology (Park and Burgess 1921; Sellin 1938; Shaw and McKay 1942). One has to be careful, however, about how the phenomenon is interpreted; too often the fear of a crime wave has resulted in an older crop of immigrants taking action against the newest wave. The report, *Crime and the Foreign Born*, of the National Commission on Law Observance and Enforcement (1931), documents earlier examples: as Cohen (1931) noted,

> "... the continued indictment for criminality of those just arrived is as old as the history of our country, and has been directed, during each period, with greatest vehemence against

---

[7] Until, of course, gridlock occurs, when none of the particles can move!

[8] "The economy" is, of course, a wave construct, based on the individual (particle) decisions of thousands of firms and individuals reacting to changes in their expenses, in their markets, and in the cost of money.

that national group whose migration here has been most recent and most marked. The Irish, Germans, Italians, and Mexicans, to mention only some of the outstanding cases, have each in turn been charged with a high susceptibility to crime."

At first the new arrivals may integrate unobtrusively into the neighborhood. At a certain point, however, a threshold is reached (Granovetter 1978; see also Crane 1991) which can change the former social structure of the neighborhood, leading to instability.

Already under some stress, these neighborhoods may face the additional burden of racial and ethnic tension. This tension can manifest itself as crime, either against the newcomers or by them, or both. Thus, a "crime wave" may result from this situation. One can visualize a wave of one ethnic group moving into a neighborhood consisting of members of other, usually more settled and (relatively) wealthier, ethnic groups, creating "turbulence" in the form of crime.

Figure 6.1 shows a (hypothetical) chronological trajectory of a neighborhood (actually, two contiguous neighborhoods)[9], superimposing crime contours on the changing ethnic mix. At first the immigrants move into a single neighborhood consisting of a few contiguous blocks (1a). The crime rate in this neighborhood is not much different than the crime rate in another neighborhood on the other side of a major artery. A slow (1b), then rapid (1c) expansion of immigrants moving into the neighborhood is accompanied by an increase in crime in the impacted neighborhood, and a further increase in immigration results in a spreading of both immigrants and crime across the artery, affecting that neighborhood's crime rate as well.

These types of phenomena occur during both internal and external migrations. They occurred as blacks from the American South moved north (Lemann 1991);[10] as people from the Caribbean and East Asian Commonwealth countries emigrated to England (Hatton and Price 1999); as various ethnic groups settled in the Netherlands (Junger and Polder 1992); and as North Africans moved to France (Zauberman and Lévy 2003). Lim et al. (2007) show how similar phenomena are found in ethnic/cultural violence (as in Serbia and India, noting that "geography is an important

[9] How does one define a neighborhood? Weisburd and Green (1995) had the same difficulty in defining a drug "hot spot," which varied by type of drug and time of day. The definition of "neighborhood" is also variable, a social-geographic "unit of analysis" that depends on the location of major streets and commercial strips, and on the racial/ethnic mix (and stability of that mix) of the area in question.

[10] During a post-doctoral year I spent in 1963–64 at the Technical University of Denmark, my colleagues there often criticized the United States about the plight of Negroes (as Blacks were then called) in the U.S. At first I felt uncomfortable about it, and pointed out that civil rights legislation was being considered (which subsequently passed). Then I noticed that virtually all of the menial jobs in Denmark were being handled by Greenlanders, who are Danish citizens but who, at that time, apparently were considered inferior by most mainland Danes – Greenland was then and is now a coequal province of Denmark. When I asked my colleagues about this situation, they became noticeably quiet, and never again spoke to me about U.S. civil rights. This anecdote can doubtless be repeated in other countries as well, as class, race, ethnicity, and even language proficiency and accents (Baugh 2000) are used to distinguish "us" from "them."

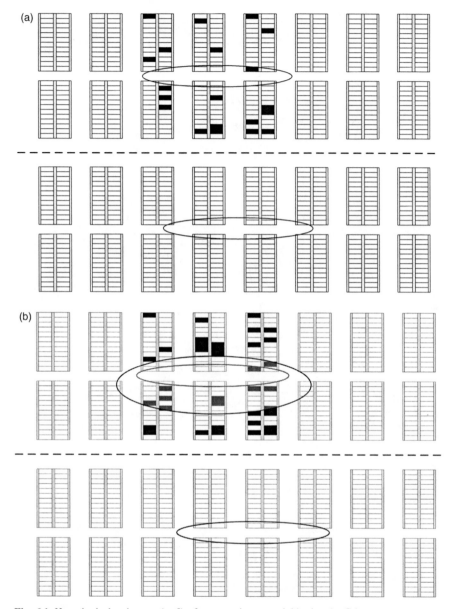

Fig. 6.1 Hypothetical trajectory (**a–d**) of two contiguous neighborhoods. Crime contours super-imposed on changing ethnic mix

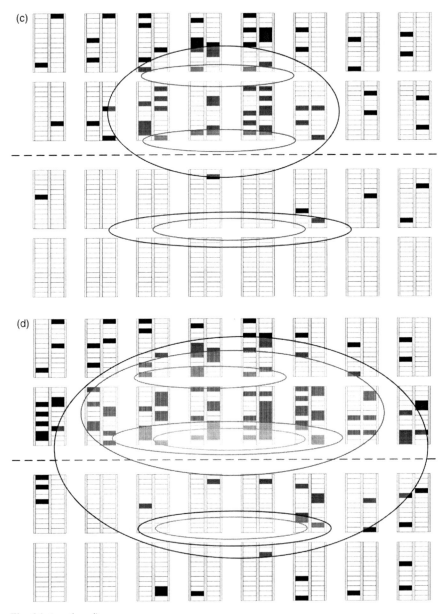

Fig. 6.1 (continued)

aspect of the dimensions of social space ... and other aspects of social behavior (e.g., isolationism, conformity, as well as violence) are correlated to it."

Some countries (and some cities within the countries) have been more successful than others in reducing ethnic tensions in such neighborhoods. It could be very useful to have a visual portrait of the extent and intensity of such waves in different contexts, depicting how it builds up, how long it lasts, who are the primary offenders and victims, and how crime fluctuates over time as the neighborhoods either change their composition or develop better methods of coping with the tensions that provoked the crime wave.

The above description is of a type of wave that occurs as a neighborhood deteriorates. Another wave-like phenomenon that may occur in urban neighborhoods has to do with gentrification, that is, with neighborhoods on the way up (Van Wilsem et al. 2006). "Urban homesteaders" may find it advantageous to move into older, deteriorated neighborhoods because of the lower cost of housing. They then make improvements to the housing stock, at the same time bringing a certain measure of wealth into a poor neighborhood. This can also lead to increases in crime.[11]

Prior studies on the relationship between neighborhoods and crime have shown varying effects. Using data from that Pittsburgh Youth Study, Peeples and Loeber (1994) found that neighborhood characteristics were more important than race in delinquency rates. Data from the same study were subsequently analyzed by Wikström and Loeber (2000), who found that neighborhood characteristics played a part in the delinquency of late-onset offenders, but not early-onset offenders. While these studies show the effect of neighborhood characteristics (determined at one point in time) on (juvenile) offenders, they do not show the effect of changing neighborhood characteristics on offending.[12]

That is, as a new racial or ethnic (or income) group moves into a previously (relatively) stable neighborhood, it can have some foreseen but unwanted consequences. What happens to crime in that neighborhood and in surrounding neighborhoods? Are there particular types of crimes that increase or decrease and to what extent? Is there a difference between crime patterns (or routine activities) in neighborhoods that are on the way up (gentrifying) and neighborhoods that are on the way down (decaying)? How does the transportation network affect crime in neighboring areas? How do zoning and land use affect crime? Are there local policies with regard to employment, schools, welfare, etc., that seem to change the dynamic, either ameliorating or exacerbating intergroup tensions? Detailing the history of such crime waves may be helpful in developing policies to reduce their impact.[13]

---

[11] Weisburd (1989) describes a more confrontational "gentrification" process that occurred in the West Bank after 1967.

[12] Green et al. (1998) document the impact of demographic change on racially motivated crime against minorities.

[13] One reviewer pointed out that not all crime waves are tied to this type of social disruption. Long-term changes such as suburbanization and women's entry into the labor market also have produced surges in criminal activity (Cohen and Felson 1979). LaFree and Drass (2002) provide

Crime and Particle Analysis

With respect to crime, the particle analysis focuses on the career trajectories of individuals, from an early age, as they experience noteworthy events[14] during their lives and move (or are moved) from place to place in a city. Residential instability is all too common an experience of youths in the U.S. in low-income areas, as the fortunes of their parents change over time and they are forced to move, leaving schools and friends behind. One question that arises is the role of residential mobility in criminality. I am especially interested in situations in which youths are moved into and/or out of poverty-ridden neighborhoods: Does residential instability affect their delinquent behavior, and if so, how?[15]

These changes are often due to divorce and separation which can have major psychological consequences for children (both positive and negative; see McCord, 1990, p. 120), as parents' fortunes change over time. They can have financial consequences as well, often causing the care-providing parents (usually the mothers) to move to less desirable neighborhoods where the schools are not as good and the dropout rate is high. The crime and delinquency rates are often correspondingly high, and the influence of gangs and peers with low life expectations can turn a youth toward delinquent behavior.

Some parents, seeing this occurring in their children, may decide to move to what they consider to be a safer neighborhood, or may send their at-risk children to live with relatives elsewhere. Such moves, however, may not accomplish what parents had expected: the youths who are moved may just bring their antisocial activities to the new neighborhood. In other words, residential mobility may not have a single effect.[16] Some factors that may make a difference are the youths' age at the time; the behavior of their peers; the length of time spent in that neighborhood; the number and ages and criminal involvement of siblings; and the "collective efficacy" (Sampson et al. 1997) of the neighborhoods from which they came and to which they moved.

I conducted a preliminary exploration of this type of particle analysis earlier (Maltz 1996). It focused on tracing the life course of youths who attended an

---

evidence that modernization of economies and other major social changes may affect national homicide rates.

[14] These events may include crimes and arrests, but also employment, military service, pregnancies and births, and other significant life occurrences (Sampson and Laub 1993; Maltz and Mullany 2000).

[15] There are doubtless different kinds of mobility that affect youths differently. For example, the children of US military personnel, so-called "army brats," also move around a lot, but they may not have the same reaction to residence change.

[16] I have seen examples of both of these effects among Mexican-Americans in Chicago. Children who became involved in gangs have been pulled out of school in Chicago and returned to their parents' village in Mexico with their families, where they eventually "straightened out" and returned to Chicago. But other nearby villages have experienced gang activity, an unwanted import from the United States. And the gang Mara Salvatrucha 13 began in Los Angeles among Salvadoran youths but spread to El Salvador when they returned there.

elementary school in a high-risk area of Chicago and were born in the years 1970–1974. It showed that this type of analysis can be accomplished to a great extent using data collected by public agencies. Data on the youths and their families were obtained from the schools, police, and juvenile court. They were combined and used to trace the trajectory of youths as they and their families negotiated their way through life and the city. Even with this limited additional information (schools and juvenile court records), it provided insight into the dynamics and sequencing of events in a youth's life that could lead to delinquent behavior. We extended this type of analysis by incorporating additional domains (employment, drug use, etc.) in the life course trajectories (Maltz and Mullany 2000). However, both of these studies focused on the behavior of a very small number of individuals; neither study was able to show how co-offending patterns might develop.

Note the two major differences between this type of analysis and standard crime analysis. First, the time period in question is *decades long*, much longer than standard crime analysis. Second, it integrates the information from *a number of different sources*, not just from police data.

There is also a difference between this type of analysis and standard academic analysis. Studies that attempt to show the relationship between offending behavior and individual and community characteristics normally use *a sampling strategy based on randomization*. One drawback is that *youths usually commit crimes in groups* (Zimring 1981; Reiss 1986, 1988; Reiss and Farrington 1991), and they normally live in the same neighborhood. Sampling precludes studying these groups *as groups*, to investigate how the offending careers of youths interact, since it is hardly likely that all youths in a network will be in a randomly selected sample. Of course, this type of study focuses on only one neighborhood, while most academic analyses attempt to determine the effect of differences in neighborhood characteristics by including a handful of variables that purport to characterize each of the youths' neighborhoods. But these cross-sectional studies overlook the fact that the social ecology of different neighborhoods, even those that appear to share the same characteristics, can be entirely different (Stark 1987).[17]

We can even go further with this type of particle analysis. Note that, unlike air molecules, the "crime particles" are not independent of one another. Given the appropriate data on crimes and residences, we could follow all of a neighborhood's youths as they commit crimes either alone or in concert with others, and even follow their behavior as they change residences. Although not all of their delinquent acts will be captured, a picture played over time, showing the geographical context of their residences and their targets, may provide additional insight into some of the dynamics of crime and criminality that are obscured by sampling and cross-sectional analyses.

Figure 6.2 shows how one can depict an individual's salient characteristics. Certain metaphors are included in the visual representations: size of icon for age,

---

[17] As noted earlier, aggregation has a way of writing off well-kept blocks within blighted neighborhoods, much to the dismay of these residents. In addition, most of the youths living in these neighborhoods, even on the most deteriorated blocks, do not enter a life of crime.

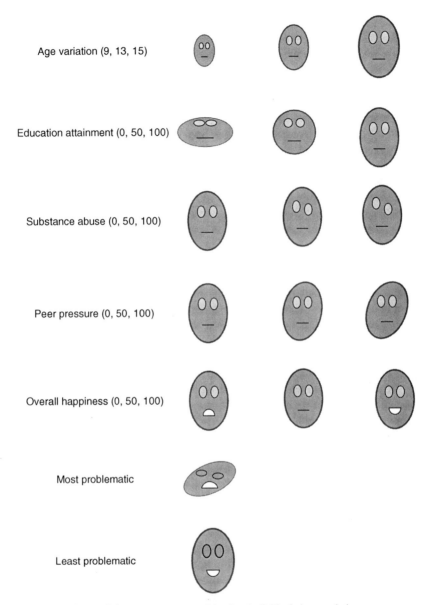

Fig. 6.2 Using Chernoff faces to represent multivariate individual characteristics

"eggheadedness" for education, skewed eyes for substance abuse, a tilted head for peer pressure.[18] This is an application of Chernoff faces[19] (Chernoff 1973; Mathematica 2006) to represent multivariate data. Although Chernoff used faces to represent complicated geological and fossil data, in this instance they are actually being used to represent personal characteristics. Moreover, an animated version can depict an individual's development over time.

This simple portrayal of individuals' characteristics can provide insight into juvenile offending. Youths change both physically and behaviorally over time; they move into and out of neighborhoods; they interact with other youths during some periods; they experiment with drugs and alcohol; they "get into trouble" and may be incarcerated for a time; their education suffers or improves, as do their families' financial and emotional resources – and all of these aspects of their lives can (theoretically) be tracked.

Although most of the data needed for such an analysis can be found in official records, I know of no agency or organization that has put such a data file together. What I have done instead is prepare a simulation of such a data set and how it might be used to visualize the delinquent activity in a neighborhood and how it changes over time. Figure 6.3 depicts the output of this simulation, using segmented circles instead of faces to represent youths and lines to represent co-offenders; an animated version (using Microsoft Visio) can be obtained from the author. In this instance, the spatial unit of analysis is the set of contiguous city blocks that form a neighborhood (see footnote 9), since the focus of youth delinquency is usually within the neighborhood. [This is not always the case; to study youth gang-related criminality and the "turf battles" associated with it the unit of analysis would be the turf of each gang, which may be within a single neighborhood or cross a number of them.]

What we can learn from such analyses is insight into how the social and geographical context can affect the behavior of different youths. On can determine who seems to be the "ringleader," the characteristics of the youths who engage in violence or in less serious crimes, how the dynamics of offending change over time and as individuals move into or out of neighborhoods, and how the individual youths change as they grow older. The *when* is as important as the *where*, since different risk and protective factors come into play at different ages.

Wave vs. Particle Analysis

There is another similarity between physics and the study of crime. No matter how complex our models of offender behavior we cannot predict which individual "particle" will commit additional crimes or when an offender will desist from offending

---

[18] Additional variables can be included using color (e.g., skin pallor for health, eye color for violence-proneness).

[19] In fact, since the simulation depicts individual youths, a face may be the best means of representing the individuals' characteristics. I have not done so in this figure and accompanying simulation, relying instead on a simpler icon.

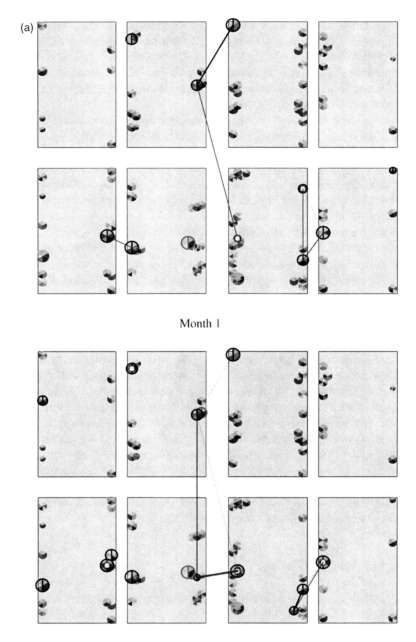

Fig. 6.3a Co-offending patterns in an 8-block neighborhood. The segmented circles represent individuals, connecting lines represent co-offenders

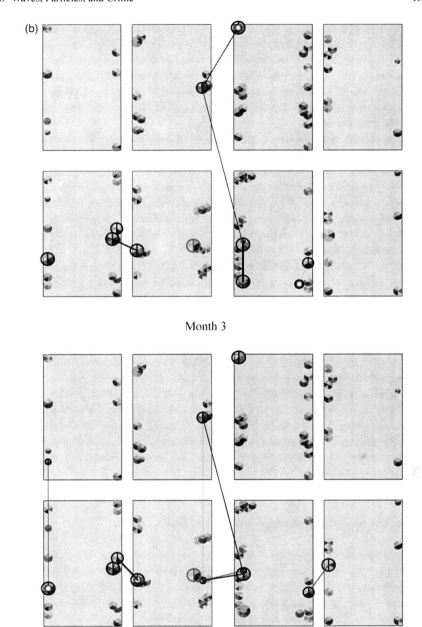

Month 3

Month 4

Fig. 6.3b Co-offending patterns in a neighborhood (continued)

(Sampson and Laub 2005). Yet different cities and different neighborhoods within them have very different crime patterns, patterns that tend to move in waves that persist (or change slowly) over time. One of the problems that some criminological theories seem to evidence is their inability to decide whether they are characterizing particle behavior or wave behavior. That is, some theories are tested using aggregate (or "wave") statistics that are then assumed to be adequate to predict how individuals will behave in the future.

For example, it is well-known that family dysfunctionality is associated with an increased propensity for offending behavior; but this does not explain why one sibling is killed while dealing in drugs and another receives a PhD (Staples 1994). Nor can it explain the fact that even though the trajectories of individuals may not be as random as molecules of air, the prediction of individual behavior is nonetheless not a real possibility – considering the unpredictable if not entirely random nature of turning points in an individual's life (Sampson and Laub 1993; Blokland and Nieuwbeerta 2005).

This does not negate the value of studying individual trajectories or criminal careers. While it may not be useful in terms what happens next to those particular individuals, or to individuals with similar characteristics, it does give some indication of how often individuals with certain characteristics behave in certain ways. In this way we can investigate the behavior of groups having different characteristics (Nagin and Tremblay 2005; Blokland et al. 2005) and estimate the frequency with which they engage in different types of behavior, with the understanding that we are dealing with the aggregate behavior of the group, not of any particular individual.

The difference between particle and wave analysis can be seen as the difference between intensive and extensive analysis. There is always a tension between descriptive richness and generalizability, and bridging the gap between the two is not a simple task. Parallel research in neighborhoods at both units of analysis, however, may add to our understanding of the micro–macro transition in social scientific models (Coleman 1990).[20]

Data Needs for Crime and Wave Analyses

The primary uses of geographic information systems in the study of crime and criminal justice have been offender-specific. That is, they tend to focus on incidents and events that are assumed to have been committed by the same offender or group. For this reason, standard crime analysis relies almost exclusively on police data, such as the location of the crime or its antecedents (where the offender first made contact with the victim, the route taken, etc.), patterns that will help to identify the offenders or forecast when and where additional crimes might occur. Thus, additional data may not *explicitly* be needed, even though contextual information concerning the

---

[20] I am indebted to an anonymous reviewer for pointing this out.

area of the city in question, such as land use and crime trends, is (or should be) imbedded in the analyst's internal storehouse of knowledge.

The study I described earlier (Maltz 1996) was essentially a "particle" analysis, in which data from the Chicago Police Department's Youth Division was integrated with data from the Chicago School Board and Cook County Juvenile Court. All of these sources keep track of the addresses of youths under their supervision, so their residential transitions can be tracked (even though the address data might not be consistent). An additional source of information about a youth's personal and family characteristics can come from the state or county welfare agency. The information thus obtained is usually in the form of reports rather than "variables," much richer than most analytic methods can accommodate, but person-based analyses can make effective use of this information (Maltz and Mullany 2000).

Data about the neighborhood can be obtained from the housing, building, zoning, tax assessor, streets and sanitation, and fire departments. They can be used to document the nature of the built environment, its deterioration or improvement over time, and insofar as crime data are geocoded, they can show the proximity of the youths in question to hot spots and other problem areas. Mapping information of this kind can be done in overlays of different colors and textures that change as the characteristics vary over time, permitting the analyst to gain insight into the complex dynamics of neighborhood activity and change.

Conclusions

Standard crime analysis using geographic information systems is focused on the detection of patterns of criminal activity for the express purpose of detecting offenders or groups of offenders who are currently active. This usually entails going through records for a few months. The goal of this paper has been to show how increasing the time scale from months to years can provide insight into the characteristics of neighborhoods and individuals that would be helpful in understanding the dynamics of criminal activity at both the neighborhood and individual level, which should be of benefit from a preventive standpoint.

The geographic units of analysis in the wave and particle analyses are, respectively, the block and the individual. What differentiates this from standard studies, however, is the fact that the analyses at both the wave and particle levels specifically eschew random sampling in both time and space, in favor of a more intense analysis of specific neighborhoods and the individuals who live (and commit delinquent acts) there, and of the interactions among and between them.

The neighborhood itself is an ecological construct. Using a GIS permits the analyst to "drill down" within that construct to the land parcel (if address information is available, as I was able to obtain for delinquent youth) and determine the interrelations among the actors on that stage. Most importantly, the analyses at both the wave and particle levels specifically eschew random sampling in both time and space, in favor of a more intense analysis of specific neighborhoods and the interactions within and between them. The goal, as always, is to better understand the dynamics of crime.

The epigraph Richard Hamming chose for his book, *Numerical Methods for Scientists and Engineers* (1962/1973), is "The purpose of computing is insight, not numbers." He went on to say (p. 3), *Thus computing is, or at least should be, intimately bound up with both the source of the problem and the use that is to be made of the answers—it is not a step to be taken in isolation from reality* (emphasis in the original). That is how geographic information systems (GIS) should be used as well – to provide insight into patterns of criminality. Map-based data at the neighborhood level, especially when it can be shown as animations over time, can be very helpful in this context, at both the wave and particle levels of analysis.

References

Baugh, J. (2000). *Beyond Ebonics: Linguistic Pride and Racial Prejudice*. New York, NY: Oxford University Press.

Blokland, A. A. J., Nagin, D., & Nieuwbeerta, P. (2005). Life span offending trajectories of a Dutch conviction cohort. *Criminology, 43*(4), 919–954.

Blokland, A. A. J., & Nieuwbeerta, P. (2005). The effects of life circumstances on longitudinal trajectories of offending. *Criminology, 43*(4), 1203–1240.

Brantingham, P.J., & Brantingham, P.L. (Eds.) (1984). *Patterns in Crime*. New York: Macmillan.

Brantingham, P. L., & Brantingham, P. J. (1993). Environment, routine and situation: Toward a pattern theory of crime. In: R. V. Clarke & M. Felson (Eds.), *Routine activity and rational choice. Advances in Criminological Theory*, Vol. 5. New Brunswick, NJ: Transaction Press.

Chernoff, H. (1973). The use of faces to represent points in k-dimensional space graphically. *Journal of the American Statistical Association, 68*(342), 361–368.

Cohen, J. (1931). Report on crime and the foreign born: Comment. *Michigan Law Review, 30*(1), 99–104 .

Cohen, L. E., & Felson, M. (1979). Social change and crime rate trends: A routine activity approach. *American Sociological Review, 44*(4), 588–608.

Coleman, J. (1990). *Foundations of Social Theory*. Cambridge, MA: Harvard University Press.

Crane, J. (1991). The epidemic theory of ghettos and neighborhood effects on dropping out and teenage childbearing. *American Journal of Sociology, 96*(5), 1226–1259.

Granovetter, M. (1978). Threshold models of collective behavior. *American Journal of Sociology, 83*(6), 1420–1443.

Green, D. P., Strolovitch, D. Z., Wong, J. S. (1998). Defended neighborhoods, integration, and racially motivated crime. *American Journal of Sociology, 104*(2), 372–403.

Hamming, R. (1962). *Numerical Methods for Scientists and Engineers*. New York: McGraw-Hill, 1962. Republished by Dover Books: New York, 1986.

Hatton, T. J., & Price, S. W. (1999). *Migration, Migrants and Policy in the United Kingdom*. Bonn, Germany: IZA Press.

Junger, M., & Polder, W. (1992). Some explanations of crime among four ethnic groups in the Netherlands. *Journal of Quantitative Criminology, 8*(1), 51–78.

LaFree, G., & Drass, K. A. (2002). Counting crime booms among nations: Evidence for homicide victimization rates, 1956 to 1998. *Criminology, 40*(4), 769–800.

Lemann, N. (1991). *The Promised Land: The Great Black Migration and How It Changed America*. New York: A.A. Knopf.

Levenson, J. S., & Hern, A. L. (2007). Sex offender residence restrictions: Unintended consequences and community reentry. *Justice Research and Policy, 9*(1), 59–73.

Lim, M., Metzler, R., & Bar-Yam, Y. (2007). Global pattern formation and ethnic/cultural violence. *Science,* 317(5844), 1540–1544.

Lodka, S. K., & Verma, A. (1999). Animations of crime maps using Virtual Reality Modeling Language. *Western Criminology Review,* 1, 2. [Online]. Available: http://wcr.sonoma.edu/v1n2/lodha.html.

Maltz, M. D. (1996). From Poisson to the present: Applying operations research to problems of crime and justice. *Journal of Quantitative Criminology,* 12(1), 3–61.

Maltz, M. D., Mullany, J. K. (2000). Visualizing lives: New pathways for analyzing life course histories. *Journal of Quantitative Criminology,* 16(2), 255–281.

Mathematica (2006). Chernoff face. http://mathworld.wolfram.com/ChernoffFace.html, accessed November 14, 2006.

McCord, J. (1990). Long-term perspectives on parental absence. In: L. N. Robins & M. Rutter (Eds.). *Straight and Devious Pathways From Childhood to Adulthood* (pp. 116–34), Cambridge, UK: Cambridge University Press.

Monmonier, M. (2002). *Spying with Maps: Surveillance Technologies and the Future of Privacy.* Chicago, IL: University of Chicago Press.

Nagin, D. S., & Tremblay, R. E. (2005). Developmental trajectory groups: Fact or a useful statistical fiction? *Criminology,* 43(4), 873–904.

National Commission on Law Observance and Enforcement (1931). *Report on Crime and the Foreign Born.* Report No. 10. Washington, DC.

Park, R. E. & Burgess, E. W. (1921). *Introduction to the Science of Sociology.* Chicago, IL: University of Chicago Press.

Peeples, F., & Loeber, R. (1994). Do individual factors and neighborhood context explain ethnic differences in juvenile delinquency? *Journal of Quantitative Criminology,* 10(2), 141–157.

Reiss, A. J., Jr. (1986). Co-offending influences on criminal careers. In: A. Blumstein, J. Cohen, J. A. Roth & C. A. Visher (Eds.), *Criminal Careers and Career Criminals* (Vol. 2, pp. 121–60), Washington, DC: National Academy of Sciences.

Reiss, A. J. Jr. (1988). Co-offending and criminal careers. In: M. Tonry & N. Morris (Eds.), *Crime and Justice: A Review of Research.* Vol. 10, edited by. Chicago: University of Chicago Press.

Reiss, A. J. Jr., & Farrington, D. P. (1991). Advancing knowledge about co-offending: Results from a prospective survey of London males. *Journal of Criminal Law and Criminology,* 82, 360–395.

Rengert, G. F., Piquero, A., & Jones, P. (1999). Distance decay reexamined. *Criminology,* 37(2), 601–619.

Rengert, G. F., & Wasilchick, J. (1985). *Suburban Burglary: A Time and a Place for Everything.* Springfield, IL: Charles C Thomas.

Rosling, H. (2006). Presentation at the Technology Entertainment Design (TED) Conference in Monterey CA, February 2006. (http://www.ted.com/tedtalks/tedtalksplayer.cfm?key= hans_rosling&flashEnabled=1). Accessed 22 September 2006.

Rosling, H. (2007). Presentation at the Technology Entertainment Design (TED) Conference in Monterey CA, March 2007 (http://www.ted.com/index.php/talks/view/id/140). Accessed 3 September 2007.

Rossmo, D. K. (1995). Place, space, and police investigations: Hunting serial violent criminals. In: J. Eck & D. Weisburd (Eds.), *Crime and Place,* Monsey, NY: Criminal Justice Press.

Rossmo, D. K. (1999). *Geographic Profiling.* Boca Raton, FL: CRC Press.

Sampson, R. J., & Laub, J. H. (1993). Crime *in the Making: Pathways and Turning Points through Life.* Cambridge, MA: Harvard University Press.

Sampson, R. J., & Laub, J. H. (Eds.) (2005). *Developmental Criminology and Its Discontents: Trajectories of Crime from Childhood to Old Age.* Volume 602 of The Annals of The American Academy of Political and Social Science. Philadelphia, PA: American Academy of Political and Social Science. November 2005

Sampson R. J., Raudenbush, S. W., & Earls, F. (1997). Neighborhoods and violent crime: A multilevel study of collective efficacy. *Science,* 277, 918–924.

Sellin, T. (1938). *Culture Conflict and Crime*. New York: Social Science Research Council.

Shaw, C., & McKay, H. D. (1942). *Delinquency and Urban Areas*. Chicago. IL: University of Chicago Press.

Staples, B. A. (1994). *Parallel Time: Growing Up in Black and White*. New York: Pantheon Books.

Stark, R. (1987). Deviant Places: A Theory of the Ecology of Crime. *Criminology*, 25, 893–909.

Van Wilsem, J, Wittebrood, K., & De Graaf, N. D. (2006). Socioeconomic dynamics of neighborhoods and the risk of crime victimization: A multilevel study of improving, declining, and stable areas in the Netherlands. *Social Problems*, 53(2), 226–247.

Weisburd, D. (1989). *Jewish Settler Violence: Deviance as Social Reaction*. University Park, PA: Pennsylvania State University Press.

Weisburd, D., Bushway, S., Lum, C., & Yang, S-M (2004). Trajectories of crime at places: a longitudinal study of street segments in the city of Seattle. *Criminology*, 42, 283–321.

Weisburd, D., & Green, L. (1993). Defining the street-level drug market. In: D.L. MacKenzie & C.D. Uchida (Eds.), *Drugs and Crime: Evaluating Public Policy Initiatives*. Newbury Park, CA: Sage.

Weisburd, D., & Green, L. (1995). Policing drug hot spots: The Jersey City drug market analysis experiment. *Justice Quarterly*, 12(4), 711–735.

Wikström, P-O. & Loeber, R. (2000). Do disadvantaged neighborhoods cause well-adjusted children to become adolescent delinquents? A study of male juvenile serious offending, individual risk and protective factors, and neighborhood context. *Criminology*, 38(4), 1109–1142.

Zimring, F. E. (1981). Kids, groups and crime: Some implications of a well-known secret. *Journal of Criminal Law and Criminology*, 72, 867–885.

Zauberman, R., & Lévy, R. (2003). Police, minorities, and the French republican ideal. *Criminology*, 41(4), 1065–1100.

Part III
Empirical Examples of Crime Place Studies: What Can We Learn?

Chapter 7
Crime, Neighborhoods, and Units of Analysis: Putting Space in Its Place

George E. Tita and Robert T. Greenbaum

Abstract Research has long established that crime is not randomly distributed, and spatial regression models of crime have clearly demonstrated that crime patterns cannot be explained merely by the socio-economic characteristics of a particular place. These findings are a reminder that "space matters" and that neighborhoods are not analytically independent units. Modeling the clustering of crime through spatial regression requires two important decisions. First, one must choose a unit of analysis that is consistent with the social processes believed to be driving the observed patterns. Second, one must consider the relationships among these units such that the model captures the influence the activities in other areas have on outcomes in the neighborhood. Within criminology, this second feature has been given insufficient consideration. Instead, the connectedness of spatial units has been taken as given and modeled solely through adjacency or a distance decay function. This chapter critiques such inductive approaches used to model and explain the spatial distribution of crime. Drawing upon the modeling of network autocorrelation within the social influence literature, we describe a deductive approach wherein specific social processes are posited, measured and modeled a priori. An empirical example using gang violence demonstrates this deductive approach and we find that the spatial distribution of violence is influenced by neighbors defined by the socio-spatial dimensions of gang rivalries rather than simply by geographically contiguous neighbors. We emphasize that a complete discussion of the appropriate unit of analysis must also consider the spatial dimensions of the social phenomena thought to be responsible for the spatial patterning.

Introduction

When examining the appropriate unit of analysis in crime research or any other examination of a social process, it is important to properly account for all of the influences that affect activity within that unit. Regardless of the choice of

G.E. Tita
Department of Criminology, Law and Society, University of California – Irvine, CA, USA
e-mail: gtita@uci.edu

D. Weisburd et al. (eds.), *Putting Crime in its Place*,
DOI 10.1007/978-0-387-09688-9_7, © Springer Science+Business Media, LLC 2009

neighborhoods, census tracts, policing districts, or some other areal units, social processes are typically influenced by actions, events, and conditions in "neighboring" spatial units in addition to the characteristics that define the focal unit. Thus, in order to understand and model these processes, it is imperative that we properly capture how these processes play out across the geography of a study region.

We begin this chapter by providing an overview of spatial studies of violence. We move quickly into a comparison between the primarily inductive modeling approach popularized within criminology with the more deductive approach used in more general studies of social influence. The goal of these first two sections is to lay the foundation for our argument that by using theory coupled with empirical evidence, it is possible to specify a spatial autocorrelation matrix that better approximates the social mechanism responsible for explaining the observable spatial patterns of crime.

Over the past decade, there has been a considerable increase in the number of published studies that explore the spatial distribution of violent crime. Much of this was fueled by the unprecedented growth in levels of youth homicide during the late 1980s through the early 1990s. Studies at the national level (Blumstein and Rosenfeld 1998; Cork 1999), the county level (Baller et al. 2001; Messner and Anselin 2004), and the local level (Cohen and Tita 1999; Morenoff et al. 2001; Griffiths and Chavez 2004) have consistently demonstrated two things. First, the subpopulation at greatest risk of homicide victimization is comprised of young urban minority males. Second, homicides exhibit a non-random pattern of positive spatial concentration, meaning that areas with similar levels of violence cluster in space. Furthermore, the concentration of high violence areas typically occur within disadvantaged urban communities.

Ecological studies of crime have clearly demonstrated that the spatial patterning of crimes can not be explained by the socio-economic characteristics of place alone. Instead, the spatial analysis of crime literature suggests that concentrations of crime are the result of particular social processes or mechanisms that are manifest in such a way that crimes in one location influence the levels and patterns of crimes in nearby or "connected" places. To date, the primary value of these studies has been to serve as a constant reminder that "space matters," thereby refuting the notion that neighborhoods, however defined, are analytically independent and that ecological models of crime need to consider the ways in which the observable outcomes in one neighborhood are dependent upon the actions and activities occurring in other areas (Sampson 2004; Morenoff et al. 2001). However, though many plausible explanations have been offered, the empirical findings offer little in the way of supporting definitive statements on the exact nature of the processes that influence crime patterns across space.

The inductive modeling strategy employed in most studies is part of the reason why the nature of the social processes responsible for relationships among crimes across space remains conjecture. Typically, the researcher takes an outcome of interest, aggregates the outcome and explanatory variables to the most conveniently available areal unit of analysis, assumes that events in only spatially adjacent areas can influence one another, estimates a non-spatial model to "test for" a particular functional form of spatial influence, and then, based upon a set of diagnostic tests, picks the appropriate statistical model. If the coefficient on the spatial term is statistically significant, ex-post explanations are constructed regarding the "importance of space." The most frequent interpretations include those social processes related to contagion (Loftin 1986), exposure (Morenoff et al. 2001; Griffiths and Chavez 2004), gangs (Morenoff and Sampson 1997; Rosenfeld et al. 1999; Cohen and Tita 1999; Griffiths and Chavez 2004), and drug markets (Morenoff and Sampson 1997; Cork 1999; Tita and Cohen 2004).

This differs from the deductive modeling approach employed in the field of social network analysis. The social networks literature recognizes both spatial regression analysis and network autocorrelation models as members of the family of models known more generally as "social influence models" (Marsden and Friedkin 1994; Leenders 2002). As the name suggests, social influence models provide a conceptual and analytical framework for exploring the structural processes by which people, organizations, or places are influenced by others. In modeling processes of social influence within the network literature, one starts with a very clear idea of the process (or processes) by which influence occurs across units of analysis, ensures that these units are linked in accordance to the pre-specified processes (e.g., geographic adjacency, status, or social similarity), estimates the appropriate statistical model, and then conducts hypotheses tests to determine whether the initial beliefs regarding influence processes are empirically supported.

In the following pages, we explore what it would mean to employ such a deductive approach to the spatial modeling of crime. We begin with a more thorough treatment of the two most important choices made in specifying both network autocorrelation and spatial autocorrelation models – choosing the appropriate unit of analysis and linking these units in a theoretically or empirically justified manner so as to be consistent with an *ex-ante* specified process. We also include a discussion of the differences between spatial error and spatial dependence/lag models. Next, we review the commonly offered interpretations in light of theoretical and empirical evidence guiding these principles. We conclude with an empirical example to demonstrate the validity of our approach. The intent of the exercise is not to answer a particular policy question. Instead, the primary question is whether additional insights can be gained by moving beyond typically employed spatial adjacency to explicitly consider the socio-spatial dimensions of social processes. Using gang-involved gun violence, we demonstrate how different specifications of the spatial autocorrelation matrix (also referred to as the spatial weights matrix) lead us to conclude that gangs do influence levels of violence in other areas but that the extent of the influence extends beyond simple geographic contiguity.

The Network and Spatial Approaches to Modeling Influence

Models of spatial autocorrelation share a number of common features with network autocorrelation models. Substantively, they both explore similar questions pertaining to influence and contagion effects, albeit among different units of observations.[1] These approaches also assume that proximity or connectedness facilitates the flow

---

[1] See Marsden and Friedkin (1994) for examples.

of information or influence across nodes in a network or across geographic space. Individuals, organizations, or places are more likely to be influenced by the actions, behaviors, or beliefs of others who are "closer," meaning observations that share either geographical or social proximity, or similarity in "status" are given the most weight in the model. Methodologically, the lack of independence among geographical units is identical in its content and construct to the interdependence inherent among the actors in a social network. The lack of independence among observations is more than a statistical nuisance that precludes one from employing standard Ordinary Least Squares (OLS) regression analysis.[2] Instead, the interdependence is at the core of our attempts to understand how links among observations matter.

Marsden and Friedkin (1994) identify three important challenges researchers face in utilizing the network approach to models of social influence. These include: (1) articulating the *substantive process* through which influence occurs, (2) correctly specifying an autocorrelation matrix, and (3) estimating the correct statistical model. After discussing these below, we compare the social network/social influence approach with the manner in which these issues are dealt with within the criminology literature.

Those interested in the adoption of innovations or beliefs differentiate between processes of communication/structural cohesion and processes of comparison/equivalence. Communication/structural cohesion presumes that influence occurs through a direct social tie, which may occur through a variety of means (e.g., face-to-face, electronic, or print media). Influence that occurs through processes of comparison or equivalence does not depend upon a formal tie among individuals. People recognize that they are part of a social system and then mimic the behaviors of others who occupy similar roles (i.e., are "equivalent") within the same social system. This sort of contagion through comparison is identical to the spatial process of "hierarchical diffusion" in which transmission occurs not along spatially contiguous geography, but rather along an ordered (often by status) route. Cliff et al. (1981, p. 9) note that hierarchical diffusion is "typified by the diffusion of innovations (such as new styles in women's fashions or new consumer good, for example television) from large metropolitan centers to remote villages."

The choice of theoretical/substantive process has direct bearing on the second challenge – the appropriate specification of the autocorrelation matrix, "W." Unfortunately, W cannot be estimated and must be specified *a priori*. This matrix is the most critical element in both network and spatial autocorrelation models, as it represents the dependence among observations in terms of the underlying social or geographic structure that explicitly links actors or geographic units with one another. As Leenders (2002, p. 26) notes:

"W is supposed to represent the theory a researcher has about the structure of the influence processes in the network. Because any conclusion drawn on the basis of autocorrelation

---

[2] However, if observations are merely correlated across space due to arbitrary political boundaries, this type of spatial autocorrelation should be modeled as a nuisance parameter by incorporating a spatial error term.

models is conditional upon the specification of W, the scarcity of attention and justification researchers pay to the chosen operationalization of W is striking and alarming. This is especially so, since different specifications of W typically lead to different empirical results".

In network models of influence, the existence of a tie between ego (one particular actor) and ego's alters (those who influence ego) is predicated upon defining the appropriate frame of reference. This step results in the specification of the actor by actor social network autocorrelation matrix (W), where each element $w_{i,j} = 1$ if i and j are tied to one another, else the cell $w_{i,j} = 0$. If friends are believed to populate the general frame of reference by which others are influenced, then $w_{i,j} = 1$, if and only if i and j are "friends." Similarly, if the frame of reference is based upon status, then $w_{i,j} = 1$, if and only if i and j share comparable levels of status attainment. Actors that belong to the same group (formal or informal) may also constitute a shared frame of reference.

The third and final step in the process requires one to choose the appropriate statistical model and assess its predictive power. Once again, the underlying substantive process guides this choice. As is the case with spatial models, the choice of models depends upon whether the process of influence operates through an autocorrelated error term or through network dependence (see Elffers 2003).

Autocorrelated error models account for the unobservable similarity or interdependence among units of analysis. When the error terms from a regression are not independent due to correlation across social or spatial units due to, for example, units of measurement that differ from the geographic scope of the phenomenon, OLS models that do not take into account the autocorrelated error term will still yield unbiased coefficients. However, estimates of the standard errors on those coefficients will be incorrect (Anselin 1988). To account for this autocorrelation among geographic units, *spatial error models*, which include spatially lagged error terms, can be estimated using maximum likelihood.[3]

If interdependence across actors or space is instead due to a particular social process, then this dependence is more appropriately modeled with a lagged dependent variable. Failure to include a lagged dependent variable in the model leads to omitted variable bias (Anselin 1988; Elffers 2003). A *spatial lag model* explicitly models the dependence or spillover across spatial units.[4]

The modeling of neighborhood effects within the criminological literature requires addressing the identical set of concerns. However, as noted in the

---

[3] $Y = X\beta + \varepsilon; \varepsilon = \lambda \varepsilon_c + u$, with $E[u] = 0$, $E[uu'] = \sigma^2 I$, where $\varepsilon = W\varepsilon$, and W is the ($N \times N$) autocorrelation weighting matrix that contains information about which spatial units are considered to be neighbors. λ measures the spatial correlation of the error term. Note that if there is no correlation among neighbors' error terms, λ equals zero and the OLS estimators are BLUE. The same holds true when modeling unobserved similarity involving individuals, groups or organizations.

[4] $Y = \rho W Y_s + X\beta + \varepsilon$; with $E[\varepsilon] = 0$, $E[\varepsilon\varepsilon'] = \sigma^2 I$, where ρ is the spatial coefficient on the lagged dependent variable, and it will be nonzero if outcomes in one location influence outcomes in another location.

introduction, criminologists tend to take more of an inductive, post hoc approach to specifying spatial models. While we have learned a great deal from the traditional approach, and each of the modeling concerns are typically addressed, they are not treated in the logical order dictated by a more careful, deductive approach. Rather than first specifying the social process, constructing the appropriate weights matrix, and then choosing the statistical method, spatial models of crime often first construct the weights matrix, choose the statistical model, and only then, in the presence of a statistically significant coefficient on the spatial term, are specific social processes considered.

The presence of positive spatial autocorrelation has been interpreted as evidence of unobserved social processes. This conclusion rests heavily upon the fact that the socio-economic composition of place (i.e., the correlated effect) fails to account for the spatial concentration of events. That is, even once factors such as race, poverty, and population density are accounted for, violence continues to exhibit spatial clustering. This remaining spatial clustering is most likely due to omitted measures of relevant neighborhood processes. While it is possible that some of these omitted variables are missing measures of local characteristics, it is more likely that the spatial clustering is due to the omission of variables that capture the influence of social processes across space.

Efforts to explain the social processes responsible for observed patterns of violence often focus on the contagious nature of violence and distinguish contagion that is driven by "exposure" versus contagion that is the result of "diffusion." Morenoff and his co-authors differentiate between the two processes by noting that diffusion "focuses on the consequences of crime as they are played out over time and space – crime in one neighborhood may be the cause of future crime in another neighborhood. The concept of exposure focuses on the antecedent conditions that foster crime, which are also spatially and temporally ordered" (Morenoff et al., 2001, p. 523).

There are two elements to exposure that researchers have considered when understanding how conditions in one neighborhood can influence levels of violence in other neighborhoods. First, violence in the focal neighborhood might be higher than predicted by structural characteristics, if it is "exposed" to offenders from other areas. The routine activities perspective (Cohen and Felson 1979; Messner and Tardiff 1986) suggests that the chances of victimization increases for those individuals living in close proximity to known offenders. In addition to offenders, crime in a focal neighborhood may by influenced by exposure to underlying criminogenic features in neighboring areas. Second, in one of the few studies that does employ a deductive modeling strategy, Mears and Bhati (2006) argue that social networks are unbounded by space and note that ties are often homophilous in terms of race, ethnicity, socio-economic status. Thus, behaviors in a focal area are presumed to be influenced by behaviors in socially similar areas because there is a higher probability of ties linking (i.e., exposing) similar areas.

In addition to processes of exposure, violence may diffuse from one area to another through various processes involving structured social interactions. Several such mechanisms have been posited. Loftin (1986) argues that the spatial concentration of assaultive violence and its contagious nature is the result of certain subcultural processes. He uses "subcultural" to refer to a process wherein violence spreads throughout the population as the result of direct social contact. Thus, an increase in violence can result in an epidemic when a small increase in assaults sets off a chain reaction of events causing local individuals to enact precautionary/protective measures in hopes of reducing their chances of victimization. At the extreme, individuals take pre-emptive actions (i.e., assault others) to protect against the possibility of being the victim of an assault, thereby feeding the epidemic. Loftin argues that the very existence of the moral and social networks that link individuals together within their local environment exacerbate the epidemic. "When violence occurs it draws multiple people into the conflict and spreads either the desire to retaliate or the need for preemptive violence through the network, potentially involving ever increasing numbers of individuals in the fight" (Loftin 1986, p. 555).

Alternatively, the notion of negative spatial autocorrelation is possible. That would imply that high crime in a neighborhood would lead to lower crime in nearby neighborhoods. For example, residents in a neighborhood spatially proximate to a high crime neighborhood might spend much more on safety or take other precautions than residents in a neighborhood with a very similar demographic composition that borders safer neighborhoods. Thus, by virtue of being proximate to a high crime neighborhood, this increased spending on crime prevention may lead to lower crime than is found in similar neighborhoods elsewhere.

Two of the most common mechanisms implicated in the literature as the source of spatial dependence include the dynamics of local drug markets and/or the presence of gang wars (e.g., Decker 1996; Wilkinson and Fagan 1996; Morenoff and Sampson 1997; Cohen et al. 1998; Cohen and Tita 1999; Rosenfeld et al. 1999; Morenoff et al. 2001; Griffiths and Chavez 2004; Tita and Cohen 2004). Several features of drug markets, especially crack cocaine, make them obvious candidates responsible for the diffusion of violence. First, guns quickly became important "tools of the trade" among urban youth dealing crack. As Blumstein (1995) hypothesized and empirically supported by Blumstein and Cork (1996), arming participants in crack markets increases the risks of violence for non-participants as well. Faced with increased risks to personal safety, youth outside crack markets increasingly carry guns and use them to settle interpersonal disputes, thereby spreading gun violence more broadly among the youth population. Second, drug markets often involve competition among rivals looking to increase their market share. Therefore, drug related murders are likely to be retaliatory in nature.

As Decker (1996) notes, there are important features that define gangs which also make them effective agents of diffusion. First, they are geographically oriented. The turf or "set space" where urban street gangs come together is a well-defined, sub-neighborhood area that remains consistent over time (Klein 1995; Moore 1991; Tita et al. 2005). Second, urban street gangs are committed to the defense of their turf. Thus, gang violence is inherently retaliatory in nature, which should promote predictable temporal and spatial tit-for-tat ordering of violence.

The above explanations where reached inductively after first producing a statistically significant coefficient on a spatial dependence term, which itself was derived primarily out of convenience (spatial contiguity). Therefore, Leender's advice that different social processes lead to different specifications of W is generally ignored. This is problematic on several fronts.

First, it assumes that the processes of exposure and diffusion operate over the same geographic dimensions and that the same unit of analysis is appropriate for both. This remains an empirical question that spatial studies relying on inductive designs are unable to study. When conducting spatial analysis, choosing the appropriate geographic unit of analysis (e.g., states, counties, census tracts) should be driven by theoretical arguments and/or empirical evidence regarding the manner in which others experience the impact or influence of the social process of interests.

Second, as Doreian (1980) points out, there are an infinite number of ways in which distance and contiguity can be measured in the spatial weights matrix. However, in specifying spatial dependence in models of crime and violence, the rule has been to follow Tobler's First Law of Geography (Tobler 1970, p. 236), which simply states, ". . . everything is related to everything else, but near things are more related than distant things." Furthermore, researchers often presume that spatial dependence follows a pattern of "spatial homogeneity," which Strang and Tuma (1993, p. 615) define as the assumption that all adjacent areas within ". . . the population have the same chance of affecting and being affected by each other." The result of following these dictums is the identification of a spatial weights matrix that is predicated solely upon geographic contiguity. Furthermore, when "row-standardized," the matrix imposes that each contiguous node impacts every other node to which the focal unit is linked and impacts them equally. The possibility of asymmetric relationships among neighbors is discounted, and the possibility that the events in non-neighboring areas can directly and strongly influence local levels of violence is ignored.

Finally, using a single matrix to capture processes of exposure and diffusion precludes the possibility of empirically differentiating between the two processes. The regression coefficient on the measure of spatial dependence provides an estimate of the overall impact that neighboring levels of violence have on local levels of violence. It does not, however, permit one to assess the relative impact of violence in neighboring areas vis-à-vis exposure or diffusion. Morenoff et al. (2001) make this point explicit by noting that their results achieved in the spatial analysis of homicide in Chicago were generally supportive of the exposure hypothesis, but that they are ". . . unable to pinpoint the relative contributions of exposure and diffusion. . . " (p. 552).

Failure to carefully account for the socio-spatial dimensions of the underlying social process in the modeling of the weights matrix leaves the interpretation of the spatial results open to criticism. The harshest criticism is that the spatial term is simply a "catch all" for any number of unobserved, residual processes. As Manski (1994, pp. 127–136) points out in his discussion of the "reflection problem," these unobserved processes may be the result of *endogenous processes* where the behavior being captured (violence) is simply the prevalence of violence within a particular reference group. This would be consistent with a process wherein similar others were grouped geographically and reacting to either exposure to violence or a set of subcultural norms that are consistent throughout the group. Alternatively, the spatial effect could be capturing a *contextual process* in which one's predilection to commit violence varies according to the characteristics of a particular reference group. Gang violence or other types of retaliatory violence in which the actors are influenced by the actions of others (the "reference group") is an example of a contextual process.

Demonstrating empirically the existence of a "spatial effect" often provides little guidance on which particular type of process is at work. This is especially true within the neighborhood effects literature because the precise mechanism by which place matters often remains unobserved or unmeasured in one's data (Manski 1994; Sampson et al. 2002).

Bringing the Deductive Approach to Spatial Models of Crime

The previous discussion makes clear that the correlation of events across nearby geographic units is not *sufficient* to establish that a process of spatial dependence exists. It is also the case that the presence of spatial autocorrelation based upon a traditional binary contiguity or inverse distance matrix is not a *necessary* condition to establish that social influence across space exists. In this section, we discuss how existing efforts to model spatial processes have moved beyond simple spatial adjacency. We explain how this can be applied to criminology by presenting a model of the influence of drug markets on patterns of violence. Our central empirical example models gun violence as a function of the location of rival street gangs.

There are several examples of innovative efforts outside of criminology that recognize that the processes by which actors in a focal area are influenced by the behaviors and actions of others are not neatly bounded by, or limited to, spatially adjacent or nearby areas. Gould (1991) finds that overall levels of resistance during the Paris Commune of 1871 were not influenced by levels of resistance in neighboring areas. Instead, resistance levels were greatest among those districts (*arrondissements*) that shared enlistments. The sharing of resources (resistance fighters) increased solidarity, which translated into greater overall effectiveness in the local insurgency's effort. More recently, Greenbaum (2002) explored the spatial distribution of wages among teachers in Pennsylvania and found that teachers' wages were more alike when contiguity among school districts was based upon the socio-economic similarity among districts. That is, wages in non-adjacent affluent school districts exhibited similar wages when compared to nearby non-affluent school districts. In addition, Babcock et al. (2005) modeled social comparisons among the same Pennsylvania school districts based upon referents identified in surveys. That is, during salary negotiations, school boards typically refer to a different set of neighbors than do the teacher unions, and the choice of reference districts affects the outcomes of the negotiations. State level budgets and fiscal policy are also known to be related to the expenditures and policies of "neighboring" states (Case et al. 1993). Not only are expenditures similar among spatially adjacent states, but they are also similar among states that are identified as "neighbors" because they share similarity in terms of median income and racial composition.

Within criminology, researchers are also beginning to take seriously the modeling of specific social processes, identified *a priori* to the specification of the *W* matrix, thought to influence the spatial distribution of violence. As noted above, recent work by Mears and Bhati (2006) examines the spatial distribution of homicide in Chicago by taking the novel approach of modeling exposure to violence by considering the impact of resource deprivation among both spatial neighbors as well as neighbors defined by social similarity that is unbounded by space. Their overall conclusion is that the impact of resource deprivation among socially similar neighborhoods is greatest when they are also spatially proximate. Interestingly, when homicides were disaggregated by type, neither spatial nor social adjacency was associated with levels of gang homicide. This finding is inconsistent with the *de facto* explanations provided in the spatial models of violence literature that often implicates the nature of gang violence as an explanatory factor in the clustering of events.

Modeling the Spatial Dynamics of Exposure

Of the ways in which events in one place can influence happenings in another, employing spatial weights matrix based upon simple geographic contiguity or inverse distance best approximates social process of exposure. There is ample evidence from the routine activities and environmental criminology literatures to suggest that living in close proximity to the types of neighborhoods that produce offenders will increase the ambient crime risk in an area.

The challenge to modeling this type of exposure spatially lies in how one chooses to implement "close proximity" in the *W* matrix. Fortunately there is a rich literature to guide this process as environmental criminologists have long concentrated on the well-traveled routes of *offenders* as the key to identifying why crimes happen where they do (Brantingham and Brantingham 1981). In fact, it has been demonstrated that the identification of abnormal spatial patterns can help uncover criminal activity (Kim 2007). Examining the journey to crime literature, one generally finds that offenders involved in homicide and assaults travel shorter distances than do offenders involved in other types of crimes (Boggs 1965; Rand 1986; Hesseling 1992). This suggests that the potential pool of victims of violence often resides close, but not necessarily in, the offender's own neighborhood. Short of constructing the *W* matrix by explicitly mapping the source and destination of all offenders, the empirical research offers at least some support for the adjacency-based approach to specifying *W*.

Two recent studies explored the influence of exposure to offenders on the spatial distribution of homicide in Chicago. Griffiths and Chavez (2004) combine Exploratory Spatial Data Analysis (ESDA) and Trajectory Analysis (Nagin 1999) and find a pattern that they identify with what they call a "defensive diffusion" effect (Griffiths and Chavez 2004, p. 967). They find that the census tracts that experienced increased gun homicide over time were located next to the tracts with the highest initial levels of violence. In other words, individuals were increasing their gun carrying, and ultimately usage, due to being exposed to violence in neighboring areas. Secondly, they point out that this spatio-temporal pattern is also consistent with offenders in the neighboring high rate tracks coming into the initially less violent tract and victimizing local residents.

By relying on a contiguity matrix, the two Chicago homicide studies assume that exposure is geographically bounded among first order neighbors. Again, this seems like a reasonable assumption. However, one could imagine instances where physical barriers such as major roads, open green spaces, or waterways inhibit such processes. For instance, drawing from environmental criminology, one could construct a travel network that measures the degree in which "neighbors" are truly accessible. Rather than using a binary contiguity or inverse distance matrix, one could then construct a weights matrix based upon the ease by which one can commute from one area to all other areas. Whether considering such impediments would alter the authors' conclusions remains an empirical question.

Modeling the Spatial Dynamics of Diffusion

Much of the spatial analysis of violence literature uses data including the homicide peak of the early 1990s, a phenomenon known to be driven by the deadly combination of youth and guns. For many cities, the period also coincides with the arrivals of crack cocaine markets as well as violent urban streets gangs. It is little wonder, then, that drug markets and gangs emerged as the two primary explanations responsible for the spatial clustering and diffusion of violence. Furthermore, as we noted above, both involve features that are inherently attractive to notion of spatial diffusion; they both have very clear geographic dimensions and (presumably) involve retaliatory violence.

The location of drug markets is not random. There is now a rich literature demonstrating that, no different from any legitimate retail business, drug markets form in environment and settings that best serve participants. Dealers must make sure that their market is accessible and known to their customers and at the same time maximize their own personal safety by making sure that they can minimize law enforcement surveillance and escape from enforcement efforts (Caulkins et al. 1993; Eck 1995; Rengert 1996). Specifically, proximity to a freeway (Rengert 1996; Caulkins et al. 1993), central business district and transit stops (Robertson and Rengert 2006), and pay phones (Eck 1995) all make particular spaces good places to set up illicit drug markets.

Because drug markets do behave like other markets and have carefully chosen locations, drug markets eschew relocation. Though enforcement efforts might temporarily suspend operations within a given location, once the efforts subside, the market typically returns to its primary niche. When the geographically targeted enforcement efforts are successful, Weisburd and Green (1995) found that crime is not displaced into surrounding areas. In fact, they find that it is the crime reduction benefits of the enforcement that diffuses.

How might the impact of drug markets on local levels and patterns of violence be modeled? Perhaps it is best to consider drug markets as a special case of exposure where the drug market serves as a special class of a criminogenic factor. This would be in line with the suggestion of Blumstein's hypothesis regarding how crack markets lead to the diffusion, and ultimate use, of guns among urban youth. Given that one cannot report the theft of one's drugs or drug money to the police, Blumstein argues that drug dealers armed themselves to protect against robbery. As more youth became involved in the crack market, more youth began carrying guns. Soon, this "arms race" expanded to youth who were not active in the market, but rather "exposed" to the participants either through residential contacts or schoolyard interactions (Blumstein 1995; Blumstein and Cork 1996).

In this light, one could model the impact of the market on all those who are exposed to it, directly or indirectly. Many drug market participants reside outside of the immediate area (see Mikelbank and Sabol 2005; Tita and Griffiths 2005). Therefore, one might choose to link together the drug market with those neighborhoods from which both buyers and sellers are drawn. This would result in a spatial weights matrix made up of a series of discontinuous "islands" with the market linking neighborhoods similar to how an axel links the spokes in a wheel.

Urban street gangs are implicated even more frequently than drug markets as responsible for the patterns spatial dependence exhibited by violent crimes. Individual level studies consistently demonstrate that gang membership greatly increases violence and gun carrying (Battin et al. 1998; Thornberry et al. 2003; Gordon et al. 2004). Given the territorial and retaliatory natures of urban youth gang violence (Rosenfeld et al. 1999), it is natural to expect that gang-related violence would follow predictable spatial and temporal patterns. Because set space is a well-defined area in which gang members spend most of their time, one might expect set space to serve as a sort of lightning rod for inter-gang violence.

Whether the impact of gangs on patterns of gun violence is limited to only geographically adjacent areas is an empirical question that has gone unaddressed. We argue that the geography of gangs and their social networks suggest a set of structural properties that researchers have not adequately exploited in terms of understanding the spatial structure of gang violence. By combining gang turf maps with social network diagrams, it becomes possible to determine whether rival gangs are located in spatially adjacent areas, and thus the impact of gangs on spatial patterns of crime would be adequately captured in a simple contiguity matrix. If the socio-spatial dynamics of gang enmity are more complex – meaning that they span both simple contiguity and serve as links among non-local areas – then the spatial dependence matrix should be specified such that it is able to capture these complexities.

We do not suggest that exposure and diffusion represent an either/or proposition with respect to the manner in which gangs can influence gun violence. The spatial distribution of violence involving gang members may be explained by both exposure as well as diffusion. Given that gang members use guns more often than do non-gang members, a community that is exposed to gang members is likely to exhibit higher levels of gun violence. Those gang members may, or may not, live in spatially adjacent areas. Similarly, diffusion driven by the social interactions among gangs involved in ongoing rivalries may also explain the observed spatial patterning of gun violence, especially if the violence is primarily gang motivated and retaliatory in nature. The extent to which the interaction patterns of gang rivalries span simple contiguity to encompass non-local areas should inform the specification of one's spatial weights matrix.

Empirical Example: Gun Violence in Pittsburgh, PA

In this section, we demonstrate a deductive approach to modeling the impact of gangs on local patterns and levels of gun violence. The main goal of this empirical exercise is to show the validity of our approach and methodology rather than to directly answer broader theoretic or policy questions. Drawing from existing theories and prior empirical evidence from a similar study conducted on gang homicide in Los Angeles (Tita 2006), two spatial models are specified in addition to a model that ignores the role of space. The first spatial model follows the conventional approach and limits the influence of violence by restricting the impact among only spatially adjacent areas. The second spatial model considers the socio-spatial dimensions of gangs. Combining spatial data on gang locations with social network data on gang rivalries, we demonstrate how neighborhoods can be conceptualized as nodes in a larger spatial network, where links between nodes are dependent upon a specific social process such as gang rivalries. The central question, then, is whether additional insights can be gained by moving beyond spatial adjacency to consider explicitly the socio-spatial dimensions of gangs and their rivalries. If gang rivalries extend beyond geographic neighbors, the network-based matrix should better explain the observed spatial distribution of crimes in the study area.

This work addresses each of the three issues outlined earlier. First, two specific social processes are offered as the mechanisms driving how events in one location influence events in other places. Second, each of the two weights matrices reflects a specific social process. Third, because an explicit social process is being measured, we model the spatial process as spatial dependence and test that assumption.

Research Design and Measurement

The empirical analysis is conducted in a subset of neighborhoods in Pittsburgh, PA. The gangs that emerged in Pittsburgh are "traditional gangs" (Klein 1995) and have a strong attachment to turf (Tita et al., 2005). Tita and Ridgeway (2007) have demonstrated that the location of gang "set space," the places where gangs hang-out and come together to as a social entity, is strongly associated with local levels of gun violence.

Measures of Gang Set Space

The mapping of set space in Pittsburgh was accomplished through the participation of gang members as well as non-gang youth who resided in gang neighborhoods.[5] Set space represents small sections of the larger neighborhood from which the informants lived. Though these areas are smaller than the geographic units (census block groups) included in our analysis, block groups offer the smallest geographic unit for which the types of ecological measures important in the spatial analysis of crime are available. Analyses such as this are necessarily limited by the level at which data are aggregated (Oberwittler and Wikström, 2009), whereas individual-level network studies have the advantage that the unit of analysis and the attribute data exhibit a one-to-one correspondence.

For this application, we limit our examination to the portion of Pittsburgh bounded on the north/northwest by the Allegheny River and on the south/southwest by the Monongahela River. This simplifies the exercise by converting significant physical barriers into boundaries. Furthermore, Pittsburgh's gangs are concentrated in this region. Though the area includes just fewer than half of all block groups (244 of 497) in the city, it includes nearly two-thirds of all block groups containing set space (36 of 57). The study region and the location of gangs are shown in Fig. 7.1.

Set Space in the Study Region

Fig. 7.1 Set space in the
study region

Legend
Non-Set Space
Set Space
Excluded Areas

---

[5] See Tita et al. (2005) for more detail on the methods used to map and validate the location of set space.

Measurement of Gang Rivalries

Gang rivalries were defined through interviews with the same set of informants who participated in the mapping project. Each participant was asked to identify those gangs that he considered to be their enemies. Though the mean number of rivals is 7.8, the gangs display a wide range in the number rivalries. The Formosa Way Crips and the Panke Way Crips have 17 and 13 rivals, respectively, though the Ehler Street Bloods, MPB, and BCK each have only three rivals.

Measures of Gang Violence

We use 911 calls-for-service to measure crime and limit the analysis to shots fired for the years 1992–1993. This is the period in which gangs formed and became embroiled in lasting rivalries, resulting in the highest levels of violence (Tita and Ridgeway 2007), especially gang-involved violence (Cohen and Tita 1999). The total number of shots fired incidents included in the study is 5762, or an average of 23.6 shots fired incidents per census block group (n = 244) over the two-year period. The spatial distribution of shots fired activity in the study area is shown in Fig. 7.2.

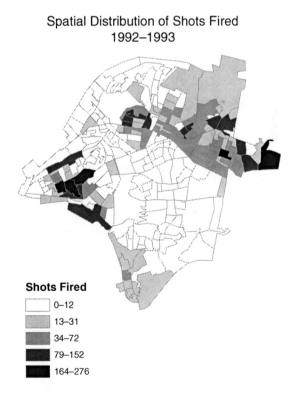

Spatial Distribution of Shots Fired
1992–1993

Shots Fired
- 0–12
- 13–31
- 34–72
- 79–152
- 164–276

Fig. 7.2 Spatial distribution of shots fired 1992–1993

Calls for service depend on the willingness of local residents to report various criminal activities rather than on the choice of the police to enforce particular laws in particular places. Klinger and Bridges (1997) found serious under-reporting bias when using 911 data as a measure of total crime. They attribute this bias to the fact that 23 percent of all crimes handled by patrol officers emanate from police-initiated actions and not from civilian 911 calls. This type of undercounting is not a problem in Pittsburgh because a unique identifier is issued for each event regardless of whether it was citizen or police initiated. Duplicate calls have also been scrubbed from the data. In addition to crime type, the data contain information on the location and date of the incident. These data do not include information on the gang affiliation of the offenders or victims. However, because the focus of our study is on modeling the spatial patterns of gun violence, knowing the gang involvement of the individual participants is not crucial.

Ecological Measures

As displayed in Table 7.1, we included pertinent variables that have been shown to be related to gangs and gun violence in Pittsburgh (Tita et al. 2005; Tita and Ridgeway 2007). These include social control, social disorganization, underclass, and economic measures at the block group level. We also adjust for the percentage of the neighborhood residents who are Black and a control for the land area of the census block group measure of area. Definitions and descriptive statistics for the independent variables, along with the dependent variable, are presented in Table 7.1.

Measurement of the Weights Matrix

The geographically based spatial weights matrix (W_g) is based on first-order contiguity and was constructed using GeoDa 1.9 software (Anselin 2004). Rook's case contiguity was chosen, meaning that two census block groups are considered to be neighbors if they shared a common border.

The second weights matrix employed in this research is derived from the ties within the enmity network and the spatial location of the gangs' activity spaces (i.e., turf or "set space"). This matrix, W_n, was constructed by first creating a location-by-gang matrix, W_l, with dimensions of $m \times n$ (244 block groups $\times$ 27 gangs). This matrix was then multiplied by the $n \times n$ (27 $\times$ 27) enmity network, E, followed by the transpose of the location-by-gang matrix (27 $\times$ 244): $W_l E W_l'$. The resulting two-mode, $m \times m$ (244 $\times$ 244) matrix, W_n, identifies census block groups that contain "enemies" of one another. That is, a non-zero value of an element of W_n, $w_{i,j}$, indicates that the pair of block groups is linked because they both contain the turf of rival gangs. For those block groups that do not contain gang set space, we retained the spatial contiguity. As discussed earlier, both W_g and W_n are row-standardized so that neighbors have equal influence.

Table 7.1 Descriptive statistics

Variable	Definition	Mean[a]	Min	Max
Shots Fired (1992–1993)	Unique 911 calls regarding shots fired	23.615 (38.396)	0	276
1990 Census Measures				
Adult:Youth	Ratio of adults (ages 25–64) to youth (ages < 12)	4.66 (4.019)	0	30
Area ($\ln(1000s \, ft^2)$)	Natural log of block group's area in 1,000s of sq. feet	7.389 (0.817)	5	10
MedRent ($)	Median monthly rent for housing units ($)	379.525 (120.196)	116	825
%Black	% African Americans in population	39.926 (39.902)	0	100
%Renters	% Rental among housing units	44.852 (22.079)	0	100
NewBlack	= 1 if substantial growth of African Americans since 1960, = 0 otherwise	0.275 (0.447)	0	1
%Vacant	% Vacant housing units	10.656 (6.921)	0	48
Underclass	Index created based upon four measures of underclass[b]	34.369 (49.467)	0	315
NewRes	% Residents who did not live in same unit 5 years ago	42.447 (17.654)	7	100
%CrimeAge (14–24 yr olds)	% Population ages 12 to 24	16.881 (9.462)	0	86
%Over 64 (65 + yr olds)	% Population ages over 64	21.803 (10.390)	0	75
Boarded	= 1 if any houses in the block group are boarded up, = 0 otherwise	0.385 (0.488)	0	1
PerCapInc (per 1000)	Per capita income ($000s)	13.459 (8.946)	2.72	54.739
%BelowPov	% Population below poverty	23.504 (18.085)	0	83
%Unemp	% Unemployed among labor force participants	11.639 (11.008)	0	60
Pov>40%	= 1 if at least 40% population < poverty; = 0 otherwise	0.189 (0.392)	0	1
PopDen	People per 10,000 square feet	0.389 (0.505)	0	2

Notes: There are 244 observations.

[a] Standard deviations are in parentheses.

[b] % Population ages 18 to 25 with no high school degree

   % Households receiving public assistance

   % Households headed by females

   % Males over age 15 not working at least 27 weeks in labor force

Models of Gun Violence

Standard OLS regression is inappropriate for estimating spatial lag models because Wy is endogenous. Maximum Likelihood Estimation (MLE) and two-stage least squares are both suitable alternatives (Anselin 1988; Land and Deane 1992), and we use MLE regressions to estimate the spatial lag model.

Results

Before reporting the results of the multivariate spatial analysis, it is customary to determine whether the spatial distribution of crime is random or exhibits a particular spatial pattern (i.e., it is spatially autocorrelated). The most common statistic used to determine the overall pattern of spatial autocorrelation is Moran's I, which is similar to a Pearson correlation coefficient.[6]

The test statistic, I, is bounded by 1.0 (perfect positive autocorrelation meaning the spatial clustering of like values) and -1.0 (perfect negative autocorrelation meaning dissimilar values cluster spatially), and statistical significance is based upon the standard normal distribution.

Using the contiguity spatial weights matrix, W_g, the Moran's I for the shots fired across all block groups is 0.325 (Z-value $= 8.562$ and P-value $= 0.000$). Repeating the analysis but using the network derived weights matrix, W_n, Moran's I is 0.442 (Z-value $= 12.046$ and P-value $= 0.000$). Based on both weights matrices, it is clear that the number of shots fired is not random across space. Though the test statistic is larger when the network-based W is used, it is incorrect to evaluate the two approaches based upon the magnitude of Moran's I. Instead, one needs to examine the significance level. Because the Z-value is greater for W_n, it would be correct to say that though the distribution of crime is both spatially and "socially" autocorrelated, the network-based measure better captures the type of dependence (social) than does the purely spatial measure of dependence.

The results of the regressions are presented in Table 7.2. Initially, the model was estimated with OLS with the constraint $\rho = 0$ imposed. The results of this estimation are reported in the first column of results in Table 7.2. The larger the physical size of the census block group, the more densely populated the block group, the block groups with the greatest growth in black residents since 1960, the higher the percentage of black residents, the higher the percentage of renters, the greater percentage of residents considered "underclass," and block groups with poverty rates greater than 40 percent based upon the 1990 census were are statistically significantly more likely to have more shots fired in the years 1992 and 1993. These results are consistent with other findings in the literature that show areas with higher levels of resource deprivation suffer higher levels of violent crime (Krivo and Peterson 1996; Morenoff et al. 2001; Mears and Bhati 2006).

---

[6] $I = \sum_i \sum_j w_{ij}(x_i - \mu)(x_j - \mu) / \sum_i (x_i - \mu)^2$

Table 7.2 Regression results

Coefficient	OLS	Geography W	Network W
Spatial lag	–	0.109	0.217**
		(0.090)	(0.086)
Adult:Youth	−0.278	−0.303	−0.266
	(0.540)	(0.518)	(0.510)
Area (ln(1000s ft^2))	11.385***	11.257***	10.907***
	(2.699)	(2.588)	(2.552)
MedRent ($)	−0.033	−0.032	−0.029
	(0.021)	(0.020)	(0.019)
%Black	0.155*	0.119	0.087
	(0.081)	(0.082)	(0.079)
%Renters	0.262*	0.282**	0.313**
	(0.144)	(0.139)	(0.137)
NewBlack	8.379*	7.983*	7.129
	(4.880)	(4.680)	(4.618)
%Vacant	−0.133	−0.157	−0.192
	(0.340)	(0.328)	(0.324)
Underclass	0.209***	0.202***	0.184***
	(0.067)	(0.064)	(0.063)
NewRes	−0.256	−0.269	−0.296*
	(0.188)	(0.180)	(0.177)
%CrimeAge (14–24 yr olds)	0.178	0.187	0.128
	(0.241)	(0.231)	(0.229)
%Over64 (65+ yr olds)	−0.362	−0.348*	−0.361*
	(0.220)	(0.211)	(0.208)
Boarded (1 if boarded properties, else 0)	7.854	7.244	5.958
	(5.411)	(5.190)	(5.130)
PerCapInc (per 1000)	0.108	0.118	0.107
	(0.309)	(0.296)	(0.292)
%BelowPov	−0.148	−0.147	−0.139
	(0.271)	(0.261)	(0.257)
%Unemp	0.143	0.150	0.111
	(0.279)	(0.267)	(0.263)
Pov>40%	14.994*	13.736*	12.562
	(8.689)	(8.330)	(8.213)
PopDen (people/10,000ft^2)	10.052**	9.434**	9.083**
	(4.359)	(4.179)	(4.121)
Constant	−66.476***	−66.694***	−64.477***
	(25.210)	(24.205)	(23.830)
R^{2a}	0.456	0.460	0.475

Notes: The dependent variable is shots fired between 1992 and 1993. N = 244
[a] For the MLE regressions, pseudo R^2 are reported
* p-value<0.1
** p-value<0.05
*** p-value<0.01
Standard errors are in parentheses.

Lagrange multiplier, and where appropriate, robust Lagrange multiplier tests were used to test the hypothesis of a spatially lagged dependent variable (Anselin et al. 1996). Despite the fact that the Moran's I indicated significant spatial correlation among shots fired across neighboring block groups as defined by the contiguity spatial weights matrix, W_g, including the set of explanatory variables in the regression model appears to account for much of the correlation across space. Lagrange multiplier tests for both the spatially lagged dependent variable (LM = 1.385 and P-value = 0.239) and spatially autocorrelated error term (LM = 0.024 and P-value = 0.877) do not indicate any remaining spatial dependence. However, as we argued above, patterns of influence are likely not bound exclusively by spatial proximity. We repeated the same tests for the network derived weights matrix, W_n. Lagrange multiplier tests help confirm the need for a spatially lagged dependent variable (LM = 7.404 and P-value = 0.007) rather than a spatially autocorrelated error term (LM = 1.421 and P-value = 0.233). The spatial lag dependence is further confirmed with a Lagrange multiplier test that is robust to any spatial autocorrelation (LM = 10.040 and P-value = 0.002).

The results of the MLE estimation of the spatial lag model using the geographic contiguity and network derived spatial weights matrices to create the spatially lagged dependent variable are displayed in the final two columns of Table 7.2. Not surprisingly given the results of the LM test, very little changed by including a spatially lagged dependent variable based upon W_g. The coefficient on the spatially lagged shots fired (0.109) is not significant at the 10 percent level and none of the other coefficients or the R^2 changed by very much by estimating this spatial model. However, inclusion of the more theoretically-justifiable lagged dependent variable based upon social networks and geography, W_n, does yield a significant coefficient on the spatial lag (0.217, P-value < 0.05). Thus, for approximately every five additional shooting incidents in neighboring tracts, all else equal, the focal tract is predicted to have one more shooting incident. Inclusion of the spatially lagged dependent variable leads to a slightly better fit ($R^2 = 0.475$). This suggests that social relationships across space do indeed impact the observed distribution of, and that that such linkages matter in ways that extend well beyond simple spatial contiguity.

Inclusion of the network generated spatial lag leads to some subtle changes in the estimated impacts of a number of the variables from the initial OLS estimation. Comparing the coefficients across the spatial and non-spatial models, we find that including the spatial lag resulted in the shrinking of the land area coefficient (11.385 to 10.907), population density coefficient (10.052 to 9.083), and percent underclass coefficient (0.209 to 0.184). The coefficients on the high poverty indicator variable (14.994 to 12.562) and percentage black (0.155 to 0.087) also shrank and became insignificant at the 10 percent level. The coefficients on the percentage of renters (0.262 to 0.313) and new residents (−0.256 to −0.296) increased slightly in absolute terms and became significant at lower significance levels. In the OLS model, all of these factors were likely capturing some of the effect of spatial dependence, thus biasing the estimated coefficients. Though such bias is important in and of itself, the true cost of ignoring the correct specification of the weights matrix lies in the ability to interpret the true impact of gang location and gang rivalries on patterns of gun violence.

Conclusions

A growing number of studies in the social sciences have adopted spatial regression in the effort to model and understand neighborhood effects (see Sampson et al., 2002). These efforts have used spatially lagged variables as proxies for social phenomena thought to be responsible for the consistent finding that spatial clustering of events related to the health and welfare of individuals remains even after controlling for local, contextual effects such as race, ethnicity, and poverty. The vast majority of these studies, however, only consider the possibility that the various social processes posited as responsible for the clustering matter only among spatially adjacent neighbors. Furthermore, even when multiple social processes are considered, the conventional modeling approach is to specify a single spatial weights matrix, thereby making it impossible to parse the impact of one process from that of another. Within the realm of criminology, models that interpret the spatial coefficient as being either the result of exposure to violence or the direct influence of diffusionary processes (especially drug markets and gangs) have no way to quantify either's independent contribution. Furthermore, the possibility that either influence process may extend beyond non-contiguous spaces is ignored.

Though our findings verify that researchers have been correct in suggesting gang rivalries play an important role in determining the observed spatial distribution of violence, the impact of these rivalries extends well beyond simple contiguity. That is, gangs have rivals, and these rivalries play an important role in influencing levels of violence in other neighborhoods, but the geographic scope of these rivalries is not limited to adjacent neighbors. By carefully considering socio-spatial dimensions of gangs in terms of the areas where they hang out and the rivalry networks that link them, it is possible to create a weights matrix that explicitly captures the geographic dimensions of the patterns of social influence among the gangs. We find that the violence, as measured by shots fired in a central part of Pittsburgh, is more a function of a social process that spans geography in such a way that violence in non-local areas impacts levels of violence in a focal neighborhood.

Though the current research focuses solely on the impact of gangs on patterns of gun violence, the lesson learned is far reaching for all types of analysis employing spatial regression in the study of violence. Most importantly, the results underscore Leenders' concern with the lack of careful consideration of the underlying social processes of influence exhibited by researchers in their construction of the weights matrices. Just as others have demonstrated the utility of disaggregating homicide by motive and other defining features in terms of understanding the social processes that lead to the commission of such crimes (Wolfgang 1958; Parker and Smith 1979; William and Flewelling 1988; Gartner 1990), it is important to consider socio-spatial processes that are specific to the type of events beings studied. For instance, testing the relationship between gun violence and drug markets would require one to specify a weights matrix that captures the important geographical information pertaining to the market (its location) as well as the spatial dimensions of the actors (mobility of customers and sellers) involved within the market. Adapting Leenders' (2002, p.26) "change one's theory, change W" statement to the current context and one is reminded to "change one's *crime*, change W."

The current research is also instructive for those who wish to use simple contiguity to capture processes beyond gangs, specifically issues addressing "exposure." Contiguity is theoretically justified when exposure is meant to capture social influence processes wherein local offenders from high violence areas transgress into *neighboring areas* to commit their crime, or when they influence residents in the *neighboring area* to carry/use guns. However, as research has demonstrated (Groff and McEwen 2006; Tita and Griffiths 2005), the distance traveled by homicide offenders differs by type of homicide. Therefore, care must be taken to construct spatial weights matrices that capture the links among neighborhoods that generate offenders and the neighborhoods where these offenders influence violence.

When the concern is tilted more to issues of social influence among peers or the contagious nature of subcultures, the geographic nature of these peers in terms of where they interact is extremely important. This is especially true among youth. As Mears and Bhati (2006) argue, the socio-spatial dimensions of these interactions is likely less dependent upon the location of residential neighbors and more likely dependent upon the geographic scale of one's social activities. This may include interactions at school, sporting events, bars/clubs, or other "staging areas" (Anderson 1999) where young people come together and interact. In fact, modeling ties among neighborhoods based upon the feeder patterns of local junior and senior high schools might offer excellent insight into the observed spatial patterns of violence and crime. Furthermore, it has also been demonstrated that homicide and gun violence have exhibited patterns of diffusion that are more consistent with hierarchical diffusion (among ordered pairs) than contagion diffusion along simple contiguity (Cohen and Tita 1999; Tita and Cohen 2004). Gun violence spread across communities not on the basis of geographic proximity, but more so in terms of social similarity. That is, violence spread along racial lines. Therefore, in modeling the diffusion of subcultures of violence or gun use, it may be necessary to consider the racial/social proximity among neighborhoods and not simply their geographic proximity to one another.

This research supports the basic conclusions reached in the spatial analysis of violence literature. First, place clearly matters. That is, levels and patterns of violence within geographic units cannot be explained by examining the structural characteristics alone. Second, the social organization of gang violence – as driven by geographic territory and enduring rivalries – is an important factor in accounting for spatial dependence. However, the common assumption that simple contiguity captures the social process of retaliation appears to be an oversimplification of socio-spatial dimensions of gang rivalries. That is, in some instances gang rivalries extend well beyond contiguous neighbors while in other cases neighboring geographic units are not linked through gang rivalries at all. As spatial analysis is used as a tool to identify the social processes responsible for "neighborhood effects," it becomes increasingly important to insure that one's spatial weights matrix is constructed in a manner that is consistent with the social process of interest.

When selecting the unit of analysis, we applaud the more recent literature that has begun to further explore the role of space. However, as we have shown, it is easy to specify a model incorporating space that does not adequately represent the social processes that underlie the spatial dependence. It is important to keep in mind that spatial autocorrelation does not necessarily imply spatial dependence – in that case, the autocorrelation is more appropriately modeled with a spatial error term that treats the spatial correlation as a nuisance parameter. However, as we make clear, many processes do lead to events in one place affecting outcomes in another, and the researcher must take care to use a deductive approach that models the social process that leads to the spatial dependence. As we have argued, this process may involve dependence among spatial units that are not geographically proximate. Future research should take care to consider this possibility.

References

Anderson, E. (1999). *Code of the Street: Decency, Violence, and the Moral Life of the Inner City*. New York: W. W. Norton & Company.

Anselin, L. (1988). *Spatial Econometrics: Methods and Models*. Dordrecht, the Netherlands: Kluwer Academic Publishers.

Anselin, L. (2004). *GeoDa. Center for Spatially Integrated Social Science*. Urbana-Champaign Urbana, IL: University of Illinois.

Anselin, L., Bera, A. K., Florax, R., & Yoon, M. J. (1996). Simple diagnostic tests for spatial dependence. *Regional Science and Urban Economics*, 26, 77–104.

Babcock, L., Engberg, J., & Greenbaum, R. (2005). Wage spillovers in public sector contract negotiations: The importance of social comparisons. *Regional Science and Urban Economics*, 35, 395–416.

Baller, R. D., Anselin, l., & Messner, S. F. (2001). Structural covariates of U.S. county homicide rates: Incorporating spatial effects. *Criminology*, 39, 561–590.

Battin, S. R., Hill, K. G., Abbott, R. D., Catalano, R. F., & Hawkins, J. D. (1998). The contribution of gang membership to delinquency beyond delinquent friends. *Criminology*, 36, 93–115.

Blumstein, A. (1995). Youth Violence, Guns, and the Illicit-drug Industry. *Journal of Criminal Law and Criminology*, 86, 10–36.

Blumstein, A., & Cork, D. (1996). Linking gun availability to youth gun violence. *Law and Contemporary Problems*, 59(1), 5–24 (special issue Kids, Guns, and Public Policy).

Blumstein, A., & Rosenfeld, R. (1998). Explaining recent trends in US homicide rates. *Journal of Criminal Law and Criminology*, 88, 1175–1216.

Boggs, S. L. (1965). Urban crime patterns. *American Sociological Review*, 30, 899–908.

Brantingham, P. J., & Brantingham, P. L. (1981). *Environmental Criminology*. Beverly Hills: Sage Publications.

Caulkins, J. P., Larson, R. C., & Rich, T. F. (1993). Geography's impact on the success of focused local drug enforcement operations. *Socio-Economic Planning Science*, 27, 119–30.

Case, A. C., Rosen, H. S., & Hines Jr. J. R. (1993). Budget spillovers and fiscal policy interdependence: Evidence from the states. *Journal of Public Economics*, 52, 285–307.

Cliff, A. D., Hagget, P., Ord, J. K., & Versey, G. R. (1981). *Spatial Diffusion: An Historical Geography of Epidemics in an Island Community*. Cambridge: Cambridge University Press.

Cohen, J., Cork, D., Engberg, J., & Tita, G. (1998). The role of drug markets and gangs in local homicide rates. *Homicide Studies*, 2, 241–262.

Cohen, J., & Tita, G. (1999). Diffusion in homicide: Exploring a general method for detecting spatial diffusion processes. *Journal of Quantitative Criminology*, 15, 451–493.

Cohen, L. E., & Felson, M. (1979). Social change and crime rate trends: A routine activities approach. *American Sociological Review*, 44, 588–608.

Cork, D. (1999). Examining space-time interaction in city-level homicide data: Crack markets and the diffusion of guns among youth. *Journal of Quantitative Criminology*, 5, 379–406.

Decker, S. (1996). Collective and normative features of gang violence. *Justice Quarterly*, 13, 243–264.

Doreian, P. (1980). Linear models with spatially distributed data: Spatial disturbances or spatial effects. *Sociological Methods and Research*, 9, 29–60.

Eck, J. E. (1995). A general model of the geography of illicit retail marketplaces. In: J. E. Eck & D. Weisburd (Eds.), *Crime and Place* (pp. 67–93). Monsey, NY: Criminal Justice Press.

Elffers, H. (2003). Analyzing neighbourhood influence in criminology. *Journal of the Netherlands Society for Statistics and Operations Research*, 57(3), 347–367.

Gartner, R. (1990). The victims of homicide: A temporal and cross-national comparison. *American Sociological Review*, 55, 92–106.

Gordon, R., Lahey, B., Kawai, E., Loeber, R., Stouthhamer-Loeber, M., Farrington, D. (2004). Antisocial behavior and youth gang membership: Selection and socialization. *Criminology*, 42, 55–87.

Gould, R. (1991). Multiple networks and mobilization in the Paris Commune, 1870. *American Sociological Review*, 56, 716–729.

Greenbaum, R. T. (2002). A Spatial study of teachers' salaries in pennsylvania school districts. *Journal of Labor Research*, 23, 69–86.

Griffiths, E., & Chavez, J. M. (2004). Communities, street guns and homicide trajectories in Chicago, 1980–1995: Merging methods for examining homicide trends across space and time. *Criminology*, 42, 941–975.

Groff, E., & McEwen, T. (2006). Exploring the Spatial Configuration of Places Related to Homicide Events. *Final Report*. Washington, DC: National Institute of Justice.

Hesseling, R. B. P. (1992). Using data on offender mobility in ecological research. *Journal of Quantitative Criminology*, 8, 95–112.

Kim, Y. (2007). Using spatial analysis for monitoring fraud in a public delivery program. *Social Science Computer Review*, 25, 287–301.

Klein, M. (1995). *The American Street Gang: Its Nature, Prevalence and Control*. New York: Oxford University Press.

Klinger, D., & Bridges, G. S. (1997). Measurement errors in call-for-service as an indicator of crime. *Criminology*, 35, 529–541.

Krivo, L. J., & Peterson, R. D. (1996). Extremely disadvantaged neighborhoods and urban crime. *Social Forces*, 75, 619–50.

Land, K. C., & Deane, G. (1992). On the large-sample estimation of regression models with spatial effects terms: A two-stage least squares approach. *Sociological Methodology*, 22, 221–248.

Leenders, R. Th. A. J. (2002). Modeling social influence through network autocorrelation: constructing the weight matrix. *Social Networks*, 24, 21–47.

Loftin, C. (1986). Assaultive violence as a contagious process. *Bulletin of New York Academy of Medicine*, 62, 550–555.

Manski, C. (1994). *Identification Problems in the Social Sciences*. Cambridge: Harvard University Press.

Marsden, P. V., & Friedkin, N. E. (1994). Network studies of social influence. In: S. Wasserman & J. Galaskiewicz (Eds.), *Advances in Social Network Analysis* (pp. 3–25). Thousand Oaks, CA: Sage.

Mears, D. P., & Bhati, A. S. (2006). No community is an island: The effects of resource deprivation on urban violence in spatially and socially proximate communities. *Criminology*, 44, 509–548.

Messner, S., & Anselin, L. (2004). Spatial analysis of homicide with areal data. In: M. F. Goodchild & D. G. Janelle (Eds.), *Spatially Integrated Social Science* (pp. 127–144). New York: Oxford Press.

Messner, S. F., & Tardiff, K. (1986). The social ecology of urban homicide: An application of the 'Routine Activities' approach. *Criminology*, 22, 241–267.

Mikelbank, K. M., & Sabol, W. J. (2005). The use of GIS and spatial analysis in responding to community concerns about local drug markets. Eighth Annual Crime Mapping Research Conference, Savannah, Georgia.

Moore, J. (1991). *Going Down to the Barrio: Homeboys and Homegirls in Change.* Philadelphia, PA: Temple Press.

Morenoff, J. D., & Sampson, R. J. (1997). Violent crime and the spatial dynamics of neighborhood transition: Chicago, 1970–1990. *Social Forces*, 76, 31–64.

Morenoff, J. D., Sampson, R. J., & Raudenbush, S. (2001). Neighborhood inequality, collective efficacy, and the spatial dynamics of urban violence. *Criminology*, 39, 517–560.

Nagin, D. S. (1999). Analyzing developmental trajectories: A semi-parametric, group-based approach. *Psychological Methods*, 2, 139–157.

Oberwittler, D. & Wikström P. (2009). "Why Small Is Better: Advancing the Study of the Role of Behavioral Contexts in Crime Causation." In: D.Weisburd, W. Bernasco & G. J. N. Bruinsma (Eds.), *Putting Crime in its Place: Units of Analysis in Spatial Crime Research.* New York: Springer.

Parker, R. N., & Smith, M. D. (1979). Deterrence, poverty and type of homicide. *American Journal of Sociology*, 85, 614–624

Rand, A. (1986). Mobility triangles. In: R. Figlio, S. Hakim & G.F. Rengert (Eds.), *Metropolitan Crime Patterns*. New York: Criminal Justice Press.

Rengert, G. F. (1996). *The Geography of Illegal Drugs*. Boulder, CO: Westview Press.

Robertson, J. B., & Rengert, G. F. (2006). Illegal drug markets: The geographic perspective and crime propensity. *Western Criminology Review*, 7(1), 2–32.

Rosenfeld, R., Bray, T., & Egley, A. (1999). Facilitating violence: A comparison of gang-motivated, gang-affiliated, and non-gang youth homicides. *Journal of Quantitative Criminology*, 5, 495–516.

Sampson, R. J. (2004). Networks and neighbourhoods: The implications of connectivity for thinking about crime in the modern city. In: H. McCarthy, P. Miller & P. Skidmore (Eds.), *Network Logic: Who Governs in an Interconnected World?* (pp. 157–166). London: Demos.

Sampson, R. J., Morenoff, J. D., & Gannon-Rowley, T. (2002). Assessing neighborhood effects: Social processes and new directions in research. *Annual Review of Sociology*, 28, 443–478.

Strang, D., & Tuma, N. B. (1993). Spatial and temporal heterogeneity in diffusion. *American Journal of Sociology*, 3, 614–639.

Thornberry, T. P., Krohn, M. D., Lizotte, A. J., Smith, C. A., & Tobin, K. (2003). *Gangs and delinquency in developmental perspective.* Cambridge: Cambridge University Press.

Tita, G. (2006). Neighborhoods as nodes: Combining social network analysis with spatial analysis to explore the spatial distribution of gang violence. Conference paper for Workshop on Space, Networks, and Social Influence. February 9th – 11th, 2006. University of California, Irvine.

Tita, G., & Ridgeway, G. (2007). The impact of gang formation on local patterns of crime. *Journal of Research on Crime and Delinquency*, 44(2), 208–237.

Tita, G., & Griffiths, E. (2005). Traveling to violence: The case for a mobility-based spatial typology of homicide. *Journal of Research on Crime and Delinquency*, 42, 275–308.

Tita, G., & Cohen, J. (2004). Measuring spatial diffusion of shots fired activity across city neighborhoods. In: M. F. Goodchild & D. G. Janelle (Eds.), *Spatially Integrated Social Science* (pp. 171–204). New York: Oxford Press.

Tita, G., Cohen, J., & Engberg, J. (2005). An ecological study of the location of gang 'Set Space'. *Social Problems*, 52, 272–299.

Tobler, W. R. (1970). A computer movie simulating urban growth in the detroit region. *Economic Geography*, 46, 234–240.

Weisburd, D., & Green, L. (1995). Policing drug hot spots: the Jersey City DMA experiment. *Justice Quarterly*, 12(4), 711–36.

Wilkinson, D., & Fagan, J. (1996). Understanding the role of firearms in violence scripts: The dynamics of gun events among adolescent males. *Law and Contemporary Problems*, 59, 55–90.

Williams, K., & Flewelling, R. L. (1988). The social production of criminal homicide: A comparative study of disaggregated rates in American Cities. *American Sociological Review*, 54, 421–31.

Wolfgang, M. (1958). *Patterns in Criminal Violence*. Philadelphia, PA: University of Pennsylvania.

Chapter 8
Predictive Mapping of Crime by ProMap: Accuracy, Units of Analysis, and the Environmental Backcloth

Shane D. Johnson, Kate J. Bowers, Dan J. Birks, and Ken Pease[1]

Abstract This chapter concerns the forecasting of crime locations using burglary as an example. An overview of research concerned with when *and* where burglaries occur is provided, with an initial focus on patterns of risk at the individual household level. Of central importance is evidence that as well as being geographically concentrated (at a range of geographic scales), burglary clusters in space *and* time more than would be expected if patterns of crime were simply the result of some places being more attractive to offenders than others. One theoretical framework regarding offender spatial decision making is discussed and consideration given to how features of the urban environment which affect the accessibility of places (e.g., road networks or social barriers) might shape patterns of offending. A simple mathematical model informed by the research discussed is then presented and tested as to its accuracy in the prediction of burglary locations. The model is tested against chance expectation and popular methods of crime hot-spotting extant and found to outperform both. Consideration of the importance of different units of analysis is a recurrent theme throughout the chapter, whether this concerns the intended policy purpose of crime forecasts made, the spatial resolution of different types of data analyzed, or the attention given to the dimension of time – a unit of analysis often overlooked in this type of work. The chapter concludes with a discussion of means of developing the approach described, combining it with others, and using it, inter alia, to optimize police patrol routes.

[1]The authors would like to thank Merseyside police and the Ordnance Survey for providing the data analyzed in this chapter, and three anonymous reviewers for their thoughtful comments. This research was supported by a British Academy International Collaborative Network grant, and additional funding from UCL Futures, NSCR and the Research Incentive Fund at Temple University.

S.D. Johnson
UCL Jill Dando Institute of Crime Science, London, United Kingdom
e-mail: shane.johnson@ucl.ac.uk

D. Weisburd et al. (eds.), *Putting Crime in its Place*,
DOI 10.1007/978-0-387-09688-9_8, © Springer Science+Business Media, LLC 2009

Introduction

Predictions about how crime will be distributed can be made for different levels of spatial aggregation, most being useful for some policy purpose. At the macro level, predictions may be made about towns or cities. These will be useful for national governments in the provision of resources and support to local policing. The meso-level employs smaller areal units such as police beats or census tracts which nonetheless may incorporate hundreds of households and businesses. These will be useful for resource decisions within police forces and for the understanding of offender spatial choices dependent on neighborhood characteristics (see e.g., Bernasco and Nieuwbeerta 2005). The micro level has the individual household or business as its unit of count and has been studied in the context of repeat victimization (e.g., see Farrell 2005) and household-specific risk factors (see Winchester and Jackson 1982; Coupe and Blake 2006). Prediction at this level is useful for the provision of advice and protective technology to individual locations at risk.

The writers contend that the unit of analysis selected should be informed by theory and/or an intended application. Data are often unavailable at the level of geographic resolution desirable, particularly where a disaggregated analysis would be appropriate. When analyses are performed using data from the less appropriate larger areal units, the temptation may be to assume that patterns observed across an area will apply equally to the mosaic of smaller areas (and individual locations) of which it is composed - the ecological fallacy. The assumption that crime experience is uniform within an area is certainly ill-founded (Bowers et al. 2005). The larger the areal unit used, the more probable it becomes that local decisions within the area will be sub-optimal. Of course, disaggregated data may be aggregated. Aggregated data cannot readily be disaggregated.

This preamble has two purposes. The first is to assert that the choice of areal unit in crime prediction should proceed in lockstep with the decisions to be informed. The second, more contentious, is to propose that there is an areal unit intermediate between micro and meso level which is the appropriate one for optimizing police patrol. This may (over-simply) be thought of as an area clearly visible within seconds by a police officer on foot, encapsulated as 'having a look around', having stopped a patrol vehicle in an area of potential interest. While vague, in the next section, we will suggest how a unit of analysis at roughly this scale emerges from research as useful in underpinning patrolling choices.

Before continuing, an overview of what follows will be provided. The general aim of this chapter is to present our most recent work and thinking concerning the forecasting of future locations of burglary, where the future relates to the next week, or so. The structure of the chapter is as follows. First, we briefly discuss research concerned with patterns of burglary at the most precise unit of analysis; repeat victimization of the individual household. This is followed by a discussion of more recent work which may be thought of an extension of the repeat victimization literature. In doing so, we discuss one theoretical framework regarding offender spatial decision making and how this might inform crime forecasting. Second, we discuss how other factors, which may be defined at different units of analysis (e.g., the street network, neighborhood characteristics), may influence offender decision making and how these might be integrated into a forecasting methodology. Third, we present an empirical test of the method discussed, comparing it to contending alternatives and chance expectation. Finally, the results are discussed, their implications articulated, and methodological issues regarding the importance of choosing the right spatial units of analysis revisited. The crime analyzed in this chapter is domestic burglary but we are actively conducting the analyses necessary for extension across crime types and across sequences of different crime types.

Risk, Contagion, and the Optimal Forager

The logic applied in the research refines and develops that focusing on repeat victimization (see Pease 1998). Briefly, for every type of crime studied (except homicide), the risk of victimization increases significantly following an initial event (e.g., Polvi et al. 1991); a small proportion of victims (e.g., 4%) account for a large proportion (e.g., 44%) of crime (Pease 1998); and, where repeat victimization occurs, it usually does so quickly, offering a narrow window of opportunity for intervention (e.g., Johnson et al. 1997). The consequence is spatio-temporal instability in crime risk at the micro-level unit of analysis. Importantly, interviews with offenders and analysis of police records suggest that repeat burglaries at the same location are overwhelmingly the work of the same offender or of groups having at least one offender in common (Ericsson 1995; Ashton et al. 1998: Everson and Pease 2001; Everson 2003; Bernasco 2008).

Research also suggests that offenders exhibit preferences, internalized as cognitive scripts (Cornish 1994; Wright and Decker 1994; Rengert and Wasilchick 2000) or templates (Brantingham and Brantingham 1993), for the types of property considered suitable targets. The prevalence of repeat victimization shows that despite the many and varied opportunities within a burglar's awareness space, he or she exhibits an inclination to return to homes already victimized. Interviews with convicted burglars (Ashton et al. 1998; Shaw and Pease 2000) suggest that where opportunities present themselves, offenders seek familiarity, which is to be found in returning to the same home or looking for near-replicas, favoring these over targets of which they know little. Prosaic reasons for return include this terse commentary of one Scottish burglar 'Big house, small van'!

Preferences (conceived as reward in relation to effort) seem to be maintained until they no longer offer an advantage over other opportunities (Brantingham and Brantingham 1981). Experience updates the templates. The discovery of a good opportunity for burglary should elevate the risk to similar households from that burglar. Thus, following a burglary at one home, those located nearby (which will share a range of physical and other characteristics) should be at an elevated risk for some time afterwards. This is termed a 'near repeat' (Morgan 2001; Pease 1998). Much recent research demonstrates this to be the case. Using techniques from epidemiology (Knox 1964), research has confirmed that burglary clusters in space and time (Townsley et al. 2003; Johnson and Bowers 2004a; Bowers and Johnson 2005). Communicable disease provides a useful simile from the policing and victim perspective, where the task at hand is to choose for attention places currently at high risk. When considering matters from the offender's viewpoint, the notion of the optimal forager (discussed below) is more apposite. In any event, we should not get too excited about similes beyond their heuristic value. For example, in disease contagion, each victim comes to carry the infective agent to his or her neighbors. In burglary contagion, the infective agent remains the same (the burglar), and it is the way in which their awareness of, or preferences for, particular opportunities may be temporarily shaped by their recent activity that is of interest.

Returning to the typical conclusions from the research concerned with near repeats, following a burglary, homes up to 400 m away have been shown to experience an elevated risk for up to two months. Importantly, data from five countries (UK, US, AUS, NDL, and NZ), demonstrated that the phenomenon is at least widespread, perhaps ubiquitous, in the developed world (Johnson et al. 2007). Arguing that the same underlying process is involved is premature but tempting. This so-far ubiquitous pattern suggests that, although some areas tend to experience enduring risks, hot spots tend to be 'slippery' (Johnson and Bowers 2004b). Offenders demonstrate by their 'spoor' (the trail of victimized homes or people) a search pattern which may be likened to foraging behavior (Johnson and Bowers 2004a). As a consequence of having exploited all favorable opportunities on one street segment, or because of a perceived elevation in the local risk of apprehension, an offender may move to other areas, typically those conveniently accessible, that is, nearby. Our understanding of the burglar's sequenced decision making is thus as follows. First, select an area/street segment, burgle the best presenting option, and then target the most similar available opportunities, returning to some before moving on when profit diminishes or physical change alerts to precautions being taken. As with foraging, the activity is intermittent.

Why is the image of the optimal forager appealing? Consider the foraging sheep. Sheep may take multiple bites of the most luscious grass, particularly since foraging involves a trade-off between, on the one hand, the energy value of food immediately available and, on the other, effort expended in reaching even more luscious grass elsewhere. Grass in the far corner of the field has to be more calorific to the extent that it offsets the energy (and possibly danger) involved in moving across the pasture. The food value of over-grazed grass diminishes until it re-grows, just as the take from repeatedly burgled homes declines until replacement goods are purchased. Even sheep get full sometimes, and so do the arms or vans of burglars. Burgled goods must be secreted or disposed of before foraging recommences. Once an area is perceived to have been grazed out (skimmed of the best opportunities) the forager moves on. This is in line with theory discussed elsewhere (e.g., Brantingham and Brantingham 1978; Cornish and Clarke 1986; Bernasco and Nieuwbeerta 2005) and is consistent with interviews conducted with offenders (e.g., Bennett and Wright 1984; Nee and Meenaghan 2006). The evident regularity in the space-time clustering of recorded burglary is, in short, a consequence of burglar as forager. It is emphatically *not* consistent with any theory predicated on a time-invariant distribution of risk factors. To put it bluntly, space *and* time are both crucial in the analysis of crime patterns. To ignore time is to diminish the value of spatial analysis and vice-versa. Ignoring time leads to a perceived paradox: that homes already victimized are liable to further victimization, but that crime risks move. The paradox is only apparent when the variable *time* is overlooked. The elevated risk to the recently burgled is transient. As time moves on, so does the foraging burglar.

We presume that crimes in a near repeat series are more often than not committed by the same offender(s). Interviews with offenders support this idea (Ashton et al. 1998), as do the findings of research which has examined patterns of offending for detected offences. For example, Everson (2003) found that having targeted one home on a street, burglars tended to target others nearby. Bernasco (2008) looked at pairs of detected burglaries at a range of spatio-temporal distances. He found that 98% of repeat burglary pairs occurring within 100 m and one week of each other were detected to the same burglar. The proportion of same-offender pairs declined as time and space between events increased. For example, events 100–200 m from an initial burglary 1–2 weeks later were the work of the same offender in only 55% of detected cases. That said, more research is required as analyses so far conducted may reflect only the targeting decisions made by the (potentially biased) samples of offenders for which data were available- those arrested or convicted.

A further test of the near repeat/same offender hypothesis (Bowers et al. 2004) involved the use of a simple mathematical model (hereafter, ProMap) to predict where burglary would next occur. The risk of crime at any location within a grid that represented the study area was derived by considering where and when burglaries had previously occurred. If burglaries clustering in space and time represent the foraging signatures of individual offenders (or co-offenders), grid locations where the greatest number of burglaries had occurred recently and nearby (rather than those locations that had just had the most crime at them, irrespective of when) were predicted to have the greatest imminent risk. Given the finding that such risk diminishes with time, the appropriate temporal interval for analysis of predictive accuracy should be short (e.g., one week into the future). The use of longer intervals (e.g., one month into the future) would be incongruent with the tempo at which offender and policing decisions are made. The areas for which the predictions were generated were also small (50 m grid cells) for the same reasons.

ProMap: Initial Tests and Introducing Accessibility

The results of the ProMap model were compared to the retrospective hot-spotting technique known as Kernel Density Estimation (KDE) and also to a thematic map generated using a police beat geography (Bowers et al. 2004). The KDE method was chosen as a comparator for two reasons. First, it is commonly used by police and researchers. Second, unlike thematic maps, the unit of analysis is flexible. 50 m grid cells were used for both the KDE and ProMap. The obvious justification for the use of thematic maps is that they correspond to areas of police responsibility (Poot et al. 2005) and that such analysis facilitates a comparison of forecast accuracy for maps derived using very different units of analysis.

To examine the relative accuracy of the approaches, we first compared the percentage of future burglaries that occurred in the 20% of cells (or beats when using thematic maps) with the highest predicted risks according to each method. ProMap proved more accurate than either KDE or thematic maps. The fact that only one prediction was generated and no comparison was made against chance expectation limits euphoria about ProMap's performance. Both of these considerations are addressed below.

A criticism of most crime mapping techniques is that crime data constitutes the sole input, (although this is not true of repeat victimization research (see, e.g., Tseloni et al. 2004; Tseloni and Kershaw 2005). The underlying opportunity structure or spatial field is essentially assumed to be uniform. This assumption is seldom tenable. Recent research concerned with spatial ecology (Matthiopoulos 2003) considered the impact on the foraging behavior of species under temporal and spatial constraints on the distribution of resources and the accessibility of locations. Where resources are unevenly distributed (the norm), the inclusion of an accessibility variable increases the predictive efficacy of mathematical models of foraging. People are likewise subject to both spatial and temporal constraints (Ratcliffe 2006), and location accessibility is hence a plausible influence on offender foraging.

In the urban environment, Beavon et al. (1994) examined how the risk of victimization at different street segments in Vancouver varied according to their ease of access. There was indeed a positive correlation between victimization and ease of access for a range of property crimes including burglary. Similar results have been found for research conducted in the UK (e.g., Armitage 2007; Hillier 2004).

The only study which considered such issues in the prediction of crime and of which the authors are aware was conducted by Groff and LaVigne (2001). They used a simple 'on-off' estimation of opportunity factors such as land use, housing tenure, and proximity to likely offenders, derived for a grid that represented the study area. These were aggregated to produce an overall risk score for every grid square (or cell). For each cell, the risk score incorporated the mean of the cells that comprised its Moore neighborhood (the surrounding cells). The accuracy of this weighted opportunity surface in predicting burglary was then tested. The results suggested that only 6% of burglaries occurred where the risk score was one to two standard deviations below the mean. At the other end of the scale, 20% of burglaries happened in cells with risk values one or more standard deviations above the mean. The model thus seemed better at predicting where crimes would not occur than where they would. Groff and LaVigne incorporated only time-invariant factors in their predictions. The model thus accurately identified areas where good opportunities for crime were always rare. Where opportunities did exist, the Groff and LaVigne procedure, neglecting variations over time, failed to help much in indicating which locations would be exploited.

How should one operationalize accessibility (or what might be thought of as pull factors)? The simplest and most obvious factor is the *number* of homes in a grid square and this is the first accessibility measure used in the study reported. The second concerns the street network and in the simplest sense the number and types of road in each grid cell. The rationale for using the latter was that the number of roads in a cell is likely to provide a crude index of how connected each cells is to those that surround it, whereas the type of road (small or large) provides an estimate of the likely volume of through traffic (pedestrian or vehicle).

A further factor that might affect offender movement is the existence of physical or perceived barriers. For example, using data for convicted offenders in The Hague, Bernasco and Nieuwbeerta (2005) examined the effect of area characteristics on offenders' target choices. After controlling for other relevant factors (such as proximity to the central business district), they found that an offender's decision to burgle was linked to ethnic heterogeneity, measured at the area level. More homogeneous neighborhoods appeared to generate impedance to offender movement, and this was particularly the case for areas hosting those not native to the Netherlands. In a further Dutch study, Poot et al. (2005) found that when offenders committed any place based crime (e.g., shoplifting, burglary, or violence) in neighborhoods other than their own, they were less likely to cross recognizable social barriers. In the same vein, LeBeau and Rengert (2006) showed that arrested drug dealers tend to deal drugs in areas with ethnic profiles similar to that of their own neighborhood. Reynald et al. (2006) also show the salience of social barriers in crime trips. In short, the evidence suggests that social barriers delineating areas shape offender choices. Observed consistencies in the target choices of offenders reflect their preferences (see Hakim et al. 2001).

Put simply, burglars have preferences for certain areas. We here hypothesize that where barriers may be perceived to separate areas of recent crime from different but contiguous areas, the established patterns whereby (offender foraging and hence) crime risk seems to spread will be impeded.

The Argument So Far and Measuring Predictive Success

Let us rehearse the arguments advanced to this point. We have argued

1. that a scale of spatial analysis between meso and micro is appropriate for patrolling choices.
2. that the range over which burglary risk might be thought of as being communicated (to use the simile) is consistent with this scale, being some 200–400 m
3. that the spatial communication of risk is temporally limited, making spatio-temporal analysis necessary.
4. that such patterns are overwhelmingly a reflection of the activity of individual offenders, with the analogy of the optimal forager being helpful in illuminating the likely search processes involved.
5. that factors of actual and perceived accessibility of places can usefully supplement the basic ProMap approach.

A further issue that is central to the theme of this book concerns the size of the areas to be identified as being most at risk. Police resources vary. A poorly resourced police area will be attracted by a predictive mapping model which identifies the most crime-prone 10% (say) of locations. The police commander in such an area will be indifferent to the model's performance for a higher proportion of the area to be policed, because he or she does not have the resources to cover more than 10% of the area. A more richly resourced area will be concerned about the model's performance up to (say) 20% of the area, if resources exist to police such a high proportion of the area. For this reason, a more sensitive means of establishing predictive accuracy than has been used elsewhere (e.g., Bowers et al. 2004; Groff and LaVigne 2001) is required. Instead of considering the fraction of events predicted by a particular proportion (such as the top 20%) of cells with the highest anticipated risks, the product which satisfies the information needs of police across a range of resourcing options is an accuracy concentration curve. This is simple to do, being generated by plotting the percentage of burglaries accurately predicted as a function of the incremental (risk ordered) percentage of cells considered. This provides a more complete understanding of how well the different models work. Crucially, it allows operational decisions to be optimized for *any* level of local resourcing and circumstance, and to be adjusted in response to changes in these factors. Consider the two hypothetical examples shown in Fig. 8.1. For the first four percent of cells considered, model 2 performs better than model 1, but thereafter the reverse is true. The functional form of model 1 is non-linear, which is desirable, whereas as that

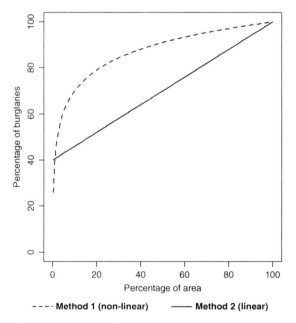

Fig. 8.1 An example accuracy concentration curve

for model 2 is linear, which is not. Patterns such as this are only detectable where a concentration curve is generated and will be missed where single cut points are used.

The aims of the analyses that follow were three-fold: (1) to provide a further test of the prospective mapping (ProMap) algorithm, by generating a series of predictions for comparison against chance expectation and the performance of retrospective methods generated using different (spatial) units of analysis (KDE and thematic mapping); (2) to examine the effect of using data concerning the distribution of opportunities and a crude index of their accessibility on the accuracy of the ProMap algorithm; and, (3) to develop the model to incorporate the potential impact of barriers. The last aim was particularly tentative as no relevant research had been conducted within the study area used in this chapter, or using the approach here proposed. It has yet to be established whether the existence of barriers of the kind discussed above affect offender targeting decisions within the UK, or what types of barrier might be chosen as most relevant. The attempt is worthwhile, if only as a marker for future research.

Data and Method

Residential burglary data were obtained for the county of Merseyside, UK. Reflecting processing limitations, data were analyzed for a (5 km × 5 km) 27,040,000 m^2 grid square in South Liverpool, a fragment of which is illustrated in Fig. 8.2. Each burglary record included information concerning date and location, the grid coordinates having a positional accuracy of one meter. The available data covered the period 1 September 1996 to 30 November 1997. Data for the first year (1 September 1996 to 31 August 1997) were used as a construction sample to generate a profile of space-time clustering, the remainder of the data were used (1 September 1997 to 30 November 1997) as a validation sample for the predictions generated[2]. Data covering a period of two months were used to generate all predictions, irrespective of the method used. To test the accuracy of predictions, data from the ensuing seven days were examined. In order to minimize spatial edge effects, data for a 500 m-buffer zone were included in the generation of the predictions.

Analysis of space-time clustering using historic data allowed calibration of the prospective mapping algorithm. Because this approach has been described elsewhere (see, Johnson et al. 2007), it will be merely outlined here. In the Knox approach (Knox 1964) and the Monte Carlo variant used here (Besag and Diggle 1977), the spatial and temporal interval between each crime and every other crime was computed. A contingency table was then populated to summarize the

---

[2] The validation sample was not used in the generation of the area-level profile of space-time clustering, but was of course used in the generation of the predictions. That is, to generate the predictions a rolling window of data were required. For the initial forecast only data from the construction sample were required, but for subsequent predictions additional data (which preceded the prediction) from the validation sample were necessary.

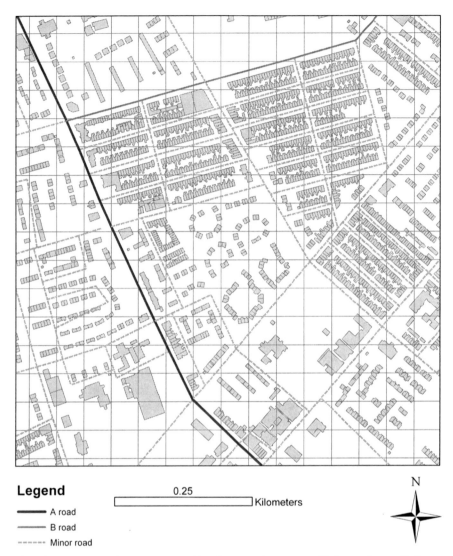

Legend

━━━ A road

━━━ B road

━━━━ Minor road

0.25 ⌐————————————————⌐ Kilometers

N

Fig. 8.2 An example of the study area grid and opportunity structure (Ordnance Survey © Crown Copyright. All Rights reserved)

resulting n*(n-1)/2 comparisons. To generate the frequencies expected (e.g., for burglaries that occurred within 100 m and 7 days of each other) under conditions where the timing and placement of crimes were independent (the null hypothesis), a Monte Carlo re-sampling approach (Besag and Diggle 1977) was used. This was completed 999 times to enable inference testing[3]. Twelve months' data from the

---

[3] The basic Monte Carlo re-sampling approach is discussed in a little detail in a later section. For the sake of brevity, readers are asked to accept that the approach was valid.

study area (N=1,662) as described above were used as the construction sample. The results showed that more burglaries occurred within 500 m and two months of another than would be expected on the basis of chance. If, as argued here, this pattern is the consequence of offender foraging behavior, the transient elevated risk for locations within close proximity of burgled homes reflects the behavior of the same offender.

As discussed, two factors contributing to the placement of burglary are the physical attributes of housing and the road infrastructure. The former defines the spatial distribution of opportunities for burglary, the latter a way of accessing homes and traveling between them. Two simple opportunity surfaces were derived to represent the two factors. Using a Geographical Information System (GIS), the study grid was divided into 50 m cells, 10,816 in all. Information on housing was generated using Ordnance Survey (OS) Land Line data. These data afforded a considerable advantage over census data, available only at the area level and consequently inviting the ecological fallacy. Processing OS data involved the conversion of building outlines to solid shapes using a GIS. The building shapes were then intersected with the 50 m grid squares which provided a target distribution 'layer'. This is illustrated in Fig. 8.2, which shows the relationship between the building outlines and the grid squares. It should be noted that some buildings were located on the boundary between two or more grid squares. Where this occurred, the building was allocated to the cell containing the midpoint of the building. It was then possible to quantify the number of buildings wholly or partially located within each grid square.

Information on road infrastructure was derived from OS Meridian data. This related to all roads in the area and provided details of the classification of the road (e.g., was it a major or minor road or a motorway?) as well as their location and length. This information was intersected with the grid square coverage and is also illustrated in Fig. 8.2. The width of the lines is proportional to the classification of the road (wide lines are wide roads). The figure shows that some grids contain no roads, others several. The following variables could then be quantified for each grid square:

- The number of road sections that were located in each grid square
- The length of each road encapsulated by each grid square
- The road classification. In the UK urban roads are categorized in terms of the volume of traffic use they are designed for, designated 'A', 'B', and 'minor', defining largest through smallest roads.

How these data inform predictions is described below. However, before proceeding, it is worth addressing a potential concern that might arise for readers most familiar with the Manhattan grid street configuration. Such readers might wonder about the orientation of the grid and why we did not align this with the street network. The simple answer is that in the UK, for most cities the street network is irregular and so in truth there was no (obvious) optimum orientation that could have been applied[4].

Crime Risk Surfaces

Thematic maps were generated in the conventional way. For a basic (concentration) map, the total number of burglaries occurring on each beat for the two months prior to each prediction was computed. To enable a direct comparison with other approaches (see below), some of the police beats were cropped so that only the area (of each beat) that was encapsulated by the 5 km grid was included. In addition to a basic police beat thematic map, others showed the historic concentration of burglary per meter squared and per 1000 households. These metrics standardize the risk experienced across beats using different denominators, with the rate per 1000 households being commonly used by both academic and operational analysts.

The ProMap and KDE event driven risk surfaces were derived as follows. Briefly, a moving window (see Bailey and Gatrell 1995) algorithm is used to generate a risk intensity value for every cell in the grid to reflect the risk experienced or anticipated for that location. For each cell, all crimes within a particular radius (bandwidth) from the midpoint of that cell are identified and a risk intensity value computed based on (for retrospective mapping) the number of crimes within the bandwidth and their spatial proximity to the center of the cell (crimes closest to the center of the cell are allocated a greater weighting). This produces a nicely smoothed map for display. A more detailed description of the approach is provided in Appendix 1.

The ProMap algorithm represents a refinement to the traditional KDE approach for three reasons. First, it provides a theoretical rationale for why risks should decay in space (distance decay is incorporated in KDE but not for theoretical reasons of which the authors are aware). Second, a temporal bandwidth is specified and an associated parameter used to model the effect of elapsed time on burglary risk. Third, the spatial bandwidth is selected for theoretical reasons and is empirically derived using the space-time clustering profile of the area concerned. Appendix 1 provides information on the equation used.

Event Driven Opportunity Surfaces

The opportunity surfaces described earlier were used to produce a variety of weighted ProMap risk surfaces, which were subsequently tested for predictive accuracy. Different layers (ProMap and the two opportunity surfaces) were generated independently and the values for each cell derived by taking the product of the relevant layers, stationary and event driven.

---

[4] Although not attempted here, it would of course be possible to repeat the analyses reported here a number of times using a different orientation of the grid each time.

The casual reader may wonder why only ProMap risk surfaces were subjected to the layering approach. The superficial answer is that the ProMap approach turned out to be the most predictive, and hence was used in the latter part of the research. The more satisfactory response is that, because the other approaches were time-invariant, other time-invariant factors like road structure (which are hypothesized to influence offender foraging) should already have their effects reflected in historic crime data. By contrast, for ProMap which particularly emphasizes short-run changes, time-stable factors like road structure provided a sort of scaffolding around which short-run changes could be modeled.

The values for each stationary surface could be generated in a number of ways, but in the current study the following simple rules were applied. A more detailed discussion of the rules used is provided in Appendix 1.

> *Road backcloth* - this surface was produced by weighting grid cells on the basis of the presence of roads alone, their length and type.
> *Building backcloth* – this surface was produced by weighting cells on the basis of the number of buildings hosted.
> *Combined backcloth* – this combined the data from the road and building surfaces.

Barriers

The first consideration for this factor concerned the identification of the boundaries that would be used to model barrier effects. A number of approaches are possible, including the identification by local offenders or police officers of likely barriers (see Poot et al. 2005). Another uses existing administrative boundaries with barriers being identified using socioeconomic data. This is the approach used here, not least because a finding of the Poot et al. (2005) study was that these aligned with practitioner perceptions. UK census Output Area geography was used as proxy for barrier location, since socioeconomic information is thus readily available. For this initial analysis a geodemographic classification system was derived using census data. The super-profiles system (Brown 1991) is one of a number of target market classification systems and was selected because of its availability to the authors. Further research will explore other market segmentation systems and alternative approaches.

Essentially, the super-profiles classes (ranging from 1 to 10) provide an indication of area affluence. Low scores reflect affluence, high scores deprivation. Figure 8.3 shows the study area with the spatial distribution of super profile lifestyle areas. Where two areas vary in terms of affluence (measured at the area level), we presume social barriers. The greater the area affluence contrast, the higher the social barrier.

The imperfections of this approach are acknowledged, and in consequence the method used was simple. Following the rationale in the introduction, this was: when deriving estimates of risk intensity, rather than weighting each crime event equally, those occurring within the same type of area as the cell for which a prediction was being made were given a higher weighting than those occurring in a different type

Fig. 8.3 Census geography and Super-profile classification for the study area

of area. To do this, each crime had to be assigned an area-level characteristic using the spatial-join command in the GIS. Each cell also had to be assigned a value using the 'intersect' command. A discussion of the equation used to model the effects of barriers can be found in Appendix 1.

Measuring Predictive Accuracy

We now return to the basic question of the relative predictive accuracy of ProMap and alternatives. The approach used to assess this was, as noted earlier, to generate the maps using two months of historic data and to determine how many of the burglaries occurring over the ensuing seven days (on average there were 70 per week, SD=7) were correctly predicted as to location. Seven days was considered sensible as each prediction would include both weekdays and a weekend, with their different routine activities (see Rengert and Wasilchick 2000). Predictions for weekdays and weekends should arguably be considered separately in future research. Nine predictions were generated using each method. Predictions were generated for the weeks from 1st, 14th, and 24th of September, October, and November 1997. Thus, test periods did not overlap. The number of predictions generated was limited to nine for two reasons. First, it was necessary to build a space-time clustering profile (discussed above) for the area to calibrate the ProMap algorithm, and with limited resources we were reluctant to do this more than once. As it is likely that space-time clustering profiles change over time, (a topic of no little interest in itself) this was deemed prudent. The second reason was simply that the work took a long time.

Statistical inference is central to theory testing. The question of interest is whether the results observed could have occurred on the basis of chance. Various types of test and method have been derived for different types of data and research questions, but the authors are unaware of any that have been used to establish the accuracy of crime forecasting techniques in anything other than a descriptive way. In the current study we use a simple Monte Carlo (MC) simulation approach (for a general discussion, see North et al. 2002). For the current endeavor, chance performance would characterize a strategy whereby cells were assigned a risk level randomly. One approach would be randomly to select 10,816 balls, one to represent each cell of the grid, from a very large bag, recording their order of selection. The cells designated as most risky would be those selected first, those least at risk last. This would generate one random selection against which the performance of the different predictive approaches could be compared. However, making one selection is not reliable and hence a series of selections was deemed necessary. If we assume that the prediction under evaluation had been drawn from a larger population, then (say) 99 random sequences or samples would enable a reasonable distribution to be produced for the purposes of inferential testing[5]. If the volume of crime predicted

---

[5] For a one-tailed test, a minimum of 19 simulations are required if the 0.05 level of significance is used, but the standard error of the estimate is inversely related to N and so a larger sample is desirable.

by the model of interest were the most extreme then the null hypothesis maybe rejected. For consistency with convention, a particular model would be considered to deviate significantly from chance if the predictions made exceeded at least 95% of the (pseudo) random sequences.

Selecting balls in this way would take a long time and result in the de-motivation of research staff. Fortunately, this MC re-sampling technique can be easily implemented by those with a basic knowledge of computer programming. The method uses a recursive algorithm shown as Appendix 2.

One criticism is that not all cells within the grid contain houses (around 29% do not). Domestic burglars would not select locations without dwellings! Consequently, the MC approach was modified so that cells with houses were selected first, and only then were cells that did not contain housing considered. This removes potential bias in favor of judging ProMap better than chance.

ProMap Accuracy and Backcloth Influences

Figure 8.4 shows the accuracy concentration curves for the first prediction for four of the models (others are not shown due to limitations of space). Each graph shows what would be expected on the basis of chance, estimated using the MC simulation described above, alongside the particular model under consideration. This enables comparisons to be made with chance expectation and, by providing consistent reference lines, facilitates comparisons across models. Considering chance expectation first, as would be anticipated there is a linear relation between the number of cells searched and the concentration of burglary identified. The slope for the average of the simulations is greater than one, indicating the effect of first sampling cells containing housing. On average around 15% of burglaries are correctly identified by searching 10% of cells. The dotted line shows the area of the graph within which 95% of simulations fall. The maximum proportion of burglaries identified by searching 10% of the cells for 95% of the simulations was 22%. If the value for a particular model exceeds the 95th percentile of the simulations, we conclude that the model was significantly more predictive than chance (for a one-tailed test, and $p < 0.05$).

For this prediction, the ProMap model has a logarithmic functional form which deviates from chance expectation across most of the distribution. This pattern reflects known facts about near repeats. The pattern for the retrospective KDE method is quite different. The KDE method appears to exceed chance expectation until around 50% of burglaries have been identified, but the shape of the concentration curve is less impressive. For example, after around 67% of burglaries have been identified, the KDE model performs below chance expectation. The thematic mapping method (computed using the rate of burglary per 1000 households) performs the worst, failing to exceed chance across the entire distribution.

The ProMap models that include opportunity layers consistently exceed chance expectation, and the area of the graph between model performance and chance expectation is larger than for the basic ProMap model. Including a parameter to model the existence of barriers (graph not shown) has little effect on model accuracy.

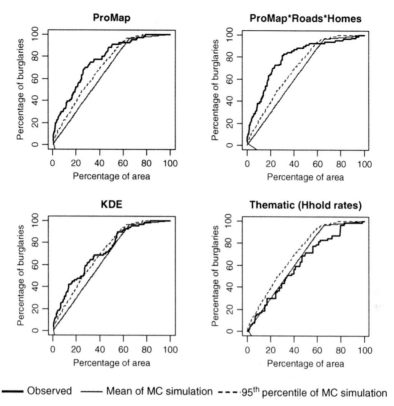

Fig. 8.4 Accuracy concentration curves for a sample of methods tested and chance expectation (for prediction 1)

The above results relate to only one prediction. Rather than reproducing each of the graphs for every prediction, a summary table was generated to provide an overview of the findings. Table 8.1 shows the median accuracy of each model across the nine predictions. It tabulates the fraction of cells that would have to be searched to identify x% of burglaries for five different cut points. Other thresholds could be used, but covering a range of values is instructive since they provide an accurate reflection of visual inspection of every finding[6].

For each cut point, the cell value for the best performing algorithm is highlighted in bold. Where ties occur, multiple cells are highlighted. Also shown in each cell as a subscript is the number of predictions for which that model exceeded chance expectation as defined by the value for the 95th percentile of the simulation results.

---

[6] An alternative approach to summarizing the data that we are yet to do is to compute a gini coefficient for each concentration curve. Frequently used to examine (for example) the inequality in the distribution of wealth across areas, the measure indicates the area between an observed (Lorenz) curve and the 45 degree line of equality. The advantage of so doing is that the coefficient summarizes the entire distribution rather than a subset of cut points.

S.D. Johnson et al.

Table 8.1 Median mapping algorithm accuracy for a subset of the results

	Percentage of burglaries identified					
	10	25	50	75	90	
Prospective:						
ProMap	1.3_9	5.0_9	14.3_9	30.8_9	55.3_6	
ProMap*Houses	1.5_9	5.0_9	14.3_9	28.3_9	48.8_8	
ProMap*RDs	1.3_9	4.8_9	13.3_9	29.0_9	52.5_7	Percentage of cells searched
ProMap*Houses*RDs	1.5_9	4.5_9	12.5_9	29.3_9	56.3_5	
ProMap*barriers	1.5_9	5.0_9	14.8_9	29.5_9	54.5_5	
Chance:						
Simulation 95th Percentile	3.8	11.5	27.3	44.8	56.8	
Simulation Mean	7.0	17.0	34.3	51.3	61.3	
Retrospective:						
KDE	2.0_9	6.5_9	16.8_9	34.8_7	59.0_4	
Thematic (concentration)	4.0_3	15.5_0	35.4_0	49.1_2	63.0_2	
Thematic (rate per area)	3.3_4	10.8_5	23.4_7	42.5_5	58.8_2	
Thematic (rate per 1000 Hholds)	6.4_1	17.6_2	31.7_0	50.0_2	69.1_1	

Note: subscripts indicate for how many of the nine predictions the model exceeded chance expectation

To take an extreme example, in predicting the locations of 90% of the burglaries, the retrospective KDE method exceeds chance on only four occasions, being worse than chance for five. For the thematic maps, two of the models (basic concentration and rate per 1000 households) failed to exceed chance for almost every trial and each cut point. It should be noted that in generating the graphs for the thematic maps, it was not possible to compute the percentage of area needed to identify a particular fraction of burglaries. This was because, unlike the regular cells used for the KDE and prospective maps, the units of analysis (police beats) for the thematic maps varied in size. Thus, when estimating how much area would need to be patrolled to identify a particular proportion of crime, one can either select the configuration of beats that identify slightly more than the threshold of interest or slightly less. The latter would overestimate the effectiveness of the thematic maps and is the approach used here. Thus the thematic approach appears to be egregious even when it is favored in the conventions applied.

We have thus established that the prospective models typically exceed chance expectation. A complementary perspective on model accuracy involves the comparison of the different models against each other. A variety of comparisons is possible. We report here comparisons between the prospective model most accurate for forecasts made over the smallest areas (that which included data on the homes and roads in each cell) and the KDE method. The results indicated that the ProMap model considered consistently performed better than the KDE method in identifying 10% ($z=1.70$, $p<0.05$, one-tailed)[7], 25% ($z=1.96$, $p<0.03$, one-tailed), 50% ($z=2.56$, $p<0.01$, one tailed), and 75% ($z=1.90$, $p<0.03$, one-tailed) of burglaries. In identi-

---

[7] A one-tailed test is here used as the direction of the hypothesis was specified a-priori.

fying 90% of burglaries, the difference was non-significant ($z=0.29$, p=ns). Thus, with one exception, the ProMap algorithm that incorporated data on the location and spatial concentration of homes and roads exceeded chance performance and consistently outperformed the KDE method. The inclusion in the ProMap algorithm of data concerning the concentration of homes *and* the road network seemed only to offer meager additional value when forecasts were generated for the largest areas (e.g., when forecasting 90% of burglary locations). Expressed in another way, the improvements in predictive accuracy offered by the ProMap model discussed were most evident for geographical areas that could realistically be targeted for police attention (i.e., smaller areas).

It is important to paint a picture of how to interpret differences in the values shown in the cells of the table. For example, what does it mean to say that to identify the locations of 50% of burglaries, using the ProMap*housing*RDs algorithm 12.5% of cells would need to be searched whereas for the KDE algorithm the equivalent fraction of cells would be 16.8? A potentially useful guide to the interpretation of these figures is that a one-percent difference in the search area required to identify a particular fraction of burglaries equates to a patrol area of $270,400\,m^2$ (or $0.27\,km^2$). If the purpose of a crime reduction intervention informed by predictive mapping is the detection of offences in progress, then even a one-percent difference in accuracy so measured will have substantial implications. The importance of a four or five percent difference needs no advocacy as to operational importance.

What Is Established? What Next?

The incorporation of short-run changes in risk via the ProMap approach to predicting domestic burglary does seem to yield a dividend in predictive performance across the spectrum of risk levels. The distances across which risks change chime well with the practice of patrolling and it is in the optimization of patrolling routes that ProMap has its most obvious potential. The various backcloth information contributed modestly to the accuracy of ProMap and with enough promise to motivate the writers to develop alternative ways of characterizing areal influence on foraging behavior. Further research will use parameters specifically calibrated to maximize prediction accuracy. Similar approaches to least squares estimation will be used, and where enough data are available, Monte Carlo Markov Chain approaches to parameter fitting may also be explored. We also intend to examine accessibility, measured using the street network, in different ways. Accessibility at a higher level of spatial aggregation than analyzed here may be considered by examining (for example) the number of roads that connect each cell to members of its Moore neighborhood. This would provide an indication of how accessible the local area is, as well as the number of roads contained within a particular grid cell. Such analysis may also be conducted at other levels of spatial aggregation.

To model the space-time variation in risk more precisely, a slightly different mathematical approach is desirable. Here, each cell (and eventually each home) would be considered a vertex or node in a graph. Each vertex would be connected by roads represented by edges in the graph. An adjacency matrix would be used to summarize how each vertex was connected to every other vertex, and weights applied to indicate the distance between each node. For nodes that are not connected by a single edge (a road), a shortest path analysis algorithm would be required (e.g., Dijkstra's 1959) to make the necessary calculations. In addition to distance, weights may also be used to indicate other factors that might encourage or impede the flow of risk through the graph network. For example, instead of assuming that the change in risk would be isotropic (uniform in all directions), the role, that the configuration of the street network plays upon people's ability to navigate their environment (and any directional biases that arise), could be modeled. Risk would be hypothesized to flow with a higher probability between nodes located near to each other, between those connected by multiple edges and along arcs which generate the least friction.

Unlike the other factors considered, the inclusion in the model of data concerned with social barriers had no observable impact on predictive accuracy. There are at least three explanations for this, some of which concern construct validity while others are more theoretical. First, the size of the effect that barriers have on offenders' target choices may be truly minimal. Second, the geography used to define the barriers considered may have been inappropriate and failed to reflect the kinds of barrier that offenders take into consideration. Given that the census geography was used, this is entirely plausible, but it should be noted that the same kinds of geographic boundary were used in the studies reviewed in the introduction for which barrier effects were revealed. Further research should use alternative geographies and, in line with the approach used by Poot et al. (2005) draw upon local knowledge when determining which boundaries to use and how to classify them.

Third, the variable used to differentiate between areas and hence to identify barriers may have been sub optimal. We here used a sociodemographic classification system developed for target marketing. Other methods of classification, such as the use of univariate or multivariate analyses of census data are possible and could be usefully explored in future research. Measures of social cohesion may be a useful next step (see Bernasco and Luykx 2003). Considering the current findings, our intuition is that the latter explanations are most likely. Whatever the answer, the current approach offers one empirical approach, easily programmed, for testing theories of this kind. A further caveat worthy of discussion, of course, is that in this study predictions were generated using the spatio-temporal distribution of historic crime events. Whilst these reflect the emergent patterns of the activity of offenders, they do not provide a direct test of the behavior of any distinct offender(s). It may (or may not) be the case that on some or all occasions there is too much 'noise' in the data to model this by proxy.

Areal Units and ProMap: Closing Thoughts

The writers believe that there is much scope for further work. Patrolling patterns are not dictated by one offence type, and establishing regularities in space-time patterns of other offence types, and integrating ProMap across offence types represents the research strategy. Research tactics should obviously incorporate salient other data as was attempted for domestic burglary in the later analyses reported above and discussed below. The point of central importance however is that the ProMap algorithm and (particularly) variants of it significantly outperformed methods extant. They did so in a way that is important not just for theory testing but also for operational policing. All variants of the ProMap algorithm produced maps that could identify the same volume of crime as other methods within much smaller areas.

With respect to units of analysis, the general theme of this book, unsurprising but important results emerged. As expected, the Thematic mapping approach was worst at predicting what happens next, but what is perhaps surprising is that the allocation of resources based on such maps may be no better than chance. This was particularly true where prioritization was informed by area-level crime rates expressed as the risk per 1000 households. It is worth briefly discussing why this might be so. The definition of the boundaries used is critical. For the task at hand, the ideal situation would be to have boundaries that circumscribe areas within which risks *tend* towards homogeneity. Unfortunately, the boundaries used by the police and others are dictated by diverse factors. Some of these are likely to be administrative and not pertinent for the anticipation of crime patterns. The units are also typically large, meaning that within them some degree of heterogeneity is inevitable. And, the boundaries (e.g., census collection areas) are often defined in advance of the data collected, rather than being derived on the basis of emergent phenomena. Rather than fully articulating these issues, which are covered in the chapter in this volume by Brantingham and Brantingham, one approach to boundary determination should be briefly discussed. This is outlined here because it may influence how the current authors attempt to delineate barriers in future work. The approach is inspired, in part, by 'lossy' image compression techniques from the field of software engineering, which attempt to reduce image file sizes by generalizing about similar elements of an image. Potential problems with any such approach are acknowledged. The idea is rehearsed here so that others might point out any weaknesses in the approach or any suitable refinements which overcome them.

To illustrate the approach, the first panel of Fig. 8.5 shows an area with three distinct geographies over which a relatively small 'meso-level' grid has been applied (one cell might encompass 10–20 properties as previously described). All cells within the area are ascribed one or a set of values relating to a multivariate description of their internal characteristics relevant to the investigator (see panel 2). For example, the values considered may include the type of housing in each cell, concentration of crime and so on. Each cell is then examined with respect to its neighbors and evaluated for similarity. Contiguous cells considered 'similar' (i.e., with values within some bandwidth of one another) are then grouped into single areas/geographies/unit of aggregation.

The degree to which cells are considered 'similar' is dictated by the level of 'compression' applied; the higher the level of compression, the less similar things need to be for them to be considered as such, as illustrated in panels 3 and 4. By applying this technique, new area boundaries can be defined which are wholly dictated by similarities important to the research question under consideration rather

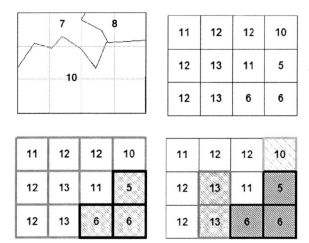

Fig. 8.5 An example of 'Lossy' Boundaries

than (say) the identification of a series of areas with similar population counts. Obviously this does not provide a complete solution to the problems associated with boundary definition as its viability relies purely upon the correct selection of those factors considered in the calculation of 'similarity'. However, it may offer an incremental step towards a more hypothesis driven approach to area boundary definition.

To reiterate in conclusion, the research demonstrates that an algorithm based on the findings from the near repeat literature predicts the future locations of crime at a level that exceeds chance expectation, and also outperforms other hot-spotting methods. Considering Thematic mapping in particular, for which the unit of analysis was police beats, this approach was not only worse than ProMap but typically failed to exceed chance expectation. Consequently, the findings provide support for the hypothesis on which the model was based. The inclusion of data concerned with the opportunity structure for the area considered improved the performance of the model, but an initial attempt at modeling barriers did not. The results have implications for both theory and practice. Maintaining a balance between theory refinement and applicability enhancement is difficult. It is contended that their implementation in practice should not wait upon further research. In the light of the research already reported, it seems difficult to justify basic KDE crime mapping in preference to ProMap as enhanced by road and building composition. The research agenda which takes enhanced ProMap as its starting point should contain at least the following elements:

1. Recalculating for periods which are operationally meaningful (e.g., police shifts and periods for which tasking and coordinating meetings plan);
2. Ensuring by calculation of patrolling routes that high risk areas are not so dispersed that transit times between high risk areas offset the advantages which ProMap offers;

3. Considering thresholds of the proportion of predicted burglaries which it is realistic to police, including consideration of policing styles which involve thorough scrutiny of the highest risk areas with more superficial search of a greater number of areas;
4. Considering other crime types, to produce a pan-crime ProMap, devising search patterns reflecting the relative seriousness of individual crime types.

Much of this drive towards applicability would appropriately be carried out by crime analysts in local areas, in a federated research programme. Winston Churchill, in World War II visited Washington to plead for assistance. He opined 'Give us the tools and we will finish the job'. A cynic's version is that for social scientists, the mantra would be 'Give us the tools, and we will spend the rest of our lives sharpening them'. This would be a fate worse than death for crime mapping. The techniques are already fit for purpose and need to be sympathetically but urgently integrated into the craft of policing.

Appendix 1 Equations Used in the Derivation of the KDE and ProMap Algorithms

KDE Equation and Callibration

To generate the KDE surfaces used, a quartic function (Bailey and Gatrell, 1995) was used. The formula is shown as equation (8.1). There exists no obvious consensus of opinion regarding the appropriate spatial bandwidth to use in KDE hotspot generation. Some suggest using a bandwidth of one-tenth of the smallest dimension of the study area. This yields a nicely smoothed map for visual display but is determined by the dimensions of the study area rather than criminological understanding or the requirements of operational policing. A variety of alternative bandwidths or methods for calibration have been proposed, but no theoretical explanations are offered to underpin the selection, or empirical studies provided to demonstrate any superior heuristic value. In the absence of a rationale for bandwidth selection, and on the basis of a suggestion by Ratcliffe (2000), we used a bandwidth of 200 m. This is relevant not least because it is used by many UK crime analysts with whom the authors have had contact.

$$\lambda_\tau(s) = \sum_{di \leq \tau} \frac{3}{\pi \tau^2} \left(1 - \frac{d_i^2}{\tau^2} \right)^2 \tag{8.1}$$

Where, $\lambda_\tau(s)$ = risk intensity value for cell s

τ = bandwidth
d_i = distance of each point (i) within the bandwidth from the centroid of the cell

ProMap Equation and Callibration

Equation (8.2) shows the formula used in the computation of the ProMap risk surface.

$$\lambda_\tau(s) = \sum_{c_i \leq \tau \cap e_i \leq \upsilon} \left(\frac{1}{(1+c_i)}\right) \frac{1}{(1+e_i)} \tag{8.2}$$

Where, $\lambda_\tau(s)$ = risk intensity value for cell s

τ = spatial bandwidth υ = temporal bandwidth
c_i = number of cells between each point (i) within the bandwidth and the cell
e_i = weeks elapsed for each point (i) within the temporal bandwidth

Similar in basic terms to that used to derive the KDE maps, the equation includes an additional parameter (e_i) to model the effect of elapsed time on the risk of crime at each location. The spatial bandwidth used is determined by the results of the Knox analysis. For example, if the Knox analysis suggests that events cluster in space and time more than would be expected on a chance basis for a distance of (say) 500 m and two months, then the spatial bandwidth used would be 500 m.

Modeling Accessibility

The basic ProMap approach was modified to try to reflect the influence of the urban backcloth on offender spatial target choices. Two factors were considered, the type and number of roads in each cell, and the number of homes:

Roads

This was used to provide a crude estimate of accessibility. The weighting considered the length, classification and number of road sections within each cell. Cells with more and larger roads were assigned a higher accessibility weighting to reflect the fact that they were likely to be more connected to surrounding cells than other cells. The following equations show the construction of the road weighting:

Road type = weighting	Length of A rds in cell +	0.8 * length B rds in cell +	0.6 * length of 'minor' rds
Road number = weighting	Number of A rds in cell +	Number of B rds in cell +	Number of 'minor' rds

Where the road type weighting was above 20 (the average length of road across cells) and the road number weighting was greater than zero, a weighting of 1.01 was applied. Where the road type weighting was less than 20 a weighting of 1.0 was used. Where there were no roads, a weighting of zero was assigned. The weights were arbitrary, but the results are robust across weighting options.

Housing

Where a cell had more than the average amount of houses (7 homes) a weighting of 1.01 was applied. Where a cell had no homes within it, a weighting of zero was used. In all other cases, a weighting of 1.0 was applied.

Roads and Homes

A multiplicative function was used to weight the cells, so that the combined weighting was the product of the above variables. These weightings were then used to generate three new event driven opportunity surfaces by taking the product of these layers and the ProMap surface.

Barriers

To model the effect of barriers, a modification of equation (8.2) was required to reflect whether contributing events had occurred in an area similar (or not) to the cell for which a prediction was being made. If we consider the ProMap formula as a form of regression equation, we can alter the slope or intercept (or both) of the model using a parameter to model the presence or absence of a barrier. Considering the effect of changing the intercept, an event will acquire a change in weight on the basis of the area within which it is located, irrespective of its proximity to a barrier. Changing the slope takes account both of the existence of a barrier and a cell's proximity to it and is thus the preferred approach here.

To model the effects of barriers, equation (8.2) is modified only slightly. In this case, the denominator in the first term of the equation $(1 + c_i)$ is replaced with the following:

$$(1 + c_i)(1 - \alpha)$$

where,

(1) $\alpha = 0$ when the lifestyle value of the cell for which the prediction is being derived and the event considered is located are the same, and
(2) $\alpha > 0$ when the lifestyle values differ.

A series of calibration trials were conducted to identify the optimum value of α. To do this, predictions were generated using values ranging from 0.5 to 0.99, with increments of 0.01 being tested across trials. The value ultimately selected of 0.98 was then fixed. That is, α was always 0.98 when condition (2) above was met. That the slope found to be optimal was virtually at the top of the range tested may be taken as a preliminary indication of the salience of social barriers as here measured.

Appendix 2 Monte Carlo Simulation Algorithm for Estimating Chance Expectation

The simulation worked in the following way:

1. Using a uniform random number generator (RNG) select the first cell from those available (1–10,816) and assign this the highest risk value
2. Select another number using the RNG

   a. If this has not previously been selected, assign this the next highest value. If it has already been selected, choose another value until a previously unselected cell is identified.
   b. Repeat step 2 until all cells have been allocated a risk value from 1 to 10,816

3. Rank order the data using the risk values assigned to each cell
4. Generate an accuracy concentration curve
5. Repeat the above steps 99 times, storing the results of each iteration

References

Armitage, R. (2007). Sustainability versus safety: Confusion, conflict and contradiction in designing out crime. In: G. Farrell, K. J. Bowers, S. D. Johnson & M. Townsley (Eds.), *Imagination for Crime Prevention: Essays in Honour of Ken Pease*. Monsey, NY: Criminal Justice Press.

Ashton, J., Brown, I., Senior, B., & Pease, K. (1998). Repeat victimisation: Offender accounts. *International Journal of Risk, Security and Crime Prevention*, 3(4), 269–279.

Bailey, T. C., & Gatrell, A. C. (1995). *Interactive spatial data analysis*. Harlow: Longman.

Beavon, D. J. K., Brantingham, P. L., & Brantingham, P. J. (1994). The influence of street networks on the patterning of property offenses. In: R. V. G. Clarke (Ed.), *Crime Prevention Studies*. Vol. 2, Monsey NY: Criminal Justice Press.

Brantingham, P. L., & Brantingham, P. J. (1993). Nodes, paths and edges: Considerations on the complexity of crime and the physical environment. *Journal of Environmental Psychology*, 13, 3–28.

Brantingham, P. J., & Brantingham, P. L. (1981) *Environmental criminology*. Rev. ed. 1991 Prospect Heights, IL: Waveland, 1991.

Brantingham P. J. (1978). A Theoretical model of crime site selection. In: M. D. Krohn & R. L. Ackers (Eds.), *Crime, Law and Sanctions: Theoretical Perspectives*. Beverly Hills: Sage.

Bernasco W. (2008). Them Again? Same-offender Involvement in Repeat and Near Repeat Burglaries. *European Journal of Criminology*, 5(4), forthcoming.

Bernasco, W., & Luykx, F. (2003). Effects of attractiveness, opportunity and accessibility to burglars on residential burglary rates of urban neighbourhoods. *Criminology*, 41, 981–1001.

Bernasco, W., & Nieuwbeerta, P. (2005). How do residential burglars select target areas? *British Journal of Criminology*, 45, 295–315.

Bennett, T., & Wright, R. (1984). *Burglars on Burglary*. Aldershot: Gower.

Besag, J., & Diggle, P. J. (1977). Simple monte carlo tests for spatial pattern. *Applied Statistics*, 26, 327–333.

Bowers, K. J., & Johnson, S. D. (2005). Domestic burglary repeats and space-time clusters: The dimensions of risk. *European Journal of Criminology*, 2(1), 67–92.

Bowers, K. J., Johnson, S., & Pease, K. (2004). Prospective hotspotting: The future of crime mapping? *British Journal of Criminology*, 44(5), 641–658.

Bowers, K. J., Johnson, S., & Pease, K. (2005). Victimisation and re-victimisation risk, housing type and area: A study of interactions. *Crime Prevention and Community Safety*, 7, 7–17.

Brown, P. J. B. (1991). Exploring Geodemographics.' In: I. Masser & M. Blakemore (Eds.), *Geographic Information Management: Methodology and Applications*, London: Longman.

Coupe, T., & Blake, L. (2006). Daylight and darkness targeting strategies and the risks of being seen at residential burglaries, *Criminology* 44(2), 431–464.

Cornish, D. (1994). The procedural analysis of offending and its relevance for situational crime prevention. In: R. Clarke (Ed.), *Crime Prevention Studies*, (Vol. 3, pp. 151–196). Monsey, New York: Criminal Justice Press.

Cornish, D., & Clarke, R. (1986). *The Reasoning Criminal*. New York: Springer-Verlag.

Dijkstra, E. W. (1959). A note on two problems in connexion with graphs. *Numerische Mathematik*, 1, 269–271.

Ericsson, U. (1995). Straight from the Horse's Mouth. *Forensic Update*, 43, 23–25.

Everson S. P., & Pease K. (2001). Crime against the same person and place: detection opportunity and offender targeting. In: G. Farrell & K.Pease (Eds.), *Repeat Victimisation*. Monsey NY: Criminal Justice Press.

Everson, S. (2003). Repeat victimisation and prolific offending: Chance or choice? *International Journal of Police Science and Management*, 5, 180–194.

Farrell, G. (2005). Progress and prospects in the prevention of repeat victimization. In: N. Tilley (Ed.), *Handbook of crime Prevention and Community Safety*. Cullompton, UK: Willan.

Groff, E. R., & LaVigne, N. G. (2001). Mapping an opportunity surface of residential burglary. *Journal of Research in Crime and Delinquency*, 38(3), 257–278.

Hillier, B. (2004). Can streets be made safe? *Urban Design International*, 9, 31–45.

Hakim, S., Rengert, G. F., & Schachmurove, Y. (2001). Target search of burglars: A revised economic model. *Papers in Regional Science*, 80, 121–137.

Johnson, S., Bowers, K., & Hirschfield, A. (1997). New insights into the spatial and temporal distribution of repeat victimisation. *British Journal of Criminology*, 37(2), 224–241

Johnson, S. D., Bernasco, W., Bowers, K. J., Elffers, H., Ratcliffe, J., Rengert, G., & Townsley, M. T. (2007). Near repeats: A cross national assessment of residential burglary. *Journal of Quantitative Criminology*, 23(3), 201–219.

Johnson, S. D., & Bowers, K. J. (2004a). The burglary as a clue to the future: the beginnings of prospective hot-spotting. *European Journal of Criminology*, 1(2), 237–255.

Johnson, S. D., & Bowers, K. J. (2004b). The stability of space-time clusters of burglary. *British Journal of Criminology*, 44(1), 55–65.

Knox, G. (1964). Epidemiology of childhood leukaemia in northumberland and durham. *British Journal of Preventative and Social Medicine*, 18, 17–24.

Matthiopoulos, J. (2003). The use of space by animals as a function of accessibility and preference. *Ecological Modelling*, 159, 239–268.

Morgan, F. (2001). Repeat burglary in a Perth Suburb: Indicator of Short-Term or Long-Term risk? In: G. Farrell, & K. Pease (Eds.), *Repeat Victimisation: Crime Prevention Studies*. Vol. 12, Monsey NY: Criminal Justice Press.

Nee, C., & Meenaghan, A. (2006). Expert decision making in burglars. *British Journal of Criminology*, 46(5), 935–949.

North, B. V., Curtis, D., & Sham, P. C. (2002). A note on the Calculation of Empirical P Values from Monte Carlo Procedures. *American. Journal. of Human. Genetics*, 71, 439–441.

Pease, K. (1998). *Repeat Victimization: Taking Stock*. The Home Office: Police Research Group: Crime Detection and Prevention Series Paper 90.

Polvi, N., Looman, T., Humphries, C., & Pease, K. (1991). The time course of repeat burglary victimisation. *British Journal of Criminology*, 31(4), 411–414.

Poot, C., Luykx, F., Elffers, H., & Dudnik, C. (2005). Hier wonen en daar plegen? Sociale grenzen en locatiekeuze. *Tijdschrift voor Criminologie*, 47(3), 255–268.

Ratcliffe, J. (2000). Aoristic analysis: The spatial interpretation of unspecific temporal events. *International Journal of Geographical Information Science*, 14(7), 669–79.

Ratcliffe, J. (2006). A temporal constraint theory to explain opportunity-based spatial offending patterns. *Journal of Research in Crime and Delinquency*, 43(3), 261–291.

Rengert, G., & Wasilchick, J. (2000). *Suburban Burglary: A Tale of Two Suburbs*. Springfield, IL: Charles Thomas.

Lebeau, J. L., & Rengert, G. (2006). The role of Racial/Ethnic barriers in the movement of drug offenders. Presentation at the *Environmental Criminology and Crime Analysis Seminar*, Vancouver, June, 2006.

Reynald, R., Averdijk, M., Elffers, H., & Bernasco, W. (2006). *Do social barriers affect urban crime trips? The effects of ethnic and socio-economic neighborhood compositions on the flow of crime in The Hague, The Netherlands*. (NSCR 2006-4) Leiden.

Shaw M., & Pease K. (2000). *Research on Repeat Victimisation in Scotland'*. Crime and Criminal Justice Research Findings 44. Edinburgh: Scottish Executive.

Townsley, M., Homel, R., & Chaseling, J. (2003). Infectious burglaries: A test of the near repeat hypothesis. *British Journal of Criminology*, 43, 615–633.

Tseloni A., Wittebrood, K., Farrell, G., & Pease K. (2004). Burglary Victimisation in the US, England and Wales and the Netherlands: Cross-national comparison of routine activity patterns. *British Journal of Criminology*, 44, 66–91.

Tseloni A., & Kershaw, C. (2005). Predicting crime rates: fear and disorder based on area information. Evidence from the British Crime Survey. *International Review of Victimology*, 12, 295–313.

Winchester, S. W. C., & Jackson, H. (1982). *Residential Burglary: The Limits of Prevention*. Home Office Research Study 74. London: HMSO.

Wright, R.T., & Decker, S. (1994). *Burglars on the Job: Streetlife and Residential Break-Ins*. Boston: Northeastern University Press.

Chapter 9
Urban Streets as Micro Contexts to Commit Violence

Johan van Wilsem

Abstract Opportunities for crime are assumed to be highly localized. Therefore, using streets as units of analysis offers insight into crime patterns that are lost when they are aggregated to the neighborhood level. Previous street-level studies on crime have concentrated on variations in the amount of incidents. According to Crime Pattern Theory, more crime is expected to occur where people's routine activities coincide with suitable targets in poorly guarded circumstances. However, the theory, if extended further, is also applicable to street-level variation in qualitative aspects of crime, such as the relation between offender and victim and the use of weapons. The reason for this is that the routine of everyday life determines spatial concentrations of certain types of people at specific locales, which may determine the way crime is committed in a particular street if the characteristics of its visitors are related to the nature of the crimes committed there. For instance, if a street attracts young people, and young people use guns more often, then gun related violence will be more frequent in that street. This chapter focuses on the volume as well as the nature of violent crime, based on a sample of approximately 600 incidents committed in certain streets in Rotterdam, the Netherlands. The results suggest that (a) accessibility and social disorganization increase the number of crimes in a street, (b) co-offending and the relation between offender and victim vary significantly between streets, while weapon use and victim injury do not, and (c) incident characteristics and the street's accessibility play an important role in explaining street-level differences in the relation between victim and offender. The latter finding supports the hypothesis derived from Crime Pattern Theory that the daily functions of streets serve as a selection mechanism for who visits the street and subsequently determine against whom violence is committed in that locality.

J. van Wilsem
Department of Criminology, Leiden University, The Netherlands
e-mail: j.a.van.wilsem@law.leidenuniv.nl

D. Weisburd et al. (eds.), *Putting Crime in its Place*,
DOI 10.1007/978-0-387-09688-9_9, © Springer Science+Business Media, LLC 2009

Introduction

The street is an interesting unit of analysis for crime research. It is possible to explore *within-neighborhood* differences of crime on this detailed level. Street-oriented research challenges the image that is often portrayed of neighborhoods as homogeneous areas. The general reason to expect substantial crime differences within a neighborhood is that the opportunities for criminal conduct are highly localized. For instance, the amount of informal surveillance is important to understand the spatial distribution of crime events, but this factor is not constant across an entire neighborhood. Some streets, within the same community, may be monitored quite well by its residents whereas others are not. As a result, the amount of crime has been found to vary across streets or street blocks (Block 2000; Roncek and Maier 1991; Sherman et al. 1989; Smith et al. 2000).

Crime Pattern Theory offers explanations for crime differences at such local levels (Brantingham and Brantingham 1993; Eck and Weisburd 1995). It assumes that the distribution of opportunities for crime across space is determined by the way people interact with their local environment. If a place is easily accessible, because of its position in the urban street network for example, a lot of people will visit that place, which increases the risk of offenders and targets converging. Such places are at risk of experiencing high volumes of crime if, on top of this, these conditions are combined with poor surveillance. Smith and colleagues, for instance, identified the presence of commercial stores and heterogeneous population structures as criminogenic risk factors for street blocks (Rice and Smith 2002; Smith et al. 2000).

The assumption that crime opportunities vary at a detailed spatial level also implies that there are street-level differences in the *nature* of criminal incidents, such as the way in which violent acts are committed and the relation between offender and victim. Streets vary in the type of public that visits them as they have different everyday functions. This has consequences for the streets' crime profile insofar as the characteristics of these visitors are related to the way that crime is committed. For instance, if certain streets attract groups of people because of local entertainment venues then the violence committed in those streets is more likely to have a group character.

However, ecological studies have almost all ignored the way in which the nature of violent crimes differs between localities. A notable exception is the work of Baumer et al. (2003), which focuses on *neighborhood* differences by looking to the qualitative aspects of violence, such as weapon possession and victim injury. Wikström and colleagues (Eisner and Wikström 1999; McClintock and Wikström 1992) have also examined the social context of criminal incidents, the victim's injuries and whether a weapon was used during the crime or not, and compared these rates across the *cities* of Stockholm, Basel, and Edinburgh. To my knowledge, a *street*-oriented study on the qualitative aspects of violence has never been conducted before.

This chapter examines the extent to which the volume and nature of violent crimes covary with the social, economic, and environmental design features of streets. For this purpose, I have used a sample of approximately 600 incidents and more than 200 streets in three neighborhoods of Rotterdam, the Netherlands. In the same vein as recent work carried-out by Hipp (2007), these data offer the opportunity to explore if the examination of *within-neighborhood* differences is a viable step. Street-level analysis also offers insight into crime variations that are lost when they are aggregated to the neighborhood level.

Determinants of Crime Volumes in Streets

The committing of crimes at specific places is assumed to be the outcome of offenders' evaluations of the costs and benefits associated with behavioral alternatives. The better places are suited to commit a crime, the higher the expected crime volume will be. Variations in target suitability and the presence of capable guardians have become the leading explanations for concentrations of crime at certain places, especially since the development of rational choice oriented crime research (Cornish and Clarke 1986). More specifically, Cohen and Felson's (1979) 'Routine Activity Theory' argues that a larger volume of crime is expected at places where informal surveillance is lacking, where large shares of offenders are easily able to enter the area, and where offenders can meet many targets eligible for a crime. According to Wikström (1995), city centers are places where these conditions co-occur, and therefore places where high crime volumes are found.

Crime Pattern Theory connects the routine activities of offenders and victims with the places where crimes are committed (Brantingham and Brantingham 1993; Eck and Weisburd 1995). It supposes that 'nodes, paths, and edges' are important concepts to understand spatial concentrations of crime. An important assumption of the theory is that crimes are committed in 'nodes', areas that are known to offenders because of their routine activities, such as work or leisure. Targets come to the attention of offenders through these activities. Therefore, large volumes of crime are expected at places where a lot of offenders routinely move about, and where they can find many suitable targets. 'Paths' are the routes connecting the nodes and which are thus used during routine activities. 'Edges' refer to the boundaries of the places where people perform routine activities and their in-between paths.

Apart from Routine Activity Theory's notion that the degree of guardianship is important to understand varying crime volumes across places, this research concentrates on the way in which nodes and paths shape local amounts of crime. In previous research on streets or street segments, social disorganization and commercial activity have been identified as risk factors for high street (block) levels of crime. For instance, Smith et al. (2000) found that street blocks characterized by many single-parent households, motels, and bars had relatively high levels of street robbery. Similarly, Rice and Smith (2002) found these patterns for automotive theft. Apart from exerting main effects, these circumstances had also conditional influence: the presence of commercial establishments induced crime, especially in the absence of informal surveillance. Roncek and colleagues (Roncek 1981; Roncek and Faggiani 1985; Roncek and Maier 1991) found that in Cleveland street blocks with facilities such as schools and bars had higher levels of crime on average, net of population characteristics in the block. These findings suggest that such facilities are 'nodes' that act as crime generators, that is, places where offenders commit violence while they are there for other reasons such as going to school or going out for entertainment (Brantingham and Brantingham 1995).[1]

In addition, the accessibility of areas also steers the direction in which offenders travel, which indicates the importance of 'paths' for the spatial distribution of crime volumes. Beavon, Brantingham and Brantingham (1994) explored street segment patterns of property crime in two Canadian suburban municipalities, and found that high levels of crime were observed in streets with many twists and turns and with a high traffic flow, also after controlling for other risk factors. Based on these findings, they argued that "city planning practices (...) create the opportunity network for crime."(p. 138) A similar argument was put forward by Wikström (1995), who claimed that the likelihood that offenders and victims will meet in a violent encounter is dependent upon 'people's patterns of movement, the street layout, and the structure of the public transport system.' (p. 441). Larger volumes of crime are expected at places where a lot of people can gain access due to transport opportunities. Indeed, higher crime rates have been documented in the vicinity of areas with public transport stops (Smith & Clarke 2000). For instance, Block and Davis (1996) found that street robberies were concentrated around rapid transit stations in several Chicago neighborhoods, while Piza (2003) found a similar result in Newark, NJ. This research will also test whether streets with public transport stops are confronted with larger volumes of violent crime. In addition, this chapter also examines the relation between crime volumes and variations in guardianship that result from street-level differences on features related to social disorganization such as concentrated disadvantage, ethnic heterogeneity and family disruption (Sampson and Groves, 1989).

Determinants of the Nature of Crime in Streets

Streets may not only differ in the amounts of crime committed there, but also in the way in which crimes are committed. For instance, some streets may experience more group violence or use of weapons than others. Two types of explanation can be applied to understand the differences, in these aspects, between streets. The first type is an incident-oriented explanation that focuses on the participants of the crime, how their characteristics affect the way the crime is committed, and how the differential distribution of these participant characteristics across places may lead to aggregate differences in the nature of crime. The second type of explanation shifts to the role of the environment itself on the violent offender's behavior and choice of target, and argues that the local context influences how violence is committed. These types have

---

[1] For instrumental violence, these modes of transportation can also serve as 'crime attractors', places where offenders go to with the specific intent to commit their crime (Brantingham and Brantingham 1995).

been labeled as 'compositional' and 'contextual' explanations in previous research (Van Wilsem et al. 2003).

The incident-oriented, compositional explanation sees concentrations of incident characteristics (e.g., the density of weapon-induced violence, or the share of group offenders) as the outcome of the type of public that visits the locality due to the street's functions for everyday use. As such, this incident-oriented approach has a close link to Crime Pattern Theory (Brantingham and Brantingham 1993). For instance, streets with bars not only attract many people, but specifically young people. Violent encounters in these streets are therefore more likely to involve youths. Because they are more likely to carry weapons than older offenders, the street's everyday function may indirectly lead to a local concentration of weapon violence.

In the compositional explanation, street-level concentration of incident characteristics lead to aggregate differences in the way crime is committed. Therefore, a specification is needed of which incident characteristics affect the seriousness of violence. For instance, Felson and Messner (1996) found that incidents involving strangers are less likely to have a lethal outcome. Wilkinson and Fagan (2001) describe how offenders with disadvantaged backgrounds are likely to use guns in violent encounters. Wilcox and Clayton (2001) documented a higher frequency of gun carrying among males and nonwhites in a large-scale survey among Kentucky students. Cook (1991) found that male-on-male homicides are mostly among young people, and that gun use is high in these cases (68%), being exceeded only by the (rare) event of the offender being significantly older than the victim. Though not aimed at explaining *ecological* differences in the way violence is exercised, these studies provide useful insights for the incident-oriented explanation of street profiles of violence. They suggest that violent incidents in streets attracting more males, youngsters, disadvantaged, and non-western people may experience a higher amount of weapon use and victim injury. For other aspects of violence, this individual-level explanation of street-level differences may hold as well. For instance, co-offending and co-victimization are expected to be more prevalent if a street attracts groups and youngsters (e.g., because of a bar being located there), as they are more likely to handle conflicts collectively.

The contextual explanation emphasizes the role of the environment in shaping the nature of violent incidents. Three perspectives can be distinguished in this type of explanation, which separately highlight the importance of (a) collective guardianship, (b) facilities that attract visitors, and (c) local culture. The first contextual explanation on guardianship stresses that the seriousness and visibility of a violent act may be tempered if opportunities for informal surveillance are present. Though not tested by previous research, the expectation would therefore be that unmonitored streets suffer from a higher prevalence of weapon use, victim injury and group violence.

The second contextual explanation suggests that the nature of violence may depend on the presence of facilities that attract people to visit the area and pursue their routine activities there. The current research tests this hypothesis by relating the presence of public transport stops to the chances of the victim and offender knowing each other. As such public transport facilities increase the accessibility of the street, the convergence of people who do not know each other becomes more likely. Therefore, it is expected that streets with public transport stops will have a relatively larger proportion of stranger violence.

A third approach to explain aggregated differences on how violence is committed is offered by Baumer et al. (2003), who use arguments from Elijah Anderson's (1999) *Code of the Street* for this purpose. They found differences between neighborhoods in the amount of weapon use, victim resistance, and victim injury in an analysis of U.S. assaults and robberies: disadvantaged neighborhoods increased gun use and forceful resistance by victims in *assaults*, and decreased the odds of non-forceful resistance in *robberies*. In accounting for these neighborhood differences in the nature of violence, Baumer et al. (2003) point toward the importance of local street culture, where 'respect, toughness, and self-reliance are highly prized forms of social capital.' (p. 41) As such, it influences which types of behavior are regular during violent interactions. For instance, because toughness is highly valued, weapon use will be more regular in disadvantaged areas where the code of the street is held in high esteem.

Apart from being an additional explanation for why the appearance of violence is different across localities, this cultural approach also raises the question at which level of explanation the impact of street codes should be addressed (Short 1998). For the current focus on differences in violent outcomes between *streets*, I argue that a cultural explanation is not suitable as these codes seem to represent a shared tolerance of deviant values on a larger scale such as neighborhoods or even groups of neighborhoods (see e.g., Sampson and Bartusch 1998). In other words, street codes are not expected to vary between (adjacent) streets but more likely between larger areas. Therefore, in my current effort to explore street patterns of violence in Dutch urban areas, I expect differences to result from the daily functions of streets, their facilities and the amount of local surveillance.

Data

The crime data used for this chapter includes all incidents of street robbery, non-lethal assault, and threats that were officially recorded by the police in 2002 and 2003 in three neighborhoods adjacent to each other in Rotterdam, the Netherlands: Hillesluis, Vreewijk, and Bloemhof.[2] Insight into police records was offered to the author as part of a research project on the development in volume and nature of violent crime in these three neighborhoods. Together, these areas comprise of approximately 40,000 residents. They are relatively disadvantaged areas within the context of Rotterdam neighborhoods. The mean annual income per inhabitant ranges from 8.900 Euro (Hillesluis) to 11.500 Euro (Vreewijk), while the city mean is 12.200

---

[2] Incidents that were reported by citizens, but not recorded by the police (e.g., because it was uncertain whether the incident happened at all, or because the police advised the reporting citizen to try and solve the matter him or her self) were therefore not included.

Fig. 9.1 Map of Vreewijk (1), Hillesluis (2) and Bloemhof (3)

Euro, and the Dutch mean is 12.900 Euro. Figure 9.1 shows a picture of their location and boundaries. In these three neighborhoods, the local police recorded 737
incidents of violent crime and complete data were available for 618 of them.

Street-Level Data

The incidents were geocoded at the street level. Information in the police file on
the street where the incident happened was used for this purpose. Dutch streets are
different from U.S. streets, as can be seen in Fig. 9.1. Bends are not uncommon in
a street and, unlike U.S. cities, the street network does not follow a matrix pattern
but is fuzzier. Lengths of streets and population sizes of streets vary considerably
between units. The smallest quarter of this selection of streets has an average population size of approximately 24 residents, while the average for the largest quarter
of streets is 408 residents. As counts of crime are the dependent variable in several
analyses, natural variation caused by differences in the sizes of streets is accounted

for by including street population size into the regression equation. Out of a total of 244 streets in these three neighborhoods, 234 offered complete data on sociodemographic characteristics and the amount of crime. Analyses with crime volumes per street as the dependent variable are based on these 234 observations.

Several variables were computed for crime counts per street. After inspecting the written accounts of recorded victim reports of the incident, each incident was categorized as (a) family violence, (b) street robbery, or (c) other type of violence (e.g., traffic disputes, conflict between neighbors). An incident was categorized as family violence if it involved a conflict between (ex-) spouses, or other types of (former) family members.[3] For every street, the number of crimes in each category was computed, as well as the total sum of violent crimes.[4]

Information was provided by the Rotterdam municipality's Centre for Research and Statistics (COS) for the independent variables of streets, except for the presence of public transport stops, which was derived from a detailed city map. The street names in the COS data were assigned the same code number as in the crime count data, in order to match the separate datasets. Data for social and demographic characteristics of streets, such as percentage of one-person households and proportion of young people, are based on population registration records of individuals and households (GBA). Data on local housing was drawn from the municipal administration's Service for Urban Development and Public Housing. Both sources of information were aggregated to the street level by COS.

An index measure for the amount of poor housing in each street was constructed by taking the mean of the summed z-scores for the percentages of abandoned housing, houses with no more than two rooms and houses with an estimated value of no more than 50,000 euros (Cronbach's alpha=0.76). Furthermore, amounts per street were available for the percentage of (a) rental homes, (b) 15-29 year olds, (c) single-parent households, and (d) people living alone. Finally, the amount of ethnic heterogeneity per street was based on a Herfindahl index (Gibbs and Martin 1962, p. 670), by subtracting the squared fractions of the main ethnic groups (Surinamese, Antilleans, Cape Verdians, Moroccans, Turks, and other Northern Mediterranean) off the value 1.

A measure on the proximity of violent crime was included to take account of spatial dependency patterns. This was done because units of analysis tend to be

---

[3] Whether the incident occurred in the parties' own homes did not influence its labeling as family violence. In fact, a quarter of all incidents in this category occurred elsewhere.

[4] Though police recorded data suffer from underrecording, the extent to which this is problematic for the interpretation of results is hard to estimate. On one hand, data from victimization surveys would offer information on incidents not reported to the police. On the other hand, there have been no surveys to date that included sufficient numbers of respondents per *street* in order to allow for reliable estimates at this level of analysis, but instead, only on higher aggregation levels such as neighbourhoods. Moreover, the police recorded data offer information on incidents that are generally poorly covered by surveys, such as family violence and violence involving drug addicts. In conclusion, although these data are not free from measurement error, they nevertheless seem to offer optimal information for the research question on the level of streets that I am trying to address.

influenced by proximate units (e.g., Morenoff et al. 2001), possibly due to diffusion of criminal activity (Cohen and Tita 1999). It was established for each street if it was next to a high-crime street (which was defined as a street with more than fifteen violent incidents over the two-year period examined here) or not. This cut-off value was used to identify the top 5% in the amount of violent crime (N=11). Ninety streets in this sample (39%) are directly neighboring a high-crime street.

Crime Incident Data

For each crime (N=618), additional information on the incident's circumstances was acquired by coding the written accounts of the victim report with a structured checklist (see also Nielsen et al. 2005). Although victim reports do not offer the full story of what happened during the incident, they often give a description of how the crime was committed on several more or less objective traits, which have been used for the current research.[5]

A variety of incident characteristics were scored. With respect to *offender char-acteristics*, dummy variables were constructed on whether a male offender was involved or not, whether an offender was of non-western origin or not, and whether the offender had used drugs or was known as a drug user by the police. Ethnicity was derived from the name if the offender was caught (with overtly non-western names scored 1), and from victim description if the offender was not caught. Offender age was also scored, and derived from the date of birth for offenders that were caught, and from estimates in victim descriptions for offenders who were not caught. If multiple offenders were involved, offender age was determined by the oldest offender. For the incidents lacking information on age, the mean offender age was imputed. This is preferred to a listwise deletion procedure, because the missings on offender age are selective and would disproportionately exclude robberies, for which few offenders are caught or are clearly described by victims. *Victim* characteristics were scored as well. For each incident, it was assessed whether a male victim was involved or not. Also, the age of the victim was derived from the date of birth given during the report to the police. In cases of multiple victims, the age of the oldest victim was used.

With respect to *the way in which the violent crime was committed*, dummy variables indicated (a) whether the offender operated with co-offenders or not, (b) whether multiple victims were involved or not, (c) if a weapon was used, (d) if the offender made a physical attack or only engaged in threatening behavior, (e) if the victim described being injured, and (f) if offender and victim knew each other prior to the incident. With respect to weapon use, guns and knifes were counted as weapons, as well as other aids used by offenders to induce force, such as paving

---

[5] As far as the victim report distorts the truth of what really happened, there is little reason before-hand to assume that this measurement error would be systematically related to incident character-istics or street characteristics. For that reason, possible measurement error associated with our type of source is not expected to bias the results.

Table 9.1 Descriptives of dependent and independent variables for street-level data and incident-level data

	Mean	Std.dev.	Min.	Max
Street-level data (N = 234)				
Total number of violent incidents	2.88	6.77	0	62
Incidents of family violence	0.70	1.45	0	12
Incidents of street robbery	0.83	2.71	0	30
Incidents of other violence	1.32	3.25	0	27
Poor housing	−0.02	0.79	−0.82	2.77
% Rental homes	91.76	13.68	9.09	100
Ethnic heterogeneity	56.06	23.65	0.00	95.20
% 15–29 year-olds	19.65	9.46	0	50.69
% Single-parent households	16.73	9.40	0	50.00
% Living alone	32.52	16.55	0	100
Public transport stop	0.06	0.24	0	1
Total number of inhabitants	171.96	189.70	1	1356
Adjacent to a high-crime street	0.38	0.49	0	1
Incident-level data (N = 618)				
Co-offending	0.30	0.46	0	1
Co-victimization	0.12	0.32	0	1
Weapon use	0.33	0.47	0	1
Physical attack	0.69	0.46	0	1
Victim injury	0.47	0.50	0	1
O+V know each other	0.45	0.50	0	1
Male offender	0.93	0.25	0	1
Age offender	29.97	10.52	9	67
Non-western offender	0.73	0.44	0	1
Offender drug user	0.07	0.25	0	1
Male victim	0.54	0.50	0	1
Age victim	33.21	14.34	7	78

stones, tools or sports utilities. Table 9.1 offers an overview of the variable used for this research.

Results

A small portion of the streets under scrutiny were confronted with a relatively large amount of crime: 40% of all recorded violence takes place in 4% of the streets. In contrast, Table 9.2 shows that four out of every ten streets do not have a single registered incident of violence. Furthermore, 50% of them had a limited amount of violence, between 1 and 5 incidents. For street robbery, the concentration of incidents is the highest, with 3% of the streets having 48% of all incidents, and 75% of the streets having no robberies at all. On the neighborhood level, average numbers of violent incidents per street vary significantly (F=7.29 (df=2), p<.01). Hillesluis has the highest average of the three neighborhoods, with 5.29 violent incidents on average per street. For Bloemhof and Vreewijk, these numbers are considerably lower, with averages of 2.13 and 1.89, respectively.

Table 9.2 Number of violent acts

	Overall violence		Family violence		Street robbery		Other violence	
	%	N	%	N	%	N	%	N
0	40	97	68	165	75	182	59	143
1-5	50	121	32	77	21	52	36	87
6-10	5	11	0	1	3	7	3	8
11-15	2	4	0	1	1	2	2	4
More than 15	5	11	0	0	0	1	1	2
Total	100	244	100	244	100	244	100	244
Mean	2.81		0.68		0.81		1.29	
Variance	44.18		2.04		7.10		10.16	
Maximum	62		12		30		27	

In order to examine the relation between population features, environmental design characteristics and the amounts of violence in streets, count data are used, with the number of violent incidents in a street as the dependent variable. Table 9.2 demonstrates that each of the available violence measures does not follow a Poisson distribution, as the variance exceeds the mean for each of them. Therefore, a negative binomial model was employed, which is a Poisson-based regression model that allows for overdispersion (Osgood 2000).[6] As the counts of violence per street are nested in neighborhoods, multilevel negative binomial models were used (see also Tseloni 2006). The multilevel model allows us to reveal remaining differences in variance between neighborhoods after adjusting for street-level influences. If substantial neighborhood-level variance would remain, then this would suggest that the neighborhood is important as a contextual determinant of street-level differences in crime. If such variance would not exist, then initial differences between neighborhoods in average crime counts can be understood as a result of compositional differences between neighborhoods in their types of streets.

The results in Table 9.3 reveal that, apart from the total number of inhabitants, there is no single predictor that is consistently related to *all* types of violence counts. However, this is mainly because the determinants of family violence are distinct from the others. The total numbers of violent acts, as well as the number of street robberies and nonfamily-related acts of violence are all positively related to (a) the percentage of residents living alone, (b) the presence of a public transport stop, and (c) adjacency to a high-crime street. The first finding is in line with the expectations derived from the social disorganization perspective, as a larger share of one-person households may decrease the capacity for social control in the street. The second finding supports Crime Pattern Theory's argument that the accessibility of streets to the general public increases the potential for the committing of violence in that place. According to an additional OLS regression analysis on the number of violent acts, a public transport stop approximately results in an additional 10 acts of vio-

---

[6] This option to allow for overdispersion resulted in significantly better model fits, compared to regular Poisson models.

Table 9.3 Negative binomial models of number of violent incidents per street on population and environmental characteristics (N = 234)

	Overall violence	Family violence	Street robbery	Other violence
Constant	−0.039**	−1.197**	−1.847**	−0.789**
Poor housing	0.048	0.124	0.054	−0.327
% Rental homes	1.605**	−0.806	0.638	2.484**
Ethnic heterogeneity	1.037**	2.075**	1.125	0.537
% 15-29 year-olds	−0.135	−1.312	−0.804	1.110
% Single-parent households	2.046*	1.783	1.338	2.059
% Living alone	1.674**	−1.657	3.032**	2.577**
Public transport stop	1.117**	0.357	1.381**	1.418**
Total number of inhabitants	0.004**	0.004**	0.003**	0.003**
Adjacent to a high-crime street	0.721**	0.332	1.210**	0.702**
Variance between neighborhoods	0.000	0.023	0.000	0.000
Negative extra-binomial variance	0.733	0.700	0.638	0.794

*$p<.05$, **$p<.01$ (one-tailed test)

lence in that street, which is considerable if we take into account the average rate of almost three acts per street in this sample. The third finding, that being adjacent to a high-crime street independently increases the number of violent crimes, suggests a spill-over effect of violence. This may be present for several reasons. First, streets close to hot-spots may serve as passage ways that need to be passed in order to reach the hot-spot. As a result, relatively speaking many people visit the street adjacent to the hot-spot, which increases the chances that violent conflicts occur in that street. Second, spatial adjacency may stimulate imitation of behavior found nearby. In this context, violence in hot-spots may 'diffuse' into adjacent areas (Cohen and Tita 1999).

For family violence, ethnic heterogeneity is the only substantive factor that is related to the number of incidents. In streets with high levels of heterogeneity (i.e., many different ethnic categories), the amount of family-related conflicts are high. This supports claims from social disorganization theory that informal surveillance decreases crime, even though many of these conflicts are conducted within the vicinity of homes. Similar to the current findings, Benson et al. (2003) suggested that the negative association they found between neighborhood income and domestic violence (net of individual factors), was indicative of social disorganization.

Turning to *the way violent crimes are committed*, Table 9.4 gives an overview of the street differences of several qualitative aspects of violence: was the incident committed with co-offenders, were multiple victims involved, was a weapon used, was the victim physically attacked, did the victim report suffering an injury, and did victim and offender know each other prior to the incident? These analyses are based on streets *in which at least one incident of violence occurred during the two-year*

Table 9.4 Deviance tests – Variance of qualitative aspects of violence between streets

Aspect of violence	Variance between streets
Co-offending	0.38**
Co-victimization	0.01
Weapon use	0.02
Physical attack	0.00
Injury	0.00
O + V know each other	0.35**

*p<.05, **p<.01 (one-tailed test)

period, and for which complete incident and street data were available. Because of missing data on one of the predictors, 10 streets were deleted. This leaves us with 137 streets (from an original 147 with at least one violent crime), in which 610 incidents occurred.

For the analysis of the incident data, multilevel logistic models were employed, with incidents nested within streets nested within neighborhoods. In order to assess the significance of differences between streets in the nature of violence, deviance tests were conducted (Snijders and Bosker 1999). The deviance test evaluates the amount of loss of fit if the random parameter of the model is dropped which, in this case, is the random intercept. The difference between the likelihood of the models including and excluding the random intercept therefore provides the deviance statistic, which follows a chi square distribution. Following Snijders and Bosker (1999, p. 90), the deviance test is conducted one-sided.

The deviance tests are performed for two-level logistic models, in which incidents are nested within streets. Table 9.4 shows that according to these analyses, streets vary significantly in their proportions of offenders operating in groups, and in the number of incidents where offender and victim know each other. Additional descriptive analysis on the 17 streets with at least 10 incidents (not shown), reveal that the range for co-offending varies from 6% of the incidents in one street to a maximum of 61%, with a mean value of 32%. For the relation between offender and victim, there is also a wide range between streets, from a minimum of 32% of the incidents where the parties involved know each other, to a maximum of 80% (mean value: 49%). Furthermore, the other aspects, such as weapon use and victim injury, do not differ significantly between streets.

Because of their significant differences between streets, co-offending and the relation between offender and victim are subjected to more detailed analyses, which are performed in two steps. The first model includes incident characteristics, while the second model adds the effect of street characteristics to the equation. This way, changes in variance between streets can be assessed after compositional differences between streets in their incident characteristics are taken into account (model 1) and, subsequently, after contextual differences are controlled for (model 2). Table 9.5 offers an overview of the results.

For *co-offending*, model 1 points out that several incident characteristics are important for understanding why some violent acts are committed with co-offenders while others are not. Co-offending was more likely if a non-western offender was

Table 9.5 Multilevel logistic regression of co-offending and relation between conflict parties on incident and street characteristics

	Co-offending		O+V know each other	
	1	2	1	2
Constant	−1.41**	−1.40**	−0.58	−0.62
Incident characteristics				
Male offender	0.84	0.87	0.23	0.26
Age offender	−0.08	−0.09	0.02	0.03
Age offender, squared	0.00	0.00	−0.00	−0.00
Non-western offender	0.79**	0.77**	−0.03	−0.01
Offender drug user	−1.37	−1.35	1.28*	1.35**
Male victim	0.69**	0.65**	−1.35**	−1.29**
Age victim	−0.01	−0.01	0.01	−0.01
Age victim, squared	0.00	0.00	0.00	0.00
Group of victims	0.85**	0.84*	−0.20	−0.09
Family violence	−1.33**	−1.32**	Ref.cat	Ref.cat
Street robbery	1.36**	1.33**	−3.46**	−3.43**
Other violence	Ref.cat.	Ref.cat.	Ref.cat.	Ref.cat.
Street characteristics				
Poor housing	–	0.01	–	−0.01
% Living alone	–	0.01	–	−0.03*
Public transport stop	–	0.22	–	−0.67*
Total number of inhabitants	–	0.00	–	0.00
Street-level variance	*0.30**	*0.32**	*0.25*	*0.00*

*$p<.05$, **$p<.01$ (two-tailed test)

involved, as well as for male victims, groups of victims, and for street robberies. Group violence was *less* likely for domestic violence and drug-using offenders. Controlling for these circumstances leads to a slight drop in street-level variance from 0.38 to 0.30. This means that the incident characteristics affecting co-offending, such as victim's gender, are to some extent distributed across streets in a way that they can explain differences in co-offending at this level. For instance, in streets with a lot of male victims, more co-offending is found. Controlling for street characteristics in model 2 does not reduce the amount of variance between streets on this aspect any further. In fact, none of the selected street variables succeed in predicting the odds of group violence. These results suggest that other factors need to be accounted for in order to explain street-level differences in co-offending.

The *relation between the offender and victim* is also dependent upon several incident characteristics (model 1). The likelihood that victim and offender know each other is greater for older offenders and drug using offenders, while these odds are reduced for incidents with male victims and street robberies. Although street-level differences remain significant after controlling for these aspects, the variance declines from 0.35 to 0.25. Adding street characteristics to the model leads to a further diminishing of the street-level differences on this point. More specifically, it appears that streets with public transport stops have a significantly lower proportion of incidents where victim and offender know each other, as well as streets with many one-person households. The former result is in accordance with our expectation that streets made accessible by public transport are confronted with larger numbers of visitors who are strangers to each other. As a result, in the emergence of conflicts, the chances increase that the parties involved are unknown to each other.

Conclusions

This chapter uses *streets* as units of analysis to explore differences in the number of violent incidents as well as the nature of these incidents. Such a detailed level of analysis enables an exploration of *within-neighborhood* differences in crime. In this study of three Rotterdam neighborhoods, we find that violent crimes are highly concentrated, especially for street robbery, where only a few streets accounted for almost half of the robberies in the period 2002–2003 in the entire area. Such concentrations within specific places in neighborhoods suggest that the opportunities to commit crime are localized as well, and are not present or absent across an entire neighborhood. In general, this result supports the idea that meaningful crime variations on a small scale get lost once data are aggregated to higher levels such as neighborhoods (see also Hipp 2007).

High volumes of crime were found in streets with a large share of single-person households and high levels of ethnic heterogeneity, which points to the disruptive effects of inadequate social control structures for the maintenance of social order. Furthermore, more violence was found in streets with public transport stops. Public transport affects the accessibility of streets by directing the everyday flow of routine behavior. It is likely that streets with public transport are busier than other streets and that more opportunities for conflict are present. As such, it is a clear example of the way in which routine activities affect the distribution of crime (Brantingham and Brantingham 1993; Cohen and Felson 1979). In addition, a spill-over effect was also found, as the spatial adjacency of streets to streets with high levels of violence independently increased the amount of violent acts in that locality.

An innovative aspect of this research was that it explored the way in which violence was committed, and how this varied across streets. For several aspects such as weapon use and the reporting of victim injury, we found no substantial differences between streets. This may have been partly due to the small sample size and the relatively uniform sample of streets in three relatively disadvantaged neighborhoods. However, the likelihood of violent acts committed by groups of offenders *did* vary significantly between streets, as well as the relation between the parties involved. In some streets, large portions of violence were characterized by the fact that the victim(s) and offender(s) knew each other, while in others the majority of conflicting parties were strangers.

Incident characteristics that were connected to co-offending, such as offender ethnicity and age, were to some extent distributed across streets in such a way that they could account for street-level differences in group violence. This was in line with our expectations, as we predicted that streets would have more co-offending if they had more young offenders and victims. Street-level characteristics, such as the concentration of poor housing or the presence of a public transport stop, were not related to co-offending, and could therefore also not account for street-level differences on this aspect. Therefore, the question why streets differ in their amounts of co-offending remains partly unanswered, which suggests we should seek additional factors that were not measured in this study. It may be that streets not only function as a selection mechanism where groups of people tend to go (and thus tend to commit violence in groups), but perhaps also as a recruiting place, where potential offenders meet. Contextual factors facilitating such recruitment for co-offenders may include places for entertainment or for hanging out, such as shopping malls.

With respect to the relation between offender and victim, both incident characteristics and street characteristics were able to explain street-level differences. Why some streets have violent incidents involving merely strangers, while others have conflicts where the majority of parties know each other depends partly upon who commits the violence, and how these offender characteristics are distributed across streets. Young offenders are more likely to victimize strangers, so the more young people choose a specific street as their offending space, the more likely it is that offenders and victims do not know each other in that locality. Also, we found that streets with public transport are more likely to yield violence between strangers, probably because public transport increases the chance that people from different neighborhoods visit the street. Strangers are therefore more likely to intersect and have a conflict, as compared to streets that are less easily accessible. Contrary to our expectations, the hypothesis on guardianship in streets was not supported, as variations in the capacity for social control did not affect how and against whom violence was committed.

Overall, the findings support the claim that the different ways of committing violence across places may be the result of the functions of streets for everyday life, which serve as a filter mechanism. These functions determine which types of people are more likely to visit the area and thus, if conflicts arise, how and against whom they are directed. This type of reasoning is akin to Crime Pattern Theory, which emphasizes how the intertwining of everyday life with illegal behavior leads to spatial distributions of crime. The results show that this is not only the case for the *volume* of crime, but also for the characteristics of violence.

An interesting direction for future research would be to assess the impact of facilities which are not in an area itself, but nearby. It may be that streets in the vicinity of people attracting facilities serve as passage ways. When we assume that routine activities are important in understanding why violent acts occur at certain places and not at others, it is expected that such passage ways also increase the likelihood of social encounters, including those resulting in violence. GIS applications that offer the possibility to identify ambient populations at specific places, such as the Landscan Population Database (Andresen 2006), may be a potentially useful tool in this respect.

Finally, it would be worthwhile to explore interactions between the type of public visiting a place and its accessibility. For instance, if motivational pressures are less among the public visiting specific places, accessibility may not lead to higher rates of violence. In order to investigate this, a more diversified sample of streets from affluent as well as disadvantaged neighborhoods is needed. It may reveal to what extent the current patterns on the nature of violent acts can be generalized for other streets.

References

Anderson, E. (1999). *Code of the Street: Decency, Violence and the Moral Life of the Inner City.* New York: W.W. Norton and Company.
Andresen, M. A. (2006). Crime measures and the spatial analysis of criminal activity. *British Journal of Criminology,* 46, 258–285.
Baumer, E., Horney, J., Felson, R., & Lauritsen, J.L. (2003). Neighborhood disadvantage and the nature of violence. *Criminology,* 41, 39–72.
Beavon, D. J. K., Brantingham, P. L., & Brantingham, P. J. (1994). The influence of street networks on the patterning of property offenses. In: R. V. Clarke (Ed.), *Crime Prevention Studies,* Vol. 2. New York: Willow Tree Press.
Benson, M. L., Fox, G. L., DeMaris, A., & Van Wyk, J. (2003). Neighborhood disadvantage, individual economic distress and violence against women in intimate relationships. *Journal of Quantitative Criminology,* 19, 207–235.
Block, R., & Davis, S. (1996). The environs of rapid transit stations: A focus for street crime or just another risky place? In: R. Clarke (Ed.), *Preventing Mass Transit Crime.* Monsey, NY: Criminal Justice Press.
Block, R. (2000). Gang activity and overall levels of crime: A new mapping tool for defining areas of gang activity using police records. *Journal of Quantitative Criminology,* 16, 369–383.
Brantingham, P. L., & Brantingham, P.J. (1993). Nodes, paths and edges: Considerations on the complexity of crime and the physical environment. *Journal of Environmental Psychology,* 13, 3–28.
Brantingham, P. L., & Brantingham, P. J. (1995). Criminality of place. Crime generators and crime attractors. *European Journal on Criminal Policy and Research,* 3, 5–26.
Cohen, J., & Tita, G. (1999). Diffusion in homicide: Exploring a general method for detecting spatial diffusion processes. *Journal of Quantitative Criminology,* 15, 451–493.
Cohen, L. E., & Felson, M. (1979). Social change and crime rate trends: A routine activity approach. *American Sociological Review,* 44, 588–608.
Cook, P. J. (1991). The technology of personal violence. *Crime and Justice,* 14, 1–72.
Cornish, D. B., & Clarke, R. V. (1986). *The Reasoning Criminal. Rational Choice Perspectives on Offending.* New York: Springer-Verlag.
Eck, J. E., & Weisburd, D. (1995). Crime places in Crime Theory. In: J. E. Eck & D. Weisburd (Eds.), *Crime and Place.* Monsey, NY: Criminal Justice Press.
Eisner, M., & Wikström, P. O. (1999). Violent crime in the urban community: A comparison of Stockholm and Basel. *European Journal on Criminal Policy and Research,* 7, 427–442.
Felson, R., & Messner, S. F. (1996). To kill or not to kill? Lethal outcomes in injurious attacks. *Criminology,* 34, 519–545.
Gibbs, J. P., & Martin, W. T. (1962). Urbanization, technology, and the division of labor: International patterns. *American Sociological Review,* 27, 667–677.
Hipp, J. R. (2007). Block, tract, and levels of aggregation: Neighborhood structure and crime and disorder as a case in point. *American Sociological Review,* 72, 659–680.
McClintock, F. H., & Wikström, P. O. (1992). The comparative study of urban violence. Criminal violence in Edinburgh and Stockholm. *British Journal of Criminology,* 32, 505–520.
Morenoff, J. D., Sampson, R. J., & Raudenbush, S. W. (2001). Neighborhood inequality, collective efficacy, and the spatial dynamics of urban violence. *Criminology,* 39, 517–560.

Nielsen, A. L., Martinez jr, R., & Rosenfeld, R. (2005). Firearm use, injury and lethality in assaultive violence. *Homicide Studies*, 9, 83–108.

Osgood, D. W. (2000). Poisson-based regression analysis of aggregate crime rates. *Journal of Quantitative Criminology*, 16, 21–43.

Piza, E. L. (2003). *Transit stops, Robbery, and Routine Activities: Examining Street Robbery in the Newark*, NJ Subway Environment. Crime Mapping, Dr. Kennedy.

Rice, K. J., & Smith, W. R. (2002). Socioecological models of automotive theft: Integrating routine activity and social disorganization approaches. *Journal of Research in Crime and Delinquency*, 39, 304–336.

Roncek, D. W. (1981). Dangerous places: Crime and residential environment. *Social Forces, 60*, 74–96.

Roncek, D. W., Faggiani, D. (1985). High schools and crime: A replication. *The Sociological Quarterly*, 26, 491–505.

Roncek, D. W., & Maier, P.A. (1991). Bars, blocks, and crimes revisited: Linking the theory of routine activities to the empiricism of "hot spots". *Criminology*, 29, 725–753.

Sampson, R. J., & Bartusch, D. J. (1998). Legal cynicism and (subcultural?) tolerance of deviance: The neighborhood context of racial differences. *Law & Society Review*, 32, 777–804.

Sampson, R. J., & Groves, W. B. (1989). Community structure and crime: Testing social-disorganization theory. *American Sociological Review*, 94, 774–802.

Sherman, L. W., Gartin, P.R., & Buerger, M. E. (1989). Hot spots of predatory crime: Routine activities and the criminology of place. *Criminology*, 27, 27–55.

Short, J. (1998). The level of explanation problem revisited. *Criminology*, 36, 3–36.

Smith, M., & Clarke, R. V. (2000). Crime and public transport. *Crime and Justice*, 27, 169–233.

Smith, W. R., Frazee, S. G., & Davison, E. L. (2000). Furthering the integration of routine activity and social disorganization theories: Small units of analysis and the study of street robbery as a diffusion process. *Criminology*, 38, 489–524.

Snijders, T., & Bosker, R. (1999). *Multilevel Analysis. An Introduction to Basic and Advanced Multilevel Modeling*. London: Sage.

Tseloni, A. (2006). Multilevel modelling of the number of property crimes: Household and area effects. *Journal of the Royal Statistical Society A*, 169, 205–233.

Van Wilsem, J., De Graaf, N.D., & Wittebrood, K. (2003). Cross-national differences in victimization. Disentangling the impact of composition and context. *European Sociological Review*, 19, 125–142.

Wikström, P. O. (1995). Preventing city-center street crimes. *Crime and Justice*, 19, 429–468.

Wilcox, P., & Clayton, R. R. (2001). A multilevel analysis of school-based weapon possession. *Justice Quarterly*, 18, 509–541.

Wilkinson, D. L., & Fagan, J. (2001). What we know about gun use among adolescents. *Clinical Child and Family Psychology Review*, 4, 109–132.

Chapter 10
Determining How Journeys-to-Crime Vary: Measuring Inter- and Intra-Offender Crime Trip Distributions

William Smith, John W. Bond, and Michael Townsley[1]

Abstract Journey to crime studies have attempted to illuminate aspects of offender decision making that has implications for theory and practice. This article argues that our current understanding of journey to crime is incomplete. It improves our understanding by resolving a fundamental unit of analysis issue that had thus far not received much attention in the literature. It is demonstrated that the aggregate distribution of crime trips (commonly known as the distance decay) does not take into account the considerable variation that exists between individual offenders' crime trip distributions. Moreover, the common assumption of statistical independence between observations that make up a distribution is something that, until now, has yet to be tested for distributions of crime trips of multiple offenders. In order to explore these issues, three years of burglary data from a UK police force were linked to 32 prolific offenders to generate journey to crime distributions at the aggregate and offender levels. Using multi-level models, it was demonstrated that the bulk (65%) of the variation of journeys to crime exists at the offender level, indicating that individual crime trips are not statistically independent. In addition the distance decay pattern found at the aggregate level was not, in the main, observed at the offender level – a result that runs counter to conventional wisdom, and another example of the ecological fallacy. The implications of these findings are discussed.

[1] We thank Forensic Intelligence Analysts Gemma Lyon and Helen Bates of Northamptonshire Police for providing data, their expertise and a great deal of their time. The willingness and co-operation of other Scientific Support Unit staff was also invaluable and very much appreciated. We would also like to acknowledge the feedback of Shane Johnson at various stages of the research and also thank both Kim Rossmo, George Rengert and the anonymous reviewers who provided insightful comments on an early draft.

W. Smith
Thames Valley Police, United Kingdom
e-mail: Will.Smith@thamesvalley.pnn.police.uk

D. Weisburd et al. (eds.), *Putting Crime in its Place*,
DOI 10.1007/978-0-387-09688-9_10, © Springer Science+Business Media, LLC 2009

Introduction

Until recently criminology 'has been devoted to finding some unicausal source of motivation' (Brantingham and Brantingham 1993, p. 273) for the commission of criminal acts. Crime control policies have traditionally echoed criminological thinking, with criminal justice systems following a predominantly offender-orientated paradigm of apportioning blame and applying penalties to act as a deterrent to whatever motive compels individuals to commit criminal acts.

Eschewing offenders as the unit of analysis, environmental criminology focuses on the 'where and when' of offending (Rossmo 2000, p. 112) and is considered a central theoretical foundation underpinning our understanding of the geography of crime. By concentrating on the place of the offence and the factors that directly affect offence instigation, it builds upon the work of human ecology and seeks to explain the spatial clustering of crime events in terms of an individual's interaction with their physical setting.

Most of the contributions to this volume deal with the issue of what the unit of analysis should be in studies of crime at place, and maybe even more importantly, what the appropriate criteria are for choosing a unit of analysis. Brantingham et al. (1976) provide clear examples of the varieties of observed patterns generated by selecting different spatial units of analysis, from national to block level, illustrating the so called geographic 'cone of resolution'.

In general, measurement is not the main problem here as criminal incidents can be measured at very fine geographical resolutions; what is problematic is determining the level of appropriate aggregation. This article will argue that the most appropriate aggregation threshold is the one which *minimizes* the heterogeneity *within* groups of observations while attempting to *maximize* the heterogeneity *between* groups of observations. Hierarchical linear models (or multilevel models) provide a natural framework in which to investigate this. These types of models attempt to control for the influence of factors that may be nested at different levels of aggregation (Snijders and Bosker 1999) by incorporating multiple geographical levels of aggregation in the same model. This means effects operating by different levels can be partitioned with a view to shedding light on unit of analysis problems. Clearly, this allows a check against the well known, but perennial, problem of committing the ecological fallacy, when relationships at a higher level of geographical aggregation are interpreted in terms of relationships at a lower level.

In a study now considered classic, Robinson (1950) calculated for each state in the USA the percentage of residents who were (a) foreign born and (b) illiterate. At the state level, the correlation was −0.53 but when measured at the individual level the correlation is 0.11! The contrasting results arise by trying to equate findings at the state level with comments about individuals and can be explained by observing that immigrants tend to move to areas where there are high literacy rates. Ultimately, the ecological fallacy is a not necessarily a *spatial* unit of analysis issue, but applies to all situations where issues of aggregation need to be resolved before proper conclusions can be arrived at.

While staying within the boundaries of the main themes of this volume, this article attempts to broaden the scope of the discussion of determining appropriate units of analysis by studying a situation in which criminal incidents are grouped not by spatially nested units but by the people who commit them. Specifically, where multiple crime locations are spatially linked to a common point (residence, say) of the offender who committed them. In this case, the 'unit of analysis' challenge is not restricted to finding an appropriate way to assign crimes to spatial entities, but instead the situation forces us to start looking at broader unit of analysis questions. For example, should we be studying offenders and the locations where they reside, should we take crime events and the locations where they take place as our unit of analysis, or should we focus on the links between offenders and their crimes, that is, should we study crime trips?

The remainder of this chapter will focus on the journey to crime literature and the well accepted principle of 'distance decay': the frequency of offending decreases with the distance from home. As we shall demonstrate, some issues have become clouded, with researchers interpreting the findings of research conducted at the crime trip unit of analysis as findings at the offender level unit of analysis. Later, we distinguish between these two levels of analysis and assesses whether the 'distance decay' principle not only applies in the aggregate, but also describes the behavior of individual offenders.

Theory and Previous Research

Within environmental criminology, a number of related theories attempt to explain the prevalence of criminal acts by focusing on factors other than, but not excluding, offender motivation. Brantingham and Brantingham (1993) describe a criminal event as 'an opportune cross-product of law, offender motivation, and target characteristic arrayed on an environmental backcloth at a particular point in space-time' (p. 259). In essence, multiple ingredients are required for the generation of a crime, motivation representing but one of these. The dominant theories include routine activities (Cohen and Felson 1979), rational choice (Cornish and Clarke 1986), and crime pattern theory (Brantingham and Brantingham 1981).

Crime pattern theory (Brantingham and Brantingham 1981) postulates that individuals have certain psychologically intimate or familiar locations (such as work, home recreation locations) called *nodes* or anchor points. Certain routes between nodes are usually preferred over others (in terms of speed, cost, aesthetics, familiarity). These *paths* contribute to the generation of an *awareness space* (a mental map). Locations with high crime risk are produced when the cognitive maps (Canter and Hodge 2000) of motivated offenders overlap with the spatial distribution of available targets (Cohen and Felson 1979).

Central to crime pattern theory and by extension spatial profiles of crime risk, therefore, is the magnitude and connectedness of offenders' node network. This observation has, in turn, fostered recent academic interest in offenders' *journey-to-crime* (JTC)[2]. The purpose of investigating JTC is to analyze the crime-specific travel behavior of offenders with a view to inferring some form of offender decision making. It also has investigative value in that findings from the JTC literature may hint at directions of inquiry. For example, the JTC literature is pivotal to the research area of geographic profiling, where crime scenes are triangulated to predict an offender's anchor point (Rossmo 2000).

The overwhelming majority of research into offender JTC has been conducted in North America. There is a general consensus within the academic community that offenders do not tend to travel far to commit crime (Rossmo 2000; Rengert et al. 1999; Rhodes and Conly 1981; Paulsen and Robinson 2004; Chainey and Ratcliffe 2005). A comprehensive review of the JTC literature can be found in Rossmo (2000, ch 10)[3] in which he compiles the results of no less than 38 different JTC studies (consisting of 80 offence-specific JTC estimates). He observes that JTC estimates are calculated in one of four ways: (a) mean distance (usually the arithmetic mean but sometimes the geometric mean is used to restrict the influence of outliers); (b) medial circle (the radius of a circle which captures a certain proportion of crime trip distances); (c) mobility triangles, and (d) distance decay functions. Rossmo concludes that the latter of these is the most advantageous as it captures a degree of the variation in crime trip distances, but out of the 38 studies considered only eight employed this method. The other three measures suffer due to an inability (to varying degrees) to capture the variability of individual crime trips. That is they are a measure of central tendency but not dispersion. Nonetheless, the key findings of Rossmo's review are that:

- crimes occur in close proximity to the offender's residence;
- there is a distance decay pattern for crime trips;
- juvenile offenders are less mobile than adult offenders; and
- JTC varies by crime type.

Wiles and Costello (2000) conducted one of the few JTC studies outside North America, carrying out extensive research into the travelling habits of offenders throughout South Yorkshire. Their main findings were broadly consistent with the Rossmo review and they further observed that in the main offenders did not set out with the intention to commit crime, but instead responded to the opportunities that presented themselves during their routine activities. They concluded that the inter-linked concepts of offender rationality and routine activities varying in accordance with the spatial distribution of opportunities were still the dominant driving force behind the JTC.

Two recent studies have sought to clarify our knowledge of JTC and its relevance to criminology van Koppen and de Keijser (1997) were sceptical that aggregate

---

[2] Levine (2005) notes that researcher interest in JTC has considerable history citing studies in the 1930s.

[3] Levine (2005) also provides an overview of the JTC literature but usefully places it in the context of the study of travel across a range of fields. Groff and McEwan (2006) also provide a thorough, recent overview of the JTC literature.

distance decay functions represented individual JTC distributions appropriately. They felt it was feasible that JTC patterns at the offender level displaying no distance decay could be combined to show an aggregate distance decay and that JTC researchers could be at the mercy of an ecological fallacy when commenting on patterns observed in the aggregate. They demonstrated this by simulating a sample of offenders, none of whom conformed to a distance decay function. When the crime trips of each offender were combined, the aggregate distribution displayed the conventional distance decay pattern.

A critique by Rengert et al. (1999) strongly rebutted van Koppen and de Keijser's argument by focussing on four areas: (a) the interpretation of the ecological fallacy; (b) assumptions of offender movements; (c) the interpretation of geographic profiling; and (d) random target selection assumptions and range of operations. The second and fourth of these are methodological issues relating to how van Koppen and de Keijser implemented their simulations. Rengert et al. demonstrated that van Koppen and de Keijser, by not properly accounting for a uniform distribution of opportunities per distance unit, inadvertently simulated offenders that *did* possess distance decay at the individual level.

Rengert et al. (1999) also take issue with van Koppen and de Keijser's use of the ecological fallacy to undermine the integrity of JTC studies. van Koppen and de Keijser (1997) state that 'the distance decay function is an aggregated function' which 'shows that the number of crimes is inversely related to the distance from criminals' residences. This, however, does not necessarily imply that *individual criminals* commit more crimes closer to their home than far away' (p. 507, emphasis added). Rengert et al. reply that because aggregate distance decay functions are generated from individual data then drawing inferences about the individual from the aggregate is not fallacious. They argue that in the context of aggregate JTC distance decay functions that 'the ecological fallacy would not be present since the analyses derive from individual-level data and inferences at this level of analysis are appropriate. This is especially true if distance decay exists at the *individual level*' (1999, pp. 432–433, emphasis added).

It appears that both groups of researchers are talking at cross purposes and the confusion is compounded as the non-specificity of the term 'individual'; it could refer to an individual offender or an individual crime trip. In the interests of clarification we will refer to a single JTC as a *crime trip*. A number of crime trips will be taken by an individual *offender*. A number of offenders will make up the *population* of offenders. The aggregate distance decay function is, therefore, an estimation[4] of the population of all crime trips taken by all offenders.

Restating the quotes above: (a) van Koppen and de Keijser argue that an aggregate distance decay function cannot be used to infer patterns at the offender level; (b) whereas Rengert et al. defend the claim that most crime trips are short because data on individual crime trips has merely been aggregated. In their respective frames of reference, both groups are right! The confusion lies with making comments about

---

[4] Assuming that only a sample of all offenders (and their crimes) are represented in the data.

offenders. While most crime trips might be short, we cannot be certain that most offenders make short crime trips. It is inappropriate to draw inferences about *offenders* from the aggregation of *crime trips*, as we have no information about how these crime trips are nested at the offender level. A possible exception is if all offender level JTC distributions take on the same (approximate) shape (as intimated in the earlier quote by Rengert et al. 1999) and they all possess similar values of central tendency.

Consideration of the distributions of individual offender crime trips have not featured prominently in the JTC literature. Exceptions include Kocsis et al. (2002), Canter and Larkin (1993), along with four replications cited in Canter et al. (2000) and Rengert et al. (1999) cite a number of studies they claim have demonstrated offender-level distance decay (Alston 1994; Rengert 1996; Rossmo 1993; and Warren et al. 1995).

LeBeau (1992) reports the travel distributions of four serial rapists (shown here in Fig. 10.1)[5]. It is immediately apparent that, while intra-offender JTC patterns conform to conventional distance decay patterns – the aggregate picture is much the same - there is considerable inter-offender JTC variation. The JTC distribution of offender 1 is well removed from the others and is easily explained by his place of employment located about 26 kilometers from a city. Offenders 2 and 3 did not travel very far to offend, offender 3 especially so with a very restricted range of JTC. The JTC distribution of offender 4 displays the most variation; although offender 2 has a wider range and greater standard deviation, this is due to the presence of an outlier and the bulk of the distribution is confined to less than five kilometers.

Snook (2004) provides an exploration of inter-offender JTC differences of serial burglars in St John's, Canada. He found that median travel distances were associated with age, method of transport and value of property stolen, but not experience, series length (events and time), offending with partners and target type. An aggregate

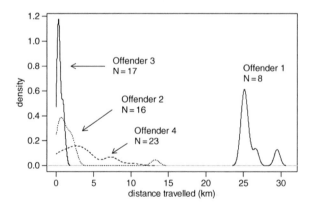

Fig. 10.1 Distributions of individual offender crime trips (with a lower bound of zero) estimated by kernel density
Source: LeBeau (1992)

---

[5] LeBeau also usefully provides a host of other data (date, time, approach method, location, relationship to victim) allowing for further inter-offender comparisons.

distance decay function is provided for the sample (347 crime trips over 51 offenders) as are descriptive statistics (N, median, mean, and standard deviation) of crime trip distributions by individual differences (age, transport, etc. as above). The degree of relative dispersion is very high. Computing the co-efficient of variation[6] for the sample across each individual difference, excluding low frequency method of transport categories, reveals ratios ranging from 50 to 120%. This suggests that summaries of the JTC distribution at the aggregate level mask considerable variation at possibly the inter-offender level, the intra-offender level, or some combination of the two.

Research Question

To summarize, the consensus in the JTC literature is that 'most offenders do not travel far to commit crime' or 'most crime trips are short(er) than long'. However, the majority of published studies have not accounted for the nesting of crime trips within offenders, making the former statement unjustified based on the evidence, and methods used. If observations are nested within a particular factor, it is inappropriate to make comments about the influence of that factor if it has been ignored! Inferring offender travel characteristics from crime trip data risks committing the ecological fallacy. Of course, just because nesting occurs does not mean it is necessarily relevant. Offenders can be grouped according to their hair colour but it would indeed be surprising if this influenced patterns greatly.

The focus of this study is to explore the extent of variability within JTC distributions with a view to better understanding the degree to which uniqueness or generality drive the well established and accepted aggregate patterns of JTC (i.e., aggregate distance decay). In other words, we seek to describe the extent of variation at the inter-offender level and the intra-offender level, with a view to determining whether the influence of grouping is large enough to raise concerns about a possible aggregation bias. If so, then comments about offender travel characteristics are not justified on the basis of aggregated crime trip data and further research is required to recover this information. If not, then comments about offender characteristics can be made on the basis of crime trip data.

This study is primarily concerned with establishing whether a methodological problem, overlooking the nesting of crime trips within offenders, has compromised our understanding of JTC.

Data and Methods

The area chosen for investigation was Northamptonshire Police Force, a semi-rural police force in the East Midlands region of the United Kingdom. As the literature

---

[6] The co-efficient of variation is the standard deviation divided by the mean expressed as a percentage. It is often used to assess the degree of variation of a group of observations while controlling for the magnitude of the observations.

revealed JTC estimates vary by crime type, only one offence was selected for the study, residential burglary. Two primary data sources were used; offence data and offender data. A three year time window for offence data was chosen after a preliminary investigation indicated that any shorter time frame would provide an insufficient sample set of offenders and their associated JTC distributions. There were a total of 14,217 offences in the period 2002–2004 inclusive. Of these, 2341 (16.5%) resulted in a detection (i.e., were linked with an offender and resulted in arrest and charging). The full postcode, date reported, crime beat, and offender name of the 2341 burglaries were extracted from the recorded crime information system.

The second source of data was offender information. All 1083 offenders featured in the detected burglary list were included. For each individual the following fields were extracted from the Force Intelligence System (FIS): name, date of birth, occupation, and full postcodes of all known residences. As some individuals had multiple addresses in the three year time period of this study, the tenure of each different address was determined by entries on the FIS. This information was originally obtained through a combination of housing records, police stop and searches, arrests for related matters, and other police intelligence placing offenders as resident at specific addresses. While a certain degree of imprecision remains, we believe the above approach is about as accurate as is possible from police data. The anchor point chosen to examine was the primary residence of the offender as the quality of police data concerning other anchor points was not of sufficient quality to warrant considering.

Location information for crime incidents and offender residence in this study was determined using the full postcode. In the UK a full postcode relates to, on average, 15 'delivery points' – literally letterboxes. In urban areas, this typically means distinct dwellings or households (in the study area there was a trivial amount of high density housing). Full postcodes, therefore, are a reasonable compromise for data protection concerns. Point information for residences of crime scenes and offender residences were determined by establishing the centroid of the corresponding full postcode areal unit (Ordnance Survey 2006).

The distribution of offending rates revealed that many offenders were responsible for only one or two burglaries. A natural break in the offending frequency was located between five and ten offences. It was decided only burglars detected for ten or more offences were included in the remaining analysis. This resulted in only 32 offenders who had been detected for 603 burglaries. In addition, three postcodes from offender residences and one from burglary locations were unable to be reconciled with the postcode list available through Ordnance Survey. These anomalies resulted in the net loss of 13 crime trip distances (all of the offenders with incorrect postcodes had valid postcodes for other periods of the time frame). The final sample therefore consisted of 32 offenders responsible for 590 burglaries and crime trips.

JTC distances were established by computing the euclidean distance between the point estimate for the offence location and the point estimate of the most likely offender residence. This distance measure was chosen as manhattan distances are usually thought to be more appropriate for grid-based urban layouts, that is, North

American cities, whereas Euclidean distances are used for European areas. Using UK data, Rossmo et al. (2004) presented the surprising result that manhattan distances provide more precise estimates than euclidean distances by using a street routing distance as a baseline. The results that follow could easily be replicated using a manhattan metric with trivial differences observed.

It should be noted that a degree of imprecision exists with the manner of the distance computed here. The derived crime trip distance is based on point estimates (centroid locations of postcode area units), not the locations themselves. Two distinct issues arise from this decision; the generation of zero distances (where the offender resides in the same postcode as the victim) and inaccurate distance measurements due to the difference between the true locations and the point estimates. The latter will be dealt with first.

The difference between a single true location and its corresponding point estimate will be called its *offset*. The *offset effect* is the difference between the true distance and the estimated distance (in other words the combined impact of both offsets). The maximum offset for any point estimate will be dictated by the geographic morphology of the postcode polygon. If the size of the postcode polygons is relatively small, the offset for any point will be small and by extension the offset effect should be minimal.

The areas of all postcode boundaries in the Northampton area (Ordnance Survey 2006) were analyzed using a GIS. The distribution of these area amounts was highly skewed toward very small areas. The 75th percentile of the postcode areas was only 0.03 of a square kilometer, or less than three football pitches.

In order to investigate how offsets might influence the estimate of distances for this study, a simulation was performed (for full details see the footnote[7]). The ratio of true to estimated distances was normally distributed around a mean of one and a standard deviation inversely proportional to the distance between the simulated postcodes. We found that when simulated postcodes were about 350 meters apart the distribution of the ratio of true to estimated distance was relatively stable[8]. The observation that the distribution of the ratio of true to estimated distances takes on a symmetric distribution indicates that the estimated distance will both over- and under- estimate the true distance, plausibly cancelling each other out in the aggregate.

---

[7] For the simulation two circular 'postcodes' were defined, with radii of one hundred metres, and located a fixed distance apart. These corresponded to the same area as the 75% percentile postcode. The postcode centroids are the centres of each circle, thus the fixed distance is the 'estimated' distance between the two locations. At each iteration, a true location was randomly located at any point within the postcode boundary (by randomly selecting polar co-ordinates). The distance between each true location was computed and compared to the estimated distance. 10,000 iterations were performed. A range of fixed distances were used to test whether the choice of fixed distance was important.

[8] Well behaved normal distributions typically have a co-efficient of variation of less than twenty percent. When the fixed distance was greater than 350 meters the standard deviation of the ratio of true to estimate distances was less than 0.2.

A more important point than these methodological issues is the purpose to which these data will be put. The focus of this study is to quantify the influence of individual offenders on the aggregate JTC distribution. That is, we seek to establish whether JTC distributions at the individual level are the same as the JTC distribution at the population level. To this end, we are not concerned with the physical distances observed (at the aggregate, offender or crime levels) as different crime types and different areas will always limit the external validity of findings, but rather whether distances are influenced by different offenders, and whether this degree of influence is large enough to be concerned about. Moreover, due to the study objectives it is the 'relative difference' between two distances which is important rather that the specific units of measurement. For instance, for two distances 500 meters and 1500 meters, the observation that one is much shorter than the other is the more pertinent issue than the values per se, with respect to the purpose of the study. For these reasons we are happy to tolerate a degree of imprecision in the distance calculations as long as we are confident this will not compromise the relative differences in distances.

The second data generation issue concerned generating a higher number of zero distances than expected. This is a problem because the presence of zero distances will tend to broaden the range of that offender's JTC distribution, possibly compromising the analysis. The data contained only 24 observations with the offender and victim residing in the same postcode (about 4% of the total). These 24 observations were distributed among nine offenders, with one offender accounting for nine of the 24 zero distance observations. The presence of the zero distances did not appear to affect the JTC distribution of this offender. The remaining 15 zero distances were distributed relatively evenly among the other eight offenders. It was felt these would not compromise the overall results.

Offender age was determined by the number of days between birth and the start of the time period. The distribution of ages revealed a trimodal distribution, with natural breaks at roughly 17 and 26 years. Offenders were partitioned into three groups - young ($n=5$), middle ($n=20$) and older ($n=7$) – according to these natural breaks. These also seemed to mirror significant legal thresholds (obtaining a drivers license) and the termination of criminal careers in early adulthood (Blumstein et al. 1986).

In order to quantify the degree of heterogeneity that resides at each level, multilevel models were employed. Multilevel models are the term used by social scientists to describe modelling approaches which take into account the grouping, or nesting, of data (Pinheiro and Bates 2000; Venables and Ripley 2002). The canonical example is that of student test performance of individuals within different school classes, some of which are located in different schools, which in turn might have different catchment areas (neighborhoods). While factors such as parent education, IQ and gender may influence *individual* test scores, there also potentially exists effects operating at cruder levels of resolution, such as the class level (quality of individual teachers may vary), the school level (some schools may foster scholastic achievement), and the neighborhood level (some catchment areas vary demographically), all of which would influence *groups* of test scores. The methodological issue is that multiple observations (pupils) exist within units (teachers, schools, etc.) and the influence of grouping factors should be partitioned from relationships that exist at the individual level. Without accounting for these grouping effects, the relationships between factors at the individual level are likely to be biased. For criminological applications of multilevel models, see Rountree et al. (1994), Sampson et al. (1997), Jang (1999), Jang and Johnson (2001), Morenoff et al. (2001), Oberwittler (2004), Tseloni (2006), and Gelman et al. (2007).

In the context of longitudinal data, where repeated measures from a group of individuals are studied, multilevel models can assist in separating the correlation between repeated measurements from correlations with potential explanatory factors. The utility of multilevel models for this study is that it will be possible to determine the proportion of total JTC variability that exists at the offender level. This is calculated using the *intra-class correlation co-efficient* (ICC). Imagine a two stage sampling design where measurements are collected at a micro level (crime trips) which can be grouped into a macro level unit (prolific offenders). The ICC is calculated as the variance *between* macro units divided by the total variance of the sample (Snijders and Bosker 1999); in other words, the ICC is the fraction of the total variance which is accounted for by the macro level[9].

So, the magnitude of the ICC implies the extent of the influence of the macro unit clustering on the outcome variable. Values of zero (or close to) mean that while observations may be clustered, this grouping does not exert an influence at the individual level (alternatively, the use of regression techniques not accounting for grouped data would be justified). It follows that the ICC statistic can be subjected to an hypothesis test to determine whether its true value is equal to zero or not (see Snijders and Bosker 1999, p. 21).

All analysis in this study was conducted in the statistical programming environment R (R Core Development Team 2004). The *nlme* package was used to implement multilevel models (Pinheiro et al. 2007).

Results

The sample of 590 crime trips yielded the aggregate distance decay distribution, estimated by a kernel density procedure, shown in Fig. 10.2. We use this method of estimating the density of these data rather than a histogram because the latter is susceptible to both choice of interval size and their locations, whereas kernel density estimation is chiefly reliant on the choice of bandwidth. The distribution had a mean of 3.7 kilometers with a standard deviation of 4.4 kilometers. The median distance travelled to burgle was 2.2 kilometers, consistent with the visual impression of skewness. The degree of variation observed is extreme, yielding a co-efficient of variation of 119%.

---

[9] There is another interpretation of the ICC - its numerical value is equal to the correlation between two randomly selected observations in the same randomly selected macro unit - but its meaning will not be appropriate in the context of this study.

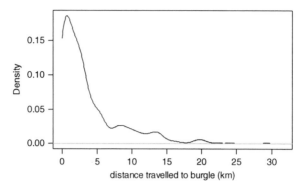

Fig. 10.2 Aggregate distribution of crime trips (with a lower bound of zero) estimated by kernel density estimation

The aggregate distance decay function in Fig. 10.2 conforms to the functional form commonly referred to in the research literature; that is, short crime trips are common and long trips are rare. The mode of the distribution is located at approximately 700 meters.

Figure 10.2 allows a preliminary picture of the general pattern of JTC trips undertaken by prolific burglars, but the magnitude of variation within the crime trip distribution is considerable. The aggregate distance decay function was recomputed, this time conditioned by the offender age group, and is shown in Fig. 10.3.

There are some fairly striking features in Fig. 10.3. The most obvious is the restricted range on the crime trip distribution of younger prolific burglars compared to the other two groups. Almost all the crime trips committed by offenders 17 years or less are located less than five kilometers from their residence. The middle and

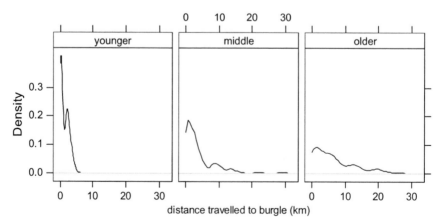

Fig. 10.3 Distributions of offender crime trips (with a lower bound of zero) estimated by kernel density estimation conditioned by age groupings

older offenders display, on aggregate, a more typical distance decay function where long trips are rare but nevertheless exist.

A second feature of Fig. 10.3 is the bimodal similarity of each age group's crime trip distribution. Each displays a global maximum value at a relatively short distance before declining rapidly, but a local maximum occurs at a distance beyond the central mass of the distribution. For middle offenders this local maximum is around ten kilometers and older offenders have one slightly further than this. When viewed on an absolute scale such as Fig. 10.3, the local maximum appears muted but in relative terms is of considerable magnitude.

Retaining the three age groups, Fig. 10.4 contains box and whisker plots of each prolific offender's crime trip distribution. Box and whisker plots were chosen here for reasons of space; they contain measures of both central tendency and dispersion and succinctly summarize a distribution. For purposes of clarity, they have been ordered on the basis of their median value.

A tremendous amount of information is contained in Fig. 10.4. The first point to note is that within each age group, there appears to be offenders whose JTC distribution is sharply restricted to a certain geographic range, whereas other distributions display a great deal of variation (indicated by the height of the boxes and whiskers on each plot). Typically, an offender with a low median crime trip displays smaller variation, although the older offenders appeared to buck this trend somewhat.

The second notable observation is that, consistent with Fig. 10.3, age appears to be correlated with extent of geographic range. Younger offenders have a lower geographic range compared to middle and older offenders. An explanation for the age-conditioned bimodal distribution observed in Fig. 10.3 presents itself. Note that

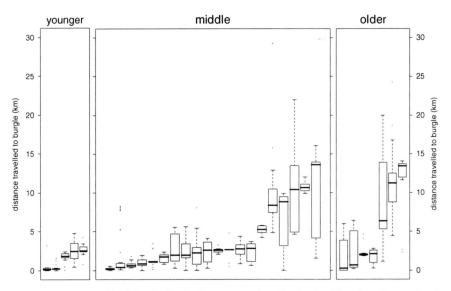

Fig. 10.4 Boxplots of individual offender journey to crime distribution. Plots have been ordered by median value within each age group

in each age group in Fig. 10.4, there appears to be two clusters of offenders, ones with low medians and those with higher medians. It seems than the local maxima (located at greater distances than the global maxima) observed in Fig. 10.3 are generated largely by distinct offenders and are *not* the result of contributions from all offenders in each age group.

The last substantial observation is that there is also a variety of combinations of central tendency and dispersion displayed by different offenders. Some offenders show very different ranges of operation, yet have equivalent medians. The degree of variation at the offender level is large. While a large number of offenders do offend at short distances there are also some prolific offenders who predominantly do not.

Figure 10.4 provides compelling initial evidence that a variation of JTC exists at both the intra-offender and inter-offender levels. The aggregate crime trip distribution does not appear to be consistent with distributions at the offender level, even after controlling for the age groupings. In other words, there appears to be an influence of nesting of crime trip distances with different offenders. This observation justifies efforts to quantify the extent of variation existing within and between offenders. In order to explore the extent of the nesting effect, multilevel models will need to be employed.

Measuring the Extent of Intra- and Inter-Offender Variation

As implied earlier, the prolific burglars' crime trips are a form of longitudinal data. For the purposes of this study, we are not trying to establish causal relationships (e.g., distance travelled increases with perceived affluence of victim), but merely to ascertain the degree to which the length of individual crime trips are influenced by the offender. In that vein, a random intercept model[10], where the intercept term is allowed to take on different values for each offender, was chosen to fit the data. As no explanatory variables are included in the model, that is, an 'empty model', no consideration towards random slopes for each level is required.

An empty model with random intercepts for each offender was fitted to the 32 prolific offenders and 590 crime trips. The estimated ICC was computed at 0.65. This means that nearly two-thirds of the total crime trip distance variation for these data exists at the offender level. Alternatively, there was a high degree of correlation of crime trip distance within offenders. A test revealed extremely strong evidence against a null hypothesis of a zero ICC ($F=32.3$, df=(31,558), $p \ll 0.0001$).

Skewness Scores

The final analysis conducted was to investigate the JTC distributions of the individual offenders separately. The approach taken here is to compute a skewness score

---

[10] Rasbash et al. (2004) use the terminology *variance components* models.

for each offender. Skewness is a measure of asymmetry in data and has positive values if the right tail of a distribution is longer than the left tail and negative if the reverse is true. If shorter trips are more common than longer ones, as suggested by the JTC literature, offenders should display positive skewness in the main. Values of zero conform to a symmetric distribution.

It is possible to compute a standard error of a skewness estimate[11], which means the skewness estimate divided by its standard error reduces to a Z score. This means that for individuals with Z scores within two standard deviations of zero, we cannot be confident (at 95%) that the actual skewness is different from zero. For example, the skewness estimate of the distribution shown in Fig. 10.2 is roughly 1.95 and has a standard error of about 0.1. The skewness Z score for the JTC distribution ignoring grouping within offenders is approximately 19.4(=1.95/0.1). Given the estimate is located almost 20 standard deviations from zero, we can be very confident that the distribution in Fig. 10.2 is not symmetric (of course, one only needs look at the figure to tell this).

Based on the consensus in the literature we would expect that most offenders would display positive values of skewness and that many of these would be reliably different from zero (i.e., with values greater than 1.96). Figure 10.5 contains the skewness Z scores for each offender in the sample.

The distribution of skewness Z scores for this sample is surprising and unequivo-cal. Nearly *half* the offenders have *negative* skewness scores, although only two of these have a magnitude reliably different from zero. Of the remainder, those offend-ers displaying the expected distance decay pattern, only seven possess a degree of asymmetry reliably different from zero (high positive scores)[12]. It appears that the source of the skewness observed in the aggregated crime trip distribution (Fig. 10.2)

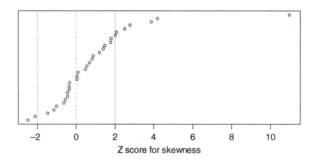

Fig. 10.5 Z score for skewness for each prolific offender. Observations have been sorted according to Z score magnitude

---

[11] Equal to $\sqrt{\frac{6}{N}}$ (Tabachnick and Fidell, 1996, p. 72).

[12] One of these positively skewed JTC distributions belonged to the individual with a sizable number of zero distances mentioned in the Data section. Thus, even though the effect of the presence of zero distances is to bias the observed skewness estimate downwards, this was not sufficient to compromise the statistical reliability for this offender.

comes from either a minority of the individuals in this sample or is a product of ignoring the grouping of these data.

Discussion

In this article, the issue of determining appropriate units of analysis was applied to a situation where multiple criminal incidents are spatially related to the residence of the offender who committed them, a situation that requires careful reflection on the proper unit of analysis. Using multi-level models, we challenged conventional wisdom and discovered another ecological fallacy: the distance decay pattern found at the aggregate level is generally not observed at the offender level.

The results presented in this study suggest that aggregate crime trip distributions contain considerable variation which was not evenly distributed among (prolific) offenders. Individual offender crime trip patterns differed remarkably in terms of their location in space (central tendency) and their spread to the extent that aggregate distance decay functions appear to be only appropriate for inferring features of the population of crime trips. Further, the fact that grouping does have an effect means that crime trip data cannot be considered statistically independent. The theoretical and operational implications of this are discussed as follows.

The theoretical importance of JTC research is that it aids in inferring criminal behavior and explaining crime patterns. Indeed, Rengert et al state no less that '[i]mplications arising from such research touches the majority of criminological theories' (1999, p. 427). The aggregate distance decay function is commonly thought to imply that the majority of offenders favour targets closer to their home (or another anchor point) compared to potential targets more distant.

The ICC statistic showed that two-thirds of the JTC variation resides between offenders, suggesting that the unit of analysis of most relevance is the offender, not individual crime trips. Consequently, a further major implication of this result is that the JTC patterns of individual offenders are far less variable than the distribution of all crime trip distances imply. In other words we can say that, compared to the population of crime trips taken, there was a greater degree of consistency of distances travelled by individual offenders.

Aggregate JTC distributions certainly give the impression that the bulk of crime trips are short: because they are! What the results of the multilevel model suggest is that there is an influence of grouping (offenders) operating which means that the observations (crime trips) cannot be considered statistically independent. Apart from the obvious issue of the presence of an aggregation effect, if statistically dependent observations are combined the resulting distribution will be biased. Thus, the aggregate distance decay function – the accepted conception of JTC patterns - as currently expressed may be invalid.

Finally, the extent of skewness at the population level is not consistent at the offender level. Almost *half* of the sample displayed skewness in the *opposite* direction that the literature would predict. Of those offenders displaying positive skewness (i.e., a distance decay pattern) only a minority could be said to be reliably asymmetric. This is further evidence of the influence of crime trips nested at the offender level.

We find support for van Koppen and de Keijser's argument that comments about offenders drawn from an aggregate distance decay function are fallacious by virtue of an ecological bias. Moreover, we found evidence of significant differences between offenders, which weakens (somewhat) Rengert et al.'s contention that the aggregation of crime trip distances is unlikely to be subject to the ecological fallacy, especially if offenders are similar to each other.

An unexpected finding in this study was the presence of a group of offenders who appeared to make no short crime trips; depending on criteria this group made up between a quarter to a third of the sample. It is conceivable that these offenders represent commuting offending behavior (Canter and Larkin 1993). If so, omitting these individuals from the analysis may alter the findings. It could be that a sizable proportion of the inter-offender variation comes from the contrasting JTC patterns of 'commuters' and 'marauders'. Even so, it at least hints at the relative proportion of both types of offending styles.

In practical terms, the results have some operational bearing. The observation that crime trips committed by the same offender are more consistent than crime trips committed by different offenders strengthens the general rationale of geographic profiling. If offenders are relatively invariant in their own JTC, then determining a node for a single offender, usually by a process of triangulation using a distance decay curve, should be possible with greater precision than previously imagined. However, if the function used to weight distances is computed by aggregating crime trip distances made by a group of offenders, our results suggest then the intensity surface generated for the single offender in question may be vulnerable to aggregation bias problems. The extent to which this is the case will depend on how typical the offender being profiled is and the degree of inter-offender variation among the group of offenders. The results of our research indicate that the latter is considerable and the very nature of geographic profiling is such that, apart from complete speculation, the former will never be known prior to apprehension.

In fact the argument could be extended to apply to *any* distance weighting function derived to emulate the general finding that most crime trips are short. If the parameter values are chosen so that the distance weighting function resembles the aggregate distance decay function then the calculation of the intensity surface does commit the ecological fallacy. Of the three major geographic profiling applications (Rigel, CrimeStat[13], and Dragnet), the second explicitly allows the use of an aggregate JTC curve to be used as a weighting function (Rich and Shively 2004).

There are three main weaknesses to the data used in this study, although they are certainly not unique to studies of this type. The first is the assumption that the most

---

[13] CrimeStat contains a Journey to Crime Estimation routine, but is geographic profiling in all but name.

relevant node for any JTC will always be the residence. The assumption here may be arguable, but it nevertheless presents a picture of territorial range. The second major weakness is data quality. These JTC represent only detected crimes, we can say nothing about those crimes not detected, whether committed by offenders in our sample or not. This is a feature common to all JTC studies and no obvious solution presents itself. Nevertheless, we have attempted to improve the quality of data by factoring in changes to offenders' residence. Finally, we have not attempted to control for the supply of opportunities between home residence and crime location. This may very well yield different patterns than those observed using a physical distance measure.

Further aspects to bear in mind are that these data relate to volume crime, so the sampling of offenders and their activities is more likely to be incomplete compared to the corresponding patterns of serious crime. The perniciousness and rarity of serious crime means that a much higher proportion of crime trips can be determined for serious offenders compared to volume offenders. Also, the offender sample used here are prolific offenders, a minority of the largely low rate opportunistic individuals who might make up the active burglar population. 'Prolifics' were selected to provide a degree of precision in the individual JTC distributions because while only comprising three percent of the known burglar population they account for about a quarter of all detected burglaries.

The design of this study is broadly consistent with other JTC studies that make comments about offenders based on the aggregate crime trip distribution. Thus, despite the shortcomings of these data and the assumptions underpinning the analysis there is no reason to suggest that the results observed here could not also be found in the datasets of other studies had the patterns been sought. In other words, the fact that these 'weaknesses' are present in this study does not take away from the validity of the findings as they also exist in an array of other JTC studies.

Some readers might be surprised at the focus and findings of this study. Surely distance decay is a fairly incontrovertible phenomenon? Our point is that much of what is conventional knowledge in criminology about JTC comes from studies which have overlooked a serious methodological problem. If our argument is persuasive, this need to be addressed. This is *not* the same as saying that everything we know about distance decay is wrong, but that for distance decay to be valid we need to demonstrate it in an appropriate way. It is not enough to be correct, we must be correct for the right reasons.

Given the results of this study, future work on JTC should focus on replicating the analysis presented here on a larger sample as well as estimating the influence of offender-specific factors from crime-specific factors. Snook (2004) attempted to investigate individual differences among a group of prolific burglars and, in a limited way, target attractiveness. A logical extension of the work outlined here would be to include explanatory variables at the crime trip and offender levels as a multi-level model. This would allow the influence of variables which operate at different levels to be isolated and estimated without running the risk of committing the ecological fallacy.

References

Alston, J.D. (1994). *The serial rapist's spatial pattern of target selection*. Unpublished Master's Thesis, Burnaby, Canada: Simon Fraser University.

Blumstein, A., Cohen, J., Roth, J. A., & Visher, C. A. (1986). *Criminal Careers and "Career Criminals," Volume 1*, National Academy of Sciences. Washington, DC: National Academy Press.

Brantingham, P. J., Dyreson, D. A., & Brantingham, P. L. (1976). Crime seen through a cone of resolution, *American Behavioral Scientist*, 20(2), 261–73.

Brantingham, P. J., & Brantingham, P.L. (1981). *Environmental Criminology*. Beverly Hills, CA: Sage Publications.

Brantingham, P. J., & Brantingham, P. L. (1993). Environment, routine, and situation: Toward a pattern theory of crime. In: R. V. Clarke & M. Felson (Eds.) *Routine Activity and Rational Choice* (pp. 259–294). New Brunswick, N.J: Transaction Publishers.

Canter, D.V., & Larkin, P. (1993). The environmental range of serial rapists, *Journal of Environmental Psychology*, 13, 63–69.

Canter, D.V., Coffey, T., Huntley, M., & Missen, C. (2000). Predicting Serial Killers' home Base Using a Decision Support System. *Journal of Quantitative Criminology*, 16(4), 457–478.

Canter, D. V., & Hodge, S. (2000) Mental mapping. Criminal's mental maps. In L. S. Turnbull, E. H. Hendrix, & B. D. Dent (Eds.), *Atlas of crime: Mapping the criminal landscape* (pp. 186–191). Phoenix, Arizona: Onyx Press.

Chainey, S. P., & Ratcliffe, J. H. (2005). *GIS and Crime Mapping*. London: Wiley.

Cohen, L., & Felson M. (1979). Social change and crime rate trends: A routine activities approach. *American Sociological Review*, 44, 588–607.

Cornish, D. B., & Clarke, R.V. (1986). Introduction. In: D. B. Cornish & R. V. Clarke (Eds.). *The reasoning criminal: Rational choice perspectives on offending*, New York: Springer-Verlag.

Gelman, A., Fagan, J., & Kiss, A. (2007). An analysis of the New York city police department's by "Stop-and-Frisk" policy in the context of claims of racial bias. *Journal of the American Statistical Association*, 102, 813–823.

Jang, S. J. (1999). Age-Varying effects of family, school, and peers on delinquency: A multilevel modeling test of interactional theory. *Criminology*, 37(3), 643–686.

Jang, S. J., & Johnson, B. R. (2001). Neighborhood disorder, individual religiosity, and adolescent use of illicit drugs: A test of multilevel hypotheses. *Criminology*, 39(1), 109–144.

Groff, E. R. & McEwan, T. (2006). Exploring the spatial configuration of places related to homicide events, Alexandria, VA: Institute of Law and Justice.

Kocsis, R. N., Cooksey, R. W., Irwin, H. J., & Allen, G. (2002). A further assessment of "Circle Theory" for geographical psychological profiling. *Australian and New Zealand Journal of Criminology*, 35(1), 43–62.

LeBeau, J. (1992). Four case studies illustrating the spatial-temporal analysis of serial rapists. *Police Studies*, 15, 124–145.

Levine, N. (2005). *User Manual for CrimeStat III*, Ned Levine & Associates: Houston, TX National Institute of Justice: Washington, DC.

Morenoff, J., Sampson, R. J., & Raudenbush, S. (2001). Neighborhood inequality, collective efficacy, and the spatial dynamics of urban violence. *Criminology*, 39, 517–560.

Oberwittler, D. (2004). A Multilevel analysis of neighbourhood contextual effects on serious juvenile offending: The role of subcultural values and social disorganization. *European Journal of Criminology*, 1(2), 201–235.

Ordnance Survey (2006) © Crown Copyright/database right 2006. An Ordnance Survey/EDINA supplied service.

Paulsen, D. J., & Robinson, M. B. (2004). *Spatial Aspects of Crime: Theory and Practice*. Boston, MA: Pearson A and B.

Pinheiro, J., & Bates, D. (2000), *Mixed-Effects Models in S and S-Plus, Statistics and Computing Serie*. London: Springer.

Pinheiro, J., Bates, D., DebRoy, S., & Sarkar, D. (2007). *Nlme: Linear and Nonlinear Mixed Effects Models*, R package version 3.1–83.

R Development Core Team (2004). *R: A language and environment for statistical computing*. R Foundation for Statistical Computing, Vienna, Austria. ISBN 3-900051-07-0, URL http://www.R-project.org.

Rasbash, J., Steele, F., Browne, W. J., & Prosser, B. (2004). *A User's Guide to MLwiN*, Version 2.0. London: Institute of Education.

Rengert, G. F. (1996). *The Geography of Illegal Drugs*, Boulder, Colo.: Westview Press.

Rengert, G. F., Piquero, A. R., & Jones, P. R. (1999). Distance decay re-examined. *Criminology*, 37, 427–445.

Rhodes, W. M., & Conly, C. (1981). Crime and mobility: An empirical study. In: P. J. Brantingham & P. L. Brantingham (Eds.), *Environmental Criminology* (pp. 167–188). Beverly Hills, CA: Sage Publications.

Rich, T., & Shively, M. (2004). *A Methodology for Evaluating Geographic Profiling Software*, Cambridge, MA: Abt Associates.

Robinson, W. S. (1950). Ecological correlations and the behavior of individuals. *American Sociological Review*, 15, 351–357.

Rountree, P. W., Land, K. C., & Miethe T. D. (1994). Macro-micro integration in the study of victimization: A hierarchical logistic model analysis across seattle neighborhoods. *Criminology*, 32 (3), 387–414.

Rossmo, D. K. (2000). *Geographical Profiling*, Boca Raton, FL: CRC Press LLC.

Rossmo, D. K. (1993). *Multivariate Profiles as a Tool in Crime Investigation*. Chicago: Workshop on Crime Analysis Through Crime Mapping.

Rossmo, D. K., Davies, A., & Patrick, M. (2004). *Exploring the geo-demographic and distance relationships between stranger rapists and their offences*, Special Interest Series Paper No 16, London: Home Office.

Sampson, R. J., Raudenbush, S., & Earls, F. (1997). Neighborhoods and violent crime: A multilevel study of collective efficacy. *Science*, 277, 918–24.

Snijders, T., & Bosker, R. (1999). *Multilevel Analysis: An introduction to basic and advanced multilevel modelling*, London: Sage.

Snook, B. (2004). Individual differences in distance travelled by serial burglars. *Journal of Investigative Psychology and Offender Profiling*, 1, 53–66.

Tabachnick, B. G., & Fidell, L. S. (1996). *Using Multivariate Statistics* (3rd Ed), New York (NY): HarperCollins College Publishers.

Tseloni, A. (2006). Multilevel modelling of the number of property crimes: household and area effects. *Journal of the Royal Statistical Society: Series A (Statistics in Society)*, 169(2), 205–233.

van Koppen, P. J., & de Keijser, J. W. (1997). Desisting distance decay: On the aggregation of individual crime trips. *Criminology*, 35, 505–515.

Venables, W. N., & Ripley, B. D. (2002). Modern Applied Statistics with S-plus, 4th Edition, Springer-Verlag.

Warren, J., Reboussin, R., & Hazelwood, R. (1995). *The Geographic and Temporal Sequencing of Serial Rape*. Final Report submitted to U.S. Department of Justice, National Institute of Justice, Office of Justice Programs, Washington, D.C.

Wiles, P., & Costello, A. (2000). *The 'road to nowhere': the evidence for travelling criminals*. Home Office Research Study 207. Research, Development and Statistics Directorate. London: Home Office.

About the Authors

Wim Bernasco

Wim Bernasco studied social psychology at Leiden University, and obtained a PhD in sociology at Utrecht University. His PhD thesis explored the interrelated nature of the occupational careers of spouses. Before joining the NSCR in 2000, he worked in different positions at various universities and at the research center of the Ministry of Justice. His current work focuses on spatial aspects of criminal activities, a broad area that encompasses a number of research questions. What drives variation in crime and delinquency between neighborhoods? Which effects do physical and social barriers have on offender travel behavior? How do offenders search and select their targets and methods? Do they offend in the communities where they used to live? Is crime spatially displaced when criminal opportunities are blocked? What causes repeat victimization? Does the risk of criminal victimization communicate spatially, and why? Wim explores many of these themes in collaboration with researchers from the United Kingdom, Australia and the United States. His recent international publications appear in Criminology, Journal of Quantitative Criminology, British Journal of Criminology, European Journal of Criminology, Crime Psychology & Law, and Journal of Investigate Psychology and Offender Profiling.

Daniel J. Birks

Dan is a Senior Research Assistant in the Justice Modelling Group at Griffith University, Brisbane, Australia. Previously is a Research Fellow at the UCL Jill Dando Institute of Crime Science, he has an honors degree in Computer Science & Artificial Intelligence and an MSc in Cognitive Science. Over the last five years, he has been involved in several crime reduction orientated research programmes and has worked with a number of UK Police forces, the Police Standards Unit and the Home Office. His research interests center around the development of innovative crime analysis and decision support techniques and tools. In particular, his recent publications have focused on prospective models of crime and the application of simulation techniques within criminology.

John W. Bond

John W. Bond is of Forensic Science for Northamptonshire Police. His research interests centre on the use of forensic science to enhance the detection of crime,

D. Weisburd et al. (eds.), *Putting Crime in its Place*,
DOI 10.1007/978-0-387-09688-9_BM1, © Springer Science+Business Media, LLC 2009

principally through the analysis of forensic data and the development of new techniques for the enhancement of fingerprints. He has research affiliations with a number of UK universities and is an Honorary Research Fellow of the University of Leicester.

Kate Bowers

Dr. Kate Bowers is a Reader at the Jill Dando Institute of Crime Science, UCL. She has worked in the field of environmental criminology for over ten years. Prior to becoming a full time criminologist, she completed a BSc in Natural Science at Durham University and an MA and PhD at the University of Liverpool. Her research has generally focused on applying quantitative methods to crime analysis and to studies of crime prevention. Some of her previous work has involved examining spatial and temporal patterns in crime, evaluating the effectiveness of crime prevention schemes and investigating business crime. Her work has been funded by a variety of organisations including the Home Office, the Police, the DfES, the ESRC, and the AHRC. She has published over fifty research papers and book chapters in criminology, has guest edited a special edition of a journal and Crime Prevention Studies and co-edited a book on Crime Mapping.

Paul J. Brantingham

Paul J. Brantingham, B.A. and J.D. (Columbia), Dip. Crim. (Cambridge), a lawyer and criminologist by training, is RCMP University Professor of Crime Analysis at Simon Fraser University. He was Associate Dean of the Faculty of Interdisciplinary studies at Simon Fraser during the early 1980s and served as Director of the Simon Fraser Centre for Canadian Studies during 1992. He taught at Florida State University prior to joining the School of Criminology at Simon Fraser University. Professor Brantingham was Director of Special Reviews at the Public Service Commission of Canada from 1985 through 1987. He has been a member of the California Bar since 1969.

Professor Brantingham is author or editor of more than 20 books and scientific monographs, and more than 100 articles and scientific papers. His best known books include *Juvenile Justice Philosophy* (1974, 2d ed. 1978), and *Environmental Criminology* (1981, 2d ed. 1991) and *Patterns in Crime* (1984) both co-authored with Patricia Brantingham.

Patricia L. Brantingham

Patricia L. Brantingham, A.B. (Barnard College), M.A. (Fordham), M.S. and Ph.D. (Florida State), a mathematician, and urban planner by training, is RCMP University Professor of Computational Criminology, Director of the Institute for Canadian Urban Research Studies and Co-Director of the ICURS Laboratory at Simon Fraser University. She served as Director of Programme Evaluation at the Department of Justice Canada from 1985 through 1988.

Dr. Brantingham is the author or editor of two dozen books and scientific monographs and more than 100 articles and scientific papers. She serves on the editorial boards of a number of professional and scholarly journals and is the leader of an interdisciplinary collaboration in computational criminology.

Gerben J.N. Bruinsma

Prof. Dr. Gerben J.N. Bruinsma, born in The Hague, studied sociology and criminology at Utrecht University. After his graduation in 1975, he became lecturer of criminology and penology at the Criminological Institute of the Radboud University Nijmegen. In 1981 he left for the Faculty of Public Administration and Public Policy at Twente University at Enschede. In 1985 he was appointed as associate professor in methodology and research methods. In the same year he finished his doctoral dissertation 'Crime as a social process. A test of the differential association theory in the version of K-D. Opp'. He was co-founder and director of the International Police Institute at the University of Twente and in 1995 he was appointed as professor of criminology at that university. From 1999, he has been director of the Netherlands Institute for the Study of Crime and Law Enforcement (NSCR), a national research institute of the National Organization for Scientific Research (NWO) and professor of criminology of the faculty of Law of Leiden University. He has been editor of various journals and had a great number of advisory and board positions in the field. He published more than 90 articles and 30 books on criminological issues like criminological theory, juvenile delinquency, policing, organized crime, and geographic criminology.

Robert T. Greenbaum

Robert T. Greenbaum is an associate professor in the John Glenn School of Public Affairs and associate director of the Center for Urban and Regional Analysis at The Ohio State University. His research focuses primarily on urban and regional economic development. In particular, he is interested both in how tax incentive policies and disamenities such as crime influence the location of economic activity. He has published a number of papers examining the adoption and effectiveness of spatially targeted economic development incentives. His research has also examined the impact of policies that are not explicitly geographically targeted but may nevertheless have policy outcomes with important spatial consequences. The primary attention of his current research concerns the investigation of relationships among crime, business location decisions, and residential choice. As part of this study, he also examines the impact of terrorism on business activity. His papers have appeared in outlets such as Journal of Policy Analysis & Management, Journal of Quantitative Criminology, Public Budgeting & Finance, Regional Science and Urban Economics, and Urban Studies.

Elizabeth Groff

Elizabeth Groff has spent the last 15 years applying spatial analysis to the study of crime-related issues at both the local and national levels. Elizabeth is an Assistant Professor of Criminal Justice at the Temple University where her current projects include a micro level longitudinal study of crime in Seattle, Washington; testing the use of simulation models for understanding street robbery; an examination of the role of parks as risk or protective factors, and the use of AVL for quantifying police presence. More generally, Elizabeth's research interests include: crime and place; modeling geographical influences on human activity; crime prevention; and policing.

Shane D Johnson

Dr. Shane Johnson is a Reader at the UCL Jill Dando Institute of Crime Science. He has a particular interest in the spatial and temporal distribution of crime, crime forecasting, computer simulation, and design against crime. He has conducted work for a variety of sponsors including the Arts and Humanities Research Council, Engineering and Physical Science Research Council, and the Home Office, and currently coordinates an international research network funded by the British Academy. He has published over 50 original research papers within the fields of criminology and forensic psychology in journals including the Journal of Quantitative Criminology, Criminology and Public Policy and the British Journal of Criminology.

Brian Lockwood is a Ph.D. student in the Department of Criminal Justice at Temple University. His undergraduate training is from The College of New Jersey where he majored in English and Law and Justice. He holds an M.A. degree in Criminal Justice from Temple University. His research interests include the spatial correlates of juvenile recidivism and near-repeat patterns of crime.

Michael D. Maltz

Michael D. Maltz is Senior Research Scientist at the Ohio State University's Criminal Justice Research Center and Adjunct Professor of Sociology at OSU. He is also Professor Emeritus of Criminal Justice and of Information and Decision Sciences at the University of Illinois at Chicago, where he taught from 1972-2002. Prior to that he was an Operations Research Analyst at the US National Institute of Justice. In addition, he edited the Journal of Quantitative Criminology from 1996-2000 and was a Visiting Fellow at the US Bureau of Justice Statistics (1995-2000), working on the development of graphical and geographical methods of analyzing data. For the past few years he has focused his attention on two areas: assessing and improving the quality of crime data, and improving the methods used to analyze criminal justice data, with a focus on data visualization methods. Maltz received his Ph.D. in electrical engineering from Stanford University in 1963.

Nancy Morris

Nancy A. Morris received her Ph.D. in Criminology and Criminal Justice from the University of Maryland in 2007. Her research interests include the development and desistance of criminal offending, criminological theory, comparative criminology, and longitudinal research methods. She is an Assistant Professor in the Center for the Study of Crime, Delinquency and Corrections at Southern Illinois University, Carbondale (USA).

Dietrich Oberwittler

Dietrich Oberwittler is a senior researcher at the Department of Criminology of the Max Planck Institute for Foreign and International Criminal Law, Freiburg/Germany, and teaches sociology at the University of Freiburg. He is currently also a PADS+ Research Fellow (University of Cambridge). From 2004 to 2006, he was a Marie Curie fellow at the Institute of Criminology, University of Cambridge, where he worked in the ESRC Cambridge Network SCoPiC (Social Contexts of Pathways in Crime) which is directed by Professor Per-Olof

Wikström. His research interests are in the fields of juvenile delinquency, social ecology of crime, urban sociology, quantitative methodology, and social history of crime. His recent publications include 'Multilevel Analysis of Neighbourhood Contextual Effects on Serious Juvenile Offending. The Role of Subcultural Values and Social Disorganization' (2004) and 'Concentrated disadvantage and adolescent adjustment – a multilevel analysis of neighbourhood contextual effects by ethnicity and gender' (2007). He is the editor of the collected volume 'Soziologie der Kriminalität' (Wiesbaden 2004, together with Susanne Karstedt).

Ken Pease

A forensic psychologist by training, Ken Pease OBE is currently Visiting Professor at University College London, the University of Loughborough and Chester University. Before retirement, he held chairs at the Universities of Manchester and Saskatchewan where he worked in the maximum security Regional Psychiatric Centre (Prairies). He has acted as Head of the Police Research Group at the Home Office, and has been a member of the Parole Board for England and Wales. He is a member of the Home Office Design and Technology Alliance and sits on the Steering Group of the current DTI review of Home Office science. The bulk of his published work over the last twenty years has concerned crime reduction and he was recently flattered by a book published in his honour under the title *Imagination in Crime Prevention*. A candidate for the Green Party in elections over 20 years, his current work includes the integration of security and sustainability in home design; patterns of dog theft; and the integration of evolutionary psychology with crime science.

George F. Rengert is Professor of Criminal Justice at Temple University. He holds an M.A. from The Ohio State University and a Ph.D. from the University of North Carolina. A geographer by training, he is one of the founders of the modern field of spatial analysis in criminology. Dr. Rengert is the author or editor of six books which include: *Suburban Burglary: A Time and a Place for Everything; Policing Illegal Drug Markets; and, Campus Security*. He also has authored more than 100 scientific articles and papers dealing with such diverse topics as the location of illegal drug markets, spatial justice, and barriers to the spatial movement of criminals. His current interests center on the application of Geographic Information Systems to the analysis of urban crime patterns.

William Smith

William Smith is a tactical analyst in the interpretation of intelligence and the delivery of analytical products to drive operational policing activity the Thames Valley Police, United Kingdom. He has an MSc in Crime Science.

George E. Tita

George Tita is an Associate Professor in the Department of Criminology, Law and Society at the University of California - Irvine. His education includes a Master's of Science in Economic Development (1993) and Ph.D. (1999) from the H.J. Heinz III School of Public Policy and Management at Carnegie Mellon. His research is anchored in the community and crime literature with a special focus on the causes and correlates of interpersonal violence. In addition to exploring how youth gangs impact spatial dimensions of crime, he is also interested in examining how racial and ethnic change at the neighborhood level impact levels and patterns of crime. Much of his research has been devoted to the design and implementation of effective strategies aimed at reducing gun violence. In addition to spatial analysis, Dr. Tita has employed diverse set of methodologies in his research including quasi-experimental methods (propensity score matching), hedonic models, agent-based models, and social network analysis. His papers have appeared in peer-reviewed journals such as Journal of Quantitative Criminology, Social Problems, Urban Studies, Journal of Research on Crime and Delinquency, and Injury Prevention.

Michael Townsley
Michael Townsley is a lecturer at the School of Criminology and Criminal Justice, Griffith University, Australia and has previously worked at the UCL Jill Dando Institute of Crime Science, and University of Liverpool. His research interests include crime analysis, crime prevention, spatial and temporal patterns of crime, and the utility of forensic science to the reduction of crime. He has published peer reviewed research in a number of leading criminological journals.

Mona Vajihollahi
Mona Vajihollahi received her MSc degree in computing science from Simon Fraser University (SFU) and is currently a PhD candidate of computing science. She is interested in formal aspects of software technology and the application of agile formal methods in novel research areas such as Computational Criminology. Her research focuses on computational modeling and analysis of patterns in crime, and application of formal modeling techniques in design and development of public safety and security systems. Since 2004, she has been collaborating with the Institute for Canadian Urban Research Studies (ICURS) at SFU, working on interdisciplinary projects aiming at developing theory-building tools for criminology researchers, and decision-support tools to be used by the police, policy makers and urban planners.

David Weisburd
David Weisburd is Walter E. Meyer Professor of Law and Criminal Justice and Director of the Institute of Criminology at the Hebrew University Faculty of Law, and Distinguished Professor of Administration of Justice at George Mason University. He is an elected Fellow of the American Society of Criminology and of the Academy of Experimental Criminology. He is also Co-Chair of the steering committee of the Campbell Collaboration Crime and Justice Group, a member of the Harvard University/National Institute of Justice Executive Session in Policing, and of the National Research Council Committee on Crime, Law and Justice. Professor Weisburd has a long interest in Crime and Place studies beginning with his involvement in a series of experimental studies of police interventions at crime places, including the Minneapolis Hot Spots Experiment, the Jersey City Drug Market Analysis Experiment and the Jersey City Violent Crime Hot Spots Experiment. Professor Weisburd is presently working on a book with Liz Groff and SueMing Yang that explores the varying factors that explain variation in developmental trends of crime at micro places over time that will be published by Oxford University

Press. Professor Weisburd is author or editor of fifteen books and more than eighty scientific articles.

Per-Olof H. Wikström

Per-Olof H. Wikström is Professor of Ecological and Developmental Criminology at the Institute of Criminology, University of Cambridge, and Professorial Fellow of Girton College. He is the director of the Peterborough Adolescent and Young Adult Development Study (PADS+), a major ESRC funded research project which aims to advance knowledge about crime causation and prevention. Professor Wikström's main research interests are the causes of crime, urban crime, adolescent offending, criminal careers, crime prevention and cross-national comparative research. His recent book publications include *The Explanation of Crime: Contexts, Mechanisms and Development* (2006, editor together with Robert J. Sampson) and *Adolescent Crime: Individual Differences and Lifestyles* (2006, with David Butterworth). Recent articles include *The Social Ecology of Crime. The Role of the Environment in Crime Causation* (2007), *The Social Origins of Pathways in Crime* (2005), *Crime as an Alternative: Towards a Cross-Level Situational Action Theory of Crime Causation* (2004), *Social Mechanisms of Community Influences on Crime and Pathways in Criminality* (2003, with Robert J Sampson) and *Do Disadvantaged Neighborhoods Cause Well-Adjusted Children to Become Adolescent Delinquents* (2000, with Rolf Loeber). In 1994 he received the Sellin-Glueck Award for outstanding contributions to international criminology from The American Society of Criminology and was elected a Fellow of the Center for Advanced Study in the Behavioral Sciences, Stanford in 2002.

Johan van Wilsem

Johan van Wilsem is an assistant professor of Criminology at Leiden University, the Netherlands. His PhD-thesis *Crime and Context* dealt with the social and spatial distribution of crime victimization. For this, he studied cross-national as well as within-national victimization patterns across neighborhoods and cities. This resulted in international and national publications on a variety of topics, such as the unintended consequences of socioeconomic neighborhood improvement on victimization, and crime displacement as a consequence of burglary prevention. Currently, he is involved in a large-scale longitudinal study of victimization, of both regular crime, and internet crime. Finally, he conducted a study of Rotterdam police files on assault and robbery in order to investigate the way violent crimes are committed. Van Wilsem's contribution to this book is one of the results of that study.

Kathryn Wuschke

Kathryn Wuschke is a PhD Student in the School of Criminology at Simon Fraser University. She has a background in Geography, specializing in Geographic Information Systems and neighborhood level spatial analysis. Katie has been a Research Assistant with the Institute for Canadian Urban Research Studies since 2005. Her research interests focus on the application of GIS within the field of criminology, developing innovative methods to spatially represent hotspots of criminal activity, and patterns of prolific offending.

Index

Note: The letter '*t*', '*f*' *and* '*n*' in the index locators refers to tables, figures, and footnotes respectively

A

Abbott, A., 13
Accuracy concentration curve, example of, 178*f*
Adderley, R., 90
Aggregate distribution of crime estimated by kernel density estimation, 228*f*
Aggregate relationships, 38–39
Aggregation effect, 39
  See also Scale effect
Amrheim, C., 113
Anderson, D., 23
Anderson, E., 166, 204
Andresen, M. A., 214
Anselin, L., 24, 72, 146, 149, 160, 162, 164
Armitage, R., 176
"Arms race", 156
"Army brats", 132*n*
Ashton, J., 173, 175
Attractors/generators, crime, 63, 89

B

Babcock, L., 153
Bafna, S., 93
Bailey, T. C., 40, 72, 73, 74, 182, 193
Balbi, A., 3, 7
Baldwin, J., 14
Baltimore, 42
Bartusch, D. J., 204
Bates, D., 226
Battin, S. R., 156
Baugh, J., 128
Baumer, E., 200, 204
BCAA, *see* British Columbia Assessment Authority (BCAA)
Beavon, D. J. K., 89, 176, 202

Behavioral contexts in crime causation, role of
  analytic strategy, 45–48
  behavior-setting, 36
  community survey data, 44–45
    OAs, 44
  multiple regression models
    aggregate-level OLS regression of 'informal social control', 53*t*
    Bayesian approach, 55
    smaller spatial units, side-effect of, 56
  neighborhood studies/unit of analysis problem, 39–42
    'zonation effect', 40
  PADS+, 43
  social cohesion/trust and informal social control (collective efficacy), results, 48–52
    conditional model, 50
    PHDCN community survey, 50
    SOA, 50
  statistical power considerations, multi-level sampling designs, 42–43
    smaller units of analysis, advantages of, 43
  'unit of analysis' problem, 38–39
    aggregate relationships, 39
    individual, definition, 38
  See also Crime causation, behavioral contexts in
Behavior-setting, 36–38, 43, 51, 56–57, 64, 82–83
Beirne, P., 4, 6, 7, 8, 11, 14
Bellair, P. E., 42
Bell, R., 15
Bennett, T., 93, 174

Benson, M. L., 210
Bernasco, W., 3, 172, 173, 174, 175, 177, 190
Besag, J., 179, 180
Bhati, A. S., 150, 154, 162, 166
Bichler-Robertson, G., 82
Birkbeck, C., 17
Bittner, T., 93
Blake, L., 172
Block, C., 18
Block, R., 200, 202
Blokland, A. A. J., 138
Blumstein, A., 71, 81, 146, 151, 156, 226
Boggs, S. L., 14, 154
Bogue, D. J., 11n, 14
Boots, B., 112, 113
Bosker, R., 42, 120, 211, 218, 227
Bottoms, A. E., 14
Boundary/edge effect problem, 112
Bounded space, edge effects of, 111–114
    boundary/edge effect problem, 112
    disregard solution, 113
    Nearest Neighbor Analysis, 112
    Torus, 113f
Bowers, K. J., 23, 171, 172, 174, 175, 178
Braga, A. A., 4, 18
Brail, R. K., 82
Brantingham, P. J., 15, 17, 18, 21, 22, 62, 63,
        64, 87, 88, 89, 90, 93, 124, 154,
        173, 174, 191, 200, 201, 202, 203,
        213, 218, 219
Brantingham, P. L., 15, 17, 18, 21, 22, 62, 63,
        64, 87, 88, 89, 90, 93, 124, 154,
        173, 174, 191, 200, 201, 202, 203,
        213, 218, 219
Bridges, G. S., 160
*British Association for the Advancement of
    Science*, 9
British Columbia Assessment Authority
    (BCAA), 91
Britt, C., 21
Brown, D. E., 90
Brown, P. J. B., 183
Bryk, A., 47
Bull, J., 18
Bulmer, M., 11
Burgess, E. W., 4, 11, 12, 14, 127
Burglaries, mean/standard deviation
    (2001–2004)
    by boundaries/borders, 99f
    Box-plot for fuzzy boundary/edge
        values, 99f
    extreme values for borders and
        interiors, 100t

by number of fuzzy boundaries, 98f
    number of land uses at selected high/low
        border areas, 101t
Burglary data, residential, 179
Bursik, R. J. Jr., 14, 15, 16
Butterworth, D. A., 22, 37, 89

C
Canter, D. V., 219, 222, 233
Cartographic display engine, 70
Case, A. C., 154
Caulkins, J. P., 155
Ceccato, V., 37
Census enhanced GIS spatial units, 118–119
Census geography and super-profile
        classification for study area, 184f
Centre for Research and Statistics (COS), 206
Chainey, S. P., 24, 120, 220
Chapin, F. S. J., 82
Chavez, J. M., 72, 74, 146, 147, 151, 154, 155
Chernoff, H., 135
Chicago Police Department's Youth
        Division, 139
Chicago School Board, 139
Chilton, R. .J., 14
City boundary on geographic profile, effects
        of, 112f
City planning practices, 202
Clarke, R. V. G., 15, 17, 18, 62, 63, 93, 174,
        201, 202, 219
Clayton, R. R., 203
Cliff, A. D., 148
Clifford, R., 11, 12, 13
Coefficient of ecological reliability
        (lambda), 47
Co-efficient of variation, 223n
Cohen, J., 166, 207, 210
Cohen, L. E., 201, 213, 219
Coleman, J., 138
'Collective efficacy' scale, 35, 48–50
    principal component analysis of, 49t
Complete spatial randomness (CSR), 73
Computational criminology, 90, 100
Computational modeling, 90
    See also Crime analysis
Conditional model, 50
'Cone of resolution', 218
Conly, C., 24, 220
Co-offending, 203
    patterns in 8-block neighborhood,
        136f–137f
Cook County Juvenile Court, 139
Cook, P. J., 203

Cork, D., 146, 147, 151, 156
Cornish, D. B., 17, 63, 173, 174, 201, 219
COS, *see* Centre for Research and Statistics
    (COS)
Costanzo, C. M., 94
Costello, A., 220
Coupe, T., 172
Co-victimization, 203
Crane, J., 128
Creating new geographies using census
    material, 118*f*
Creation of torus to correct for edge effects,
    113*f*
Crime
    analysis , *see* , Crime analysis
    causation , see, Crime causation, behavioral
        contexts in
    definition, 88
    ecological studies of, 146
    hot spots, 62, 125
    incident data, 207–208
    mapping techniques, 176
    places, 61–62, 83
    in streets, *see*, Crime in streets, nature of
    trip, 221
Crime analysis
    computational criminology, 90
    crime pattern theory and scale of analysis,
        88–90
        problems for analysts, 89
    fuzzy topology, 90
    GLM model, 99–100
    methodology
        data sources, 91–92
        micro-meso-micro analysis, 92–93
        urban backcloth, 93–95
    results
        fuzzy and sharp borders, 98–101
        micro level of analysis, 101
        residential burglary, 96–97
Crime causation, behavioral contexts in
    analytic strategy, 45–48
        Bayesian approach, 47
        collective efficacy, 48
        Cronbach's alpha, 46
        data quality, 46
        ecological reliability, 47
        'ecometric' approach, 46
        empty model, 48
        ICC, 47
        informal social control, 48
        social cohesion/trust, 48
Crime and the Foreign Born, 127

Crime mapping techniques, 176
Crime/neighborhoods and units of analysis
    deductive approach to spatial models
        spatial dynamics of diffusion, 155–157
        spatial dynamics of exposure, 154–155
    gun violence in Pittsburgh, 157
    modeling influence, network and spatial
        approaches, 147–153
        autocorrelated error models, 149
        gangs, agents of diffusion, 151
        positive spatial autocorrelation, 150
        spatial error/lag models, 149
    research design and measurement
        descriptive statistics, 161*t*
        ecological measures, 160
        gang rivalries, measurement of, 159
        gang set space, measures of, 158
        gang violence, measures of, 159–160
        gun violence, models of, 162
        regression results, 163*t*
        results, 162
        spatial distribution of shots fired
            (1992–1993), 159*f*
        weights matrix, measurement of, 160
    spatial analysis of violence literature,
        166–167
"Crime particles", 133
Crime Pattern Theory, 199
    and scale of analysis, 88–90
Crime in streets, nature of, 202–204
    Code of the Street, 204
    compositional explanation, 203
    contextual explanation, 202–204
"Crime waves", 127, 131
Criminal Statistics of Preston, 8
"Criminology of place", 5
Cromwell, P. F., 93
Crow, W., 18
CSR, *see* Complete spatial randomness (CSR)
Curtis, L. A., 18

D
Dacey, M., 113
David, W., 3, 19, 61
Davis, S., 202
Deane, G., 162
Decker, S., 151, 173
"Defensive diffusion" effect, 155
de Keijser, J. W., 220, 221, 233
Diggle, P. J., 74, 179, 180
Dijkstra, E. W., 190
Disregard solution, 113
Dissemination Area (DA), 92

Distance decay, 145, 182, 217, 221–223,
    227–229, 232–234
  principle of, 219
Dolmen, L., 40, 48
Donnelly, K., 114
Doreian, P., 152
Drass, K. A., 131
Drug
  markets, impact of, 156–157
  user, 207
Ducpétiaux, E., 6–7
Duffala, D. C., 18
Durkheim, E., 10

E
Eck, J. E., 62, 63, 151
EDA, *see* Exploratory data analysis (EDA)
'Edges', 201
Eisner, M., 200
Elffers, H., 93, 149
Elmer, M. C., 11
'Empty model', 230
Environmental criminology, 62, 63,
    154–155, 219
Erickson, M. L., 5
Ericsson, U., 173
ESDA, *see* Exploratory spatial data analysis
    (ESDA)
Everson, S. P., 173, 175
Exploratory data analysis (EDA), 72
Exploratory Spatial Data Analysis (ESDA),
    72, 154

F
Fagan, J., 151, 203
Faggiani, D., 201
Family violence, 210
Faris, R. E. L., 11
Farrell, G., 23, 172
Farrington, D. P., 133
Felson, M., 62, 63, 81, 131, 150, 201,
    213, 219
Felson, R., 203
Fidell, L. S., 231
FIS, *see* Force Intelligence System (FIS)
Fletcher, J., 9, 10
Flewelling, R. L., 165
Force Intelligence System (FIS), 224
Forrester, D., 23
Fotheringham, A. S., 72, 73, 79
Friedkin, N. E., 147, 148
Friendly, M., 7
Fuzzy topology, 90, 94

G
Gang
  rivalries, measurement of, 159
  set space, measures of, 158
  violence, measures of, 159–160
Gartner, R., 165
Gatrell, A. C., 40, 72, 73, 74, 182, 193
Gelman, A., 227
General Linear Model (GLM), 98
Gentrification, 131n
Geocoding, 70, 92
Geographical crime research, France/Belgium,
    6–8
Geographical Information System (GIS), 181
Geographical units and analysis of crime
  aerial units and statistical analysis, 119–120
  edge effects of bounded space, 111–114
  modifiable aerial unit problem, 114–116
  problems associated with politically
    bounded space, 111
    metropolitan areas, 111
  units of analysis and statistical criteria
    census enhanced GIS spatial units,
      118–119
    GIS enhanced census spatial units,
      117–118
    GIS enhanced spatial data, 117
Geographic criminology, analysis in
  criminological context
    geographical crime research, 6–8
    micro crime places, study of, 15–18
    neighborhoods/square miles, unit of
      analyses, 11–15
    pioneers in England, 19th century, 8–11
  theory/data, problems of, 21–24
Geographic Information Systems (GIS),
    116, 140
Geographic profiling, "high probability
    surface", 112
Getis, A., 72, 112, 113
Gibbs, J. P., 206
GIS enhanced census spatial units, 117–118
GIS, *see* Geographic Information Systems
    (GIS)
GLM, *see* General Linear Model (GLM)
Global cluster analysis, 112
Glyde, J., 10, 20
Gold, M., 5
Gordon, R. A., 14
Gordon, R., 156
Gottfredson, 15, 81
Gould, R., 153
Gove, W. R., 71

Granovetter, M., 128
Greenbaum, R. T., 23, 24, 145, 153
Green, D. P., 131
Green, L., 4, 18, 62, 124, 128, 156
Greg, W. R., 7, 9
Griffith, D., 113
Griffiths, E., 72, 74, 146, 147, 151, 154, 155, 156, 166
Groff, E., 19, 20, 90, 166
Groff, E. R., 61, 64, 166, 176, 178, 220
Groves, W. B., 15, 202
Guerry, A. M., 3, 7, 8, 9
Gun violence, models of, 162

H
Haining, R., 72
Hakim, S., 177
Hamming, R., 140
Harvey, L., 11
Hatton, T. J., 128
Henry, D., 11, 13
Hern, A. L., 124
Herting, J. R., 72
Hesseling, R. B. P., 154
Hillier, B., 64, 176
Hipp, J. R., 16, 22, 201, 213
Hope, T., 93
"Hot spots of crime", 4
Hox, J., 47
Human interactions, waves and particles in, 126–127
Hunter, R. D., 15, 18
Hypothetical trajectory (a–d) of two contiguous neighborhoods, 129f–130f

I
IMD, see Index of Multiple Deprivation (IMD)
Incident characteristics, 199, 203, 211–214
Index of Multiple Deprivation (IMD), 44
Individual criminals, 221
Individual offender
    crime trips estimated by kernel density, 222f
    journey to crime distribution, box plots of, 229f
Inductive modeling strategy, 146
Instrumental violence, 202n
Intra-class correlation coefficient (ICC)
    and ecological reliability of social cohesion/trust and informal social control, OA and SOA levels compared, 51f
    of social cohesion/trust and informal social control in three-level models, 52f

J
Jackson, H., 172
Jacobs, J., 64, 82
Jang, S. J., 227
Jefferis, E., 71
Jeffery, C. R., 18
Jensen, G. F., 5
John, G., 10
Johnson, B. R., 227
Johnson, S. D., 23, 64, 171, 173, 174, 179, 217
John, W., 217
Journey-to-crime (JTC), 220
Journeys-to-crime
    Box plots of individual offender, distribution of, 229f
    data/methods, 223–227
    discussion, 232–234
    individual offender crime trips estimated by kernel density, 222f
    offender crime trips estimated by kernel density estimation conditioned by age groupings, 228f
    research question, 223
    results
        extent of intra/inter-offender variation, 230
        skewness scores, 230–232
    theory/previous research, 219–223
Junger, M., 128
Juvenile crime
    analysis of spatial patterns, see Spatial patterns, analysis of juvenile crime
    definition of, 70
    location, benefits of measuring, 71
    spatial autocorrelation, see Spatial autocorrelation, juvenile crime
    spatio-temporal patterns of, see Spatio-temporal patterns of juvenile crime
    street blocks, see Street blocks, juvenile crime
    trajectories, 66

K
KDE, see Kernel Density Estimation (KDE)
Kenwitz, J. W., 3
Kerlinger, F. N., 71
Kernel Density Estimation (KDE), 175
Kershaw, C., 176
Kim, Y., 154
Klein, M., 5, 151, 157
Klinger, D., 160
Knox, G., 173, 179, 194
Kobrin, S., 15, 16

Kocsis, R. N., 222
Krivo, L. J., 162
Kubrin, C. E., 40, 72

L

Labor, type of/cause of crime, 9
LaFree, G., 17, 131
Lagrange multiplier tests, 164
Landau, D., 8
Lander, B., 14
Land, K. C., 56, 162
Landscan Population Database, 214
Larkin, P., 233
Laub, J. H., 132, 138
LaVigne, N. G., 64, 176, 178
Lazarsfeld, P. F., 8
LeBeau, J., 177, 222
LeBeau, J. L., 15, 18
Leenders, R., 147, 148, 165, 166
Lemann, N., 128
Level of 'immorality' of populations, causes
        of, 9
Levenson, J. S., 124
Levine, N., 220
Lévy, R., 128
LISA, see Local indicators of spatial
        association (LISA)
Liu, L., 90
Local indicators of spatial association
        (LISA), 73
Localities of crime in Suffolk, 10
Lockwood, B., 16, 19, 21, 23, 109
Lodka, S. K., 125
Loeber, R., 131
Loftin, C., 147, 150, 151
Lombroso, C., 10–11
Low rate trajectory groups, 67f
Luykx, F., 190
Lynch, K., 94

M

Maier, P. A., 117, 200, 201
Male
    offender, 207
    victim, 207, 212
Male-on-male homicides, 203
Maltz, M. D., 18, 21, 23, 123, 132, 133, 139
Manhattan grid street configuration, 181
Manski, C., 152, 153
Marsden, P. V., 147, 148
Martin, D., 44
Martin, W. T., 206
Matthiopoulos, J., 176
Mayhew, H., 10

Mayhew, P., 18
Mazerolle, L., 18
McClintock, F. H., 200
McCord, E. S., 41, 89
McCord, J., 71, 132
McCullagh, M. J., 5
McEwan, T., 220
McEwen, T., 3, 17, 166
McKay, H. D., 4, 5, 11, 13, 14, 15, 16, 19, 40,
        88, 89, 90, 110, 127
McVie, S., 42
Mears, D. P., 150, 154, 162, 166
Meenaghan, A., 174
Meier, R. F., 42
Messerschmidt, J., 11, 14
Messner, S., 146
Messner, S. F., 72, 150, 203
Micro–macro transition, 138
Miethe, T. D., 42
Mikelbank, K. M., 156
Miller, L. L., 48
Modifiable area unit problem (MAUP), 5, 40,
        114, 116
    effect of modifying area of region on
            spatial pattern of point data, 115f
    problems of aggregation, 115f
Moland, J. Jr., 5
Monmonier, M., 124
Monte Carlo (MC)
    Markov Chain approaches, 189
    re-sampling approach, 180n
    simulation approach, 185
Moore, J., 151
Morenoff, J. D., 24, 146, 147, 150, 151, 152,
        162, 207
Morgan, F., 173
Morris, N., 19, 20, 61, 91
Morris, T., 9, 10, 14
Mullany, J. K., 132, 133, 139
Multivariate individual characteristics, using
        Chernoff faces to represent, 134f
Murrey, D. M., 42

N

Nagin, D., 65, 138
Nagin, D. S., 154
Nearest neighbor analysis, 112
'Near repeat', 173
Nee, C., 174
Negative binomial models of number of violent
        incidents per street on population
        and environmental characteristics,
        210t

Neighbor equation, correction factor to
    nearest, 114
Neighborhood, 128*n*
    hypothetical trajectory, 129*t*
Nettler, G., 22
Newman, O., 18
Nielsen, A. L., 207
Nieuwbeerta, P., 138, 172, 174, 177
Nlme package, 227
'Nodes', 201
Norris, P., 42
North, B. V., 185
*Numerical Methods for Scientists and
    Engineers*, 140

O
OAs, *see* Output areas (OAs)
Oberwittler, D., 20, 22, 23, 35, 50, 91, 158, 227
Offender
    age, 226
    characteristics, 207, 209, 223
    crime trips, kernel density estimation
        conditioned by age groupings, 228*f*
    and victim, relation between, 212
Offset effect, 225
Okihiro, N., 93
OLS, *see* Ordinary Least Squares (OLS)
Openshaw, S., 5, 40
Opportunity theories, 63
Ordinary Least Squares (OLS), 116
Orleans, P., 82
Ouimet, M., 41, 54
Output areas (OAs)
    20-page questionnaire, 45
    'normal'/'deprived', 40

P
PADS+, *see* Peterborough Adolescent and
    Young Adult Development Study
    (PADS+)
Parent-Duchâtelet, A. J. B., 7
Parker, R. N., 165
Park, R. E., 4, 10, 11, 12, 13, 127
Particle analysis, crime and, 132–135
Particle *vs.* wave analysis, 135–138
'Paths', 201
Paulsen, D. J., 24, 220
PCS, *see* Peterborough Community Survey
    (PCS)
Pease, K., 23, 171, 173
Peeples, F., 131
Peterborough Adolescent and Young Adult
    Development Study (PADS+),
    35–36, 43

aim of, 37
topics covered
    environment, individual 43
    individuals' exposure to different
        environments, 43
Peterborough Community Survey (PCS), 43
Peterson, R. D., 162
Physical attack, 207
Physical world, waves and particles in, 125
Pierce, G., 18
Pinheiro, J., 226, 227
Piza, E. L., 202
Placement of burglary
    physical attributes of housing, 181
    road infrastructure, 181
    See also Predictive mapping of crime
Poisson-based regression model, 209
Polder, W., 128
Politically bounded space, problems associated
        with, 111
Polvi, N., 23, 173
Poot, C., 176, 177, 183, 190
"Positivist criminology", 4
Potchak, M. C., 64
Predictive mapping of crime
    areal units and ProMap, 190–193
        'Lossy' boundaries, example of, 192*f*
    barriers, 183–185
    crime risk surfaces, 182
    data and method, 179–182
    equations used in derivation of
        KDE/ProMap algorithms
        KDE equation/callibration, 193
        modeling accessibility, 194
        ProMap equation/callibration, 194
    event driven opportunity surfaces,
        182–183
    measuring predictive accuracy, 185–186
    Monte Carlo simulation algorithm for
        chance expectation, 196
    predictive success, measuring, 177–179
        aims of analyses, three-fold, 179
    ProMap
        accuracy and backcloth influences,
            186–189
        accuracy concentration curves, 187*f*
        initial tests, 175–177
        median mapping algorithm accuracy,
            188*t*
    risk/contagion/optimal forager, 173–175
    roads, 194–195
        and homes, barriers, 195
Price, S. W., 128

ProMap (prospective mapping)
  accuracy and backcloth influences,
    186–189
  algorithm and KDE approach, 182
  elements, essential, 191–192
  initial tests, 175–177
  risk surfaces, 182
  See also Predictive mapping of crime
"Property crime", 89
Prospective mapping (ProMap), 179
Pyle, G. F., 18, 94

Q
Quetelet, L. A. J., 4, 8, 88

R
"Racial inferiority", 11
Rand, A., 154
Rasbash, J., 230
Ratcliffe, J., 24, 120, 176, 193
Ratcliffe, J. H., 5, 89, 94, 220
Raudenbush, S. W., 16, 35, 42, 46, 47, 50,
    51, 56
Rawson, R. W., 9
Reboussin, R., 109
Reiss, A. J. Jr., 4, 5, 15, 16, 133
Rengert, G. F., 15, 16, 18, 19, 21, 23, 24, 93,
    94, 109, 117, 118, 119, 120, 124,
    155, 217, 220, 221, 222, 232, 233
Rengert, G., 82, 173, 177, 185
Residential burglary, 96–97
  repeat, 96f
  study area land use, 97f
  See also Crime analysis
Residential instability, 132
Respondents' assessment of the vicinity of
    police stations, external validation
    of, 46
Reynald, R., 177
Reynolds, H. D., 40
Rhodes, W. M., 24, 220
Rice, K. J., 200, 201
Rich, T., 233
Ridgeway, G., 157, 159, 160
"Ringleader", 135
Ripley, B. D., 70, 73, 74, 75, 76, 77, 226
Ripley's *K*, 70n, 73–75, 76f, 77f
Road
  infrastructure, information on, 181
  weighting, equations showing construction
    of, 194
Robertson, J. B., 82, 155
Robinson, M. B., 24, 220
Robinson, W. S., 14, 15, 19, 218

Roncek, D. W., 15, 18, 117, 200, 201
Rosenfeld, R., 146, 147, 151, 156
Rosling, H., 125
Rossmo, D. K., 24, 124, 217, 218, 220,
    222, 225
Rountree, P. W., 227
Routine activity theory, 62–63, 201
Rowlingson, B. S., 74

S
Sabol, W. J., 156
Sampson, R. J., 4, 15, 16, 35, 40, 41, 42, 43,
    46, 47, 48, 50, 51, 52, 54, 56, 132,
    138, 146, 147, 151, 153, 165, 202,
    204, 227
Sarnecki, J., 5
Scale effect, 40
Schmid, C., 88, 89
Schuerman, L. A., 15, 16
Sellin, T., 127
Shaw, C. R., 4, 5, 11, 12, 13, 14, 15, 16, 19, 40,
    88, 89, 90, 110, 127
Shaw, M., 173
Sherman, L. W., 4, 5, 15, 18, 22, 62, 200
Shively, M., 233
Short, J., 204
Short, J. F. Jr., 5
Shots fired (1992–1993), spatial
    distribution, 162f
Silver, E., 48
Situational action theory, 35–37, 56
Situational crime prevention, 63
Skogan, W., 15, 18
Small number problem, 56
Smith, M., 200, 201, 202
Smith, M. D., 165
Smith, W., 217
Smith, W. R., 15, 24, 41, 64, 71
Snijders, T., 42, 120, 211, 218, 227
Snook, B., 222, 234
SOA, *see* Super output areas (SOA)
'Social cohesion/trust'/'informal social
    control' scales, variance
    components of, 49t
Social disorganization, 4, 22, 83, 160,
    201–202, 209–210
  concept of, 12
Social influence models, 147
Space-time budget technique, 37
Spatial autocorrelation, juvenile crime
  for high rate groups, 80f
  for low rate groups, 78f
  for middle rate groups, 79f

Spatial dependence, mechanisms, 151
Spatial homogeneity, 152
Spatial patterns, analysis of juvenile crime
    autocorrelation, types of, 73, 74
    cross K (also called a bivariate-K)
        function, 74
    Ripley's K-function/LISA, 73
    toroidal shift, 74n
Spatio-temporal patterns of juvenile crime
    background, 63–65
    discussion, 81–83
        implications for practice, 83–84
    methodology
        analytical approach, 72–73
        geocoding process, 70
        geographic distribution of trajectory
            group members, 70
        juvenile crime, 70–71
        spatial patterns of trajectory group
            members, 73–75
    results
        comparing spatial distribution of
            trajectory groups, 79–81
        spatial autocorrelation among trajectory
            groups, 77–79
Staples, B. A., 138
Stark, R., 63, 133
Statistical Society of London, 8
Strang, D., 152
Street blocks, juvenile crime, 65
    per trajectory group, 66t
    preferred unit of analysis, reasons for, 64
    spatial heterogeneity, 64
Street-level data, urban, 205–207
    incident, categories, 206
    variables, 206
Streets, determinants of crime volumes,
        201–202
Super output areas (SOA), 50
Super-profiles system, 183
Symons, J., 10

T
Tabachnick, B. G., 231
Tarde, J. G., 11
Tardiff, K., 150
Taylor, P. J., 40
Taylor, R., 42, 48
Taylor, R. B., 4, 15, 18, 64, 82
Thematic maps, 182
Thomas, W. I., 11, 12
Thornberry, T. P., 156
Thrasher, F. M., 4

Tita, G., 23, 24, 145, 146, 147, 151, 156, 157,
        158, 159, 160, 164, 166, 207, 210
Tobler's First Law of Geography, 82n, 152
Tobler, W. R., 82, 109, 152
Tonry, M., 4, 15
TOPO algorithm, 94–95
    See also Crime analysis
Torus, 113
Townsley, M., 24, 90, 174, 217
Trajectory groups
    moderate to high rate, 69f
TRAJ procedure, 65, 72
Treiber, K., 36
Tremblay, R. E., 138
Tseloni, A., 64, 176, 209, 227
Tukey, J., 72
Tuma, N. B., 152
"Turf battles", 135

U
"Urban homesteaders", 131
Urban street gangs, 156–157
Urban streets, as micro contexts to commit
        violence
    crime volumes in streets, determinants of,
        201–202
    data
        crime incident, 207–208
        street-level, 205–207
    dependent/independent variables for
        street/incident-level data, 208t
    deviance tests, variance of qualitative
        aspects of violence between
        streets, 211t
    multilevel logistic regression of
        co-offending and relation between
        conflict parties on incident/street
        characteristics, 212t
    nature of crime in streets, determinants of,
        202–204
        'compositional'/'contextual'
            explanations, 203
    results, 209–213

V
Vajihollahi, M., 87
van Koppen, P. J., 220, 221, 233
Van Wilsem, J., 24, 131
Venables, W. N., 226
Verma, A., 125
Victim
    characteristics, 207
    injury, 199–200, 203–204, 211, 213

Violence
    acts, number of, 210, 210*t*
    encounters, 203
    in neighborhoods, influencing
        elements, 150
"Violent crime", 8–9, 11, 24, 71, 89, 146, 156,
        162, 199, 200, 204–207, 210–211,
        213
Virtual Reality Modeling Language
        (VRML), 125
Vold, G. B., 12
VRML, *see* Virtual Reality Modeling
        Language (VRML)

W
Waller, I., 93
Wallman, J., 71, 81
Waring, E. J., 5
Warren, J., 222
Warr, M., 5
Wasilchick, J., 93, 94, 124, 173, 185
Wave analysis and crime, 127–131
    data needs for, 138–139
Waves/particles and crime
    crime and particle analysis, 132–135
    crime and wave analysis, 127–131
    data needs, 138–139
    in human interactions, 126–127
    in physical world, 125
    preliminary considerations, 123–126
    wave *vs.* particle analysis, 135–138
Weapon use, 199, 203–204, 207, 210, 211, 213
Webb, J., 15, 16

Weisburd, D., 3, 4, 17, 18, 19, 20, 21, 24, 91,
        93, 124, 128, 131, 156, 200, 201
Weisburd, D. L., 61, 62, 63, 64, 65, 70, 71, 72,
        84
Weitzer, R., 40
Wikström, P. O. H., 20, 21, 22, 23, 35, 36, 37,
        40, 48, 89, 91, 131, 158, 200, 201,
        202
Wilcox, P., 203
Wilcox, S., 89
Wiles, P., 220
Wilkinson, D. L., 151, 203
Winchester, S. W. C., 172
Wolfgang, M., 165
Wolfgang, M. E., 22
Wooldredge, J., 41, 43
Wright, R., 93, 174
Wright, R. T., 173

X
Xue, Y., 90

Y
Yeates, M., 115

Z
Zauberman, R., 128
Zero Inflated Poisson (ZIP), 119
Zimring, F. E., 133
Zorbaugh, F. M., 13, 20
Zorn, C., 119
Z score for skewness for each prolific
        offender, 231*f*

Breinigsville, PA USA
17 December 2009
229387BV00003B/58/P